SPATIAL, REGIONAL AND POPULATION
ECONOMICS

EDGAR M. HOOVER

SPATIAL, REGIONAL AND POPULATION ECONOMICS

Essays in Honor of Edgar M. Hoover

Edited by

MARK PERLMAN

CHARLES J. LEVEN

BENJAMIN CHINITZ

GORDON AND BREACH

New York   London   Paris

Edgar M. Hoover

Harvard College in the 1920s was still an institution whose students were about equally divided between gilded youths acquiring gentlemanly C's while seeking pleasures on wider circles, and serious minded boys who came to Cambridge for an education. There was no doubt from the beginning to which group the gangling boy from Boise, Idaho, mysteriously called Bump, belonged. To his tutor and instructor, not many years older than this Bump, he was not only a teacher's delight but living proof of his instructor's ability, at that stage little recognised, to instruct. Hoover was his first tutorial student to graduate *summa cum laude* thus conferring distinction not only on himself but on his preceptor. His interests at that time seem to have been about evenly divided between the analytical aspects of economics and music and these have persisted as his two main interests throughout his scholarly career.

That career has brought us together again on a number of occasions though unfortunately never very frequently or for very long periods. During the Second World War when I was Chief Economist in the Office of Strategic Services, he, on assignment from the Navy, was one of the distinguished analysts in that unusual organization. When as Dean of Harvard's School of Public Administration, I initiated the New York Metropolitan Region Study, he was one of the principal participants. And in government and in academic circles our paths occasionally crossed. The only period when we served together as academic colleagues was in the years 1957–1959 when he was a Visiting Professor at Harvard.

Economists, like other segments of the human species, come in different shapes and sizes. Some are glib and flashy, others serious and reserved. This particular economist belonged on the serious side, reserved and deliberate in speech but with a wry humor that persisted in breaking through. Orderly in his habits he never failed to meet a deadline or to honor an engagement. A first rate analytical mind was joined to a passion for empirical research and this combination of interests and qualities has illuminated all his work. Very few of his writings have been devoted to pure theory but neither is any of it to be characterized as the mere accumulation of data. He has principally been concerned with stating hypotheses and testing them through a rigorous examination of the facts.

Hoover's first publication, his doctoral dissertation on "Location Theory and the Shoe and Leather Industry," set the stage for a life-long preoccupation with spatial economics. This was a relatively new field of economics in the United States and Hoover was one of the early developers. At the time there was no one on the Harvard Economics Faculty particularly concerned with this subject. Alfred Weber's classical work on the theory of location had just been translated into English by a Harvard Faculty member, C. J. Friedrich, but he was in another department. A very able young German spatial economist, August Lösch, spent a year or two in Cambridge and was a close friend of Hoover's, but in the main it was Hoover, pursuing his own course, who stimulated interest in this branch of Economics in this country. After publishing a considerable number of journal articles on this subject he drew his ideas together in a book on *The Location of Economic Activity* published in 1948, and translated into a number of languages.

His interest in spatial problems inevitably took him into the area of regional economics in which he has been a prolific writer and a notable contributor. Among the most important of these contributions was his work on the New York Metropolitan Region Study. He wrote, with Raymond Vernon, "Anatomy of a Metropolis" and participated in two other contributions to that ten volume study. His work on the New York study led to his appointment as Director of the Economic Study of the Pittsburgh Region which he not only directed but in which he participated as a principal author. Hoover's work on regional economics was recognized in 1962 by his election to the Presidency of the Regional Science Association.

Although the economics of location and regional economics have been his principal areas of interest Hoover has wandered widely and fruitfully in other fields. His work on population has been notable and, with Ansley J. Coale, he published a frequently cited study of *Population Growth and Economic Development in Low-Income Countries* in 1958. His interest in spatial economics formed part of a broader concern with industrial organization and this concern was expressed not only in a number of papers on industrial financing and capital expenditures but was central to his regional studies in the New York and Pittsburgh areas and elsewhere. In addition he was a frequent contributor in the field of natural resource problems as evidenced by his study for the U.S. Department of Commerce on "The Economic Effects of the St. Lawrence Project," and his participation in the publications of the National Resources Planning Board.

One thinks of Hoover primarily as an academic economist and, indeed, not only were most of his years spent in the university but all his writings bear the stamp of academic excellence. But his curriculum vitae indicates that at various stages he served on the staffs of the National Resources Planning Board, the Office of Price Administration, the Office of Strategic Services, and the Council of Economic Advisers. Furthermore, he acted as consultant to various other government agencies, foundations, research institutes and business firms. As I have frequently observed, the ablest academic economists are often the most sought after advisers to government and business. Economics is not an ivory tower subject and Hoover has not been an ivory tower economist.

His teaching career has been mainly divided between the University of Michigan and the University of Pittsburgh. Both institutions have been generous in granting him leave to pursue his interests in government and elsewhere. It is fitting that he should end his academic career with the bracing and embracing title of "Distinguished Service Professor of Economics and Professor of Regional Economic Development." His former teacher, his colleagues, and a host of former students and present admirers are happy to welcome this book in his honor.

EDWARD S. MASON

Table of Contents

Resistance to the Wired City

HAROLD J. BARNETT*

Professor of Economics
Washington University,
St. Louis, Missouri

A major innovation in mass communications is in prospect for developed nations. This is the "wired city." Many television programs plus hundreds of voice and data services can be carried to homes on a wire. The cost of transmission is small. The variety of services is large. They include entertainment, education, and and other public services. In "The Wired City Innovation," I characterize technology, costs, and services. In "Implications

---

* This research was assisted by a grant from the National Science Foundation, by accommodation as a visiting scholar at the London School of Economics, and by presentation and discussion in seminars at the Universities of Southampton and Essex. I am also grateful for comments on the larger draft monograph of the same title (mimeo, March 1970) from which this paper has been drawn to: E. Greenberg and K. Cowling at Washington University; R. Gabriel, Rediffusion, Ltd.; P. Barnett, Dubner Computer Systems; R. Caves, R. McKenzie, H. Townsend, B. Weisbrod and P. Wiles at London School of Economics; J. Norman, U.K. Ministry of Posts and Telecommunications; C. Pratten, Cambridge University; and H. Christie and P. Seglow, U.K. National Board for Prices and Incomes. The responsibility for any errors, of course, is mine alone. Submitted for publication December 27, 1970.

for Cities," I illustrate some of the services significant for urban society, particularly in the United States.

But it is charged that the wired city is a dangerous innovation. Arguments are made that rural areas would lose their television service entirely and cities their free TV; that wire monopolies would inevitably arise; and that local governments and advertising excesses would reduce and corrupt television service. Some of the allegations have small elements of truth. To a much larger degree, they are maneuvers by the economic interests that might lose in competition with the innovation and its expanded offerings of entertainment, news, and other services: present TV oligopolists, newspapers, cinemas, and others. In "Alleged Defects or Dangers," we consider the arguments against the wired-city innovation, and in "Economic Pressure Groups," we appraise the forces which are resisting it. The paper closes with "Conclusions."

THE WIRED CITY INNOVATION

Let us pretend that the innovation which we named "the wired city" has already occurred and is present in the society [(3) Barnett and Greenberg, 1967; (32) Smith, 1970].

Network

The wired-city technology is a broadband cable network to homes and other establishments which have TV sets.

In the cable technology which has been developed in the U.S., a pencil-thick coaxial cable of 300 megahertz band width has a theoretical capacity to carry up to 50 television programs (restricted, at the present stage of development, to about 25 in practice, or much larger numbers of other data and voice services). A 150 megahertz cable carries half as many, or dual cables, twice as many. The network is switched for convenient-sized areas but not switched within them and has limited return band width for signals by individual users [(12) EIA, 1969].

A more flexible system has been developed in British cable television technology. This provides a separate connection from a program exchange box to each television set in the homes within a radius of about 500 yards, on very similar lines to a conventional telephone network. The program exchange boxes are linked by a coaxial cable network. But the connection from the program exchange box to the home is several wires of 6 megahertz band width. The subscriber selects the program of his choice from those available at the program exchange by dial impulses [(14), (15) Gabriel, 1967, 1968; (16) Gargini, 1970].

With both techniques, there are at convenient points input studios, stations or other devices. (The British system could accept inputs at each program exchange box, and, indeed, from individual homes.) The output points are the drop lines to individual homes. The wired city provides high-quality sound and pictures irrespective of atmospheric conditions.

The network is operated as a common carrier on public utility principles. It accepts any sender's signals to any one or several areas. Senders can lease a 6-megahertz TV channel or another channel by the year, month, day or fraction of an hour, subject to a published, nondiscriminating tariff. They use their own input facilities or rent them for the occasion. Wire and other facilities are expanded as demands justify, as in electricity, gas, and telephone industries. Charges in most instances are very low [(4) Barnett and Greenberg, 1969].

TV Programs

Television programs go directly onto the wire from studios without need for towers or transmitters. Present over-the-air broadcasters probably lease full-time channels. In addition, other senders enter broadcasting. They have been frozen out for lack of spectrum assignments [(37) U.S. Department of Commerce, 1966] or because of the high cost of operating an over-the-air station for each signal relative to audience [(1) Barnett, 1964; (18) Greenberg, 1969]. TV program guides are available in magazines and newspapers to inform homes of what is to be broadcast on each channel, or one or two channels may be allocated to provide up-to-date program information on the subscriber's television screen.

One new entrant into broadcasting is the pay-TV company, which provides programs for a fee [(43) Wiles, 1963; (7) Caine, 1968]. There are series subscriptions for a whole channel, or for a firm that has leased certain hours, or for individual programs. An inexpensive time meter records viewing (where the subscription is not for a full channel).

Politicians use the system for electioneering, confining themselves to one or more particular constituencies. Instructional stations send programs on the wire to homes or schools. In the U.S., public television is offered by so-called ETV stations. Other public service programs are available from legislative bodies, municipal bands, chapters of the League of Women Voters, the Art Museum, and the Zoo. The franchise conditions of the wired city may provide for free channels for educational and public-service programming, as today governmental units enjoy tax-free gasoline and non-profit organizations, other free or subsidized services. Newspapers are likely to lease channels. Political action groups such as trade unions, Black organizations, veteran groups, and peace societies rent time on occasion. So do music societies, drama groups, dog lovers and bowling leagues. In each case, there is advertising or not, depending on the sender's desires and his willingness to bear the whole cost of the program and channel time. In addition, department stores and other advertisers rent channel time to present sales pitches, straight or diluted with programs, if they think it worthwhile [(41) President's Task Force, 1968; (3) Barnett and Greenberg, 1967; (32) Smith, 1970].

Not all programs are local. There are ground stations connected to the wired city. They receive inputs on tall antennae by microwave and from communication satellites. Satellites are already economical for point-to-point transmission in telephone. But they are enormously more efficient for relays to *many* ground stations at one time in broadcasting. A program sent to a communication satellite can be simultaneously relayed to 100 ground stations in America at only slightly greater cost than to one station. In Europe, programs can be sent to all the ground stations on the continent at only slightly greater cost than to one. Such re-reduction in transmission cost per receiver increases the volume and variety of TV programs potentially available. It gives access to the whole world's output of programs [(9) d'Arcy, 1969; (30) Rydbeck and Ploman, 1969].

Wire Services

Other services are also available from the wired city. [(41) President's Task Force, 1968; (38) FCC, 1968; (32) Smith, 1970; (12) EIA, 1969; (4) Barnett and Greenberg, 1969; (17) Goldmark, 1970]. Unmanned television cameras are placed at appropriate traffic points, street and dock areas, etc., to provide surveillance for police and fire stations on one or more of the channels not available for general use. The same channels can be used for circulating notices and pictures to the stations. It is possible that another private channel will be useful in health activities—for hospitals, doctors and nurses. In homes with proper connections to telephone, gas, electric, and water meters, automatic readings of these measuring devices can be taken.

When facsimile printers become cheap enough, first-class mail can be delivered and printed in individual homes by electronic addressing. This may be done late at night when the wire network is not fully in use. Even before then, facsimile printers can be economical in business and government offices. First-class mail is in crisis in the United States because it continues as a labor intensive industry. About 80 per cent of cost is wages and salaries, with manual or foot performance in many of the tasks. Crises will develop in other countries also as living levels rise and postmen's wages increase. The need is to devise labor-saving techniques, to substitute capital for labor. One way to do this is to use wire transmission. Facsimile transmission on telephone lines is now in use, but equipment costs and the unsuitable wire rental costs are too high.

As equipment is perfected and costs reduced, the facsimile mail innovation could be generally extended. Materials other than the usual run of letters can be sent (i.e., library, reference, and data bank materials). Twenty years ago in a demonstration at the U.S. Library of Congress, the entire text of *Gone With The Wind* was transmitted in facsimile over a television micro-wave circuit in slightly over two minutes [(12) EIA, 1969, p. 21]. Even before printers are widespread, video or "soft copy" display is possible, as in stock price quotations and weather notices.

The computer interacts with these and other uses. Computer use in data banks, time-sharing, and computation is facilitated by existence of the wired city. And computers assist development of the wired city in the first instance by providing switching between people and information sources and for storage and queues. Computer programs also provide controls for use of open electronic spaces in other signals.

Recently, TV tape casettes have been developed for home use. They also permit tape-rental libraries on unused channels through dial-a-program service in wired cities. Such service increases availability and reduces cost. Eventually, tape libraries could respond to requests automatically as in jukebox record selection. Just as a book lending library economizes on numbers of books and radio broadcasting on records by reducing inventories relative to use, so also would this form of tape rental be inexpensive—to an extraordinary degree since the tape would be "out" only when actually being played.

Network Costs

Costs have been estimated from experience with cable television (CATV) in the United States and Canada, wire relay exchanges in Britain and other countries, and telephone and electricity wiring [(31) Seiden, 1965; (3) Barnett and Greenberg, 1967; (15) Gabriel, 1967]. Under average conditions, the installed street wire for a twelve-channel system costs roughly $4,000 per mile for overhead construction, and the dropline to the home perhaps $10 or $20. Costs would rise slightly for double this number of channels, and substantially to put cables underground. If the bulk of homes were connected under public utility conditions, the average cost of the wired network per home might be between $2 and $5 per month in the United States, and possibly less in other countries where labor costs for installation are lower. (CATV companies in the United States and Canada have been charging about $5 per month per home. Their density of subscribers is frequently less than 50 per cent of the homes, which increases cost per home; and their profits have been high. Also, they provide some TV services, beyond simple provision of the wire network.) The cost could be entirely borne by the program senders, rather than the homes. Or the drop line which connects the home to the street cable could be viewed as consumer equipment and borne by him; he saves much more than that amount in cost and maintenance of antenna and television receiver. An outside antenna costs $40 to $80; and in Britain, a wire-TV set costs one-third less than an identical over-the-air set. Maintenance costs are correspondingly lower also. The British form of wire service also provides high fidelity FM radio service through the TV set or on a high fidelity speaker; an FM receiver is unnecessary. The wired city network costs are quite small relative to the national investments in receivers and annual costs for operating and maintaining them, as may be seen from the cost data in Table 1 and in various references.

National Implications

The wired city innovation has implications for nations and the world society. It has always been widely believed (although quite without proof) that if communications improved and thereby nations knew each other better, they would be less likely to wage war. Large changes are occurring in money and credit systems. Computers and wire are moving us to a cashless society. Advanced nations are beginning to drown in paper records; wired services can reduce the volume of paper and improve access to record storage. Mail delivery is becoming increasing expensive. Securities exchanges are moving to wire *cum* computer in transfers, storage, and evidence of ownership of shares and bonds, in place of present paper, bank vaults, and certificates. The wired city, thus, has important implications for national politics, economic welfare, and TV diversity [(3) Barnett and Greenberg, 1967; (41) President's Task Force, 1968; (38) FCC, 1968; (32) Smith, 1970; (22) Johnson, 1970; (19) Greenberg and Barnett, 1971].

IMPLICATIONS FOR CITIES

Without attempting to be exhaustive, we wish now to show that the innovation has important implications for cities. The Sloan Commission on Cable Communications is currently (1970) engaged in a very large-scale study of these; results will be available in 1971.

Localism and Community Ethos

The present crises in cities derive in part from their decline as cohesive societies. Communal identification of people has lessened. The sense of community is disappearing. Community pride and spirit are down, and with them, citizen willingness to participate and serve. Responsibility is less. The results are unsafe and dirty streets, neglected and cannibalized buildings, political apathy and indifference. There is helplessness in the dispossessed. There is widespread a sense that there really is no community but only a mindless, corrupt, bureaucratic monster termed city government.

The wired city provides for powerful mass communication in cities and neighborhoods. With great efficiency and vitality, it offers the equivalent of town meeting, village square assembly, and neighborhood newspaper. The electronic moving pictures and voices are in some respects stronger, more intimate, and more

B

moving. On the video screen, one sees close up and hears well. One does not even have to be a "reader." Moreover, local video permits one to be seen and heard *himself.* In his own belief, he becomes more real because others see him and are listening. He is encouraged to participate.

The significance of local wire "stations" in building community ethos has been pressed for Black ghetto neighborhoods. The idea is simply that local television can help to build community spirit and purpose. It is not a new theory. School rallies have always been used to build school spirit; political rallies for similar purposes; and veterans, religious, and sales conventions to warm up ex-soldiers, congregations and salesmen. There is hope that the wired city would improve local identification and increase participation in community affairs. There is alleged evidence from the effects of ethnic radio stations and newspapers, in testimony before the Federal Communications Commission, and in the successful operation of neighborhood improvement associations [(42) White, 1968; (41) President's Task Force, 1968; (11) Dordick, et al., 1969; (38) FCC, 1968].

There are, however, some uncertainties. Is it likely that the wired city programs would exert *powerful* force in arresting the decline of communities? The technological and other trends which have been dissolving communities may be too strong to be overcome by improved community voice. Further, the very notion that improved mass communications could *create* an important sense of identification in American cities is unproved. Second, what will the voices of the urban slums say in the wired city? They would call not merely for improvement on traditional lines. They would shout also "burn baby, burn." An open access wire system would convey also hate and disruption, the voices of revolutionaries, demagogues and sometimes even the insane. It *is* the fact that some believe society to be so corrupt and malformed that it must be destroyed, and only then can a better society emerge.

The second question, in short, is whether powerful local television would exert greater centripetal force to build the community than centrifugal force to dissolve it. Improved communications might magnify existing differences.

Transportation and Congestion

A major problem in cities is traffic volume and congestion. From these, derive a host of city difficulties: fiscal crises; accidents and their costs; need for roads; delays; air pollution; housing problems; and others. The wired city has potential for reducing these social costs, to the extent that it provides alternatives to road movement. Too little is known at the present time to estimate these. The near term reductions in traffic would be very small. But combined with other innovations over the long term, the reductions associated with the wired city could become substantial. For example the wired city could show supermarket goods on "shoppers channels." The housewife could order without driving to the shop if the necessary assembly, packaging, and delivery innovations also occurred in supermarkets. It has also been proposed that cities, industries, and employment could be decentralized: "Broadband communication networks will make it possible to live and work without major pollution, crime and traffic problems in the new rural society." [(17) Goldmark, 1970].

Education

Education, the largest element in city finance, is also at crisis stage. The problems are many, but central are shortage of money and need for innovation. Funds are inadequate, the productivity of teachers is low, and bureaucracy is widespread. The wired city has major potential in providing many very low-cost channels for closed circuit TV education. In school education, it is now known that TV can be very effective on multiple channels. Regarding home education as a substitute for school and for pre-schoolers, the experience is less but favorable. For ghetto areas in Head-Start-type programs and also in educational efforts related to local culture, there is evidence that the wired city would be helpful after time for experimentation ad trial [(11) Dordick, et al., 1969]. In all these, the potential is to extend education and improve its quality and productivity. The means are reducing teacher cost per student in the presentation and display aspects of education; allocating best talent to these lecture and demonstration activities; saving on building costs; reallocating funds; and introducing innovations [(2a) Barnett and Denzau, 1971].

Also, adult education programs on television can be effective if offered and repeated when adults can watch. The British Open University, largely on television, begins with more than 20,000 students already enrolled. Other countries are also beginning university-level programs. They could be greatly improved if more channels and times were available and transmission costs lower, as in the wired city [(28) Perry, 1970].

Employment Exchange

Day workers in ghettos spend large amounts of unproductive time trying to connect with jobs, while prospective employers cannot find workers. In construction, the employment exchange is sometimes a street corner, where workers gather in the hope that prospective employers will drive up. The market for part-time labor of housewives and teen-agers could also be improved. Community labor information could be more effectively exchanged if timely notices and announcements could be made over a TV channel, and if these could be adjusted as they were filled or withdrawn.

Health Service

Some services now provided by visiting nurses are educational—pre-natal care, handling of babies, sanitation, etc. Many of these lessons could be usefully provided on wire TV to homes. Hospitals and physicians have considerable need for presentation of records or facsimile transmission. They also need access to data banks. Also, formal and clinical medical education—post-graduate for both doctors and for nurses—can be carried on closed channels of the wired city.

ALLEGED DEFECTS OR DANGERS

We consider now several possible defects or dangers in the wired city. They are (1) that the wired city would damage rural areas; (2) that pay-TV offerings on the wire would bid away all or most of the desirable free TV programs; (3) that dangerous wire monopolies would develop and frustrate the service potential of the wired city; (4) that local governmental units would impose undue taxation and impair wire service; and (5) that there will be advertising excesses and abuses.

   In this section, we appraise the allegations. In the next section, we examine the economic pressure groups that offer these arguments in their efforts to persuade the public to abort the innovation.

Service to Rural Areas

Argument is sometimes made along the following lines: because of low population density in rural areas, the cost of the wire network per home would be higher than in cities, and therefore they would not be economical to serve. This being so, the wired city should not be permitted anywhere because urban dwellers should not have public-utility benefits which are not also available to the rural population. Further, if cities were wired, television stations would cease over-the-air broadcasts to save this transmission expense; and rural dwellers would lose their present television services.

   These arguments may be refuted. First, wiring up small towns and rural areas is not necessarily more expensive than wiring cities. In cities, cables have to be put under busy city streets and carried into apartment walls in order to reach individual apartments. Network and drop lines to homes can be inexpensive in rural areas. This is why it was feasible for rural areas and small towns, in their effort to acquire TV service, to become the leaders in cable television in the United States and Canada. Second, even if wiring costs are higher in rural areas than in urban, costs and charges may be satisfactorily economical in both. Despite cost differences in installations and rates, the greater numbers of people in the U.S., Europe and other advanced nations are served by telephone and electricity grids. There is no reason that the rates charged to consumers or senders of signals need be identical over the breadth of a nation. They are not identical for many other services.

   Third, if social policy required that charges for wire service to homes be identical over county or larger areas, the cost could be averaged out by the common carrier. Or government could subsidize the rural area in one way or another. In the United States, rural electrification and telephone have, in fact, been assisted by preferential lending terms to cooperatives. Electricity and telephone companies in America and Europe have a long history of averaging costs in an effort to serve widely. The diseconomies of small scale in the country or of large-scale service in the great

metropoli are old public utility problems that have been prag-
matically solved over and over.

Fourth, it might be required that the wire system companies
radiate at least the same number of over-the-air signals as before
the wiring, so that homes without wire service would be no worse
off than now. Broadcast authorities in the United Kingdom, Norway, Sweden, Finland, Switzerland, the Soviet Union, and other
European countries have a strong tradition of providing nation-
wide radio and television service to quite remote and inaccessible
places, on grounds of social policy. In the United States, the same
type of effort occurs for a different reason, although perhaps to a
lesser degree—because advertisers pay according to number of
viewers who can receive the signal. The present use of unmanned
stations (boosters, repeaters, and ground satellites) to reach
shadowed areas in mountainous terrain or low-density sections is
already extensive and economical in the United States and
Europe. These are inexpensive, low-power transmitters without
studios that receive input signals over the air or from wire and
propagate them to areas of difficult access. For example, Norway
already uses 125 low-power television repeaters. Switzerland and
Sweden each use more than 100 low-power boosters. France has
800 low-power relay stations, Finland 20 low-power repeaters, and
West Germany more than 500 low-power stations [(44) WRTV
Handbook, 1969]. Norway describes its plans or hopes: " . . . owing
to the topography and scattered population of Norway, approximately 50 main transmitters and 1,500–2,000 low-power repeater
stations are necessary for 100 per cent coverage of the country with
television of good technical quality." [(26) Norwegian Broadcasting
Company, 1968/69].

Finally, there will be much, much time to make whatever adjustments are necessary to protect rural viewers. Entrance and
diffusion of the wired city would be massive undertakings in organization and construction—similar to the building of a highway
system. The spread of wire services would be gradual. It would
take at least a decade or so before the major fraction of the population could be on wire, and still more years before the figure
approached 80 or 90 per cent. During this time, broadcasting
stations would surely be transmitting both on wire and over the
air [(4) Barnett and Greenberg, 1969]. As the innovation diffuses
and load factors improve, the costs per home would decline. Meantime, there would have occurred new developments in this dyna-

mic field, such as technical advances which could further reduce cost of transmission to remote areas. The difficulties in providing rural areas with their present or an increased volume of television would be even less than today. For example, there have been recent developments in extremely short-wave (18,000 megahertz), unmanned transmitters for multiple TV signals to substitute for wire links in cable television systems. These are received by automatic exchanges or low-power stations, which then translate the signals to VHF or UHF frequencies and rebroadcast them locally on wire or over the air for a 20-mile radius. In the United States the Teleprompter Corporation, the leading U.S. CATV company, and Hughes Aircraft Company are now conducting experimental operations of this Amplitude Modulated Link in New York City and several small Oregon and New Mexico communities, under FCC authorization [(25) NCTA Bulletin, 1968].

Pay-TV

The argument is made that the wired city should be prohibited because its extra channels would permit pay-TV. As noted earlier, pay-TV is the provision of special programs or series on a "view-for-pay basis." In effect an admission charge is levied. The evil of pay-TV, it is said, is that their suppliers would seek to purchase or produce desirable programs and films to show to their viewers. The advertiser-supported networks and stations like London Weekend, Columbia Broadcasting System, and WTOP could not compete successfully against pay-TV companies. Nor could the BBC which is supported by license fees, nor the U.S. educational TV stations. The more desirable programs of all these would be bid away, and viewers would have to pay for what it now free TV. Low-income viewers, in particular, would be the losers, stemming from an inability to subscribe to pay-TV programs and substantial disappearance of free TV.

The argument has been given major and respectful attention by the Federal Communications Commission in the United States. It is responsible for policy decisions which have quite emasculated pay-TV, made by that body up to and including the present. It is the establishment view in Great Britain. It appeared in the British Pilkington Report of 1960, and more recently in a letter to *The Times* (20 June, 1968) from Lord Pilkington: ". . . his Committee concluded unanimously that if Pay-TV supplied a service for which viewers were prepared to pay fees sufficient to cover its costs, 'it would significantly reduce the value to viewers of the BBC and ITA services:' programs broadcast on Pay-TV services in return for fees would not be available to BBC viewers who paid by license duty or to ITA viewers who paid nothing." [The entire quotation is from the Editor's Preface to (7) Caine, p. 5; the inner quotation is from Lord Pilkington's letter]. The Pilkington Report concluded in its summary of recommendations: "No service of subscription television, whether by wire or by radio, should be authorized. There should be no experiment in subscription television" [(33) Pilkington, 1962, p. 295 and pp. 262–71, see a critical review in (43) Wiles, 1963]. Similar arguments have been made whenever pay-TV has been suggested and frequently when wire TV is proposed. They must be taken seriously.

One answer is that the wired city is not pay-TV. If pay-TV is an objectionable service, public policy could most easily deny it access to the wire. The wired city need not be rejected in order to reject pay-TV. Pay-TV is an option that the wired city offers conveniently to society, and very cheaply as compared with over-the-air pay-TV in metering,, billing, and preventing unpaid reception [(21) L. Johnson, 1970]. It need not be accepted if society believes it unwise.

A second answer is that the dichotomy of "pay-TV" and "free TV" is a fallacy. Free TV is not free. In the United States TV homes pay directly about $7,000 millions per year for purchase and operation of TV receivers. This is the annual cost for amortization and maintenance of the TV set, antenna and for electricity. In addition, they pay the entire cost of programs indirectly in supporting TV advertising outlays for broadcasting—another $2,500 millions per year. Similarly in the United Kingdom, the TV homes pay a large sum for reception service and a considerable, but lesser, amount for the broadcasting. The 1968 figures for the 56 million TV homes in the U.S.A. and the 15 million in the U.K. are roughly as in Table 1.

Now we consider whether pay-TV would significantly reduce program supply for viewers of free TV. It is the case that the wired city innovation would easily and economically accommodate pay-TV. This is because of much larger channel capacity at low cost, and because of ease, economy, and flexibility in metering pay-TV customers and filtering out the noncustomers. We consider the markets involved in pay-TV, assuming introduction of the wired city and its numerous open channels.

Pay-TV will enter the entertainment and sports market. In this market, firms purchase talent, performances, exhibition rights, concerts tapes, and the like, and offer them to consumers for pay. For instance, the cinema offers moving pictures, athletic teams

Table 1   Costs of "Free TV"—U.S.A. and U.K. Per TV Home, Per Year

	U.K. (£)	U.K. ($)	U.S.A. ($)
Broadcasting Cost			
BBC TV license revenue (a)	£4	$10 (c)	—
Broadcasting revenues (b)	7	17 (c)	$45
Subtotals (d)	£11	$27	$45
Reception cost (e)	30	72	120
Total cost of free-TV	£41	$99	$165

Notes:

(a) The BBC license figure is after deduction of the Post Office collection charge and excludes the portion of the combined license fee attributable to radio.

(b) The advertising sales and other broadcast revenue figures, both U.S. and U.K., are net of agency commissions and discounts, but gross otherwise. They are thus equal to the sum of selling, administrative, program, and technical expenses; taxes and government levies; interest, dividends, and retained earnings. Advertisers pay this aggregate sum to broadcasters and collect it from the viewing-consuming public.

(c) The BBC would appear to be a very efficient TV supplier since it provides $1\frac{1}{2}$ or 2 channels for $10 as against 1 ITV channel for $17. But ITV pays substantial income taxes and levies.

(d) As between the U.K. and U.S., the aggregate for BBC and ITV is much lower than U.S.—$27 vs. $45. Although both U.K. and U.S. provide an average of 3 channels per TV market, the U.S. provides many more hours per day. A further reason for lower British cost is lower pay scales and less lavish operations in the U.K. (as in Europe relative to Hollywood in film operations, until recently).

(e) U.K. reception costs are taken from National Board for Prices and Incomes, *Costs and Charges in the Radio and Television Rental and Relay Industry*, Report No. 52, January 1968 (London, H.M. Stationery Office), based on TV rental data per set for the half of British sets which are rented in a competitive market. I have added a small allowance for antenna and electricity. U.S. receiver costs are my estimates. They are based on $1\frac{1}{4}$ sets per TV home, of which one-fifth are color; an allowance for antenna and electricity; and annual rates of about 15 per cent of capital cost for maintenance and about 20 per cent for interest and amortization.

sell admissions to games, and present broadcasters offer programs for which advertisers pay on behalf of viewers. The "show-for-pay" TV entrepreneurs who now enter the market will be competing with these firms and with each other in purchase of talent and programs. And all of these organizations will compete for consumer viewing and dollars paid for viewing.

In some cases, the pay-TV firm will be successful in outbidding the present broadcaster. The equivalent of this happens time and again, everyday. The closed circuit TV prize fights which are shown in cinemas are cases where show-for-pay operators outbid the free TV broadcasters for initial showings. Cinemas usually outbid TV for film showing during the first few years following their production. Hundreds of show-for-pay theaters and concert halls outbid broadcasters for talent and performances at particular times. The U.S. ball parks which "blank out" TV during home games and many away-games are showing for pay in the ball parks, and denying or outbidding broadcasters at these times.

The pay-TV firm will engage in buying talent, films, game rights, etc. The owner will learn to limit his offerings to what he can sell at a profit. He has no captive audience or assured revenue. He will buy as shrewdly as he can. Some of the pay-TV showings will be "new"—that is exhibition rights not previously available, new talent, shows the firms produce themselves, ball games not previously shown, foreign shows and tapes, and satellite events from abroad. Some will be bid away from others, who will have to find and produce replacements. This happened when ITV entered to compete with BBC, and also when BBC 2 was added to the existing two networks. It happened when TV first entered to compete with radio, theaters, and other exhibitions for talent and for audiences. It happens when cinema or broadcasters bid for the local nightclub comic and take him to London, Hollywood, or New York.

The question essentially involved is the long-term elasticity of supply of entertainment material, ball games, concerts, theatrical talent, moving pictures, comedians, and newscasters, domestic and foreign, old and new combined. Are all these employed on television in full degree? If so, then additional demands will only raise price. If not, then volume can be expected to increase. The evidence is that the supply is very, very elastic. There would seem to be no danger that the viewers of free TV will not be offered first-rate programs. In London, as I write this paper, there are operating about forty first-rank legitimate theaters, many minor ones, five symphony orchestras, several opera companies, and other entertainments. They have not appeared on TV this season. Nor, in general, have the great number of artists in these companies. The same is generally true in the United States. Live theater and music performances would lose some talent and audience to the competition of pay-TV, but there is no danger that free TV will not offer expensive programs.

Increased demand in entertainment, sports, and news is not an undesirable phenomenon. Unemployed artists get work; new artists are encouraged; minor leagues become major, as in U.S. baseball and football; lesser sports become major; salary rates rise somewhat; new programs are created; young people break into theater, news, sports, and other public offerings.

We now comment on the financial competition between advertiser-sponsored broadcasters and pay-TV in the U.S. Advertisers are powerful bidders. They spent around $2\frac{1}{2}$ billion on U.S. television in 1967. Consumer expenditures in the category most competitive with television (admissions to such spectator amusements as motion picture and stage theaters, opera, entertainment of non-profit institutions, and spectator sports) were less—$1.8 billion, about $150 million per month, on *all* these activities [(36) U.S. Survey of Current Business, 1969.] It seems clear that pay-TV could not generally outbid advertisers wishing to reach the mass audience with free programs. One hears statements about how 50 million homes, each paying $1 to view each of the U.S. National Football League games would provide $50 million in pay-TV revenues per game, and leave free-TV barren of first-class sports offerings. But three such events per month would exhaust the *total* of consumers' budgeted expenditures on *all* forms of admission to spectator amusements, and one event per month would exceed the entire U.S. budget for sports.

The American public spends only $35 million per month on spectator sports—on all of professional baseball, football and hockey, horse and dog race tracks, college football and baseball, and other amateur sports. Let us even assume that it blows its entire spectator sports budget on a single NFL football game on TV each autumn month. Then this still leaves available for bid by advertiser-sponsored TV the dozens of other NFL games, the AFL games, the college games, the Bowls, the major league baseball season of 2,000 games, the minor leagues, the minor sports, and so forth. In Great Britain, there are dozens of esteemed football (soccer) teams and dozens of games each week. Only a few are shown on television. If one or more were to be bid away from free TV, there are many more still available. The fact is that advertising budgets are of enormous size and power in sports and TV generally.

Turn now to the competition for viewer time. The American home averages over 40 hours per week of watching commercial TV. With the foregoing budget limitations of American payments for admissions, pay-TV could capture only a small portion of the national viewer audience each week. The cost to the viewer of a pay-TV program is after all very much greater than that of a free one!

Actually, the major effects of pay-TV are likely to be in competition with other paid attendance. Assume, for example, that first-run movies come down the wire with perfect picture quality and without advertising interruptions or the need to pay baby sitters and to look for parking places and then stand in line. Cinema attendance might be significantly reduced again, as it was when TV first competed for audiences on a large scale.

Monopoly in the Wired City
The network of the wired city is characterized by strong economies of scale in each area. For any city, other things constant, the network costs are smaller for one firm than if competitors entered, laid down duplicate wires, and they all fought for subscribers. Electricity, telephone, water and gas grids are comparable in this respect. There will thus be a strong tendency for development of wire network monopoly [(22) N. Johnson, 1970; (29) Posner, 1970; (10) Dean, 1970; (21) L. Johnson, 1970; (4) Barnett and Greenberg, 1969]. On the other hand, the "natural monopoly" characteristics of the network do not extend to programs. There is no technical reason to permit monopolization in TV program origination. There is, indeed, every reason to ensure that the operation of the network be conducted as an open access, common-carrier system, and this enterprise be kept entirely out of program and message activity.

The danger that the wire network monopoly will use its power to acquire program and message monopoly is acute in the United States and Canada. CATV firms are both developing wire networks and providing the television programs thereon. They have no common carrier obligations. There is not open access to their channels. Once well established in an area, a CATV firm has overwhelming advantage over any other prospective firms in view of the scale economies in the wire network. Thus, even though the company has only a non-exclusive license in the first instance, there has been a very strong tendency for it to acquire a monopoly of the wire network and programming. There may be several CATV firms in a county but each is a monopoly in its own area and they do not effectively compete once established.

What might the monopolist do if he is not subject to common carrier obligations and is offering programs himself? He might prefer certain politicians over others. He might decline to import desirable programs of distant stations if this would reduce advertising sales on his own originated programs. He could be uncooperative in providing time for public-affairs activities if these reduced audience for pay-TV or advertiser programs. He could avoid controversial offerings and people, and censor what he did offer. He could exert monopoly force and toll on other television groups and services. In sum, there could be a concentration of economic and political power equal to the present concentrations in monopoly broadcast organizations in Europe, but without the public interest concerns and controls customary in these enterprises. Extensive development of this type could quite frustrate the objectives of the wired city. The wired city would then become a danger in a free society, even beyond present television oligopolies.

Some of the principles for avoiding the danger are immediately apparent. First, the network company should be a public utility, regulated to be an open access common carrier. Second, it is doubtful that it should be permitted to engage in offering programs or wire services other than operation of the network. It is also questionable as to whether it should be permitted to own or engage in publishing or entertainment activities. It would be safer if it could not do these things. But if it did, safeguards should be introduced to prevent exploitation of its network monopoly power in the related activities of communication, entertainment, sports, politics, and social persuasion. The dangers in concentrated control over a variety of communications are very serious in the United States [(22) N. Johnson, 1970] and all developed countries. Concentration is already far advanced in most nations. Fourth, the service area of any single network company should not be very large in order that there might be competition among alternative companies in bids for installing and operating wire networks. This also would permit comparative operations to be appraised, would provide alternative firms when a utility's performance was unsatisfactory and franchise was to be withdrawn, and would permit independent efforts in technological progress. Fifth, franchise periods and buy-out or reversion terms, which would permit change in ownership or direction of the wire network monopolist, should be stipulated.

Excess Franchise Charges and Taxes

The form of CATV development in the U.S.A. and Canada is posing still another obstacle to desirable development of the wired city. CATV companies earn high returns at the conventional subscription fee of $5 per month. In general, municipalities have chosen not to regulate rates of return despite the *de facto* monopoly privilege they grant in the so-called "non-exclusive" franchises. Instead, as municipalities have become aware of how profitable CATV systems are, they have begun to exact large payments in exchange for the franchise. For example, the New York City proposals are 5 per cent of gross receipts from residents, 10 per cent from lease of channels to communications services, and up to 25 per cent for pay-TV, in addition to usual taxes [(10) Dean, 1970, p. 44]. More and more communities will procure high franchise fees, either from negotiation or by requiring CATV applicants to bid against each other. Franchise taxes of a third or even a half of revenues to the city are possible when the franchise authority is less concerned about the rate that will be charged to consumers than it is over its own revenues [(4) Barnett and Greenberg, 1969].

Municipalities tend to be so impelled by their chronic, sometimes desperate, shortage of revenues. But this high-tax behavior prejudices the major question of whether the CATV should not have charged a much lower rate in the first place. It also tends to force CATV rates even higher [(29) Posner, 1970; (32) Smith, 1970]. A preferable policy for the wired city would be rates closer to cost of service plus a reasonable return on capital and for risk. At the lower prices which would then result, more homes would subscribe, permitting still lower rates in this declining marginal cost industry. Monthly subscriber rates might fall to half of present levels.

A similar phenomenon has occurred in British television. The independent television companies licensed by the ITA have monopoly access to TV advertisements, and they share audiences only with BBC. The result was extraordinarily high profits— almost 40 per cent on capitalization *after taxes* in the five years 1957–62. The British government, in 1964, imposed levies on the gross advertising revenues of independent television in an attempt to recoup these monopoly gains thereafter. It could have, as in Switzerland, Netherlands, Germany, Italy, and some other countries, allocated the funds to the public broadcast corporations (BBC and ITA) to improve and enlarge their efforts. Broadcasting was the industry that provided the funds. Instead, the very large levies, about one-fourth of the gross advertising revenues, are discharged into the general funds of the Chancellor of the Exchequer. The result is that television has been differentially taxed, to a far heavier degree than other entertainment, news, advertising, or communication industries. [35 UK NBPI, 1970]. (It could be argued, but has not been, that the broadcasting industry should be differentially taxed because it preempts a portion of the scarce electromagnetic spectrum space and thus denies it to other economic uses.)

Advertising Excess and Abuse

The major European countries have avoided advertising abuse in broadcasting. The volume of advertising per hour is constrained. Program disruption is limited. Advertiser sponsorship of and influence on programs was prevented. While the many channels of the wired city would increase broadcasting outlets and thereby advertising, the past European record suggests that advertising would not be permitted to devalue programs.

In American commercial broadcasting, on the other hand, advertising practices have severely degraded program value in television and radio by excessive volume and disruption [(13) Friendly, 1967, p. 287, 288]. The difficulty is now deeply rooted in American political life.

According to the U.S. National Association of Broadcasters (NAB) voluntary code, advertisements should not exceed 20 to 25 per cent of the hour, plus two advertising spot announcements between programs, plus opening and closing "billboard" announcements, plus station ID and coming program announcements.

But, as the FCC officially stated [(40) Federal Register, 1963, (28) p. 5158]:

> ... the NAB has only been able to enlist about 38 percent of all radio stations and 70 percent of television stations to subscribe to the codes. And with respect to those that have subscribed, the NAB, by itself, lacks effective sanctions to prevent abuses.

Beyond the amount of advertising time in the code which, even if not abused, far exceeds European standards, there is the placement of the advertisements. While there is no intention by advertisers or stations to be sadistic to viewers, there is obviously intent to reach the viewers' attention when strongly fixed. This frequently results in severe disruption, particularly in dramatic programs and motion pictures.

In 1963, the FCC issued a "Notice of Proposed Rule Making With Respect to Advertising on Standard, FM and Television Broadcast Stations," [40, Federal Register, 1963, (28) p. 5158]. It recited over-commercialization, advertising abuses, the failure of self-regulation by the industry, complaints by the public, and other difficulties and proposed official adoption of the Radio and Television Codes of the industry's trade association—the National Association of Broadcasters.

The House of Representatives, Committee on Interstate and Foreign Commerce, reacted in wrath. A bill was immediately introduced, "H.R. 8316 (1963)" which proposed to amend the Communications Act by adding a provision, ". . . that the Commission may not by rule prescribe standards with respect to the length or frequency of advertisements which may be broadcast by all or any class of stations in the broadcast service" [(23) Jones, p. 1229]. As reported in the press, the Committee angrily and forcibly informed the FCC that it was way out of bounds in undertaking to regulate or even appraise station autonomy in advertisements. It reported its bill favorably, stating that the FCC's rule-making proceeding with respect to advertising was without statutory authority.

The FCC, having been publicly whipped, was thoroughly cowed. It terminated the rule-making proceeding on January 15, 1964, expecting that the Congress would permit it a scrap of face-saving in its retreat. The Committee nevertheless brought HR 8316 to a vote in the House on February 27, 1964, where it passed by a vote of 317 to 43. (There was no action in the Senate.)

In summary, the FCC cannot regulate over-commercialization

and advertising abuses by stations because Congress will not permit it to do so. Anthony Lewis pointed out (*International Herald Tribune*, 24 September 1969, London dispatch): "The American broadcasting industry has rightly been called one of the most powerful of lobbies. It is not just that many members of Congress have television interests. Much more important is the fact that members regard television appearances as a potent aid to re-election and so hesitate to offend station owners." The extent of members' direct and indirect financial interests and political alliances with the broadcasting stations in their constituencies is not generally known. Nor is the financial fecundity of a station broadcasting license, nor how strongly a station will fight to protect its private mint.

There is more than a little danger in the United States that advertising excesses and abuses will occur on many of the channels of the wired city. This is a matter for public policy concern now, before the cable innovation becomes widespread and the wired city arrives. Perhaps European-type standards should be set to control excess volume, disruption, and sponsor's influence. The Federal Communications Commission has already proposed such standards on advertising volume and disruption for CATV, and Congress has thus far not objected. Congressmen's links with the small-size CATV industry are far less than with the powerful broadcasting industry. And, of course, advertising restraints on CATV finances and growth serve the financial interests of broadcasters and their unrestrained advertising scales. CATV is willing to accept constraints to enter and develop. It is possible, therefore, that public policies along European lines could at this time be successfully imposed to restrain advertising on wired city channels. When one compares present European and American television advertising practices and their effects on programs, one is fervently inclined to hope for this.

But a policy of strong restriction on advertising is not clearly necessary in the logic of the wired city, and may be inconsistent with it. *If* the wired city were to be a genuinely open-access and common carrier with strong competition among program suppliers, competition would provide what consumers wanted and were willing to pay for. As with newspapers and magazines, some channels would be a massive barrage of advertising, but some would have little or none. Similarly, as in cinemas, some would have advertising and some not.

c

There are difficulties with betting entirely on perfect competition and *laissez-faire* for control, however. Perfect competition usually does not occur, and then restraints on advertising might yield a preferred "second-best" economic solution. It is also possible that governments will decide against a strong libertarian, *laissez-faire,* economic market solution for operation of the wired city for reasons of social and political stability. It may be decided that advertising beyond limited amounts and types constitutes pollution which should be controlled. Finally, it is possible that the TV medium has such extraordinary powers in excitation, persuasion and manipulation that unlimited advertising dosage at the discretion of wealthy companies and individuals can warp society and persons. In summary, television advertising generates wide-ranging social costs including effects on children which may be serious enough to require control [(2) Barnett, 1970 and references therein].

ECONOMIC PRESSURE GROUPS

It is inevitable that innovations be resisted by the economic interests that would be adversely affected. Innovations partially displace products or factors of production by shifting demand to others that become more desired or efficient. Society tends to benefit from an innovation voluntarily accepted by consumers or producers, acceptance implying greater efficiency in providing consumer satisfaction or in production. Suppliers of the displaced product, however, are not necessarily better off and they resist the innovation and strive for protection. Sometimes the resistance is violent, as when the Luddites smashed textile machinery which would have enabled fewer workers to produce the same output. More usually, it is by the exertion of economic pressures and political efforts to persuade government and the public that the innovation is undesirable. The allegations that the wired city would damage rural areas, that pay-TV is undesirable, and that there are other dangers, discussed above, are examples of such efforts.

Which economic interests oppose this innovation? The press, cinemas, and other broadcasters would be strongly opposed.

Press

The press has a three-fold competitive interest *vis-a-vis* television. Both media present news. Both are usually supported in significant degree by advertisements. And they compete for the limited leisure time of the public, for readers or viewers. In Japan, for example, homes view TV for 21 hours per week and listen to radio for three hours a week, a total of 24 hours of broadcasting. This compares with only $3\frac{1}{2}$ hours per week for newspapers and magazines.

In Britain, the history of radio and television is studded with continual press opposition to the broadcasting of news and advertisements. The press preferred monopoly in broadcasting and restricted service:

> The Press has always been conscious that broadcasting and the Press were, or might be, competitive. The broadcasting of news, commentaries and talks might reduce the sales of newspapers and periodicals; if broadcasting were financed by advertisements, the advertisement revenue of the Press might suffer. The Press was aware of the danger in the earliest days of broadcasting and was able to protect its interests even before the broadcasting scheme in 1922 was brought into existence [(8) Coase, 1950, p. 103].

The BBC license of 1922 and a supplementary agreement with the press provided that BBC would not broadcast news or related information except as obtained from named news agencies, nor broadcast news at all before 7 p.m. It was only in 1972 that BBC, bargaining with great skill, reached agreement with the Press and the four main news agencies that allowed the BBC to broadcast its first news bulletin at 6.30 p.m. and to transmit a strictly limited number of eye-witness descriptions [(6) Briggs, 1965, p 153]. BBC refrained from introducing a regular radio news bulletin earlier than 6 p.m. until the outbreak of the war in 1939.

The newspapers were very influential in prohibiting broadcast advertising in Britain from the 1920's until the 1950's: "It is in the national interest that newspapers should be safeguarded against unfair competition from a monopoly given by the State . . . what is for the good of the race it not always for the good of the individual immediately concerned. . . . It is very hard to convince a man who is going to lose his living that it is to the national advantage that he should be sacrificed. So far as the newspapers are concerned, they are not prepared to be sacrificed." [(8) Coase, 1950, pp. 105–6, quoting Lord Riddell on his testimony on behalf of the Newspaper Proprietors' Association (NPA)]. In 1945, the Newspaper Proprietors' Association continued to protest that radio advertising ". . . is unnecessary from the point of view of advertisers, whose requirements can in normal conditions be fully and adequately met by the Press and other existing media of publicity" [(8) Coase, 1950, p. 106, quoting a policy statement issued by the NPA].

Newspaper interests consistently fought broadcasting and its extension through the years. They have opposed reporting of test matches and boat races, skimming headlines off the news, foreign broadcasts to England, broadcasts by "pirate" stations, the printing of foreign broadcast schedules in newspapers (the *Daily Worker* refused to go along [(8) Coase, 1950]), and the publication of *The Listener* and the *Radio Times* by the BBC (and in any case wanted limitation of the advertisements in these journals) [(6) Briggs, 1965, pp. 286–288].

Switzerland had a difficult problem in introducing television. The country has a population of only 6 million. It has three major linguistic groups to serve: German, French and Italian, as well as a small one in Romanche. The nation is a federation of strong provincial governments. Local newspapers, all with very small circulations, are major in the nation's political and cultural life. Its mountainous terrain makes broadcast transmission difficult and expensive. After experimentation, it was decided that television could not be suitably financed from license fees only, but would need advertising support. Newspapers were alarmed. Their trade association subscribed a large annual subsidy fund to support, for up to ten years, limited television offerings by the public broadcasting monopoly, on the proviso that advertising would not be permitted. This successfully delayed the entrance of television advertising from 1958 until 1964. In 1964, the publishers, who by the 1958 agreement could legally have delayed advertisements until 1968, agreed to commercial television in order to acquire a favorable bargaining position. Advertising sales of television time at fixed prices are permitted, limited to fifteen minutes per day. (In the U.S.A. this much advertising appears each hour!) Local advertising is prohibited, and every effort must be made to prevent injury to the Swiss press. Radio advertising is prohibited. A public corporation, the Society for Swiss TV advertising, has been established as a monopolist for sale of all TV advertising time in Switzerland. It is controlled 40 per cent by the newspaper publishers, 40 per cent by the Swiss Broadcasting Corporation, and the remainder by representatives of commerce, industry, press association, farmers, and tradesmen.

In the Netherlands the government fell in 1964 on a controversy concerning increase in television service and introduction of advertising. The press was strongly opposed to the introduction of advertisements and expansion of television broadcasting, in fear of adverse effects on newspaper circulation and advertising revenue. A new government was constituted. It provided for television advertising of up to fifteen minutes per day on either one or the other, or a combination, of the two television networks; and twenty-four minutes per day for each of the three radio networks. Reversing the Swiss arrangement with respect to newspapers, 40 per cent of the advertising revenue for several years was reserved for compensating the press in the event of advertising losses, which have indeed occurred. All advertising is handled by a public foundation, the board of which is appointed by the Government and on which various media, including the press, are represented.

In most other European countries, the history of press resistance to television expansion and advertising is similar. In Western Germany, there is a continuing battle between broadcasters and press over advertising income. Although there are severe time limits on TV advertising in order to protect the press, nevertheless, in 1965 a law was drafted by the German Newspaper Publishers Association proposing to forbid all radio and TV advertising. In Italy, as a result of pressure from the press, the broadcast monopoly's charter of 1952 decreed a strict limit (5 per cent) on the ratio of advertising to program time. Actual levels have never reached this. In 1962, only about 3 per cent of each of television and radio time was taken by advertisements. "RAI intentionally allows only enough advertising to support its activities adequately without seriously affecting press income" [(27) Paulu, 1967, p. 104].

In the United States, increase in broadcasting and support by advertising was early authorized in the Radio Act of 1927 and the Communications Act of 1934, and occurred even before then. In these Acts, it was explicitly decided that there would not be a broadcasting monopoly. The broadcasting industry in legislative purpose and operating fact had been opened for commercial growth and exploitation. There seem to have been no real opportunities for the press to prevent the growth of commercial television. The corporations that owned magazines and newspapers entered the great competition to acquire frequency assignments and enter the profitable business.

As broadcasting grew in influence and power and particularly when television arrived, newspaper and magazine working staffs and the publishers without broadcasting subsidiaries came to greatly resent their powerful broadcasting competitors. Financial stringencies from the competition forced many of the leading magazines to close down and added greatly to the financial problems of newspapers. During television's quiz scandals and at other times of public criticism, television circles believed that the large volume of magazine and press space devoted to their embarrassments reflected the deep press resentment at its gradual replacement as the major news and advertising media.

The history of world press reaction to the introduction of radio and television tells us a good deal about their attitude to the prospective wired city innovation. The press will, in general, be strongly opposed to large increases in television offerings and advertising times, and to reductions in television advertising rates. In the United States, press opposition is likely to be relatively ineffective. The press lost its dominant position in mass communications many years ago. In Europe, however, the press is most likely to exercise strong restrictive influence, as it has heretofore.

The strategy for resistance in Europe is roughly predictable. First, the press will argue for preservation of the existing public broadcasting monopolies; for license fees as the financial basis of operation to the maximum extent possible; and for limited over-the-air transmission. All these tend to restrict the growth of television. Thus, if there are to be new television services, these should be offered by the existing monopolies, as in Netherlands and proposed in Sweden, and not by a new authority, as when Britain introduced ITV. Second, the press will try to continue the strong limitations on volume and range of advertising, through legislative pressures, agreements, and participations on councils and boards. Third, government should continue to exercise discretionary controls on broadcasting. This is achieved in several ways. One is traditional European monopoly or oligopoly control of programs in the public interest. Another is the usual PTT (government post, telegraph, and telephone monopoly) restrictions with respect to all over-the-air and wire transmissions. A third is monopoly control on volume and types of broadcast advertising, as in Britain, Italy, Switzerland, Netherlands, and other countries. Finally, the press will attempt to acquire stakes and participations in the enlarged television industry, as they have done whenever such commercial ownership was possible, e.g., by substantial ownership of program production companies. In Britain, the press ownership figure was 23 per cent in 1959 [(20) Harris and Seldon, 1959, p. 174]. In W. Germany, the Axel Springer press combine has been pushing strongly to extend its mass communications empire into commercial television.

Cinemas

We distinguish between cinemas (exhibition houses) and motion picture producers. There is now a substantial history in the United States and Europe of very severe declines in cinema motion picture attendance due to substitution of TV.

In the United States, opposition to the wired city has already begun. In California, a well-financed commercial organization, headed by the former president of the National Broadcasting Company television network, attempted to innovate pay-TV on wire in the early 1960's. The showings were first-run films, major sports events, and other exceptional offerings without advertising, on a pay-basis-per-program. Led by motion picture exhibitors and assisted by broadcasters, a crusade to eliminate the competitive threat was launched. A referendum on the California ballot, making such pay-TV illegal was approved by the electorate in a large vote, as the result of extensive publicity in cinemas, on theater marquees, and in other advertisements. The company was enjoined from operation by the new statute. Several years later, the California Supreme Court declared the referendum law unconstitutional, but by then the company's wire pay-TV activity had been liquidated.

A few years ago, a major nationwide campaign was launched by American motion picture exhibitors against CATV. The campaign theme posted on theaters was "Save Free TV." Moviegoers were shown a film in which cable TV begins as a small serpent but grows to terrifying proportions and blots out free TV. For months, cinemagoers speculated on why theater owners, of all people, were concerned to save free TV. U.S. over-the-air TV has already been a traumatic experience for cinemas, and the prospect now of competition from the many channels of the wired city strikes terror in the pockets of theater owners. The wired city would provide imported programs from other cities, programs for so-called minority tastes, movies without frequent advertising interruptions, and pay-TV, none of which is readily available now. In addition, the wire system would multiply conventional TV offerings, which are competitive with the cinemas for audience.

Broadcasters

In the United States, each local group of several broadcasters is an oligopoly relative to the local viewers. Entry of new stations is very difficult from a combination of factors. One is limited spectrum and TV assignments. Second, network affiliation is important for both advertising revenues and popular network programs. But there are only three networks, and existing stations have pre-empted the affiliations in virtually all cities. The fact of only three networks is itself largely due to the limited number of local stations, since most cities have three or fewer stations. A third factor is the cost of operating a station, including the substantial fixed cost of transmitting each over-the-air signal from a main transmitter—$2,000 to $3,000 per week.

Oligopoly makes for high profits. In 1965, the $102 million of profits (before Federal income tax) of the 15 *stations* owned and operated by the three networks exceeded their investment in tangible broadcast properties. For the 473 other VHF stations, the profits were $287 million on tangible broadcast property investment of $316 million [(39) FCC, 1965].

In the United Kingdom, the level of monopoly profits of the independent companies was also shockingly high for a number of years—for example, 40 per cent on capitalization (*after* tax) in 1961–62—until Parliament provided for special levies [(7) Caine, 1968, p. 19]. Lord Thomson, owner of a newspaper empire and then a major holder in Scottish Television, had commented that a television contract was "a license to print money."

Clearly, private commercial television broadcasting is usually very profitable under conditions of large audience and monopoly or oligopoly. Large audiences tolerate the massive and disruptive barrage of advertisements of the U.S. system. Advertisers find television a very productive sales instrument or one in which competitors' actions must be countered or escalated. And, advertiser expenditures on TV tend to rise over time. The holder of a commercial television license has every reason to fight entrance of the wired city. It would fragment his captive audience for which advertisers pay. And it would provide alternative advertising time, outside his control, for sale to merchants, politicians, and industries.

The networks, stations, and their trade associations and attorneys in the United States, have understandably fought CATV and the prospective wired city. For example, the National Association of Broadcasters (NAB) commissioned preparation of a major book, *Television and the Wired City* [(24) Land, 1968], for submission to the U.S. President's Task Force on Communications Policy in an effort to show that the wired city would not increase program diversity [(19) Greenberg and Barnett, 1971]. The NAB and other broadcaster groups have also been very vigorous before the Federal Communications Commission in measures to prevent the growth of CATV.

In other countries, the governmental broadcasting organizations can also be expected to resist the wired city innovation. BBC has fought the wire exchanges, imported programs, and the establishment of ITV [(8) Coase, 1950; (5) (6) Briggs, 1961, 1965]. It opened a second channel in order to forestall for a time ITV's extension to a second channel. It is now (1969/70) creating a BBC local radio system in the hope of forestalling entrance of local commercial radio.

It is inevitable that a state broadcaster should attempt to protect its monopoly. If it operates on license fees, then entrance of competing television service takes audience and reduces political support for prospective fee increases. It may even be argued that the license revenue should be shared with the interloper. A competitive service would also bid for talent and shows. This breaks the monopsony controls of the input markets, and usually causes some rise in the cost of programs and talent, as in Great Britain with the advent of ITV. If the monopoly enjoys advertising revenues, the entering service acquires a share of these and causes advertising rates to be less than if there were no competition. The political relations and compacts which the monopoly enjoys with other government agencies and the legislature are disturbed. Government empires and bureaucracies are shaken up. Alternatives against which to gauge performance come into being. The state monopoly is distressed by the need to compete for audiences. As Judge Learned Hand once pointed out, a monopolist enjoys a quiet life, competitors do not. ". . . The State broadcasting agencies, well entrenched and strongly backed by the national establishment, often fought the introduction of advertising especially if the creation of competitive broadcasting organizations was also involved" [(27) Paula, 1967, p. 95].

The state broadcasting agencies will resist introduction of the wired city. Self interest accounts for much of this attitude. But the opposition of the State monopolist also rests upon public interest policies and arguments, which partly accounted for creation of the state monopoly in the initial instance. These will be mentioned in the concluding section of this paper.

Others

Other diverse persons and groups will resist the wired city. In Britain, it might include orchestral groups subsidized by the BBC. The Chancellor of the Exchequer who now levies, in addition to usual taxes, more than a quarter of the gross revenues of a so-called independent television system has a major stake in its high profits. In the United States, leading television performers and others who enjoy a degree of monopoly control of television inputs might lose somewhat if the wired city entered. The same is presently true of the owners of copyright television material under a recent U.S. Supreme Court decision that CATV pick-up of television broadcasts and relay to its subscribers is not subject to copyright payment. But this decision is likely to be reversed in new copyright legislation now before Congress. The several classes of exhibitors which would lose audience and not gain correspondingly by opportunity to broadcast on the wire would oppose the innovation.

The telephone and telegraph bureaucracies—the PTT's in Europe and the corresponding utilities in the U.S.—have been disturbed and feel their monopolies threatened by the wired city innovation. Generally, their initial reaction has been to resist or try to kill the innovation as a bothersome nuisance. Their later reactions, as the wired city potential becomes more manifest and its thrust stronger, is to try to take it over [(2) Barnett, 1970, pp. 39–41, 61–63].

Comment

Undue respect is given to arguments that the innovation may damage established economic interests—rural residents, press, cinemas, broadcast stations, etc. No economic innovation imposes uniform costs and provides uniform benefits for each individual in society. Extensive school improvements benefit mostly the families with children, but all pay the cost. The advent of air transport has benefited those who travel so, but (together with the automobile) has so reduced inter-city rail traffic that the service is no longer economical for those who prefer rail travel. Automobiles have not benefited all uniformly, nor have they imposed their burdens only on those who buy them. The advent of television has had severe impacts on the profitability and availability of substantial radio programs, magazines and newspapers, and even cinemas. The benefit from increased television services may be greater in rural areas, which have less access to big-city entertainment and other services.

All innovations are uneven in their benefits and cost burdens over the population. The criterion for introducing the innovation cannot be that there is no damage to existing economic interests from the innovation. If this were so, the horse-breeder could have persuaded society to reject the train and automobile. In one way or another, society has to cast up the accounts for prospective benefits and costs from each prospective innovation.

In the concluding section, below, I offer some judgements on the probable social response in the U.S. and Europe to the thrust of the wired city innovation in the near term.

CONCLUSIONS

It is likely that the wired city innovation as an economic market will develop strongly in the United States, for three main reasons. One is that CATV has demonstrated that wire systems are extremely efficient devices—economically, physically, and in quality —for feeding the voracious appetite for television in our affluent society. Second, U.S. public policy since the beginning has been that broadcasting should be governed by consumer and advertiser demands and the efforts of profit-seeking enterprises. The fits and starts and turnings and failures of the FCC should not obscure the fact that the basic statutes and durable policies have been to promote broadcasting as a competitive economic market. Third, the multiple, low-cost channels of the wired city provide important opportunities for the troubled public goods sectors—urban improvements, ghetto assistance, education, mail, public and private health, surveillance of streets, and others.

The major uncertainties are what institutional forms the wired city will take and whether it will become a "market" for free speech, discourse, and ideas. Specific uncertainties are the extent of monopoly and cross-media ownership; whether the networks will be public utility common carriers with open access; whether advertising and commercial excesses and abuses will extend to the wire; and what will the opportunities be for varied pay-TV.

In most of Europe, there is no early prospect for strong development of an open access wired city, either as an economic market or as a "market" for unlimited discourse. The major European countries have followed the British lead in adopting highly restrictive public service broadcasting. They have rejected the view that broadcasting is a member of the Fourth Estate and subject to advertiser and consumer economic dictates. In Europe, it is believed that the powerful television medium should be used in substantial degree to provide "merit goods"—education, culture, national history, art—no less than for popular programs. It is also believed that television service should be limited in volume and hours, in service to popular tastes and in seeking advertiser support. It should not be influential in politics, should be impartial, and should be detached from controversy.

The Europeans have thus opted for severe limits on television. In these circumstances, the productivity of the wired city in the near term is limited. While the basic physical elements of wired cities will sometimes come into being for physical, aesthetic, or efficiency reasons, as in the English "New Towns," in the present state of policy, program originations and imports are likely to be denied or restricted.

What will happen in the wired city in the longer term—say 1984—I shall not venture.

REFERENCES

(1) Barnett, H. J. *Economics of Television Markets.* St. Louis, Mo.; Washington Univ., mimeo. 1964. Filed with Federal Communication Commission 32 FCC 811 C Docket 14223, 1962.

(2) Barnett, H. J. *Resistance to the Wired City.* St. Louis: Washington Univ., mimeo, 1970.

(2a) Barnett, H. J. and Denzau, *Future Development of Instructional Television.* Washington University, 1971.

(3) Barnett, H. J. and Greenberg, E. *A Proposal for Wired City Television*. P-3668. Santa Monica, Calif.: RAND Corp., 1697. Subsequently published in *Washington Univ. Law Quarterly*, Winter 1968, pp. 1–25, and reprinted in *The Radio Spectrum*, Washington, D.C.: Brookings Institution, 1968. Condensed version in *American Economic Review*, June 1968, *58*.

(4) Barnett, H. J. and Greenberg, E. "Regulating CATV systems," *Law and Contemporary Problems*, 1969, 34, pp. 562–85.

(5) Briggs, A. *The Birth of Broadcasting*. London: Oxford Univ. Press, 1961.

(6) Briggs, A. *The Golden Age of Wireless*. London: Oxford Univ. Press, 1965. (v. II of the *History of Broadcasting in the U.K.*)

(7) Caine, Sir Sydney. *Paying for TV*. Hobart Paper 43. London: Institute of Economic Affairs, 1968.

(8) Coase, R. *British Broadcasting, A Study in Monopoly*. Cambridge: Harvard Univ. Press, 1950.

(9) d'Arcy, Jean. "Direct Broadcast Satellites and the Right to Communicate," *European Broadcasting Union Review*, Nov. 1969. 118B, pp. 15–18.

(10) Dean, Jr., S. "Hitches in the Cable," *The Nation*, July 20, 1970. 211.

(11) Dordick, H., Chesler, L., Firstman, S., and Bretz, R. *Telecommunications in Urban Development*. RM-6069-RC. Santa Monica, Calif.: RAND Corporation, 1969.

(12) Electronic Industries Association (EIA). *The Future of Broadband Communications*. Washington, D.C.: EIA, 2001 Eye St., N.W. Submitted to the Federal Communications Commission, Docket 18397, October 27, 1969.

(13) Friendly, F. *Due to Circumstances Beyond Our Control*. London: MacGibbon & Kee, 1967.

(14) Gabriel, R. P. "A Comparison of Wired and Wireless Broadcasting for the Future," *Royal Television Society Journal*, 1968, 12.

(15) Gabriel, R. P. "Wired Broadcasting in Great Britain," *IEEE Spectrum*, 1967, 4, pp. 97–105.

(16) Gargini, E. J. "Dial-a-programme Communication Television," *Royal Television Society Journal*, 1970, 13, pp. 95–106.

(17) Goldmark, Peter. *Broadcasting Magazine*, Dec. 21, 1970, 79, p. 32.

(18) Greenberg, E. "Television Station Profitability and FCC Regulating Policy," *Journal of Industrial Economics*, July, 1969.

(19) Greenberg, E. and Barnett, H. J. "Program Diversity—New Evidence and Old Theories," *American Economic Review*, May, 1971, 61.

(20) Harris, R. and Seldon, A. *Advertising in a Free Society*. London: Institute of Economic Affairs, 1959.

(21) Johnson, L. *Future of Cable Television: Some Problems of Federal Regulation*. RM-6199-FF. Santa Monica, Calif.: RAND Corporation, 1970.

(22) Johnson, Nicholas. *How to Talk Back To Your TV Set*. New York: Bantam Books, 1970.

(23) Jones, W. *Regulated Industries*. Brooklyn: The Foundation Press, 1967.

(24) Land, H. and Associates. *Television and The Wired City*. Washington D.C.: National Association of Broadcasters, 1968.

(25) National Cable Television Association *Bulletins* weekly. Washington, D.C.: NCTA, 918-16th St. N.W., 20006.

(26) Norwegian Broadcasting Company. *Fact Book*. Oslo: Aas and Wahl, 1968/69.

(27) Paulu, B. *Radio and TV Broadcasting on the European Continent*. Minneapolis: Univ. of Minnesota Press, 1967.

(28) Perry, W. "The Open University," paper presented at Royal Television Society Convention, March 21, 1970.

(29) Posner, R. "Cable Television: Problem of Local Monopoly." Santa Monica, Calif.: RAND Corporation.

(30) Rydbeck, Olof and Ploman, Edward W. *Broadcasting in the Space Age*. EBU Monograph No. 5. Geneva: European Broadcasting Union, 1969.

(31) Seiden, Martin H. *An Economic Analysis of Community Antenna Television Systems and the Television Broadcasting Industry*. Washington, D.C.: U.S. Government Printing Office, 1965.

(32) Smith, R. "The Wired Nation," *The Nation*, May 18, 1970, **210**.

(33) U.K. House of Commons, Committee on Broadcasting (Pilkington). Report, Command 1753. London: H.M. Stationery Office, 1962.

(34) U.K. National Board for Prices and Incomes. *Costs and Charges in the Radio and Television Rental and Relay Industry*. Report No. 52. London: H.M. Stationery Office, January, 1968.

(35) U.K. National Board for Prices and Incomes. *Costs and Revenues of Independent Television Companies*. Report No. 156. London: H.M. Stationery Office, October 1970.

(36) U.S. Dept. of Commerce. *Survey of Current Business*. Washington, D.C.: U.S. Government Printing Office, 1969.

(37) U.S. Dept. of Commerce, Telecommunication Science Panel. *Electromagnetic Spectrum Utilization—The Silent Crisis*. Washington, D.C.: Dept. of Commerce, 1966.

(38) U.S. Federal Communications Commission. Docket No. 18397, Relative to CATV, Washington, D.C., Dec. 12, 1968. Various FCC documents and hearings.

(39) U.S. Federal Communications Commission. *TV Broadcast Financial Data, 1965*. Washington, D.C.: FCC.

(40) U.S. *Federal Register*. Washington, D.C.: U.S. Government Printing Office.

(41) U.S. President's Task Force on Communications Policy. *Final Report*, Chapter 7. Washington, D.C.: U.S. Government Printing Office, 1968.

(42) White, Stephen. "Toward a Modest Experiment in Cable Television," *The Public Interest*, Summer 1968, pp. 52–66.

(43) Wiles, P. "Pilkington and the Theory of Value," *Economic Journal*, June 1963, **73**, pp. 183–200.

(44) *World Radio and Television Handbook, 1969*. Hellerup, Denmark.

2

The Spatial Dimension of the Economy as a Social Outcome: Some Theoretical and Empirical Issues

JAMES L. BARR and CHARLES L. LEVEN*

Washington University

Nineteenth century economics, at least of the British neoclassical variety, was essentially spaceless in its construction. The economic problem with which it was concerned was that of how to organize a set of economic markets so that, with firms and consumers each trying to optimize their own economic position, there would result the most efficient (or *an* efficient) allocation of resources possible, given the state of technology. Problems involving the movement of resources to firms, the movement of commodities to consumers, or the locational adjustment of either producers or consumers so as to make the total production-distribution process more efficient were largely ignored.[1]

While neoclassical economics can and has been described as "spaceless," it is the case, of course, that economists have been aware of the fact of spatial relationships at least since Von Thünen.[2] His immediate concern was in establishing an *a priori*

---

*The authors wish to acknowledge support of the research underlying this paper by National Science Foundation Grant number GS–1814.

[1]Also, ignored was the withdrawal of resources for public sector use and the allocation of these resources within the public sector. While we are here concerned much more with the ignoring of the impact of spatial separation, the leaving aside of the matter of resource allocation in the public sector also will be relevant to the position we wish to establish in this essay, although in a somewhat indirect way.

[2]Johann H. Von Thünen. *Thünen's Isolated State.* Translated by C. M. Wartenberg. Edinburgh: Pergamon Press, 1966.

theoretical basis for the existence of negatively sloped rent gradients as one moved outward from city centers into various zones of the agricultural hinterland. He was also interested in demonstrating that different activities would arrange themselves not in a helter-skelter checkerboard pattern, but rather in concentric circles (abstracting from topographical irregularities) with like activities grouped with like.

But while it is easy to identify the dependent variables in Von Thünen's theory, it is not, as indicated above, especially easy to identify just why these variables are relevant to the performance of an economic system. True, they can be regarded as part of the general concern with the origins of rent from the standpoint of income distribution. In addition, they might have had some "managerial" relevance from the standpoint of regional planning or enterprise location. But as to broader questions such as the desirability or efficiency of a negative, flat, or positive rental gradient, for example, answers are hard to come by. Accordingly, while Von Thünen's ideas may represent an important contribution to modern theories of urban land rent,[3] they have had no obvious impact on welfare theory.

Much of the same kind of observation can be made about the later path-breaking work of Alfred Weber on the theory of the location of industry.[4] Obviously Weber's work was a very important beginning point for modern theories of location, but in its own time, it is hard to find an application for it—except to the calculation of an optimum location selection for a particular enterprise, and, perhaps, to a weak explanation of more generalized locational patterns. The possibilities of empirical application were limited to selected cases in light of the rather severe assumptions of the theory as developed at that time.[5] But in any case, within

---

[3]See essay by Fales and Moses in this volume, for example.

[4]Alfred Weber. *Theory of the Location of Industries.* Translated by C. J. Friedrich. Chicago, Ill.: Univ. of Chicago Press, 1929.

[5]And the assumptions of modern location theory are not much less stringent, although programming routines for determining equilibrium locational patterns for an industry under a wide variety of conditions have been worked out. See, for example, E. M. Hoover, "Computerized Location Models for Assessing of Indirect Impacts of Water Resources Projects." Working Paper CWR 1, Institute for Urban and Regional Studies, St. Louis, Mo.: Washington University, 1966. Also, this is substantially reprinted in C. L. Leven, ed. *Development Benefits of Water Resource Investments.* Springfield, Va. Clearinghouse for Federal Scientific and Technical Information. 1969.

Weber's theory itself, it is very difficult to draw any conclusions with regard to more or less efficient, or more or less utilitarian locational outcomes.

The first real synthesis of the impact of spatial separation on the economic efficiency of resource allocation can be found in Hoover.[6] Here for the first time, the costs of overcoming distance are treated as a constraint on the production process itself. Output can no longer be regarded as an unambiguous function of labor, capital and raw material inputs; nor can equilibrium output be regarded as a single valued function of consumer demand. Hoover's work clearly showed the need for taking into account the location of production relative to the location of raw materials and the location of consumers, not only to solve for optimum location but for optimum output as well. Moreover, a truly general solution would have to allow for shifting movements of raw material supply and market locations as well as a shifting of production locations. Hoover's concept of transport costs was explicitly incorporated into the theory of the firm by Isard.[7]

In essence then, contemporary location theory can be thought of as a reformulation of neoclassical economics wherein outputs can no longer be regarded as unique transformations of inputs, and sales can no longer be regarded as unique transformations of F.O.B. prices.

SPACE AS AN ASPECT OF CONSUMPTION

A conclusion of the introductory discussion is that the effect of spatial separation should be incorporated into the theory of production as a constraint on the transformation of resources into commodities, given the state of technology. We argue here that the spatial configuration of an economy affects the relationship between commodity production and economic welfare as well. Spatial configuration will have an impact on final consumption, moreover, in two ways. First, different spatial arrangements will lead to different income-consumption relationships, i.e., different resource allocations in competitive equilibrium. Second, and more

---

[6]Edgar M. Hoover. *Location Theory and the Shoe and Leather Industry.* Cambridge: Harvard Univ. Press, 1937.

[7]See, for example, Walter Isard. "Location Theory and Trade Theory: Short-Run Analysis." *Quarterly Journal of Economics,* May 1954.

D

important, the spatial arrangement itself can be thought of as an argument of individual or community preference functions.

It is important to distinguish between the impact of "space" and the impact of "geography." Obviously, geography has an influence on the relationship between production possibilities and consumer welfare. First, it will affect the bill of goods produced—at seashore locations, boating and fishing will be more important; in the northern plains, fuel oil will be a larger part of household budgets. Second, non-pecuniary returns can be imputed to climate and other physical features *per se*. These are what we mean by the impact of "geography." They exist on the supply as well as the demand side of economic markets, e.g., production functions will be affected by differences in climate, topography, etc. But when we are speaking of the impact of space—or, distance—on production we have something more basic in mind, namely the impact of spatial separation *per se*, say on a uniform plane, *a la* Lösch. And especially if we add uneven natural resource location to the Löschian network, we can see a clear impact of space. Everything cannot be located next to everything else, and depending on the way that the locational pattern is arranged, production possibilities will differ. In essence, space itself makes a difference over and above the irregular appearance of geographic features.

In quite the same way, we would contend, space makes a difference in the utilitarian value of consumption, as well. As Lösch has shown, a set of consumers on a uniform homogeneous transport plane will arrange themselves in a hierarchy of central places. With limited transport connections or topographical irregularities, the hierarchy would be further displaced from an even distribution, but in any event, a hierarchy would exist under normal initial conditions.[8] The nature of this hierarchy, however, would affect both income-consumption and consumption-utility relationships, as suggested above.

Income-consumption relationships would be affected in two ways. On the one hand, the size and type of city in which one resided and the location of the city with respect to other settlements

---

[8]It has been argued that the particular initial conditions of even distribution of population are required for the particular equilibrium Lösch describes, but in any event, except under extreme initial conditions, a hierarchy of some sort or another would emerge. See C. L. Leven. "Determinants of Size and Form of Urban Areas." *Papers and Proceedings of the Regional Science Association.* 22, 1968.

would alter one's preference function for private goods. For example, in a large metropolis, people would probably spend relatively more on "culture," somehow or other defined—say, theatre, music, and professional athletics. In smaller centers, easier access to nonurban settings would promote more spending on the "outdoors"—say, hunting, fishing, and camping. In any event, the point we want to make is the fairly obvious one that depending on the frequency distribution of urban places by type (i.e., size and "other" characteristics) different patterns of consumer demand would emerge; and they would not all be equally adaptable to a given technology.[9]

The other way in which income-consumption relationships could be affected would be by way of the influence of the resultant set of urban places on the division of resources between the private and public sectors. In short, the kind of place in which one lives does have a direct impact on the need for collective goods. Where population is small, the needs for police surveillance are low; where density is low, a much simpler fire protection system will suffice. And so, different urban configurations would lead to different patterns of demand for collective goods, again not all of which would be equally amenable either to available technology or to the political mechanisms for allocating resources to the public sector. That the "degree of urbanness" would affect the pattern of demand for private goods and the extent of demand for public goods is hardly a very novel point, although more empirical research on the nature of such relationships clearly would be helpful.

More to the point of our present interest is that the degree of urbanness would itself affect the consumption-utility relationship. In other words, the kind of place one lives in and its location relative to other places would enter one's welfare function independent of other more conventional arguments like the kind of goods consumed and the kinds of services performed. The main point of this essay will be to discuss how one could analyze "place" as such, as a commodity, and how one could determine the conditions

---

[9]These comments are made reluctantly, because we feel that too much attention has been given to the so-called urban amenities. The cultural attractions of the city are probably attended by a very small proportion of the population, of which university people represent a disproportionately large fraction. A potentially interesting research topic is an inquiry of whom and how many urbanites take advantage of the cultural activities available.

for a socially optimal emergence of place. Essentially, for such discussion to be meaningful, it is necessary to believe that "place" matters, and that the emerging pattern of places is not necessarily the (or *a*) best of all technically possible patterns.

Although further research on the question of whether place matters clearly would be helpful, we will not much pursue that issue here—essentially we will regard it largely as axiomatic in much the same way that we accept the notion that people prefer more to less commodities as axiomatic in conventional price theory. Our ultimate defense for such an axiom is its intuitive sense. We do, however, note that people frequently express a preference for living some place other than where they actually do live. This reflects the fact that considerations other than "kind of place" enter one's residential choice decision—such things as income opportunity, family ties, fear of uncertainties connected with movement to a new community, etc. Moreover, only in rare cases, would we expect that "place" alone would dominate the total decision, so that in the end, people might choose a somewhat less preferred place in order to achieve more of some other objective—say income. What this means, of course, is that other things being equal, they would rather live someplace else, or, in other words, that "place" does matter independently.

"PLACE" AS A COMMODITY

Given the foregoing discussion we feel it would be useful to think of "place" as a commodity, which comes into being by a process which could be regarded as analogous to production and which enters individual or community preference functions in much the same way as do conventionally thought-of commodities. Places are, of course, produced in the sense that their coming into being involves a resource-consuming process of production. Having come into being, they then exert an influence on welfare, indirectly through their impact on income-consumption relationships, and directly through the impact of "placeness" as such on consumption-welfare relationships.

Seen in this light it makes sense to ask whether the "place-producing industry" is or is not functioning efficiently from an economic welfare point of view, broadly conceived, much in the same way that we can question whether the composition of production in agriculture or manufacturing, for example, does or does not reflect an efficient response to societal preferences. Moreover, even if people are completely free to choose any community they prefer (which, given the cost of relocation, is not so), and even if they have access to complete information on all available places (which also does not hold), it would not be the case that the set of "places" necessarily was optimal without the further assumption that they were "produced" under something like competitive conditions. In other words, the "place-producers" had an incentive to move toward more socially profitable and away from less socially profitable forms.

The process by which the physical structure incident to "population holding capacity" comes into being, however, is so complex and institutionally mixed, that we have little confidence in the notion that it necessarily responds in anything like a competitive way. In part, it does represent private market response, mainly for residential housing. In part, if the resultant place is to be economically viable, it represents private response in the private market for labor. But it also depends on the laying down of a quite intricate system of infrastructure (transportation, comunication, sanitation, regulation, circulation, etc.) which comes out of the combined responses of public utilities, regulatory commissions, and a wide variety of governmental agencies at all three levels of government. The notion that this complex of decisions somehow or other automatically is coordinated to produce a socially desirable distribution of places would seem to us to be highly unreasonable.

Given an unwillingness to accept that assumption, the alternative, it seems to us, is to build a theory of place formation and utilization into the theory of resource allocation and commodity consumption. Essentially, it would represent a further extension of neoclassical economics whereby "space," in addition to being a factor in the production of private goods, would also become a factor of consumption of private individuals. The building of this theory will be a very difficult undertaking.[10] It can probably be simplified considerably, however, by not trying to consider every possible case of locational difference at one time. For example, we can probably confine ourselves to a theory of "urban places" quite safely. That would seem to be the case not only because non-urban

---

[10]For a more detailed discussion of what might be involved in the building of a theory of city size and form, see Leven, *op. cit.*

locations are not very important quantitatively, but also because, to a large extent, they come into existence simply as part of the private market system.

And even among urban locations, we can make an important differentiation, namely as between "resource-oriented" and "agglomeration-oriented" urban places. Resource-oriented places can be thought of as collections of population which exist essentially for the purpose of exploiting some geographic feature existing at some particular location. This could be a natural feature like a mineral deposit, a harbor, or a ski slope. It could be a particularly geographic economic feature like the existence of a number of farmers who need a trading center. It could be a man-made feature like a state capital, an army camp, or a university. In any event, in all of these cases, the process of change and response is not particularly interesting. Such places could either exist in perpetuity as very small communities, or could easily disappear when the resource played out, fell out of use, or was transferred. To the extent that places are totally resource-oriented, we probably are fairly safe in assuming that they are "produced" under something like competitive conditions.

Of more interest and of much greater importance quantitatively, are the agglomeration-oriented urban places; these are the places that exist essentially to exploit themselves as a collection of people. Typically, their historical origination is resource exploitive (St. Louis, for example, is at the highest point of the Mississippi reachable without navigation locks), but they seldom achieve any significant size on that basis.[11] Essentially, such urban places of any size are based on the exploitation of scale economies and the division of labor. Their particular location certainly is related to the location of other urban places, but is rather unrelated to geographic features, in general, except for the accident of an earlier resource exploitation phase which provided a stock of accumulated physical capital at a particular spot on the map. In other words, the location of a sizable city somewhere near St. Louis makes sense in terms of the location of Chicago and the cities of the Southwest. Its

---

[11]Perhaps the most notable exception in the U.S. is Pittsburgh which achieved quite considerable size on the basis of a very narrow geographically based specialization—but it is a very exceptional case. See Pittsburgh Regional Planning Association, *Region in Transition*. Vol 1 of the *Economic Study of the Pittsburgh Region*. Pittsburgh, Pa.: Univ. of Pittsburgh Press, 1963; especially Chapters 7–10.

exact location probably would be free to vary within a circle of at least a hundred miles or so, but one would see the sense of putting it in that circle where the "left-over" accumulated capital of the river port happened to be situated. In actuality, of course, all places probably are partly resource oriented and partly agglomeration oriented, but probably little would be lost if we thought of a theory of agglomeration oriented urban places.

Another simplification is that we will primarily be thinking of a theory in which the observation units will be metropolitan or, in the case of smaller places, urbanized areas. In short, we will not be directly concerned with the distribution of population and the building of urban environments *within* urban communities. However, this cannot literally be the case since we have to deal with the reality that whenever the population size of a place changes, it either must expand territorially at the margin or undergo an increase in average density of land use internally— in either case, the place will change form when it changes size. It is for this reason that we cannot think of an "urban outcome" simply as the frequency distribution of urban places by size, but rather, an urban outcome will have to refer to a joint frequency distribution of urban places by size and type.

Accordingly, we would look at the allocation of resources to the production of an "urban environment" as a question of whether among all possible frequency distributions of urban places by size and type, was the resultant outcome such that no other possible outcome would be preferred? Clearly different "types" would refer, among other things, to differences in internal arrangements. Thus, while we will not be concerned with the problem of an individual's choice of location within an urban area, we will be concerned with choice among areas, in part as a function of their various internal arrangements. In essence, our interest here is a return to the somewhat older concern for the emergence of a particular "system of cities,"[12] but it is an interest in the system of cities not as a feature of geography but as an independent variable impinging on social welfare.

A theory of the system of cities seen from this vantage point, ultimately would be aimed at evaluating the outcome of the system

---

[12]See Eric Lampard. "The Evolving System of Cities in the United States: Urbanization and Economic Development" in H. S. Perloff and L. Wingo, Jr. *Issues in Urban Economics.* Baltimore, Md.: Johns Hopkins Univ. Press, 1968.

of cities. We would hope, however, that this would involve more than a benefit-cost evaluation of particular alternative urban outcomes. Hopefully, conditions of optimality could be defined, and, eventually, the institutional conditions for insuring that the produced outcomes would be optimal could be derived.

Building such a theory would involve three kinds of research. First, a meaningful way of describing urban outcomes must be devised (definition of dependent variables). Second, the factors affecting urban outcome must be specified (identification of independent variables) and hypotheses about the effects of such variables specified and tested. Third, the nature of the dynamics of change (not necessarily adjustment to disequilibrium) must be articulated.

The remainder of this essay will be concerned mainly with the first of these problems and to some extent with the third. So far as the second aspect—identifying significant factors affecting city size and form—is concerned, what seems in order is a fairly ambitious research effort in testing behavioral relationships.[13] But as will be seen, even the seemingly elementary process of describing the urban outcome, toward which the system of cities is tending, is more complicated than appears at first glance.

DESCRIBING URBAN OUTCOMES

In this section, we report on some attempts to more fully specify the problem of describing the system of cities, as opposed to a city. Our interest in this problem stems, on the one hand, from the sterility of findings expressed solely in terms of size distribution and, on the other hand, from the difficulty in specifying urban descriptors that have straightforward interpretations. As a first step in arriving at a more complete specification, we here consider population density of urban places in conjunction with their (population) size. In doing so, we distinguish between the population of particular incorporated places and the scale of the urban area in which they participate. This distinction leads to a consideration of urban descriptors that are useful for static or dynamic analyses. Finally, we present some descriptive data on size density relationships of urban places in the United States since 1890.

---

[13]For some preliminary suggestions for this kind of research, see C. L. Leven, *op. cit.*

Our original research plan was eventually limited by the availability of data on urban places, and so the data presented later on are not as complete as we would prefer. But it does seem worthwhile, however, to describe our original plan since research beyond that completed in this paper certainly is called for.

The original plan started with a consideration of all urban places (cities)[14] in the United States as a single urban system. For each census year, we can describe this system in terms of two attributes—city population density and the scale of the urban area in which the city is located. A city is associated with one and only one urban area; if a city is isolated, its association could be with itself. By considering connected intervals of urban area scale and city density, we can define a scale-density matrix where the entries a_{ij} would represent the proportion of the urban population residing in cities of density i, and enjoying a scale of urbanization j.

Such an exercise is intended to identify long-run trends in urbanization. Our immediate purpose is simply to assess the extent to which the pattern of city size (population) and density has changed over the last several decades. Casual observation suggests that the proportion of the total population living in the more populous and denser regions has increased over the years. We can summarize these urbanization trends in terms of scale-density matrices for the census years. Ideally, we would want to scrutinize scale-density patterns and their changes well back into the nineteenth century. This would allow us to test hypotheses with regard to how changes in tastes, technology, and communication may have affected the evolution of the urbanization pattern. We can, of course, think of many *ad hoc* reasons why scale-density patterns have changed, but these can only be regarded as conjectures at this time.

A useful outcome of the present kind of exercise might be the identification of agglomeration and density levels with discrete "jumps" in technology, e.g., railroad commuting, the automobile, and the elevator. Another outcome might be the identification of agglomeration limits for a given technology phase. For example, it might be argued that changes in scale density patterns would not be affected much after 1960 by an increase in the extent of automobile ownership, but rather, by increases in the provision

---

[14]An urban place is defined by the Census Bureau as a community with more than 2,500 residents and a minimal population density. The latter requirement is intended to exclude essentially rural environs.

of expressways and federally subsidized mass-transit systems. But preliminary to such speculations is the problem simply of describing the outcomes that have occurred, and so we will now turn to the underlying rationale and problems encountered with these descriptors.

THE CHOICE OF DESCRIPTORS

Taken by itself, average population density does not leave one with a clear impression of an urban place. Even if the statistic is net residential density, its descriptive power is quite limited. For example, if the city density is very low, we might consider it a "hick" town or a very wealthy residential area, depending on whether it is located in an urban area of very small or very large scale. However, it is this kind of ambiguity associated with population density when taken by itself, that makes it a rich descriptor when considered with other attributes like scale, average income, or access to large commercial centers. Certainly, the population density of urban places depends to some extent on the scale of the urban area in which it is located. However, cities with the same population density in urban areas of different scale connote different characteristics. For this reason, we chose to use population density in conjunction with urban scale.

A second reason for using average population density is its widespread use as an intracity descriptor. Clark, Muth, and others have found that the negative exponential distribution explains population density within cities rather well, where distance from the city center is the distribution parameter.[15] Furthermore, these intracity density patterns can be related in a simple way to transportation costs and construction technology.[16] To the extent that large metropolitan areas can be considered as a central place subsystem, we would expect city population densities within larger urban areas to reflect these intracity findings.

---

[15]C. Clark. "Urban Population Densities." *Journal of the Royal Statistical Society.* Series A, 1951 and R. Muth, "The Spatial Structure of the Housing Market." *Papers and Proceedings of the Regional Science Association.* 7. 1961.

[16]See R. Muth. *Cities and Housing.* Chicago, Ill.: Univ. of Chicago Press, 1969; E. Mills. "Urban Density Functions." *Urban Studies.* Feb. 1970; and Martin Beckman. "On the Distribution of Urban Rent and Residential Density." *Journal of Economic Theory.* June 1969.

Another empirical regularity found in intra-urban population density studies is a gradual movement over time toward equalization of central city and suburban densities.[17] Mills has demonstrated this tendency in a group of eighteen cities,[18] and we have substantiated the same result for a larger sample of one hundred cities over the last five decades. These results suggest that, for the population residing in the large urban areas, the proportion of people in urban places of "intermediate" density has increased over time. This tendency is weakly born out by our scale-density matrices for the period 1940–1960. Before presenting these results, we discuss the urban scale attribute.

Classification of urban places according to scale is less straightforward than is classification by density. The most direct classification scheme would be according to the population of the city itself. However, this descriptor is clearly misleading for incorporated places within large metropolitan areas. To a large extent, these places enjoy (suffer) the scale of the larger metropolitan area. This fact has been recognized in the designation of Standard Metropolitan Statistical Areas (SMSA) by the Census Bureau. Accordingly, we have designated the scale of an urban place by the population of its SMSA if it is located in such a designated area. This is a rather large compromise, but we felt it more representative than the use of the population of the city itself.

For urban places not in SMSA's, the scale definition chosen was the population of the county in which it is located. This definition is clearly less than satisfactory since county population includes rural residents; and counties are in many cases, sufficiently large as to include regions beyond the environs of individual cities. The only justification is that SMSA's are collections of counties, and hence, the single county population is the scale analogue for non-SMSA urban places.[19] The usefulness of the present classification scheme will have to be judged on the basis of the empirical descriptions that follow.

As mentioned above, the availability of Census data has limited

---

[17]Assuming a negative exponential decline in population density from the city center and using average central city and suburban densities, a density gradient can be calculated for each census year. In virtually all cases that we have considered, the density gradient falls over time, as does the population density at the city center.

[18]E. Mills, *op. cit.*

[19]We investigate this classification problem further later in the paper.

our empirical inquiry to the more recent years. Area figures for cities with population under 50,000 are unavailable for the census years before 1940. The only exception to this is a set of data for cities with population of at least 10,000 inhabitants for the year 1890. Unfortunately, here, there is no convenient way to designate the equivalent of SMSA areas so the comparability of this data to the 1940–1960 data is limited. We nonetheless make some alternative scale classifications, using this data later on.

Table 1　Percentage Distribution of Population

1940 Density (000)	$S_1 \leqslant 86.3$	$< S_2 \leqslant 496.7$	$< S_3 \leqslant 2858$	$< S_4$	$\sum_j a_{ij}$
Scale (000)					
$0 \leqslant d_1 \leqslant 4$	14.0	8.6	4.9	1.2	28.7
$4 < d_2 \leqslant 8$	7.3	15.5	6.2	1.2	30.2
$8 < d_3 \leqslant 12$	0.7	4.5	6.1	0.6	11.9
$d_4 > 12$	1.0	1.5	8.8	18.0	29.3
$\sum_i a_{ij}$	23.0	30.1	26.0	21.0	100.0%

Total Population Represented: 73.2 million

1950: Density (000)	$S_1 \leqslant 86.3$	$< S_2 \leqslant 496.7$	$< S_3 \leqslant 2858$	$< S_4$	$\sum_j a_{ij}$
Scale (000)					
$0 \leqslant d_1 \leqslant 4$	14.6	8.1	4.6	1.8	29.1
$4 < d_2 \leqslant 8$	7.1	14.0	7.7	4.6	33.4
$8 < d_3 \leqslant 12$	0.3	3.2	3.2	0.8	7.5
$d_4 > 1$	0.8	1.0	10.3	18.0	30.1
$\sum_i a_{ij}$	22.8	26.3	25.8	25.2	100.0%

Total Population Represented: 88.7 million

1960 Density (000)	$S_1 \leqslant 86.3$	$< S_2 \leqslant 496.7$	$< S_3 \leqslant 2858$	$< S_4$	$\sum_j a_{ij}$
Scale (000)					
$0 \leqslant d_1 \leqslant 4$	13.9	13.3	12.7	2.1	42.0
$4 < d_2 \leqslant 8$	4.1	9.6	10.3	6.8	30.8
$8 < d_3 \leqslant 12$	0.6	0.9	5.3	1.6	8.4
$d_4 > 12$	0.0	0.4	4.8	13.7	18.9
$\sum_i a_{ij}$	18.6	24.2	33.1	24.2	100.0%

Total Population Represented: 114.8 million

The main empirical results we wish to present are scale-density matrices for urban places for 1940, 1950, and 1960. The are formulated, using a log-linear interval scheme, with density intervals in thousands per square mile, and scale intervals depending on exponential formulae. We experimented with different interval ranges with as many as sixteen different intervals of scale and density. For the scale-density matrices presented here, the interval ranges were chosen so as to distribute the urban population into many cells.[20] The matrix entries in Table 1 are in percentage terms, that is a_{ij} represents the percentage of the population in urban places in density interval i and residing in an urban area of scale j.

The third and fourth columns of each matrix in Table 1 mainly represent that portion of the urban population located in SMSA's. The figures indicate that there has been an increase in the proportion of the population in these large-scale areas, particularly during the 1950's. However, this apparent shift is, in part, a result of the redefinition and creation of multi-county SMSA regions between 1950 and 1960.[21] In some cases, an additional county(ies) was added to 1950 SMSA designates; and in others, multiple county SMSA's were created in the 1960 designations. These definitional changes cause area scale to increase in a way analogous to city growth by annexation. In most cases, however, SMSA's have been defined as single counties, which would make the changes in urban scale comparable for the three census years.

Perhaps the most remarkable movement has been toward lower density urban places. This shift, as best seen between the 1950 and 1960 matrices probably reflects the massive flight to the suburbs that went with postwar affluence and increased home and auto ownership. A slight movement toward density equalization in the SMSA areas can be detected in 50–60 matrices. This trend, however, can be regarded only as a conjecture at this level of aggregation. One final remark should be made on the stability of the scale-density pattern between 1940–1950. Even though the urban population increased by roughly 25 percent, the percentage of the population in most cells remained fairly constant.

The density-scale pattern of urban places presented above gives a different view of urban structure than does the existing city

---

[20] The density intervals are in units of 4,000 people/square mile. The scale intervals follow the formula, $S_j = 15000\ e^{1.75j}$. The largest density encountered was for New York City, which was about 20,000/square mile.

[21] The SMSA definitions were not created until 1950, but we have constructed comparable definitions for the 1940 census data. In most cases, SMSA definitions are the same for these two census years.

size distribution literature.[22] In those studies, empirical regularities such as the "rank size rule" are explained in terms of stochastic growth tendencies of individual cities within the larger system. It is argued that if population growth in percentage terms is, (1) small and independent of city size, and (2) stochastically independent over time, then the distribution of population sizes will tend toward a log-normal distribution.[23] The justification for the observed size distribution is in terms of this stochastic growth process and the stability of the process over time. Empirical analyses based on this hypothesis usually pertain to only the very large cities, where each city is regarded as an isolated organism following the uniform stochastic growth rules.[24]

On the other hand, the scale-density structure depicted here explicitly recognizes the importance of scale by association or proximity and attempts to represent all urban places, however small, within that framework. The justification for such a view is more agnostic than the dynamic theories referred to above. We would argue, however, that the very rapid development of modern suburban communities and their density in metropolitan areas can be traced to changes in tastes and technology more easily than to the constancy of factors that influence city growth. We would argue further that the emerging pattern of urban living conditions can be deduced more easily from Table 1 than from the log-normal size distributions of central cities. Of course, the inclusion of other coincident attributes such as income and access would improve this description considerably.[25]

We noted above that the heart of this problem lies in the appropriate designation of contiguous urban areas. This is particularly

[22]For example, see Berry B. and Garrison W. "Alternate Explanations of Urban Rank-Size Relationships." *Annals*, Association of American Geographers, 1958; Simon H. "On a Class of Skew Distribution Functions." *Biometrika*. April 1955; Weiss H. "The Distribution of Urban Population and an Application to a Servicing Problem." *Operations Research*. October 1961.

[23]Simon, *op. cit.*, has shown that if the system is "open at the bottom," that is, new cities can enter the system in the lowest population bracket, a varient of the lognormal, the Yule Distrbution, will obtain in the steady state.

[24]Weiss, *op. cit.*, found the rank size rule to fit rather well for the hundred largest U.S. cities, but the empirical power of this formula deteriorated when smaller cities were considered.

[25]Access could be defined by mileage or travel time to the nearest urban place of some minimal size (e.g., 100,000 people).

true when we examine changes in urban structure over time when political boundaries are changing. We would like to identify real growth and structural change rather than political reorganization that leaves structure essentially unchanged. In particular, city growth by annexation of adjoining (similar) territory often leaves the scale of the urban area unchanged; this should be considered as distinct from an actual influx of population into existing political boundaries. The scale-density matrices successfully distinguish between these kinds of change (provided annexation occurs within county boundaries).

The major deficiency in our descriptive scheme is that the scale intervals are so large that a substantial increase in a city's population may, in fact, change the scale of its environment; but they will not be sufficient to change its designated scale. This can be remedied to some extent by a finer gradation of intervals, but the problem still exists in that our urban areas are of an order of aggregation above individual cities.[26] This specification problem seems unavoidable, however, if we wish to capture the notion of agglomeration beyond individual city boundaries.

AN HISTORICAL GLANCE

We now turn to some additional data in an attempt to get a longer view of scale-density changes in urban areas. Population and area figures are available for cities with over 10,000 inhabitants for the 1890 census year. While it would be difficult to construct comparable SMSA classifications for that year, county population data are available; and these have been used as a measure of area scale.[27] For the sake of comparison we present a second scale-density matrix, which defines the scale of an urban place by *city* popula-

---

[26]Appendix A includes a finer description of the same data presented in Table 1 for the years 1940 and 1960. Individual cells are subject to much more variation than in the more aggregated Table 1.

[27]The use of county population as a scale indicator is probably better for 1890 than for non-SMSA cities in the more recent period since population tended to be more concentrated around the urban centers. The county scale definition accommodates the obvious political distinctions (for example Allegheny City was what is now the immediate North Side area of Pittsburgh, Pennsylvania) within the same county, but does not agglomerate adjoining cities that are in different countries (e.g., Minneapolis–St. Paul).

tion size (Table 2B), as opposed to *county* population size (Table 2A) as a measure of scale.

Looking at Table 2, nearly 50 percent of the total urban population resided in places with an average density of over 8,000 people per square mile. And four places of fewer than 25,000 inhabitants had an average population density of over 12,000 per square mile (Matrix 2, B, a_{41}). This high proportion of people living in close quarters can be understood in view of the transportation facilities available at that time. Virtually all the urban places (346) in the list can be easily identified as railheads, river-towns, or pre-nineteenth century cities.

Table 2   1890 Scale-Density Patterns for Urban Places of over 10,000 Inhabitants.

A. Scale Based on County Population:

Density (000)	Scale (000)				
	$S_1 \leqslant 50 \leqslant S_2 \leqslant 250 \leqslant S_3 \leqslant 750 \leqslant S_4$				$\sum_j a_{ij}$
$0 \leqslant d_1 \leqslant 4$	7.7	9.2	2.0	0.1	19.0
$4 \leqslant d_2 \leqslant 8$	5.2	13.4	7.3	6.4	32.3
$8 \leqslant d_3 \leqslant 12$	0.8	6.2	9.0	6.1	22.1
$d_4 > 12$	0.8	5.9	6.6	13.5	26.8
	14.5	34.7	24.9	26.1	100.0%

B. Scale Based on City Population:

Density (000)	Scale (000)				
	$S_1 \leqslant 25 \leqslant S_2 \leqslant 100 \leqslant S_3 \leqslant 250 \leqslant S_4$				$\sum_j a_{ij}$
$0 \leqslant d_1 \leqslant 4$	10.6	6.7	1.7	0.0	19.0
$4 \leqslant d_2 \leqslant 8$	5.4	9.8	4.9	12.2	32.3
$8 \leqslant d_3 \leqslant 12$	1.2	4.2	6.4	10.2	22.0
$d_4 > 12$	0.5	3.7	4.8	17.7	26.7
	17.7	24.4	17.8	40.1	100.0%

Total Population Represented: 17.3 million

Now compare the 1890 figures to the more recent scale-density patterns presented earlier in Table 1. First, we note that the density intervals for all years were left unchanged; but due to a general movement over time to urban areas of larger scale (and the recent designation of SMSA's), the scale intervals for the comparable Table 2A are smaller. As expected, there has been a definite trend toward lower population density in urban places on a per-centage basis, within any urban scale interval.[28] For the overall trend in population density, one can look at the row sums shown for each matrix. It should be noted that much of this density change occurred in the 1950–1960 decade. Trends in urban scale are more difficult to identify, as they are confounded by the definitional changes.

Finally, we note that the choice between scale defined on county or city population does not alter the scale-density pattern very much for 1890. Except for the difference in scale intervals, the two matrices presented in Table 2 are qualitatively similar. The reason for this similarity seems to be that, in 1890, cities generally were not located so as to create an urban scale beyond that given by their own size.[29] This isolated nature of urban places in 1890 makes our scale designation less important here than for the more hierarchial urban structure that has emerged in recent years. This assertion can be seen by looking at the scale-density pattern for 1960, when scale is defined as the population of the urban place —a 1960 table constructed with the same definition of scale (*city* as opposed to *county*) as in Table 3. A comparison of this matrix with the 1960 matrix presented in Table 1 yields some striking differences.

Table 3 1960 Percentage Distribution of Population Scale based on City Population

Density (000)	Scale (000)				$\sum_j a_{ij}$
	$S_1 \leqslant 50$	$< S_2 \leqslant 250$	$< S_3 \leqslant 750$	$< S_4$	
$0 < d_1 \leqslant 4$	27.2	8.3	5.4	1.1	42.0
$4 < d_2 \leqslant 8$	12.3	10.2	6.0	2.3	30.8
$8 < d_3 \leqslant 12$	1.9	2.7	2.2	1.6	8.4
$12 < d_4$	0.7	1.2	2.9	14.1	18.9
$\sum_j a_{ij}$	42.1	22.5	16.5	20.2	100.0%

Total Population Represented: 114.8 million

[28]Note that the population covered in these urban snapshots has increased by 500 percent during the period 1890–1960.

[29]Notable exceptions to this statement could be found in areas along the eastern seaboard. Differences in the scale intervals accommodate the larger county population. Typically, however, there was only one urban place of over 10,000 people per county in 1890.

E

SOME OBSERVATIONS ON THE PROCESS OF CHANGE

We have argued above that it has become increasingly more important to view the system of cities as a set of urbanized areas that extend beyond the political boundaries of a single city. The designation of the SMSA, in fact, recognized this need. Within these urbanized areas there is a hierarchy of urban activities, and the presence of many activities would seem to depend on the scale of the entire area. Such activities that readily come to mind are symphonies, professional sports, major airports, and franchises for nationally marketed specialty goods. Within each area, the distribution of population among individual urban places depends on transportation facilities, topographical differences, zoning constraints, and importantly on differences in their areal size.[30]

Normalizing urban population by area, of course, yields density. We have argued here that the distribution of this characteristic within the set of urban areas deserves more recognition. The importance of density has been established by the intracity location models. Land values reflect the derived demand for land in residential housing, and this depends on (among other things) access costs to other sites in the urban area. If these costs fall, this tends to equalize the cost of land and thereby equalize population density. Federally subsidized expressways that connect central places of work with suburban residential areas have reduced commuting costs and have led to this density (and land value) equalization trend.

While population density has been given prominence in intracity location analyses, it has been largely overlooked in the system of cities literature. But population growth in urban places appears to have occurred so as to distribute population density more evenly within urban areas. This would suggest that prospective population growth in an urban place depends not only on its initial size, but on its initial density *vis-à-vis* other places in its urban area. Certainly, the rapid growth (and incorporation) of suburban communities has to be viewed as being conditional on the existing residential alternatives in their urban area. The same remarks would seem to apply to the rate of growth of urban area relative to other areas within the urban system.

---

[30]The story is more complicated than this, as the intracity locational models point out.

It has been suggested by some authors that the growth of cities and the evolution of a city size distribution can be characterized as a Markov process. States of the system are city size intervals, with changes in the distribution of cities among these states over time governed by a stationary probability matrix. Size "jumps" are stochastic and contained in a narrow range about the current size. That is, the transition probabilities are loaded heavily along the main diagonal, but it is possible to reach any city size from any initial state. In the limit, this growth process yields an equilibrium distribution of city sizes.

We would object to this simplistic approach to the system of cities problem on at least two grounds: (1) There is ample evidence that the urban growth process is not stationary, and (2) City growth depends on coincident conditions such as density within larger urban areas, as well as among the urban areas themselves.

SOME FURTHER DIRECTIONS

The research efforts reported on here admittedly are only a beginning. If a solid theory of urban spatial arrangements as an economic *outcome* is to be developed a great deal of work lies before us—both conceptual and empirical. Perhaps the most salient conclusion that can be drawn from the empirical work presented above is the recognition of just how much difficulty is encountered even with regard to the seemingly simple job of describing urban outcomes. Moreover, this is the case even where we are attempting to deal only with a two-dimensional descriptor, namely scale and density. First of all, there are the problems of the physical assembly of the data itself. Here, the most serious difficulty is in obtaining measurements of the land area of urban places. The hard reality is that the Census simply does not have any data on the area of incorporated places before 1940, except for special studies such as the one from which the 1890 data were extracted. Possibilities for reassembly of area data from Census material for 1930 and earlier years could and should be investigated, although it was beyond the scope of present effort. Such documentation does exist in the National Archives, but it is neither organized nor complete.

It seems clear that we must begin to think of extending our use of urban descriptors into more than two dimensions. In this regard, there are really two kinds of extensions that could be made. One would refer to additional aspects of each urban area, as a whole; such things as median or per capita income, an index of occupational composition, the age of the inhabitants or the structures, etc. Other kinds of descriptors would refer to the internal physical structure of the urban area, i.e., measures of the area's physical form.[31] In this regard, however, the problems of constructing meaningful indices are extensive. In part, they involve data collection; but in part, they involve conceptual perplexities as well.

Insofar as further conceptualizing as to the nature of the urban outcome is concerned, it seems important to note that we must think of developing standardized descriptors for urban areas with some reasonably small number of dimensions—perhaps about ten as an upper limit. We want characterizations of urban outcome, not detailed descriptions of actual urban places. This point might be made clear by analogy to the way we describe industries in economics. Here we characterize according to number and average size of firms, conditions of entry, degree of product differentiation, and also by such factors as bulk-value ratio, degree of product perishability, etc. In any event, we can characterize an industry in terms that are very meaningful for analysis in terms of three or four, or perhaps a half-dozen factors—far short of a complete description of the product produced or the production function. It is at this level of generality that we feel we should be aiming in developing a theory of urban outcome; and, moreover, we should get additional encouragement from this analogy. For example, even from a specification of only two factors, the number of firms and the degree of product differentiation, we can get a wide variety of useful generalizations in the theory of industrial organization. There seems to be no reason similar success could not be achieved in the theory of urban outcome with, say, only scale and density. Moreover, some of the independent variables that we have suggested for such a theory—say, the intraurban transportation system or the set of local fiscal instruments—are really no less tractable of specification than such things as product differentiation or ease of entry. Accordingly, we are fairly optimistic about the possibilities for reworking neoclassical economics to include

---

[31]An argument for why city form must be observed along with changing scale is contained in Leven, *op. cit.*

urban outcomes as an end product of the resource allocation process.

APPENDIX A

Detailed Matrices, 1940 and 1960 Census Data

In the tables that follow, the density intervals are multiples of 2,000 inhabitants per square mile, with the last row covering all places having a population density greater than 14,000/sq. mile. The scale intervals are constructed from the formula,

$$V_i = 20,000 \ e^{.81}, \qquad V_0 = 0$$

with

$$V_{i-1} \leq S_i \leq V_i$$

Entries are in percentage terms.

1940				Scale (000)				
	S_1	S_2	S_3	S_4	S_5	S_6	S_7	S_8
Density	(44.5)	(99.1)	(220.5)	(490.7)	(1092)	(2430.2)	(5409)	($\geq S_7$)
$d_1 \leq 2000$	4.1	1.4	1.4	1.4	0.5	1.0	0.5	0.1
$2000 \leq d_2 \leq 4000$	5.6	3.9	3.0	1.7	1.1	0.8	2.3	0.2
d_3 .	2.4	3.4	4.3	4.3	3.1	1.0	0.6	0.2
d_4 .	0.5	1.0	2.1	5.6	0.7	0.6	0.1	0.2
d_5 .	0.1	0.3	0.5	0.9	1.3	0.3	0.3	0.1
d_6 .	0.0	0.9	0.3	0.3	1.8	4.5	0.3	0.0
$12000 \quad d_7 \quad 14000$	0.0	0.0	0.2	0.0	2.0	2.3	7.7	0.6
$d_8 \geq 14000$	0.0	0.0	0.3	0.4	2.0	2.8	0.4	10.6
$\sum_j a_{ij}$ (%)	12.7	10.9	12.1	14.6	12.5	13.3	12.2	12.0

1960	S_1	S_2	S_3	S_4	S_5	S_6	S_7	S_8
d_1	4.0	2.3	2.0	1.9	2.1	0.8	0.9	0.3
d_2	4.5	4.4	4.2	3.5	6.8	2.3	1.0	1.1
d_3	1.9	2.1	3.1	4.2	4.1	2.0	1.2	3.5
d_4	0.3	0.4	0.8	1.2	1.7	1.8	1.1	1.3
d_5	0.0	0.6	0.1	0.5	0.7	0.3	1.1	1.2
d_6	0.0	0.0	0.1	0.1	0.1	2.9	0.4	0.8
d_7	0.0	0.0	0.0	0.1	1.1	1.1	2.5	3.4
d_8	0.0	0.0	0.0	0.2	0.9	1.5	0.9	7.2
$\sum_j a_{ij}$ (%)	10.7	9.8	10.3	11.7	17.5	12.7	9.1	18.8

Note that the population is distributed roughly evenly among the scale intervals, particularly in the 1940 pattern. This regularity implies a log linear distribution of population with regard to our definition of urban scale (in the interior intervals).

ADDITIONAL BIBLIOGRAPHIC REFERENCE

(1) Berry, B. "Cities as System Within Systems of Cities." *Papers and Proceedings of the Regional Science Association,* 1964.

(2) Bourne, L. and Maher, C. "Comparative Extrapolation of City-Size Distribution: The Ontario-Quebec Urban System." Working Paper. Toronto, Can.: Univ. of Toronto, 1970.

(3) Fano, P. L. "Organization, City Size Distributions and Central Places." *Papers and Proceedings of the Regional Science Association.* 22, 1969.

(4) Mills, E. "An Aggregative Model of Resource Allocation in a Metropolitan Area." *Proceedings of the American Economic Association.* May 1967.

3

Federalism and Regional Policy

JESSE BURKHEAD*

Maxwell Professor of Economics
Syracuse University

The endemic crises of our time may be generally attributable to a common cause—the lack of responsiveness of established institutions, whether they be governmental, social, economic or educational. The discontent of the youth, the deterioration of our central cities, the oppression of ethnic minorities, environmental pollution and our continued aggression in Vietnam—all of these are a reflection of institutional rigidity, of tyrannical majoritarianism. The conventional methods by which value changes are recognized and incorporated into new political programs, such as through coalition politics, seem no longer to be adequate. New techniques for inducing value shifts and resource re-allocations, such as confrontation politics or community action programs, thus far at least, seem incapable of serving as the necessary change agents. Thus, frustration abounds, both among silent majorities and among vocal minorities.

It is the purpose of this essay to examine one of the prevalent patterns of institutional rigidity—that which is associated with our federal system. It will be argued that many of the basic features of federalism have outlived their usefulness and that some of the

*The author is indebted to his colleagues, Jerry Miner and Alan K. Campbell, for comments on an earlier draft, but they should not be held responsible for the conclusions.

crises of our time, particularly those associated with racism and the deteriorating urban scene, are attributable to that fact. However, since moderate incrementalism is the most likely structural change that can be anticipated, only the most modest new directions will be proposed. There is no "revolution" in prospect in intergovernmental relations in this country.

THE FOUNDING FATHERS

It is sometimes useful to go back to the beginnings, in this case to inquire about the origins of our federal system. As every student of eighth grade civics learns, our governmental structure incorporates a system of checks and balances. The legislature, the executive and the courts were established as equal partners in the common enterprise, each with authority that is intended occasionally to countervail. What is overlooked in the civics courses is that the federal system itself is a part of the checks and balances. The federal system was intended as a deterrent to popular will. As Madison said, the Union is ". . . essential to guard them [the people of America] against those violent and oppressive factions which embitter the blessings of liberty . . ." [(8) Madison, No. 45, p. 298]. The sharing of power between the states and the national government will serve to isolate these "factions." The recent memory of Shay's Rebellion weighed heavily. Madison makes the point:

> The influence of factious leaders may kindle a flame within their particular States, but will be unable to spread a conflagration through the other States. . . . A rage for paper money, for an abolition of debts, for an equal division of property, or for any other improper or wicked project, will be less apt to pervade the whole body of the Union than a particular member of it; in the same proportion as such a malady is more likely to taint a particular county or district, than an entire State.
>
> In the extent and proper structure of the Union, therefore, we behold a republican remedy for the diseases most incident to republican government [(8) Madison, No. 10, pp. 61–62].

Madison was quite clear as to the causes of these "conflagrations": "But the most common and durable source of factions has been the various and unequal distribution of property" [(8)

Madison, No. 10, p. 56]. But this condition is almost a "natural law" heritage. Madison argued that diversities in the faculties of men gave rise to diversities in the faculty for acquiring property. It was as important to protect diversity in property ownership as diversity in opinion. [(8) Madison, No. 10, p. 55].

A federal system would thus contain the radicals who would strike at the roots of property ownership, but a federal system would always be threatened both by the power of the national government and by the power of the states. Either could destroy the structure. The authors of *The Federalist Papers,* however, were more impressed with the dangers from the latter than from the former, conditioned in their thinking, apparently, by the disintegrating and decentralizing experiences of the Greek city states, the feudal baronies of western Europe and in particular with the recent experience of the Confederation. Madison states:

> Several important considerations have been touched on in the course of these papers, which discountenance the supposition that the operation of the federal government will by degrees prove fatal to the State governments. The more I revolve the subject, the more fully I am persuaded that the balance is much less likely to be disturbed by the preponderancy of the last than of the first scale [(8) Madison, No. 45, p. 299].

Hamilton writes:

> It will always be far more easy for the State governments to encroach upon the national authorities, than for the national government to encroach upon the State authorities [(8) Hamilton, No. 17, p. 102].

Seventy years later, a Civil War confirmed this observation, and a hundred years after that, the continued interposition of state authority against national government desegregation orders reconfirmed it. The general unwillingness of state governors or state political organizations to become seriously concerned about urban problems within their borders represents a different kind of interposition. In this case, it is interposition by nonresponsiveness.

Thus, the federal system is inherently conservative on two counts: it suppresses popular "factions," and it strengthens the authority of state "factions." Federalism is a system that provides for multiple vetoes on popular movements and on national policy. Depending on one's values in these matters, the U.S. federal system can thus be described as "Perhaps the greatest mark of American political genius . . ." [(12) McConnell, 1966, p. 357]. It has also been described as a system which ". . . favors capitalists, landlords and racists. . . . Thus, if in the United States one disapproves of racism, one should disapprove of federalism" [(16) Riker, 1964, p. 155].

MACRO-ECONOMIC OBJECTIVES

This inherent conservatism not only makes the U.S. federal system unresponsive to the forces of economic and social change, but also makes the system ponderous in the pursuit of contemporary economic objectives.[1] This is the case with the economic objectives of growth, an equitable distribution of income and efficient allocation of resources, both public and private.

State-local governments have very little responsibility for the achievement of economic stabilization in the U.S. federal system, and, indeed typically behave with fiscal perversity.[2] Theirs are open economies, with a substantial volume of interstate trade, with the demand for a state's exports determined nationally and with substantial mobility of capital and labor. In consequence, any effort to expand employment within a state, during periods of national recession, may be offset by increased in-migration of labor. Multiplier effects from increased state-local expenditure will be small, with substantial spill-outs to other states. If states were to pursue anti-inflation policies by way of increased tax rates without corresponding expenditure benefits, the state's taxpayers would suffer a relative disadvantage with a consequent loss of economic activity. Expenditure reductions, with tax rates unchanged, would bring similar results.

Neither do states possess the conventional tools of monetary policy, including access to a central bank. Therefore, states must be concerned about their external debt and do not engage in

---

[1] For a more detailed discussion, see Jesse Burkhead and Jerry Miner, chapter on "Fiscal Federalism" in *Public Expenditure*. Chicago, Ill.: Aldine 1971.

[2] The term was first introduced to the literature in Alvin H. Hansen and Harvey S. Perloff, *State and Local Finance in the National Economy*. New York: Norton, 1944. There have been no important structural or policy changes in the intervening twenty-five years to alter the pattern of perversity.

deficit financing for stabilization purposes. Balanced budgets for the current account thus become the rule, often enforced constitutionally. Borrowing must be justified on grounds of intergeneration equity. This conforms with both the political and the economic requirements of an open system.

Down the years, a good many proposals have been made that look toward integrating state and local governments in a national stabilization policy [(9) Hansen and Perloff, 1944, pp. 194–222]. It would be possible to devise coercive techniques that would achieve this end. Federal grants-in-aid, for example, could be made conditional on state acceptance and implementation of specified stabilization policies. But such policies are not likely to be acceptable since they fly in the face of a degree of fiscal autonomy characteristic of the federal system itself. The result is that state-local governments do not initiate stabilization policy but rather adapt to what is initiated elsewhere by the national government. The adaptation, as noted, is very often counter-productive. As Netzer says, ". . . there is little evidence that state-local governments have had a positive, purposeful counter-cyclical role" [(15) Netzer, 1969, p. 2].

The pursuit of distributional objectives is also difficult in a federal system, and the pursuit is not made easier by the lack of clarity among economists as to the objectives that are to be attained. In a rarified model where a "proper distribution of income" is to be implemented solely by taxes and transfers, it is usually concluded that the appropriate objective must be specified in relation to the distribution of income by size class. Then it is concluded that states may seek an initial modification in the distribution of income, but the national government must determine the final distribution [(13) Musgrave, 1959, p. 181]. This reduces the possibility that states will erect uneconomic barriers or provide uneconomic inducements to the location of economic activity or the migration of labor by way of tax/transfer policies.

But reality differs—distributional objectives are implemented, more in state-local finance than in national finance, by way of resource allocations, not by way of taxes and transfers. State-local expenditures for education will have different distributional consequences than state-local expenditures for streets and roads. Expenditures for recreation will bring a different distribution of real income than do expenditures for public health.

A second approach to distributional objectives is represented by

Buchanan's search for horizontal fiscal equity among individuals in a federal system [(5) Buchanan, 1950, pp. 583–599]. The criterion is that all citizens should receive equal treatment with respect to taxes and benefits from governmental services, regardless of the state in which they live. This will avoid the condition that would obtain as the citizens of low-income states are subject to excessive fiscal burdens when states tax heavily to maintain an adequate level of governmental services. It will also avoid the distortions that result as citizens move to higher income states where services can be provided at lower tax burdens in relation to income.

Buchanan's distributional objective would be attained by equalizing the fiscal residua of individuals—the net difference between tax burdens and expenditure benefits. If it may be assumed that within a state, individuals' tastes and preferences are such that all persons value equally the services of the state-local system, then the residua can be equalized by varying the national rate of personal income tax among the states. Aside from constitutional infirmity (recognized by Buchanan), there is an economic infirmity. The true test of equality among individuals in a federal system would assure that all individuals attain an optimum on their indifference curves between public and private goods [(17) Scott, 1964, pp. 253–55]. This will not be achieved by equalizing the residua since some individuals will prefer to live in a high-tax, high-benefit jurisdiction.

The third conceptualization of the appropriate distributional objective runs not in terms of individuals in the federal system but rather in terms of jurisdictions within the federal system. This is undoubtedly the "popular" view of the matter, expressed in concern over the position of poor states and rich states in relation to each other and in relation to the central fisc. This objective implicitly assumes that individuals within a state are homogeneous with respect to tastes and preferences. However, even with this questionable assumption, there is no clear guide as to what shall be equalized. There remains a choice among 1) actual outlays or performance, 2) differentials in need and capacity and 3) fiscal potentials [(14) Musgrave, 1961, pp. 97–116].

The practical implementation of any of these choices encounters formidable obstacles. Spill-ins and spill-outs of benefits and costs would have to be estimated, together with estimates of taxable capacity. These latter are most unsatisfactory since they are typically based on ratios to state personal income or yields of "model" tax systems. Neither of these approaches makes allowance for the distribution of income within a state or the circumstantial parameters that affect taxable capacity. Some of these parameters are political leadership, citizen preference for public vs. private goods or the existence of tax handles such as extractive industries that may enhance the fiscal capacity of a given state.

It must be concluded that distribution objectives are very difficult to specify in a federal system and almost incapable of implementation even if they could be specified.

The economic rationale for a federal system must therefore reside in the allocations branch. The case here rests on an assumption that tastes and preferences for public goods, and the costs of such goods, will differ less within regions than among regions. With this assumption, a federal system will be more efficient in optimizing preference patterns than will a unitary system where differences in preferences and costs would presumably be obliterated. But against this efficiency consideration it should be pointed out, as Scott has urged, that there is an economic cost of federation [(17) Scott, 1964, p. 242]. Any degree of regional authority with respect to economic or fiscal policy will interpose some barriers to factor and product mobility. This means that gross product will be lower than in a unitary system, although higher than in a "Balkanized" system. Barriers to the free flow of economic activity will, to some degree, reduce the level of that activity.

If the cost of federation has been paid, then allocational efficiency must be attained within the limits of this lowered GNP. As with the distribution branch, there is a choice betwen optimizing with respect to the position of individuals within the federal system, or optimizing with respect to the positon of state or local government units within the system.

The "pure" individualistic solution was outlined by Tiebout, who argued that optimization is obtained as households move from place to place within a metropolitan region to secure that bundle of public goods and services and tax costs that satisfies the preference patterns of the household [(19, 20)] Tiebout, 1956 and 1961]. The Tiebout option is, however, available to some but not to others. Those with sufficient income or wealth, or whose occupation requires frequent movement, will be Tiebout-responsive. But some will be left behind [(17) Scott, 1964, p. 268].

In consequence, clustering does indeed occur in the metropolitan area. The tastes and preferences of middle and upper income families in the metropolitan area are reinforced by exclusionary zoning and subdivision regulations. The resulting concentration of low-income families in the central city gives rise to a serious burden of social costs, as is commonly observed, that is not shared by the optimizing families who reside in the suburbs.[3]

The second approach to allocational efficiency looks to the conditions for collective rationality for the state or local government unit. The conventional assumption of homogeneous tastes, preferences and costs is employed, and the possibilities of attaining an optimum for the collective then rests on whether the political domain of benefits coincides with the political domain of costs. If there is a net spill-out of benefits of local government goods, these goods will tend to be underproduced within the jurisdiction [(21) Weisbrod, 1964]. If there is a net spill-in, there will tend to be over-production of local government goods. The issue then turns on whether the spill-ins and spill-outs can be estimated with sufficient accuracy to arrange a pattern of compensating taxes and transfers.[4] If this were the case, it would be possible to implement a theory of optimizing grants [(4) Break, 1967, Chapter 3; (15) Netzer, 1969, pp. 7–10]. Each level of government would be responsible for the support of the proportion of benefits defined as national, state or local.

The reality of existing grant patterns hardly conforms with this concept of optimality. Education, usually thought to reflect national benefits, is supported primarily by state and local finance. Urban renewal, housing and highways, whose benefits are more largely local or regional, are supported by federal grants. A National Social Diseconomies Board would be required to estimate the appropriate externalities and arrange the taxes and transfers. In the absence of such a Board, functional grants-in-aid are far from optimizing.

---

[3]A second individualistic solution is Breton's, which rests on the heroic assumptions of equal tastes for local government goods within the jurisdiction, taxes levied on the basis of objective benefits to individuals and no externalities. This is a conceptually interesting but rather rarified view of the problem. Andre Breton, "A Theory of Government Grants." *Canadian Journal of Economics and Political Science.* May 1965, pp. 175–87.

[4]The best empirical study is Werner Z. Hirsch, Elbert W. Siegelhorst, and Morton J. Marcus, *Spillover of Public Education Costs and Benefits.* Institute of Government and Public Affairs. Los Angeles: Univ. of California, 1964.

FUZZY THEORY AND BAD PRACTICE

If our constitutional forefathers started the nation out with a theory and practice of federalism that made for inaction and the frustration of the popular will, matters have not been much improved by the rationalizations of subsequent generations of economists and political scientists. Economists have tended, with few exceptions, to accept a federal system as an ideal type, and to theorize about generally unworkable ways by which the systems could optimize legitimate economic objectives prespecified without reference to the federal structure itself. Political scientists have tended, with only a few exceptions, to accept the Madisonian rationalization of a federal system as a technique for containing popular movements, preserving property rights and permitting the interposition of state authority against national authority. The inevitable economic tendencies toward centralization have been rationalized in terms of concepts such as "dual federalism," "cooperative federalism" or "creative federalism."

There may be no exit. Fiscal arrangements and program decisions are the heart of the matter. On the former, Hamilton wrote:

> Money is, with propriety, considered the vital principle of the body politic; as that which sustains its life and motion, and enables it to perform its most essential functions. A complete power, therefore, to procure a regular and adequate supply of it, as far as the resources of the community will permit, may be regarded as an indispensable ingredient in every constitution [(8) Hamilton, No. 30, pp. 182–183] . . . . the federal government must of necessity be vested with an unqualified power of taxation in the ordinary modes [(8) Hamilton, No. 31, p. 190] . . . the individual States should possess an independent and uncontrollable authority to raise their own revenues for the supply of their own wants [(8) Hamilton, No. 32, p. 193].

Although experience in 1787 with federal systems was limited, Hamilton might have surmised that such appealingly simple prescriptions would not work very well. Sources of revenue in a federal system are never "independent"; they are dependent on the wealth and income of a body of taxpayers that are identical for the nation and for the aggregate of states.

The devices that are available or have been employed for purposes of fiscal accommodation in a federal system are legion. They include centralization of functions, separation of revenue sources, tax supplements, revenue sharing, deductibility, tax credits and grants-in-aid. Of these the grant-in-aid is at all odds the most significant lubricant for the stresses and strains of a federal system. Beyond doubt, the great appeal of grants-in-aid lies in the choice that the device affords to the administration and the Congress. As new program responsibilities emerge in response to a broad range of political, social and economic concerns, it is possible for the national government to choose to administer the program directly, or to administer it indirectly through the grant-in-aid device. As noted above, an optimizing support pattern for grant programs would require that, for a given program, national benefits be supported by national revenues, state benefits by state revenues, and local benefits by local revenues, all at the margin. Casual observation would suggest that this is not quite how it all works out. Rather, grant programs emerge, and financing arrangements are adopted in accordance with program concerns, and where interest group support is strong, such concerns will dictate a large measure of national government support.

The consequences have often been the subject of rather bitter commentary. They include, but are not limited to the following:

1. The numbers and complexities of federal grants, grant formulae and administrative patterns boggle the mind. The Advisory Commission on Intergovernmental Relations counted 379 grant-in-aid authorizations in 1967, of which 219 had been adopted in the years 1963–66 [(1) ACIR, 1967, p. 151]. Twenty-five new grant programs were enacted in the First Session of the 89th Congress. More have been added since.

2. Only occasionally is it possible to simplify the structure. In 1966, the Partnership in Health Act did consolidate a number of small grants in public health, but the President does not yet have general authority to consolidate grants in broad program categories.

3. State and local officials, particularly mayors and governors, complain continuously about administrative requirements, auditing, and overcentralized controls. The costs of agreement in grant programs, in their administration if not in their initiation, appear to run high.

4. Many federal programs have contributed to the fiscal and economic imbalance of metropolitan areas. Suburbs have been built with the assistance of FHA, and access to these suburbs

has been made possible by the federal highway program. Federal aid programs have not offset the fiscal disparities between central city and suburb [(3) Bahl, 1970, pp. 88–92].

5. The federal policy of channeling major aid programs through the states, since the states have been relatively insensitive to urban needs, has contributed to metropolitan fiscal disparities.

6. Federal aid has indeed increased in the past decade, from $7.0 billion in FY 1960 to $24 billion in FY 1970. This brings federal aid from 12.7 percent of state-local revenue to 17.4 percent of state-local revenue in FY 1970. This is a 40 percent improvement in 10 years, but total aid is only 12 percent of federal outlays and only 2.5 percent of GNP.[5]

7. Many urban grant programs are grossly underfunded in relation to their original authorizations. Whether this is attributable to the dominance of military spending, the need to control inflation, the lack of effective urban representation in the Congress, antagonistic local interest groups, or whatever, the condition of under-funding appears to be endemic. Housing, urban renewal, community facilities, urban education, manpower training and Model Cities all operate at levels far below initial legislative intent.

8. Federal programs in urban areas have not served to catalyze or require reform in metropolitan government organization. The "federal presence" has left undisturbed the patterns of maladministration and governmental fragmentation that have been so persistent in America's metropolitan areas. Indeed, in some cases, as with poverty programs, manpower training and Model Cities, new federal programs have accentuated structural deficiencies.

NEW DIRECTIONS?

If the general problem, as suggested at the outset, is the non-responsiveness of existing institutions, what can be done? It is not possible to be very optimistic. We are not about to abolish the federal system and move toward unitary government notwithstanding that the costs of federalism are high.

Any progress toward shifting additional resources to urban areas and rationalizing government programs therein must proceed on

[5]Data are from *Special Analyses, Budget of the United States, Fiscal Year 1971.* Washington, D.C.: Government Printing Office, 1970, pp. 225–26.

F

two broad fronts: fiscal and organizational. The former may be easier than the latter.

Revenue sharing obviously provides an unparalled opportunity for rechanneling to areas of greater rather than lesser need [(10, 11) Heller, 1966, pp. 117–72; (6) Heller, 1968, pp. 3–38]. Under President Nixon's proposal the amounts shared will be based on a specified proportion of the personal income tax base, and such amounts are expected to increase from $275 million in the last quarter of FY 1971 to $4 billion for FY 1975. The shares are to be based on population, with an adjustment for state-local tax effort. Municipalities, but not school districts, would receive a pass-through in proportion to the local share of revenue collection in the state-local total. Since in most large cities, school districts are dependent and not independent, the omission of the independent districts from revenue sharing will improve the relative position of the central cities.

At $4 billion for 1975, the amounts of revenue sharing are, of course, ridiculously small. If, in that year, state-local tax revenues are $100 billion, a not unlikely figure, revenue sharing will have added an additional 4 percent. This will hardly be sufficient to meet the wage demands of policemen, firemen and hospital and sanitation workers in that year. But it may be hoped that the Nixon proposal is an opening wedge for actions that might make a much more realistic contribution to the alleviation of central city fiscal pressures.

It would be nice to imagine that a new device, such as revenue-sharing, would rationalize the structure of federalism. Unfortunately, fiscal devices will not get at very much of the task of moving toward a restructured federal system. Increased resources for the cities will help; the imbalances are serious. But fiscal imbalances are only a part of the reason for the absence of a regional rationality. The more pervasive obstacles lie in the fragmented decision structures that abound in every metropolitan region, the competitive anarchy that prevails among local governmental units, and the ease with which strong local interest groups can frustrate national policy. And there are no forces that will countervail the resulting state of competitive anarchy that will fill in the program gaps, in short, that will plan and execute programs for the region as such.

There are those who feel that the recent and rapidly-growing movement represented in the Councils of Governments (COGs) in metropolitan areas is the wave of the future, and that voluntary associations among governments of goodwill will provide the necessary force and fiber, and eventually the necessary fiscal resources to fill the existing vacuum. The record of frustration that has accompanied most of these efforts provides no grounds for such optimism.

There is, whether one likes it or not, only one center of political authority that is capable of organizing for regional rationality and that is the federal government. A basic restructuring of the federal system is very much in order if regional goals are even to be defined, much less to be met.

Ten years ago, Marion Clawson proposed an organizational form that represents the kind of direction that federal regional policy must take [(6) Clawson, 1960, pp. 69–83]. It was a proposal for the creation of suburban development districts to be organized under federal statute, with state enabling legislation. The districts would have responsibility for planning and executing comprehensive programs for suburban land use, with appropriate attention to the orderly development of community facilities, transportation patterns and water and sewerage facilities. The districts would have fiscal authority and authority to purchase property and to reserve open space. Under Clawson's proposal, development would not be prohibited outside such districts, but the financial incentives to develop within the district would be substantial. These would be assured by state subvention and by federal assistance for planning and public facilities grants and possibly by the denial of FHA assistance outside the districts. After a period of time, the development districts would cease to exist as governmental units, once the basic pattern of land use and control was established. Their functions would be assumed by other local governmental units.

The Clawson proposal was based on a philosophy of permissiveness—no area would be required to participate. It was also directed solely to suburbs. But this kind of approach could well be adapted to the regional needs that have emerged in the last ten years. The events of the past decade have brought to the forefront, not the needs of the suburbs, significant as they are and will be, but the needs of the central city. The past decade has brought far greater participation in central city policies on the part of the federal government than was true in 1960. It has also brought new requirements for community participation in programs that affect the lives of those in the neighborhoods.

Thus, there is a new setting for a new federalism and the time has come for some organizational innovation. It would be foolhardy to attempt to sketch the precise lines along which such innovation will proceed, but the following would appear to be possible new directions.

First, there must be some rationalization at the national level with strenuous efforts to coordinate existing programs of direct federal expenditure and federal grants. This can come only through the traditional mechanism for such coordination—the Executive Office of the President.

Second, there must be some coordinating authority in the metropolitan region. Unless one puts great faith in the on-going voluntary regional organizations of governments, it will be necessary to extend national government authority into the regions, once more through mechanisms that have traditionally been successful only when mounted through the Executive Office of the President.[6] The coordinating authority and the resources must be combined.

Third, the reality of the private federalism must be recognised. The concept of "maximum feasible participation" has been one of the most controversial of public policy experiences in recent years; but one lesson, at least, should have been learned from this experience. The residents of the inner city will henceforth claim and secure the participation in the control of programs, a prerogative that has long been enjoyed by suburbanites and central city elites. In the inner city, program participation has become as important as program output and this condition will not soon be changed.

There is some scattered evidence that there are movements in all three of these directions. At the level of federal coordination since 1967, the Bureau of the Budget has been required to submit drafts of grant-in-aid regulations for review and comment by state and local government agencies prior to the promulgation of such regulations. Apparently the procedure is working, although

---

[6]The Committee for Economic Development recently called for both a community level and a metropolitan level of government in each region but would leave this to the states and cities to effectuate. It was suggested that the federal government might stimulate such organizations with appropriate aid mechanisms. Committee for Economic Development, *Reshaping Government in Metropolitan Areas*. New York: CED, 1970. A more direct federal intervention than this is likely to be required for any significant organizational change.

slowly and painfully [(2) ACIR, 1970, pp. 3–4]. In 1969, President Nixon established an Office of Intergovernmental Relations within the Executive Office, headed by Vice-President Agnew, with a former governor as staff director.

Movement in the second direction, toward assuring a stronger federal presence within the regions, has been miniscule in relation to the progress that is required, but again, some things have been done.

The Demonstration Cities and Metropolitan Development Act of 1966 required that all applications for federal grants or loans for open space, hospitals, airports, libraries, water supply, sewerage facilities, highways and other transportation facilities, law enforcement facilities and land conservation projects within any metropolitan area must be submitted to area-wide planning agencies for review and comment. The Intergovernmental Cooperation Act of 1968 provided that the President should establish rules and regulations governing the formulation, evaluation and review of federal programs with a significant impact on area and community development. The Act also provided that federal agencies could extend technical services to state and local governments on a reimbursement basis.[7] To bring some order out of the federal chaos of non-coterminous departmental field offices, President Nixon required, in 1969, that five major federal agencies harmonize their boundaries into a ten-region pattern.

The new directions in community participation are best illustrated in Model Cities, which requires that the Community Demonstration Agency organize a pattern of participation as a condition of securing funds. In most cities this has been a painful experience [(7) Department of Housing and Urban Development, 1969], even as "maximum feasible participation" under OEO was painful.[8] But it is here to stay, and as far as innercity residents are concerned, offers the major hope for means to overcome the non-responsiveness of local government institutions.

In addition to resident involvement, Model Cities agencies are to be innovative and coordinating. It is this latter requirement that is unattainable in the absence of organizational re-structuring.

---

[7]The appropriate regulations are contained in Bureau of the Budget Circular A-95, July 24, 1969.

[8]The most critical view of this experience is contained, of course, in Daniel P. Moynihan, *Maximum Feasible Misunderstanding*. New York: The Free Press, 1969.

As Sundquist and Davis point out, the community action agencies were a total failure as coordinators [(18) Sundquist and Davis, 1969, pp. 32–78]. In part, this was attributable to the basic conflict between confronting city hall and working with city hall, but the roots of the failure went even deeper. No one agency or department can "coordinate" another agency or department at the same level of government. If the coordinating agency has substantial resources at its disposal, it may purchase some minimum cooperation; the community action agencies did not possess sufficient resources even to purchase cooperation. But bringing together the total resources of federal, state and local agencies, working out program inter-relationships, developing patterns of relationship with private agencies, filling in the program gaps and providing for periodic reassessment and evaluation—these kinds of coordinating tasks must be undertaken, not by a line agency, but by a superior staff agency.

Sundquist and Davis, after a careful review of the requirements of a workable federalism conclude that:

> It makes little sense for the federal government to encourage the communities to construct elaborate coordinating systems that the federal government's own agencies are then left free, individually and collectively, to ignore. It make little sense to foster complicated and laborious planning processes unless the government—and that necessarily means all its agencies—supports the plans and projects that come out of the community processes [(18) Sundquist and Davis, 1969, pp. 247–48].

> Somewhere in the Executive Office must be centered a concern for the structure of federalism—a responsibility for guiding the evolution of the whole system of federal-state-local relations, viewed for the first time as a *single* system [(18) Sundquist and Davis, 1969, p. 246; italics in original].

This approach would require Executive Office assumption of responsibility for coordinating urban and regional programs at the national level. It would also require Executive Office authority for coordinating regional councils. The coordinator would not administer—unlike OEO or Model Cities agencies. The coordinator would ". . . monitor the workings of the federal system at the regional level" [(18) Sundquist and Davis, 1969, p. 275].

None of this is very simple and straight-forward. The role of the states, in most instances totally incompetent or disinterested in regional problems, would remain very obscure. Neither will it be a simple matter to work out the necessary deference for local wishes and local innovations that is called for in an era of community involvement and participation. It may be easier, for example, to visualize a federal coordinating presence with respect to Model Cities, where machinery is now being fashioned, than in region-wide manpower policy, where the failure of planning has been pervasive, or in the control of land use in suburban areas, which now seem totally immunized from the social and economic problems of the region as a whole. But the federal system can no longer remain, as Hamilton and Madison wished, as a device for thwarting local initiatives and local "revolutions."

It can at least be hoped that more effective organization for regional programs and for their coordination will serve to attract some additional resources out of the military and into the cities—to remedy the fundamental imbalance that cursed the 1960s and still promises to curse the 1970s. Organizational innovation without the resources necessary for program implementation can never succeed. But with additional resources, organizational change is possible.

REFERENCES

(1) Advisory Commission on Intergovernmental Relations. *Fiscal Balance in the American System,* Vol. I. Washington, D.C.: Government Printing Office, 1967.

(2) Advisory Commission on Intergovernmental Relations. *Eleventh Annual Report.* Washington, D.C.: Government Printing Office, 1970.

(3) Bahl, R. "State Taxes, Expenditures and the Fiscal Plight of the Cities" in A. K. Campbell, ed., *The States and the Urban Crisis.* Englewood Cliffs: Prentice-Hall, 1970, pp. 85–113.

(4) Break, G. F. *Intergovernmental Fiscal Relations in the United States.* Washington, D.C.: The Brookings Institution, 1967.

(5) Buchanan, J. M. "Federalism and Fiscal Equity." *American Economic Review.* Sept. 1950, pp. 583–99.

(6) Clawson, M. "Suburban Development Districts." *Journal of the American Institute of Planning.* May 1960, pp. 69–83.

(7) Department of Housing and Urban Development. *The Model Cities Program.* Washington, D.C.: Government Printing Office, 1969.

(8) *The Federalist.* From the original text of Alexander Hamilton, John Jay, James Madison. New York: The Modern Library, [1788] 1937.

(9) Hansen, A. H. and Perloff, H. S. *State and Local Finance in the National Economy.* New York: Norton, 1944.

(10) Heller, W. W. *New Dimensions of Political Economy.* Cambridge: Harvard Univ. Press, 1966, pp 117–72.

(11) Heller, W. W. "A Sympathetic Reappraisal of Revenue Sharing" in H. S. Perloff and R. F. Nathan, eds., *Revenue Sharing and the City.* Baltimore, Md.: John Hopkins Press, 1968.

(12) McConnell, G. *Private Power and American Democracy*. New York: Knopf, 1966.

(13) Musgrave, R. A. *The Theory of Public Finance*. New York: McGraw Hill, 1959, pp. 179–83.

(14) Musgrave, R. A. "Approach as to a Theory of Fiscal Federalism." *Public Finances: Needs, Sources and Utilization*. National Bureau of Economic Research, Princeton Univ. Press, 1961, pp. 97–122.

(15) Netzer, D. *State-Local Finance and Intergovernmental Fiscal Relations*. Washington, D.C.: The Brookings Institution, 1969.

(16) Riker, W. H. *Federalism*. Boston, Mass.: Little, Brown and Co., 1964.

(17) Scott, A. "The Economic Goals of Federal Finance." *Public Finance*. No. 3, 1964, pp. 241–88.

(18) Sundquist, J. L. with the collaboration of D. W. Davis. *Making Federalism Work*. Washington, D.C.: The Brookings Institution, 1969.

(19) Tiebout, C. M. "A Pure Theory of Local Expenditures." *Journal of Political Economy*. October 1956. pp. 416–24.

(20) Tiebout, C. M. "An Economic Theory of Fiscal Decentralization." *Public Finances: Needs, Sources and Utilization*. National Bureau of Economic Research, Princeton Univ. Press, 1961, pp. 79–96.

(21) Weisbrod, B. A. *External Benefits of Public Education*. Princeton: Princeton Univ. Industrial Relations Section, 1964.

4

The Economy of the Central City:
An Appraisal

BENJAMIN CHINITZ

Brown University, Providence, R.I.

INTRODUCTION

It is virtually impossible to be original in describing the status of
the central cities of our major metropolitan areas. The problems
abound: congestion, pollution, slums, poverty, racial strife, crime,
drug addiction, dirt, noise. People still argue about whether conditions are better or worse than they used to be and whether the
people who now live in these cities are or are not better off than
they used to be. This much is certain: not many are happy with
conditions as they are.

What also seems to be beyond debate is that the fiscal condition
of the local governments of these cities is as bad as or worse than
it has ever been. The diagnosis is quite simple. The problems put
pressure on the demand side: more money for welfare payments;
more money for education; more money for police and fire protection, sanitation, and almost everything else on the list of locally
provided goods and services.

Then there is the pressure for higher wages for city employees.
That pressure stems, in part, from the general rise in earnings in
the private sector of the economy, which makes it increasingly
difficult to recruit people to the public sector at lower wages. But
it also reflects the impact of the unionization of public employees

and explicit pressure, via strikes and other devices, to increase wages and improve working conditions even for those who may not have the option of moving over to the private sector.

Finally, and this is my main concern in this paper, there is the faltering private sector of the central city that provides a weak base for local taxation. The big city Mayors—Republican and Democrat and Independent—are all pleading for greater financial aid from their respective states but mainly from the federal government. Federal money and state money, one might suppose, are to be preferred over local money in all circumstances. But whether or not that is true, there can be no doubt that the urgency in the current plea for outside support reflects greater reluctance than ever to impose higher taxes on local business and households.

Such reluctance, in turn, can be attributed in part to the political consequences of proposing higher local taxes. Voters persist in an illusion which can be fatal to the incumbent, namely, that while the "old" man wants new taxes, the "new" man is likely to get by with the old taxes. But even a daring Mayor has to contend with the competitive aspects of local taxation. Households and businesses can move to nearby suburbs where taxes are more favorable. Some people and some enterprises might even be induced to move to more distant areas.

This constraint, which was always there to some extent, is now deemed to be much more binding because it is assumed that the central city, taxes aside, is increasingly vulnerable to competition for the location of people and jobs. Nobody really knows with any precision how that competition is affected by increased local tax burdens. But when the city's hold on industry and people is assumed to be weakening, increased taxes are not likely to help matters.

In this paper, I will focus on the central city as a location for private sector activities. I want first to examine the assets and liabilities of the city as a location, much as we viewed them in the early days of urban economics, before the current sense of crisis set in. I then want to show how these assets and liabilities interact with exogenous forces to shape the changing competitive position and the growth of the city's economy. Third, I want to suggest that municipal policies can affect the local economy's competitive posture and that taxation is only one of many issues in this regard. Finally, I want to speculate about the future of the city as a place of employment.

THE CENTRAL CITY: A BALANCE SHEET

There is a vast literature on the subject of the city as a location for industry to which the man whom we honor in this volume has made substantial contributions [(3) Hoover, 1959; (4) Hoover, 1963; (10) Vernon, 1959]. But in the heat of the current preoccupation with the urban crisis, many of the simple points have been submerged if not forgotten.

By *assets*, I mean those characteristics of a city location that increase productivity and reduce costs. By *liabilities* I mean the converse: those characteristics of a city location that reduce productivity and increase costs. The latter are more readily identified and articulated; the former are more subtle and require greater elucidation. Let me take the easy side first.

The city's liabilities should perhaps more appropriately be termed "constraints" rather than liabilities. These are *rents* and *congestion*.The competition for space increases rents and acts as a deterrent to the location of some activities which might otherwise prefer to be located in the city. Outside the city, we assume the supply of land to be much more elastic.

The density of activity creates congestion. In simple terms, it takes more driver time and more gasoline to traverse a given distance. The same density that gives you congestion may also yield a lower cost per unit of business transacted, despite the higher operating costs but that's on the other side of the equation. Congestion gets translated into higher rents for space by increasing construction costs. Lately, particularly in New York, congestion has assumed other dimensions: deterioration in telephone service and power cut-backs on very hot days. Some of these manifestations of congestion are also experienced in the suburbs.

Rents and congestion are inherent in the logic of central city growth. Their precise levels are of course not inherently determined. Elevators make a difference; size of cars makes a difference; relative use of private and public transport makes a difference; street layout and building design make a difference. We shall deal with some of these as "exogenous" influences in the next section. But planning and clever design can only temper the inelasticity of supply of space for activity and mobility; they cannot render supply completely elastic.

Do we capture all of the liabilities under the twin concepts of rent and congestion? How about higher wages and higher taxes? How about crime and insurance rates? On wages the evidence is mixed [(9) Segal, 1959]. On taxes, congestion is again the root problem to the extent that public services are in greater demand and harder to provide in conditions of high density. But the welfare burden and such problems as crime insofar as they affect the cost of doing business directly or indirectly via taxation, would be hard to subsume under the heading of congestion. These are more appropriately dealt with in the next section as "exogenous" developments.

The asset side is more complex. Face-to-face contact with a wide variety of related individuals and activities is often defined as the root or fundamental advantage of a city location. This is the other side of the congestion coin. You can't walk too fast, traffic is bumper-to-bumper, telephone service is unstable, restaurants are crowded; but you can achieve a great variety of contacts in a day because of the sheer number and diversity of people and activities concentrated in such a small area. What it boils down to is that the unit cost of information is cheaper.

But the facilitation of face-to-face contact is only one of the assets of high density, and high density does not exhaust the asset side of the balance sheet. More basically, the city derives its strength from Adam Smith's famous dictum about specialization and the extent of the market. Density permits a much higher order of specialization because proximity of specialists, one to the other, keeps down the costs of trade for a given scale of operation. Thus each unit can concentrate on doing one thing very efficiently and on drawing its auxiliary needs at low cost from neighboring units. In short: the city is a mechanism for enlarging the market by containing transportation and communication costs, thus permitting a greater degree of specialization and hence higher productivity. Face-to-face communication and short-haul goods movements are the visual byproducts of the process.

Another way to view the favorable impact of high density is in terms of capital saving. An enterprise in isolation must substitute capital for what might be current expenses for an enterprise in the city. It might take the form of higher inventories, more workers on the payroll, a computer, cars and trucks—all of which are designed to shield the firm against its isolation. In the city, the firm can augment its supplies on short notice and can purchase transport services, computing services, and the like from other firms which—to get us back where we were before—can afford to specialize in these services because there is a large market at close call.

All these considerations relate to concentration *per se*. They would be relevant if the city were lifted up bodily and put down in the middle of a desert. They might even apply with equal force if part of the city were lifted up and relocated. This is why the thought of relocating the whole garment center out of New York City, for example, is so tempting to some city planners. To the extent that the most vital inter-firm linkages are contained within a given industrial complex, the dream has a certain appeal.

But there are at least two other forces making for concentration in the center that do not derive their fundamental logic from the economies of concentration *per se*. One has to do with the natural attributes of the areas where most cities are located, principally, their access to water. The other has to do with the "centrality" of the city in relation to the metropolitan area. These advantages motivate firms to seek city locations to minimize transport costs on freight and to maximize access, on average, to the region's labor supply. Each firm independently seeks a central location, and concentration is the *result*. By contrast, the gains which accrue from specialization, easy face-to-face contact, saving of capital, result *from* concentration. When you put the two sets of forces together in some kind of historical dynamic model, you have the essentials of the well-known concept of agglomeration.

Before we move on to consider those exogenous forces which erode the city's assets or aggravate its liabilities (and vice-versa), a few further comments on the balance sheet may be helpful. First, the relevance of and the weights attached to each asset and liability will vary according to the needs and the objectives of the prospective locator. That's why we observe at any point in history that the city is relatively more attractive to some activities than to others.

Second, the flavor of my comments suggest a preoccupation with the Central Business District (CBD) of the central city rather than the whole central city. This is a correct inference, but it should not be overdrawn. Obviously, the asset-liability balance will come out differently for the same firm at a given point in time, for different locations in the city. But we want to keep the whole city in view, at least through the next section.

Finally, we should distinguish between *micro* dynamics and

macro dynamics. The same firm over its own lifetime, even when the parameters of the larger system are constant, will strike a different balance for the city as a location because of its *own* changing needs and requirements. Hoover and Vernon have told that story well in *Anatomy of a Metropolis* [(3) Hoover and Vernon, 1959]. Furthermore, the city itself, as it grows and ages, even if the exogenous forces are unchanging—technology, tastes, etc.—will go through a revision of its balance sheet from the perspective of a given firm with fixed requirements. The latter tale is unfolded in Hoover's essay, "The Evolving Firm of the Metropolis" [(5) Hoover, 1968].

In other words, there is a lot of dynamics—internal to the firm and internal to the city—that would prevent the city from taking on a very static image even if nothing were happening "outside" to shake things up. But in the sections that follow, we want to focus on the external dynamics.

Dynamics I: The Changing Industrial Mix

It is an elementary proposition in regional analysis that the relative growth of different areas will inevitably be affected by the changing industrial composition of the national economy. It is equally well established that the industrial composition of a nation's economy is roughly related to the state of development. At first, agriculture and other resource-oriented activities predominate. As productivity in these activities increases, labor is released for industrialization, and the manufacturing sector grows very rapidly as a share of the total. Finally, at very high levels of income, the service sectors—government, trade, finance and the like—move into first place. Currently in the United States, these service sectors account for 64 per cent of total employment, manufacturing[1] 31 per cent and extractive industries 5 per cent.

This transformation of the national economy, it is generally agreed, is responsible for, or at least is highly correlated with the relative decline of rural areas and the rapid growth of cities and metropolitan areas. Progress and urbanization go hand in hand. What is not so obvious is how these industrial trends have affected *intra*-metropolitan patterns and the competition between city and suburb. The fact is that the city has been favored by these trends

---

[1]Manufacturing in this context includes Construction which, in a more detailed classification, is treated as a separate category.

because precisely those sectors for which the city has a stronger attraction have grown most rapidly in the national economy. While the city continues to yield ground to the suburbs in almost all sectors, the overall performance of the city is sustained by the favorable industrial composition of national economic growth.

The impact of these trends is manifested in the very dramatic growth of "office" employment in the nation as a whole, and particularly in cities. By office employment, we mean employment that occurs in detached buildings that are entirely devoted to paper work. Office employment cuts across all sectors as traditionally defined, but as one might expect, it is far more important in the service sector than in the manufacturing sector. Corporate headquarters in the manufacturing sector do give the "office" component considerable status even in that sector. According to the only study of the office sector done so far, "jobs in detached office buildings account for about one-quarter of all white-collar jobs in the nation (or 12 per cent of total employment) and 40 per cent in the New York Region. These proportions have been rising in recent years, both here and abroad" [(1) Armstrong, 1970, p. 3].

In the simplest terms therefore the central city, which always boasts a larger share of the metropolitan area's offices than of its factories, while losing ground in each, is benefiting from the fact that the national trend favors offices over factories.

If nothing else had happened, central cities would have been expected to grow even faster in response to *Dynamics I* than they had before. So now, we must turn to the factors that have adversely affected the city in its competition with the suburbs.

Dynamics II: Transport Technology and Transport Policy

Economic theory suggests that reductions in transport costs extend market areas and expand the opportunities for specialization and trade. From this point of view, the city would be expected to gain from the transport revolution of the twentieth century. In some respects it has, but one would be hard put to argue that the city has not lost out, on balance.

The gain occurs if, and only if, the city retains its advantage as a production site; all that happens is that it can now serve a wider market. For example, if the Metropolitan Opera remains in New York City, as it apparently must, then New York City stands to gain from the fact that more people can now reach the opera for a given amount of travel time and cost than before automobiles and highways were available. Similarly, if the Port of New York retains its hold on international traffic, then the fact that a trailer-truck can bring freight in from 200 miles a lot faster and cheaper expands the market area served by the Port.

Unfortunately for the city, however, the automobile and the truck and even the airplane do more than simply reduce the cost of transport relative to other things, which would favor greater concentration. As alternatives to traditional modes—rail and water—they alter the balance of advantages and disadvantages at different locations and therefore undermine the very motive for concentration at particular points, e.g. the central city, for particular activities. The central city cannot accommodate highway and air facilities too well. The substitution of these new modes for the old modes, therefore, favors other locations in the metropolis as logical points at which to concentrate activities that make heavy use of these new modes.

The substitution of automobiles for public transit further undermines the special advantage of the center for labor supply. True, the automobile makes it possible for the worker to commute longer distances. The employer who sticks to the center for other reasons will benefit from the extension of the radius of the labor market. But now a large labor force can be conveniently assembled at almost any point served by the highway network; and the center is hardly the best place to assemble an auto-oriented work force.

The auto and the truck also modify the basic spatial character of specialization and concentration. Assume an employer who calculates that he must retain a presence in the center despite its liabilities—old and new. Under the old technology, that decision would entail a much greater commitment to the center than it does now because with improved mobility, there is greater opportunity to "fine-tune" one's commitment to the center. The front-office, the showroom, and those related activities that call for face-to-face contact can be located in the center while production and distribution activities can be located further out where space is cheaper, access to transport service is better, and access to labor as good or better. This spatial separation is facilitated by the new transport technology. In the extreme case, the production can go to Japan, to be linked to the home base by air freight.

Thus, every asset of the city is challenged by new transport technology, and some of its liabilities are aggravated. The substitution of automobile travel for mass transit to and from the center and within the center increases the desired space per capita, and in a very real sense, diminishes the overall capacity of the center to accommodate people and jobs. More space is taken up for parking. The greater speed and maneuverability of the truck compared to the horse-and-wagon by itself represents an improvement. But the potential gain from that source is frustrated by the high cost of re-arranging the already developed center to accommodate the new vehicle. A city that is built with the new technology in mind can better compete with its suburbs.

On the whole, public policy has supported the thrust of the new technology. Nobody can tell us with certainty what would have happened if transport investments were entirely managed by the private sector and if the prices of all transport services reflected marginal social costs. The fact is that the public sector was relatively quick to supply the complementary capital investments in roads and terminals for the new modes and relatively slow in responding to the agonies of decline in the old modes. Since the center city had more to gain from the preservation of the old, it certainly was not favoured by the dominant thrust of public policy.

Nevertheless, there is one aspect of *Dynamics II*, as suggested earlier, that has worked in the city's favor. *Dynamics I* has enlarged the national basket of activities, as symbolized by the growth of the office sector, in which the city retains a strong comparative advantage. The potential for the continued concentration of such activities in the center is enlarged by the revolution in air transport, which makes it easier for an activity of this type to serve an ever-wider market. In this respect, the classic theorem about the impact of transport costs on specialization and trade applies.

When you add it all up, you have to conclude that the center has been adversely affected competitively by technological progress in transport and the public policies which have embodied that progress in physical investments. The impact, however, is not only to hold back the city's growth but also to refine the character of the city's economy forcing it to specialize increasingly in those activities that gain most from the city's assets and suffer least from its liabilities.

Dynamics III: Technological Progress in Other Sectors

There are at least three other kinds of technological progress that

G

have important implications for the competition between city and suburb. We will refer to them as *Dynamics III (A)*, *III (B)*, and *III (C)*.

Dynamics III (A) is technological change in goods handling in plants and warehouses other than those occasioned by *Dynamics II*. The key here is the use of electric power, in combination with engineering design, to favor horizontal as against vertical layouts in such facilities. As a result, the twin pressures of high rents and congestion in the city act even more forcefully to favor outlying areas for the location of production and distribution facilities.

Dynamics III (B) is technological progress in communication and data processing, as symbolized by TV and the computer, which are well established but continuously evolving new forms and remote access. At first, these new gimmicks favor the center because their limited availability and high unit costs compel sharing of a kind that is more readily achieved in a dense market. But as unit costs go down and remote access is achieved, they tend on balance to reduce the disabilities of remote locations and alleviate the pressure to be in the center. They also contribute to the potential, as with *Dynamics II*, of achieving a finer spatial specialization by permitting the top decision-makers in the center to be in close contact with the information and other paper processing activities that can then be located at lower cost in outlying areas.[2]

Many have speculated that further progress in communication will ultimately undermine entirely the "face-to-face" aspect of concentration which favors the center of the city. Even if that were true, it would not necessarily lead to the demise of the center, in terms of our balance sheet above. "Face-to-face" is the reflection of a complex pattern of specialization, the logic of which, rests essentially on a large dense market. Easy communication removes one motive for employers to want to be located in close proximity to each other. But they can substitute close-circuit TV for lunch at the club and retain their location in the center if there are other good reasons for doing so.

Dynamics III (C) takes us farther away from our subject but its relevance is soon obvious. I have in mind the technological revolution in agriculture which was alluded to above under *Dynamics I*. There we stressed the shifting industrial mix of the economy and

---

[2]The reader is referred to another chapter in this volume, "The Wired City" by Harold Barnett.

the implications of such shifts for the city center, from the per-spective of growth in employment. Here I want to stress the population migration effects.

Historically, the city, especially in the Northeast, was favored in its growth by a very elastic supply of labor. Hordes of immi-grants came to these cities from abroad and from America's rural areas because they, like their contemporary counterparts, found the center city a more congenial atmosphere for launching their assimilation into the modern American economy. The happy coincidence of demand and supply worked in everybody's favor.

In recent decades, two factors have operated to create a very serious divergence of interests. On the demand side, the city's economy generates fewer opportunities for the uneducated, un-trained, immigrant worker. On the supply side, these workers con-tinue to favor the city voluntarily for the traditional reasons, or involuntarily because of suburban discrimination against racial minorities and poor whites. The City would prefer to make more living space available for workers who are in demand at the center. The immigrants frustrate this objective, in part by competing for scarce space, in part by adding to the tax burden because of their public service requirements, and in part by making the center generally less attractive to the middle- and upper-income groups. Obviously the movement of these groups to the suburbs has been motivated by "pull" factors as well, but the "push" factors cannot be denied.

In summary, *Dynamics III (C)* cuts into the labor supply advantages of the center. *Dynamics III (B)* reduces the need for proximity insofar as it rests on easy communication. *Dynamics III (A)* feeds the demand for space per worker and aggravates a long standing liability.

Dynamics IV: Capital Accumulation and Higher Incomes

The city, as we said, is a capital-saving device. It is a device for sharing the costs of indivisible units of capital, thus reducing the unit cost per capita or per unit of output. In part, this saving is achieved at the expense of higher operating costs arising from congestion.

Dynamics I, II, and III all relate to various facets of progress. But if you can imagine achieving economic progress through capital accumulation alone, a process certainly theoretically possible, you would already have identified a reason for the relative decline of central cities. As wages rise relative to interest rates, there is increasingly less incentive to economize on labor. You go outward, where you can reduce operating costs, even if you have to incur higher capital costs in the process.

The same logic applies to the resident as to the employer. Living in relative isolation calls for a greater commitment of capital. You have to own your own home, provide for your own mobility and for a host of other services, available on a current account basis, albeit at higher prices, in the congested center. As your assets and borrowing power improve, you have less incentive to conserve capital and can give vent to your desire for easy, spacious living.

Thus, even with the state-of-the-art held constant, capital accumulation and rising incomes render the savings arising from density less relevant and the advantages of sparsely settled territory more relevant for both producers and consumers.

THE ROLE OF MUNICIPAL POLICY

In the previous section, we view the changing location of jobs and people as reflecting inexorable forces in the economy and society at large. Rural to urban migration is mainly attributed to the decline of job opportunities in agriculture and other resource-oriented industries and the concomitant growth of employment in service industries, which are city-oriented in their location. Technological change in transport—people and goods—accompanied by higher incomes are held to be responsible for the far more rapid rate of growth of the suburbs as compared to the central cities.

Typically, when we think of public policy as an influence on geographic patterns of development, we are more likely to consider aspects of federal government policy than local policy. We credit the Federal Interstate Highway Program and the Federal Housing Program with having accelerated the impact of the automobile on metropolitan growth patterns. We think of the geographic distribution of federal contracts as having significant effects on the distribution of economic activity and population. By contrast, we generally think of local policy as being restricted to a passive role. "How do we adjust to what is happening to us?" is the perspective we have on local policy.

In recent years, there has been a growing presumption that local policy can assume an active role in determining what happens, at least as far as employment is concerned. Local governments have increasingly adopted the view that they can influence the demand for labor in their jurisdictions by adopting and implementing policies that improve their competitive position. Some communities have offered subsidies in one form or another to prospective employers; others have attempted to ease local tax burdens. These measures directly affect the operating costs of the firm. Other measures operate indirectly by enhancing potential productivity. These include improved public services, better transport, and friendlier bankers.

Communities have, of course, also used local policy to discourage the location of certain industries inside their boundaries. The main instrument is zoning, which establishes the legal basis for saying "NO" to a prospective employer. Such communities also have the power to influence the composition of population within their borders. They do so not by inducing changes in the demand for labor but by defining the terms under which people can locate their residences within their borders.

Whether or not localities pursue explicit policies to influence employment and population inside their borders, programs and policies designed to serve other objectives are bound to have such side effects. Taxes are the prime example. The aggregate tax burden and the way that burden is distributed within the community both affect job and residential location even if they are largely decided on other grounds. But other policies are also relevant in this regard.

New York City, for example, is undergoing considerable change in the pattern of job and population growth. In the main, these changes reflect the workings of forces far beyond the control of city government. On the demand for labor side, the impact of these changes has been to retard the overall growth of jobs in the city but mainly to reduce absolutely the number of low-skill jobs. On the supply side, the reverse has occurred. On balance, the city as a place to live is increasingly less attractive to high-skill, high-income employees while low-skill, low-income populations are increasingly attracted there.

Insofar as city policy has been at all addressed explicitly to this problem, the focus has been on the supply side. Very simply, the city has attempted to arrest the decline of blue-collar low-wage employment by assisting employers who might otherwise leave the city to find suitable space for their operations. Although one cannot estimate with certainty the importance of space as a factor in relocation of production facilities, it is reasonable to assume that, in many instances, the proximate if not the ultimate factor motivating relocation is the lack of an adequate site at an acceptable price. Sometimes, the difficulty arises from plant expansion; at other times, from displacement caused by renewal or private preemption for higher value uses. In any case, it is felt that intervention by the city can augment the supply of space to those producers who would otherwise find it in their own best interests to locate outside the city.

The merits of this particular policy instrument will not be appraised here. Suffice it to say that it appears to have been of limited impact in dealing with the fundamental supply-demand imbalance. Moreover, there are other city policies motivated by non-economic objectives of the city that have tended to exacerbate, not resolve the basic labor market imbalance. In this paper I will focus on two such policies which have received detailed treatment in research: housing and welfare.[3]

The essential dilemma of the government has been clear for some years. To finance a very large and growing welfare burden along with conventional city services whose costs keep rising rapidly, it has had to extract revenue from a productive sector that is growing very slowly and is increasingly sensitive to comparative cost pressures. The dilemma seems difficult enough to resolve by itself; yet it is further aggravated by city policy. In other words, the city is actually making worse an already bad situation.

Let me suggest two criteria for judging such policies. The first is short run and static: it says that you should pursue those policies that do the least damage to your productive capacity while yielding the maximum effectiveness in combating poverty. The second criterion is longer run and dynamic: it says that you should prefer those policies which contribute to the automatic or natural resolution of the problem over policies which perpetuate or even exacerbate the problem. Generally, although not always, the two

---

[3]The research referred to here is in progress at the New York City Rand Institute which the author serves as consultant. So far, the only published work is that of Lowry [(7) 1970].

criteria reinforce each other to create a strong preference for one set of policies over another.

As applied to the case in hand, these criteria would argue for bringing relief to the needy in ways that do least damage to the local economy and provide maximum incentive to escape from poverty through gainful employment. A federally-financed family-assistance plan which does not tax earnings at 100 per cent is readily seen as passing these criteria with the highest possible scores. In the absence of such an ideal resolution of the city's dilemma, it is unfortunately hard to argue that the second-best alternative is being pursued.

The sad fact is that the city is transferring *assets* to the poor, rather than just *income*. It is doing so by creating artificial incentives for the poor to occupy space that is either directly or indirectly in great demand for productive use. The full force of city policy can be made clear by imagining that the Pan-American Building were to be condemned by the city so it could be made available as housing for the poor. Nothing like this has happened to my knowledge; yet this is the logical limit of current city policy.

Which aspects of city policy give rise to this interpretation? First, there is the welfare practice of treating housing costs as an extra. Within reason, a household on welfare can compete for housing with no budget constraint; the city will simply pay whatever bill is incurred. Thus, space, which in its current condition or more likely through clearance or renovation would be attractive to firms or their employees wishing to locate in the city, is likely to be retained in the "poverty" market. Instead of deriving maximum value from the property and taxing that value to subsidize poor people to live elsewhere where the alternative uses are not so productive, the city, in effect, transfers assets to the poor, which they are not able to use anywhere nearly as productively. The net social loss is large and unambiguous.

The policy not only fails on the first criterion but its failure on the second is equally apparent. Paradoxically, the space which is most valuable to the potential producer, e.g., in Manhattan, is least relevant to the welfare recipient in terms of ultimately providing him with job opportunity and wages to displace welfare benefits. If the welfare recipient could be induced to seek cheaper space elsewhere, thus preserving a vital productive asset, he could, at the same time, increase the probability of locating closer to the relevant potential employer who is compelled by the nature of his business also to seek out cheaper space.

Again, to bring the point home, let us imagine the (politically) impossible: the city of New York derives revenue from its own industry to subsidize the co-location of low-skill jobs and workers in open tracts in the suburbs. But failing this, can we justify the indiscriminate use of space within the city for anti-poverty purposes?

The illogic of this policy is reinforced by the city's housing policy, specifically, rent control. To begin with, rent control is a very inefficient anti-poverty policy for the simple reason that 45 per cent of the occupants of rent-controlled housing are not poor [(7) Lowry, 1970]. Viewed as a tax on the rich landlord, rent control is deficient in the sense that landlords can escape the tax through disinvestment. But what is most relevant to the issue at hand is the effect that rent control has on relative prices. Rent control confers a far greater bargain on the occupant in Manhattan than it does in other boroughs of the city. Median rents for controlled housing hardly vary from borough to borough ($21.80—$26.90 per room per month) whereas median rents for uncontrolled housing substantially ($30.00—over $50.00 per room per month), suggesting that rent control conceals the relative opportunity cost of space within the city.

The very high figure for Manhattan attests to the ongoing validity of a Manhattan location in the private sector despite all the heralded pressures to suburbanize. There is every reason to suspect that the city could enjoy greater private output and greater public welfare if its scarce resources—mainly space—were more strategically employed. At the same time, the resolution of the labor market imbalance might better be served in the long run by such policies.

NET IMPACT AND FUTURE PROSPECTS

Despite the widespread interest in the economic welfare of the central city, there are no standard data sources that permit easy calculation of comparative rates of growth of employment except for manufacturing, wholesale, retail, and a category called "Selected Services" in the U.S. Census. These four categories account for only slightly more than half of total employment. More comprehensive measures have been developed for a limited number of areas for selected time periods by painstaking research.[4] [(2) Birch, 1970; (6) Lewis, 1969; (8) Noll, 1970].[4]

Both the standard sources and the special studies show a very mixed picture as between areas and as between time periods if we look only at the absolute growth of employment in the central city. When, however, we compare the central city to the rest of the metropolitan area and control for industrial mix,[5] the trend to the suburbs is rather persistent and pervasive. There are also some interesting surprises. For example, in a study of twelve metro areas over the period 1953–1965 [(6) Lewis, 1969] the author found that New York City, which grew very slowly, experienced less suburban competition than places like Atlanta, Denver, and Washington, D.C., which grew much more rapidly in absolute terms.

The pattern of national growth was found to be favorable to the growth of central city employment in every case but one, as suggested above in *Dynamics I*. Also, while the suburbs grew faster than the central cities in all industrial categories, the suburban drift was more pronounced in manufacturing and retail trade than in the service sectors, as suggested in *Dynamics II*. When the national economy is growing rapidly, the favorable effect of national growth tends to outweigh the unfavorable impact of competition from the suburbs.

What will happen to employment in the central city in future decades? *Dynamics I* should continue to operate with considerable force in favor of the central city. The triple trend to white collar, service, and office employment shows no signs of abatement. *Dynamics II* offers considerable ground for speculation. Although the automobile is still chipping away at mass transit patronage and

---

[4]In the New York Metropolitan Region Study, for example, estimates were developed for New York City, covering all categories of employment. Similar estimates have been developed for other areas in connection with special studies of these areas. The most comprehensive attempt to go beyond the readily available sources is that of Wilfred Lewis Jr., in an unpublished paper entitled "Urban Growth and Suburbanization of Employment—Some New Data."

[5]That is, we take into account the industrial structure of the city's economy and control for the influence of overall national rates of growth by industry.

finances in many cities, there are significant counter-developments. New transit systems are being built, and there is some hope that rail-commuter travel will be put on a more solid basis by federal action. The revolution in differential access wrought by the automobile is irreversible, but we don't see in the cards another revolution with similar effects and small incremental measures in favor of the city are definitely possible.

Dynamics III (A) is the great imponderable. We need more research on the extent to which sophisticated communication devices do, in fact, substitute for face-to-face contact before we can make any assessment of the locational implications of *Dynamics III (A)*. The relevance of *Dynamics III (B)* will wane as goods handling activities continue to shrink as a share of the total economy. The rural-to-urban shift that underlies *Dynamics III (C)*, the 1970 Census already tells us, is less of a factor in shaping the demographic characteristic of metropolitan areas. As for *Dynamics IV*, I see no reason why it should not continue to work in favor of lower densities.

What all this adds up to is that the city will most likely continue to lose competitively to the suburbs, but the aggregate demand for labor in the city will be sustained by overall national growth and the favorable "mix" aspects of that growth. To the extent that we continue to rely on local revenues to finance city needs, extreme caution is called for to protect the goose that lays the golden egg.

REFERENCES

(1) Armstrong, R. B. *The Office Industry.* New York: Regional Plan Association, 1970, Final Pre-Publication draft.

(2) Birch, D. L. *The Economic Future of City and Suburb.* New York: Committee for Economic Development, 1970.

(3) Hoover, E. M. and Vernon, R. *Anatomy of A Metropolis.* Cambridge: Harvard Univ. Press, 1959.

(4) ————. *The Location of Economic Activity.* New York: McGraw-Hill, 1963.

(5) ————. "The Evolving Form and Organization of the Metropolis." in Perloff, H. S. and Wing, L., Jr., eds. *Issues in Urban Economics.* Baltimore, Md.: Johns Hopkins Press, 1968.

(6) Lewis, W., Jr. *Urban Growth and Suburbanization of Employment.* Some New Data, Unpublished, Revised Draft, 1969, available through Mr. Lewis at *National Planning Association.*

(7) Lowry, I. S. *Rental Housing in New York City.* Volume 1. *Confronting the Crisis.* New York: New York City Rand Institute, 1970.

(8) Noll, R. *Metropolitan Employment and Population: Distribution and the Conditions of Urban Poor.* Washington, D.C.: The Brookings Institution, 1970 (Reprint).

(9) Segal, M. *Wages in the Metropolis.* Cambridge: Harvard Univ. Press, 1959.

(10) Vernon, R. *The Changing Economic Function of the Central City.* New York: Committee For Economic Development, 1959.

5

The Demography of Constantly Changing Birth Rates

ANSLEY COALE

Princeton University

INTRODUCTION

The core of theoretical demography is the stable population, a concept developed to a surprising degree by Euler in the eighteenth century,[1] then independently rediscovered and much more fully elaborated by Lotka beginning in 1907.[2] The stable population is the closed population of one sex that is generated by unchanging schedules of fertility and mortality. It illustrates the full implications of any combination of schedules—one of fertility and one of mortality. It recently has aroused revived interest because stable population analysis serves as the basis of an array of techniques of estimation that are proving valuable in providing approximate values of birth rates, death rates, and other basic measures for the large fraction of the world's population whose births and deaths are not recorded at

---

[1]Leonard Euler. "Recherches générales sur la mortalité et la multiplication du genre humain," *Histoire de l'Académie Royale des Sciences et Belles-Lettres*, Belgium, 1760, pp. 144–64.

[2]Alfred J. Lotka wrote more than thirty articles and a book on stable populations. The first article was "Relation between Birth Rates and Death Rates," *Science*. N.S. **26**; 1907, 653, pp. 21–22; and the last was "Application of Recurrent Series in Renewal Theory," *The Annals of Mathematical Statistics*, **29**, 1948, 2, pp. 190–206.

all fully, and whose numbers and age are recorded in censuses with large margins of error.[3]

The fact is, of course, that real populations are never genuinely stable. All populations of large areas gain or lose to some degree through migration (although sometimes the effect on growth and age composition is minor). Schedules of fertility and mortality are never, in fact, unchanging from year to year so that the properties of a stable population usually fit those of actual populations only very approximately, and occasionally, to a good approximation because of offsetting effects in different directions of changes that sometimes occur. A natural question to raise is whether it is possible to find a simple analytical structure that relates the birth rates, death rates, and age composition of populations, subject to changing rather than fixed schedules.

The basic theorem of stable population analysis is as follows: any closed population, with no matter how irregular an initial age distribution, experiencing fixed schedules of fertility and mortality, approaches, with the passage of time, a state in which its age composition is fixed and its birth rate, death rate, and rate of increase all are constant. In other words, the stable population is established by fixed fertility and mortality, no matter what the initial conditions: the stable population is independent of its remote past history. In 1957, I made a conjecture to the effect that the age composition of *every* closed population is determined by the particular recent sequence (fixed or changing) of schedules of fertility and mortality to which it has been subject—and is independent of its remote history.[4] This conjecture has been formally proved by Alvaro Lopez and David McFarland.[5] This broader theorem, of which the basic

[3]See especially, United Nations, Department of Economic and Social Affairs. *The Concept of a Stable Population. Application to the Study of Populations of Countries with Incomplete Demographic Statistics.* By Jean Bourgeois-Pichat; Population Studies, 39, New York, 1968; and A. J. Coale and P. Demeny, *Methods of Estimating Basic Demographic Measures from Incomplete Data.* United Nations, Manuals on Methods of Estimating Population. Manual 4. Population Studies, 42, New York, 1967.

[4]A. J. Coale. "How the Age Distribution of a Human Population is Determined." *Cold Spring Harbor Symposium on Quantitative Biology*, **22**, 1957, pp. 83–88.

[5]A. Lopez. *Problems in Stable Population Theory.* Princeton, Office of Population Research, 1961.

———, "Asymptotic Properties of a Human Age Distribution under a Continuous Net Maternity Function," *Demography*, **4**, 1967, pp. 680–87. David D. McFarland, "On the Theory of Stable Populations: A New and Elementary Proof of the Theorems under Weaker Conditions." *Demography*, **6**, 1969, pp. 301–22.

theorem of stable populations is a special case, implies that it is possible to calculate the sequence of births, and the number of persons at each age, whenever a sufficiently long sequence of fertility and mortality schedules are known. It is not necessary to know the age composition or the fertility and mortality of the population in the remote past. Concretely, one can assume an arbitrary age distribution a hundred years ago and project the population by standard techniques from year to year on the basis of recorded age-specific rates of fertility and mortality. The recent sequence of births and the current age composition calculated in this way will be essentially the same as the actual birth sequence and age composition in a closed population experiencing the given sequence of fertility and mortality. Thus it is, in fact, possible to determine the influence of a sequence of fertility and mortality schedules on the birth rates, death rates, and age composition of a population. However, it has not been possible to date to find, under unrestricted conditions of change in fertility and mortality, succinct expressions relating birth rates, death rates, rates of increase, and various basic parameters of age composition, to fertility and mortality schedules, as is possible with the stable population.

There is, however, a particular instance of changing schedules for which approximate formulae have been presented. In this essay, I wish to explore this special case further. The particular circumstances that can be analyzed in a manner roughly analogous to stable population analysis is the sequence of births, and the number of persons at each age that evolve when fertility continuously declines (or continuously rises) while mortality remains fixed. It is possible as will be shown below to derive a simple equation that provides a close approximation (and a more complicated equation that provides a *very* close approximation) to the sequence of births generated when fertility persistently declines, and to determine the birth rate, death rate, and rate of increase of the population. The characteristics of the population generated under these circumstances can be related to characteristics of stable populations to show just how a history of declining fertility (as compared to a history of constant fertility at the current level) affects the age composition, and hence the birth rate, the death rate, and the rate of increase of a population.

Demographic analysis of this sort is relevant to (among others) the French and American populations from 1800 to the 1930's, when both experienced prolonged declines of fertility, and to some extent to the populations of most highly industrialized countries during an extended part of their histories.

A decrease of fertility to replacement at low mortality levels is the only alternative, in the long run, to an increase in mortality. Rapid reduction to, or below, replacement is a goal strongly advocated by some groups today—advocated as a goal for almost all populations. The demography of a population in which fertility has just reached replacement after a sustained decline thus has some special topical interest.

AN APPROXIMATE ANALYTICAL EXPRESSION FOR THE SEQUENCE OF BIRTHS WHEN MORTALITY IS CONSTANT AND FERTILITY IS SUBJECT TO A CONSTANT ANNUAL CHANGE

In any closed population of one sex there is a simple-appearing relation between the births at a given moment and births in the past:

$$B(t) = \int_{\alpha}^{\beta} B(t - a)m(a, t)p(a, t) \, da . \qquad (1)$$

When α and β are the upper and lower limits of the childbearing span, $m(a, t)$ is the proportion of women at age a and time t giving birth to a female child, and $p(a, t)$ is the proportion of women surviving from births occurring t years ago to age a at time t. Equation (1) can be expressed in a different form as

$$B(t) = R(t) \int_{\alpha}^{\beta} B(t - a) f(a, t) \, da , \qquad (2)$$

where $R(t)$ is the "net reproduction rate" at time t, and $f(a, t)$ is $m(a, t)p(a, t)$ divided by $\int_{0}^{\beta} m(a, t)p(a, t) \, da$. Thus, births at t are equal to the net reproduction rate at time t (defined in a peculiar way) and the weighted average of births occurring α to β years ago. Note that $f(a, t)$ has the characteristics of a frequency distribution. $R(t)$ is a "net reproduction rate" defined by the age-specific maternity rates at time t, combined with the survival to age t of cohorts born a years ago. Thus, at each age, the past mortality over a different time span enters the definition of this "net reproduction rate." The case that we shall explore is one wherein $p(a, t)$ is fixed, and can be written as merely $p(a)$, and $m(a, t) = m(a, o)e^{kt}$—fertility is fixed in age structure, but changing in level at a constant annual rate. Our goal is to find out what we can about the birth sequence, and also the age composition, birth and death rates, that result when

$$B(t) = R(o)e^{kt} \int_\alpha^\beta B(t - a) f(a) \, da \, .\tag{3}$$

If we can find an analytical expression for the birth sequence that satisfies Equation (3), we can be sure that it is indeed the birth sequence that would be approached as a constant rate of fertility change continued for a long time because of the proven tendency for the effect of initial conditions to vanish with the passage of time.

Our general procedure in finding a solution to Equation (3) will be to use some possibly contrary-to-fact simplifications to obtain an approximate solution and then to verify whether or not the approximate solution is appropriate by substituting it in Equation (3). The basic simplification that we shall employ is an assumption that the birth sequence satisfying Equation (3) is very similar to one that would occur if births were concentrated at a single age rather than being spread over an interval from ages α to β. Indeed it follows from the mean value theorem of the integral calculus that the weighted average of the births from α to β can be replaced by the births at a single age in the interval. It follows that

$$B(t) = R(o)e^{kt}B(t - T(t))\tag{4}$$

where $T(t)$ is a number (that may be constantly changing) lying between α and β. Our first approximate solution is obtained by assuming that $T(t)$ is a fixed number, and the second approximation makes allowance for the fact that: (a) $T(t)$ is different in different stable populations according to the level of fertility even with the same age structure of fertility (in short, $T(t)$ varies with $R(t)$); and (b) the second order exponential that arises in the first approximate solution implies a slight systematic difference in the relation between $B(t - T(t))$ and $\int_\alpha^\beta B(t - a) f(a) \, da$ in the stable population on the one hand, and a population with constantly changing fertility on the other. We now proceed to carry through the two successive approximations. To simplify the subsequent analysis, we shall set $t = o$ at the point where changing fertility brings the net reproduction rate to unity. We now assume that the value of $T(t)$ is held fixed at T_0 and use as an estimated value of T_0 the mean age of the net fertility function, i.e.,

$$T_0 = \frac{\int_\alpha^\beta a p(a) m(a) \, da}{\int_\alpha^\beta p(a) m(a) \, da} \, .\tag{5}$$

H

Thus, the version of Equation (4) that we are trying to solve is

$$B(t) = R(o)e^{kt}B(t - T_0) .$$ (6)

If we let $\Upsilon(t) = \log B(t)$, Equation (6) can be rewritten as

$$\Upsilon(t) - \Upsilon(t - T_0) = \log R(o) + kt .$$ (7)

Equation (7) is a simple difference equation that is readily solved; for example, by assuming that $\Upsilon(t) = b_1 t + b_2 t^2$. Substituting this form of $\Upsilon(t)$ in Equation (7), and solving for the undetermined coefficients b_1 and b_2 leads to the solution

$$B(t) = B(o) \, e^{(k/2)t + (k/2T_0)t^2}.$$ (8)

(Note that by choosing the origin at the time when the net reproduction rate is unity, we are sure that Log $R(o)$ is zero.) The number of persons at age a in a population with this birth sequence would be

$$
\begin{aligned}
\mathcal{N}(a, t) &= B(t - a)p(a) \\
&= B(o) \, e^{(k/2)t + (k/2T_0)t^2} \, e^{-(k/2)a + (k/2T_0)a^2} \, e^{-(kt/T_0)a} \, p(a)
\end{aligned}
$$ (9)

or

$$\mathcal{N}(a, t) \doteq B(t) \, e^{-(k/2)a + (k/2T_0)a^2} \, e^{-r(t)a} \, p(a) .$$ (10)

The indicated approximate nature of Equation (10) arises from the fact that $r(t)$—$r(t)$ means the rate of increase in the stable population defined by the fertility and mortality at time t—is not exactly equal to kt/T_0. It may be recalled from stable population analysis that $r(t) = (\log R(t))/T(t)$. Thus kt/T_0 differs from $r(t)$ to the extent that T_0 and $T(t)$ are different. The proportionate age distribution at time t is given by

$$c(a, t) = \frac{\mathcal{N}(a, t)}{\mathcal{N}(t)} = b(t) \, e^{-(k/2)a + (k/2T_0)a^2} \, e^{-r(t)a} \, p(a) .$$ (11)

But the stable age distribution based on the fertility and mortality at time t is

$$c_s(a, t) = b_s(t) \, e^{-r(t)a} \, p(a) .$$ (12)

Hence, Equation (11) can be rewritten as

$$c(a, t) = (b(t)/b_s(t)) \, e^{-(k/2)a + (k/2T_0)a^2} \, c_s(a) .$$ (13)

Thus, the age distribution, according to this approximate formula, of a population with a history of changing fertility is equal to a constant (the ratio of the birth rates) times the stable age distribution modified by a second order exponential term. Equation (13) is derived, of course, from the approximate solution for the birth sequence given in Equation (8). As an empirical test of how good this approximate solution is, we have projected a population for many years with fertility falling each year by 1 per cent. The initial population had an age distribution consisting of a stable population modified according to Equation (13). It was deliberately chosen with very high fertility (gross reproduction rate 4.07) and low mortality (e_0^0 70 years). The age structure of fertility was arbitrarily selected as that of the Swedish population from 1891 to 1900 (with the level of fertility approximately doubled). T_0 is 32.1 years. The population was projected for 200 years. The natural logarithm of the births for each subsequent year divided by the births in the initial year is shown in Figure 1 on the basis of two different calculations; first, based on a precise projection that was carried out by single years of age and single years of time, and secondly based on Equation (13). The fit is quite close, although there is a gradual divergence that reaches a maximum of about 6 per cent after more than a century. The example shows clearly enough that, at least for this fertility schedule, the approximation is quite serviceable. We now turn to an examination of an improvement in the approximation, an examination that leads to a virtually perfect second approximation, which in turn shows what factors cause divergence of the first approximate solution from the accurately calculated birth sequence.

The basic source of the failure of the approximation to fit the actual birth sequence perfectly is that it began with Equation (6), in which the value of $T(t)$ in Equation (4) is held fixed at T_0 rather than being allowed to vary. As a first step in improving the approximation, consider Equation (4) for the special case where k is zero, implying, of course, fixed fertility. Then the proper relationship between births in one generation and births at a fixed point a generation earlier is

$$B(t) = RB(t - T) . \qquad (14)$$

If Equation (14) is solved in a manner analogous to the solution of Equation (6), the solution is found to be

$$B(t) = B(o)\ e^{[(\log R)/T]t}, \qquad (15)$$

which is precisely the correct solution for the birth sequence in a stable population, provided T is the mean length of generation in the stable population, since, as is well known, in a stable population the rate of increase $r = (\log R)/T$. However, the mean length of generation differs in stable populations with different levels of fertility even when the stable populations share the same age structure of fertility and the same mortality schedule. In fact, as shown by Lotka,

$$T = T_0 - \frac{\sigma^2}{2} r + \ldots\ldots \tag{16}$$

where T_0 is the mean age of childbearing in the net fertility schedule and σ^2 is the variance of the net fertility schedule. Since $\sigma^2/2T_0$ is in the order of 0.6 to 0.9 in most recorded fertility schedules, T differs from T_0 by a proportion that is approximately $-0.7r$. Thus if the intrinsic rate of increase is 3 per cent, the mean length of generation is slightly more than 2 per cent less than the mean age of the net fertility schedule. In other words, if we look again at Equations (3) and (4), it is apparent that the value of $T(t)$ that produces the same result as the weighted average of the births during the preceding generation varies with the level of fertility. The higher the level of fertility, the lower the value of $T(t)$, even though $f(a)$ in Equation (3) remains unchanged. We shall now construct a second approximation by modifying the basis of the first approximation—Equation (6)—in a way that allows for a value of $T(t)$ that varies with the level of fertility rather than retaining the incorrect assumption that $T(t)$ is fixed at T_0. We shall actually incorporate two adjustments. One is to assume that we can use as a value of $T(t)$ the mean length of generation in the stable population defined by the fixed mortality schedule and the fertility schedule at time t. The second adjustment will make allowance for the fact that the second order exponential indicated by the approximate solution in Equation (8) introduces a systematic difference between the weighted average of the births α to β years ago, and the births T years ago (where T is the mean length of generation in a stable population)—a systematic difference between this relationship in the stable population on the one hand, and in the population with a second order exponential birth sequence on the other.

We are searching for a solution to an equation of the form shown in Equation (4). However, if we try to allow the interval between the births at different times that are related by the equation to vary, it is not possible to convert the equation into a difference equation and apply standard difference equation techniques for a solution.

What we shall do then is indicated in Equation (17).

$$B(t) = R(o) \, e^{kt} \, B(t - T_0) \frac{B^*(t - T(t))}{B^*(t - T_0)}. \qquad (17)$$

If the B^* values in Equation (17) were identical with values without the *, Equation (17) would reduce simply to Equation (4). The * indicates values taken from the approximate solution given in Equation (8). In other words, we shall assume that the relationship of births at $t - T(t)$ to births at $t - T_0$ is the same in the exact solution as in the approximate solution. The next step is to determine the value of $B^*(t - T(t))/B^*(t - T_0)$. Since $T(t)$ differs only slightly from T_0, we can assume that

$$\log_e \left(\frac{B^*(t - T(t))}{B^*(t - T_0)} \right) = (T_0 - T(t)) \left(\frac{d \log B^*(t)}{dt} \right)_{t = t - T_0}; \qquad (18)$$

but $T_0 - T(t)$ is one half $\sigma^2 r$, or approximately $\sigma^2 kt / 2 T_0$ and

$$\left[\frac{d \log B^*(t)}{dt} \right]_{t = t - T_0} = \frac{k}{2} + \frac{kt}{T_0} - k = -\frac{k}{2} + \frac{kt}{T_0}; \qquad (19)$$

Hence,

$$\log \left(\frac{B^*(t - T(t))}{B^*(t - T_0)} \right) = -\frac{\sigma^2 k^2}{4 T_0} t + \frac{\sigma^2 k^2}{2 T_0^2} t^2; \qquad (20)$$

and

$$\frac{B^*(t - T(t))}{B^*(t - T_0)} = e^{-(\sigma^2 k^2 / 4 T_0)t + (\sigma^2 k^2 / 2 T_0^2)t^2} \qquad (21)$$

If we modify Equation (6) as indicated in Equation (17) by using the value of $B^*(t - T(t))/B^*(t - T_0)$ indicated in Equation (21), there remains another minor adjustment still to be allowed for. As indicated in Equation (14), the relationship between the births at a given time and the births T years earlier in a stable population depends on the level of fertility; but if the birth sequence that we are trying to find resembles $B^*(t)$—the function given in Equation (8)—it will be a second (or possibly higher) order exponential, and when substituted in the integral in Equation (1), will fail to satisfy it exactly. If $B^*(t)$ is substituted in this equation, we find, after simplification,

$$B^*(t) = B^*(t) \int_\alpha^\beta e^{-(k/2)a + (k/2 T_0)a^2} \, e^{-(kt/T_0)a} \, p(a) m(a, t) \, da . \qquad (22)$$

The modifications that we are proposing above should produce a solution in which T_0 is, in effect, replaced by $T(t)$, in which case we can see that the integral equation would be satisfied provided

$$\int_\alpha^\beta e^{-(k/2)a+(k/2T(t))a^2}\, e^{-r(t)a}\, p(a)m(a,\,t)\, da = 1.0 \,. \qquad (23)$$

The new term $r(t)$ appears because $r(t)$ is equal to $\log R(t)/T(t)$, and $\log R(t) = kt$. The terms after the second order exponential in a in Equation (23) represent a non-negative continuous function with finite values in the range from α to β that has the aggregate value of 1.0, according to the fundamental equation of stable population analysis, namely $\int_0^\beta e^{-ra}p(a)m(a)\, da = 1.0$. Thus our solution will fail to satisfy the integral equation to the extent that the integral in Equation (23) differs from 1.0 with a non-zero value of k (it clearly equals 1.0 if k is equal to zero). First we define $Z(t)$ as

$$Z(t) = \int_\alpha^\beta e^{-(k/2)a+(k/2T(t))a^2}\, e^{-r(t)a}p(a)m(a,\,t)\, da \,, \qquad (24)$$

and find the value of $(d\,Z(t)/dk)$ when $k = 0$.

$$\left(\frac{dZ(t)}{dk}\right)_{k=0} = \int_\alpha^\beta \left(-\frac{a}{2} + \frac{a^2}{2\,T(t)}\right) e^{-r(t)a}\, p(a)m(a,\,t)\, da \,, \qquad (25)$$

or

$$\left(\frac{dZ(t)}{dk}\right)_{k=0} = -\frac{\bar{A}}{2} + \frac{\gamma_2 + \bar{A}^2}{2\,T(t)} \,, \qquad (26)$$

where $\bar{A}$ is the mean age of fertility in the stable population and γ_2 is the variance of net fertility in the stable population. If we accept the approximation that the mean length of generation is about equal to the mean age of fertility, we find

$$\left(\frac{dZ(t)}{dk}\right)_{k=0} \doteqdot \frac{\gamma_2}{2\,T(t)} \doteqdot \frac{\sigma^2}{2\,T_0} \qquad (27)$$

Thus, for small values of k the value of the integral $Z(t)$ is

$$Z(t) \doteqdot 1.0 + \frac{k\sigma^2}{2\,T_0} \doteqdot e^{(k\sigma^2/2\,T_0)}. \qquad (28)$$

Incorporating the expression in Equation (21) in the appropriate place in Equation (17), multiplying by the factor very close to 1.0 indicated in Equation (28), we finally reach

$$B(t) = R(o)B(t - T_0)\, e^{kt-(\gamma k^2/2T_0)t + (\gamma^2 k^2/4T_0^2)t^2 + (\gamma^2 k/2T_0)} \qquad (29)$$

or, if $Y(t) = \log B(t)$,

$$Y(t) = Y(t - T_0) = a_0 + a_1 t + a_2 t^2, \text{ where}$$

$$a_0 = \frac{\sigma^2 k}{2T_0}, \quad a_1 = k\left(1 - \frac{\sigma^2 k}{2T_0}\right), \quad \text{and} \quad a_2 = \frac{\sigma^2 k^2}{2T_0{}^2}. \tag{30}$$

The solution of this difference equation leads to the following expression for $B(t)$.

$$B(t) = B(o) \, e^{[k/2 + (\sigma^2 k/2T_0)(1/T_0 - k/12)]t + k/2T_0(1 + \sigma^2 k/4T_0)t^2 + (\sigma^2 k^2/6T_0{}^3)t^3} \tag{31}$$

Thus, allowance for a changing value of T, and for the effect on the relationship between births in consecutive generations of a higher-order exponential birth sequence converts a second-order exponential function of t, depending only on the annual rate of change of fertility and on the mean age of the net fertility function, into a third order exponential that depends on the variance of the net fertility function as well. When numerical values are substituted in Equation (31), the fit with projected fertility is extraordinary. The maximum difference between projected births and births calculated by Equation (31) is 6/10ths of a per cent over a 200-year span, a difference that cannot be shown on the scale of Figure 1. The numerical differences in the parameters found in Equation (8) and those found in Equation (31) are small, as might be expected. In Equation (8), the coefficient of t is 3.764 times 10^{-2} and the coefficient of t^2 is -1.604 times 10^{-4}. In Equation (31), the coefficient of t is $3.723 - 10^{-2}$; the coefficient of t^2 is -1.637 times 10^{-4}; the coefficient of t^3 is 2.14 times 10^{-8}. Given the values of σ^2 and T_0 found in actual human fertility schedules, the adjustments incorporated in Equation (31) become important only for relatively rapid changes in fertility and large values of t; and in reality, a combination of a large value of k and a large value of t is not possible, i.e., it would not be possible to maintain a large proportionate rate of increase or decrease in fertility for a long period of time without either fertility approaching zero or surpassing biologically or socially possible levels. In fact then, the approximate solution provided by Equation (8) is perfectly adequate to indicate the nature of the age composition in a population with changing fertility, the nature of the birth sequence, and the like. To avoid carrying the cumbersome expressions developed from Equations (14) to (31), we will, in the remainder of our analysis, accept the approximation expressed in Equation (8).

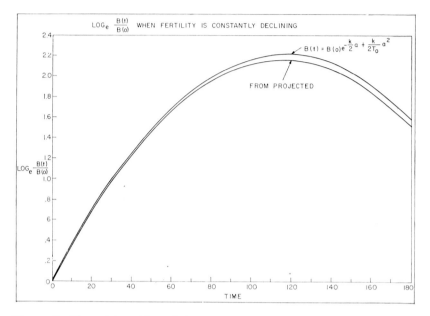

Figure 1   Natural logarithm of the ratio of births at time *t* to births at time *o* when fertility is constantly declining by 1 per cent annually; exact value from projection and approximate value from Equation (8).

CHARACTERISTICS OF THE BIRTH SEQUENCE AND OF THE POPULATION RESULTING FROM CONTINUOUSLY CHANGING FERTILITY

As is evident in Figure 1, if fertility declines continuously from a high level, the birth sequence rises at a diminishing rate, reaches a maximum, and begins to fall at an accelerating pace. Were we to plot a birth sequence resulting from continuously rising fertility from low levels, we would find a curve that fell ever less rapidly until it reached a minimum and then began to rise at an accelerating pace. We shall now consider the rate of increase of births under these circumstances. If we accept the approximate solution given in Equation (8), it is readily seen that the rate of increase of births in a population with changing fertility is

$$\frac{d \log B(t)}{dt} \doteq \frac{k}{2} + \frac{kt}{T_0} \doteq r(t) + \frac{k}{2}; \qquad (32)$$

the intrinsic rate of increase plus one-half the annual rate of change of fertility. The rate of increase of the population may be found as follows:

$$P(t) = \int_0^\infty B(t-a)p(a)\,da \doteq$$
$$B(o)\,e^{(k/2)t+(k/2T_0)t^2}\int_0^\infty e^{-(k/2)a+(k/2T_0)a^2}\,e^{-kta/T_0}\,p(a)\,da\;; \quad (33)$$

Hence,

$$\frac{dP(t)}{dt} = \left(\frac{k}{2} + \frac{kt}{T_0}\right)P(t) +$$

$$B(t)\int_0^\infty -\frac{ka}{T_0}\,e^{-(k/2)a+(k/2T_0)a^2}\,e^{-(kt/T_0)a}\,P(a)\,da \quad (34)$$

or

$$\frac{dP(t)}{dt} = P(t)\left[\frac{k}{2} + \frac{kt}{T_0} - \frac{k}{T_0}\bar{a}(t)\right]. \quad (35)$$

Hence

$$\frac{d\log P(t)}{dt} = \frac{k}{2} + \frac{k}{T_0}(t-\bar{a}(t)) \doteq \frac{k}{2} + r(t-\bar{a}(t)) \quad (36)$$

The rate of increase of the population is equal to the rate of increase of births at the time that the cohort whose age is now the average age of the population was born.

The births reach a maximum (if fertility is continuously declining) when the rate of increase in births is zero. From Equation (32) we can see that this occurs when the intrinsic rate of increase of the population is $-k/2$, or at a time equal to $-T_0/2$ (recalling that our origin has been maintained at the moment when the net reproduction rate becomes 1.0). In other words, the births reach a maximum a half a generation before the population is at replacement. It is interesting to note that the sequence of white births in the United States reached a maximum in the early 1920's, just about half a generation before the net reproduction rate fell to 1.0. The population reaches a maximum $\bar{a}(t)$ years later than the births do. In the projection with fertility falling at 1 per cent a year represented in Figure 1, the mean age of the net fertility function is 32.1 years so that the maximum of births is reached more than sixteen years before the net reproduction rate reaches unity. At the time that the projected population reaches a maximum, the mean age is about thirty-seven and one-half years, so that population continues to increase for about twenty-one years after the intrinsic rate of increase is zero.

An expression for the age distribution of the population with changing fertility relative to the stable population has already been given, and is repeated here for convenience:

$$c(a, t) = (b(t)/b_s(t)) \; e^{-(k/2)a + (k/2 T_0)a^2} \; c_s(a) \qquad (13)$$

The easiest way to visualize the relationship between a stable age distribution and the distribution of the population with changing fertility is first to imagine two populations that have the same number of births at time t, one of which has always experienced the current fertility and mortality schedules, and the other of which has experienced a history of constantly changing fertility. One, of course, would be the stable population, and the other, the population whose age distribution we are now examining. The number of persons at each age in the stable population would be $N_s(a, t) = B(t) \, e^{-r(t)a} p(a)$; the number of persons at each age in the population with a history of constantly changing fertility would be $N_k(a, t) = N_s(a, t) \, e^{-(k/2)a + (k/2 T)a^2}$. The second order exponential multiplying $N_s(a, t)$ is shown in Figure 2 for various values of k. The salient characteristics of the second order exponential relating $N_k(a, t)$ to $N_s(a, t)$ are: the number of persons at age zero and at an age equal to the mean length of generation are the same in the two populations. When fertility has been declining, the number of persons at ages between zero and the age equal to the mean length of generation is slightly greater than in the stable population. The ratio of N_k to N_s reaches a maximum of $e(-kt/8)$ at an age equal to one half the mean length of generation. At ages above the mean length of generation, the ratio of N_k to N_s falls rapidly below 1.0.

In sum, the effect of a history of declining fertility on the numbers at each age (relative to a stable population) is to produce slightly greater numbers (assuming the number of births to be equal) from ages zero to T and sharply diminishing numbers above age T. The effect of a slight increase at ages from zero to T and increasing diminution above age T on the *proportionate* age distribution depends upon the age structure of the stable population itself. A proportionate distribution is defined as the number at each age divided by the total number. If the total number in the two populations were the same, the proportionate distributions would be related to each other precisely by the functions shown in Figure 2; that is, if the total number in each population were the same, the ratio of the proportions in the population with a history of declining fertility to that in the stable would be $e^{-(k/2)a+(k/2T)a^2}$. However, the number of persons in the two populations would be the same only if the small proportionate increases below age T somehow offset the large proportionate decreases above age T. Such a balance might occur in a stable population that declines very steeply with age. In fact, such a balance occurs in a stable population where the mean age is about 57 per cent of the mean length of generation. Thus if the mean length of generation is thirty years, a stable population with a mean age of a little over seventeen years would have about the same number of persons as a population with the same births and a history of constantly declining (or constantly rising) fertility. (With a life expectancy of seventy years, a stable population with a mean age of seventeen years would have a gross reproduction rate of about five, and a rate of increase of about 5.3 per cent per year. It is doubtless more plausible in such an instance to analyze the age distribution of a population with a history of rising rather than declining fertility. The effect of multiplying by the function shown in Figure 2 on stable populations that diminish at a more moderate rate with age is to decrease the total number. Hence the ratio of $c_k(a)/c_s(a)$ is usually a function like those shown in Figure 2 multiplied by a constant greater than one. In fact, as is shown in Equation (13), the multiplier is the ratio of the birth rate in the population with changing fertility to the birth rate in the stable. Since we have been assuming that the number of births in the two populations is the same, the ratio of the birth rates is simply the reciprocal of the ratio of the population sizes.

In a given stable population, as the above consideration suggests, the ratio of b_k/b_s will be less for a given value of k, the greater is the mean length of generation—the greater the age at which the function shown in Figure 2 crosses unity. Conversely, in a population with a given mean length of generation, the ratio of b_k/b_s will be greater the greater are the proportions in the stable population at the older ages. b_k/b_s depends upon the extent to which the function shown in Figure 2 diminishes the stable population. The younger the stable population, the less it is diminished; the greater the age at which the function crosses unity, the less the stable population is diminished. These considerations suggest the hypothesis that the ratio of b_k/b_s will be the same in two stable populations if the relationship

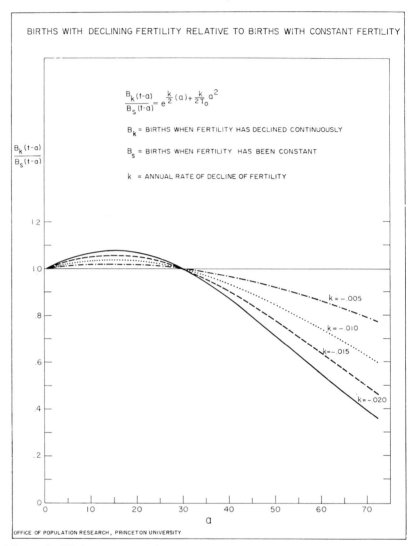

BIRTHS WITH DECLINING FERTILITY RELATIVE TO BIRTHS WITH CONSTANT FERTILITY

$$\frac{B_k(t-a)}{B_s(t-a)} = e^{\frac{k}{2}(a) + \frac{k}{2T_0}a^2}$$

B_k = BIRTHS WHEN FERTILITY HAS DECLINED CONTINUOUSLY

B_s = BIRTHS WHEN FERTILITY HAS BEEN CONSTANT

k = ANNUAL RATE OF DECLINE OF FERTILITY

$\frac{B_k(t-a)}{B_s(t-a)}$

$k = -.005$

$k = -.010$

$k = -.015$

$k = -.020$

a

OFFICE OF POPULATION RESEARCH, PRINCETON UNIVERSITY

Figure 2   Births *a* years ago in a population with a history of declining fertility relative to births in a population with constant fertility when births at given moment are equal in two populations, for varous rates of decline. (from Coale & Zelnick, "New Estimates of Fertility and Population in the United States")

between the point where the function shown in Figure 2 has a value of unity, and the average age of the population is the same—in other words, in stable populations with the same ratio of $\bar{a}_s/T$.

We have calculated b_k/b_s for thirty-six stable populations (e_0^0 20, 30, 50, 60 and 70 years, growth rates -0.01, 0.00, 0.01, 0.02, 0.03, and 0.04) for values of k ranging from -0.005 to -0.030 with values of T at 28 and 30 years. The calculations involved a numerical evaluation of the integral in Equation (38). Figure 3 shows the values of b_k/b_s for different values of $\bar{a}_s/T$. Some of the closely clustered points are derived from stable populations with very different growth rates and mortality schedules; for example, the stable population with $e_0^0 = 30$ and $r = -0.01$ has a mean age only slightly different from the stable population with $e_0^0 = 70$ and $r = 0.01$. The stable populations that we utilized were drawn from the "west" family of model stable populations.[6] By fitting curves to the values of b_k/b_s calculated for these populations, we arrived at the following empirical relationship between b_k/b_s and k for a given value of $\bar{a}_s/T$.

$$\frac{bk}{bs} = 1.0 + \left[3.807 - 1.039\,\frac{\bar{a}s}{T} - 9.839\left(\frac{\bar{a}s}{T}\right)^2 \right] k + \left(66.0 - 149.0\,\frac{\bar{a}s}{T} \right) k^2 \quad (37)$$

Equation (37) provides estimates of b_k/b_s within about 1 per cent of the true value over the stated range of k except at very large values of $\bar{a}_s/T$. Its accuracy would be within the same margin for positive values of k up to 0.03.

Equation (37) is based on a geometric argument suggesting that b_k/b_s should be a function of $\bar{a}_s/T$ and k. It is also possible to express b_k (as well as b_s) in terms of integrals that can be evaluated as accurately as one pleases by numerical methods, and finally to express b_k/b_s in terms of the moments of the stable age distribution. If we note that the total population at time $N(t)$ is $\int_0^\infty N(a, t)\, da$ and that $N(a, t)$ is as given in Equation (10) it follows that

$$b_k = \frac{1}{\int_0^\infty e^{-(k/2)a + (k/2T)a^2}\, e^{-ra}\, p(a)\, da} \quad (38)$$

We shall now approximate b_k by expanding the expression in Equation (38) in a McLaurin series, and accept the first two terms

---

[6] A. J. Coale, and P. Demeny, *Regional Model Life Tables and Stable Populations*. Princeton, N.J., Princeton Univ. Press, 1966.

as a usable approximation. According to this expansion,

$$b_k = (b_k)_{k=0} + \left(\frac{db_k}{dk}\right)_{k=0} \cdot k + \left(\frac{d^2 b_k}{dk^2}\right)_{k=0} \cdot \frac{k}{2} + \ldots \ldots \tag{39}$$

But

$$\left(\frac{db_k}{dk}\right)_{k=0} = (-b_k^2)_{k=0} \int_0^\omega \left(-\frac{a}{2} + \frac{a^2}{2T}\right) e^{-ra} \, p(a) \, da, \tag{40}$$

or

$$\left(\frac{db_k}{dk}\right)_{k=0} = \frac{b_s}{2}\left(A_1 - \frac{A_2}{T}\right),$$

where

$$A_n = b_k \int_0^\omega a^n e^{-(k/2)a + (k/2T)a^2} \, e^{-ra} \, p(a) \, da,$$

and

$$A_n = b_s \int_0^\omega a^n \, e^{-ra} p(a) \, da \text{ when } k = 0. \tag{41}$$

Note that

$$\left(\frac{dA_n}{dk}\right)_{k=0} = \left(\frac{db_k}{dk}\right)_{k=0} \cdot \frac{A_n}{b_s} + b_s \int_0^\omega \left(-\frac{a^{n+1}}{2} + \frac{a^{n+2}}{2T}\right) e^{-ra} p(a) \, da, \tag{42}$$

or

$$\left(\frac{dA_n}{dk}\right)_{k=0} = \frac{1}{2}\left(A_1 A_n - A_{n+1}\right) + \frac{1}{2T}(A_{n+2} - A_2 A_n) \tag{43}$$

Thus,

$$\left(\frac{d^2 b_k}{dk^2}\right)_{k=0} = \frac{b_s}{2}\left(\frac{dA_1}{dk} - \frac{1}{T}\frac{dA_2}{dk}\right)_{k=0}, \tag{44}$$

or, after substitution and rearrangement,

$$\left(\frac{d^2 b_k}{dk^2}\right)_{k=0} = \frac{b_s}{4}\left[A_1^2 - A_2 - \frac{1}{T}(2(A_1 A_2 - A_3) + \frac{A_4 - A_2^2}{T})\right] \tag{45}$$

Hence

$$b_k = b_s\left\{1 + \left(A_1 - \frac{A_2}{T}\right)k + \left[A_1^2 - A_2 - \frac{1}{T}\left(2(A_1 A_2 - A_3) + \frac{A_4 - A_2^2}{T}\right)\right]\frac{k^2}{8}\right\} \tag{46}$$

In trial calculations, Equation (46) yielded estimates of b_k a little less exact than those produced by Equation (37). Equation (37) shows the dependence of b_k/b_s on two parameters ($\bar{a}_s/T$ and k) whereas (46) relates the same ratio to k, the first four moments of the stable age distribution, and T. In principle, Equation (46) should indicate how b_k/b_s depends on the structure of the stable age distribution, but it is hard to visualize the influence of the properties of the age distribution in this somewhat complicated expression. Equation (37) provides at least as good an approximation because of the existence of systematic relationships among the moments of stable age distributions. Equation (37) arises from intuitively appealing geometric relations; the relations in Equation (46), on the other hand, would apply to the age structure of any growing aggregate, whether in a human population or not, characterized by constantly changing fertility.

We are now in a position to explain, in succinct terms, how the birth rate, the death rate, and the rate of increase of a population with a history of changing fertility are related to the corresponding parameters of a stable population. Figure 3 shows the relation of b_k/b_s to k and $\bar{a}_s/T$, a relationship expressed analytically in Equation (37). The larger is $\bar{a}_s$ relative to T; the larger is the birth rate with declining fertility relative to the birth rate in the stable population. When $\bar{a}_s/T$ is a little less than 60 per cent, the slightly greater proportions in the population with declining fertility below T just offset the smaller proportion above age T, and the population with changing fertility has the same birth rate as the stable. However, such equality could occur only in a population with an extremely low average age, a population not likely in fact to occur. From Equation (36) it is possible to derive a direct relationship between the rate of increase of the population with declining fertility and the stable population. This relationship is

$$ r_k = r_s + \left(\frac{1}{2} - \frac{\bar{a}_k}{T} \right) k \qquad (47) $$

If k is negative, it is evident that the rate of increase in the population with a history of changing fertility is greater than the intrinsic rate of increase, provided the mean age of the population is greater than one half the mean length of generation. It is hard to imagine a population with a history of declining fertility where $\bar{a}_k$ is less than one half of T, since very high fertility—a gross reproduction rate of five or more—is required to produce a low $\bar{a}_s$, and $\bar{a}_k$ is generally less than $\bar{a}_s$. It is certainly hard to picture arriving at such a gross reproduction rate after a long history of steadily declining fertility. However, it is possible to imagine a population with steadily *increasing* fertility in which r_k would be less than r_s, contrary to the relationship at moderate levels of fertility.

The death rate in a population with constantly changing fertility can be expressed as the difference between b_k and r_k. In populations with very high fertility, it is imaginable that d_k would be no greater than d_s, but within the range of fertilities commonly observed (especially in view of the assumption that d_k is based on a history of declining fertility), the death rate in the population with declining fertility is lower than the death rate in a stable population, based on the same mortality and fertility schedules. The tendency towards a lower death rate is easily visualized by considering the typical relationship of the age distributions in the two populations. The population with a history of declining fertility has substantially lower proportions at the older ages and slightly to moderately higher proportions under age T. This relative age structure is favorable to lower population death rates, especially in populations where the mortality schedule has moderate to low rates. In such low mortality schedules, death rates at the older ages are especially prominent, and the fact that the population with a history of declining fertility has higher proportions in early childhood offsets only to a very slight degree the reduction in the overall death rate caused by the low proportions above age sixty. In a very high mortality life table, the relative advantage in producing a lower death rate enjoyed by the population with a history of declining fertility is much less. Table 1 (which is located at the end of this article) shows birth rates, death rates, and rates of increase for stable populations and for populations with a history of declining fertility at an annual rate of 2 per cent for various levels of fertility and mortality.

Another point to be noted is the substantial growth potential in a population whose fertility has fallen to replacement during a sustained decline. How much would the population grow if fertility fell steadily until a net reproduction rate of unity were attained and then remained constant? This question is readily answered by comparing the population with a history of declining fertility to a stationary population with the same number of births as the declining fertility population has when it reaches a net reproduction rate of one. The future sequence of births from this point generated with no further changes in fertility by the population with a history of declining fertility depends only on the number of persons there are at each age under the highest age of childbearing. The population with a history of declining fertility has the same number at

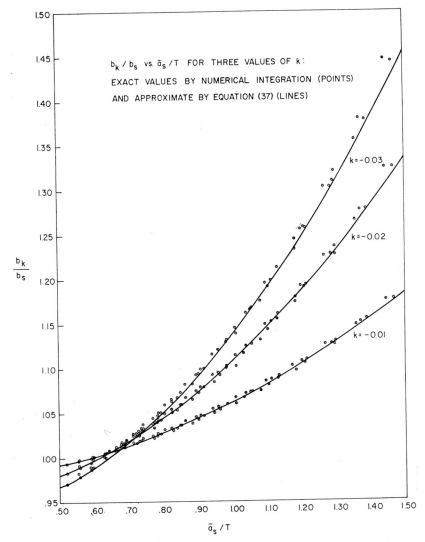

Figure 3 The birth rate in populations with a history of declining fertility relative to the birth rate in a population with a history of constant fertility, for various values of the ratio of the mean age of the stable population to the mean length of generation, and various rates of decline in fertility.

J

age zero and the same number at the mean age of childbearing as does the stationary population, as is evident in Figure 2. For the next few years the number of births occurring to the population with a history of declining fertility would be greater than to a stationary population with the same number of births at $t = 0$ because the changing fertility population has slightly larger numbers at ages from zero to T. If fertility remains constant at replacement, the ultimately constant stream of births will be at a level between those experienced by the stationary population and those experienced by the stationary population multiplied by $e^{kT/8}$ (the value of $e^{(-k/2)a + (k/2T)a^2}$ at $a = T/2$). The ultimate annual number of births in fact exceeds those in the year at which net reproduction rate reaches one by a factor of about $e^{-kT/11}$. The ultimate population would have the age structure of the stationary population and the number of annual births just given. But the stationary population with a given annual number of births is related in size to the population with a history of declining fertility and a given annual number of births as the ratio of b_k/b_s. Hence the remaining growth in the population at the time its fertility reaches replacement multiplies it by $(b_k/b_s) e^{-kT/11}$. If e_0^o is seventy years, and the mean length of generation is twenty-eight, the population would increase by $17\frac{1}{2}$ per cent after reaching replacement if the rate of decrease of fertility were 1 per cent annually, by 32.5 per cent if the rate of decrease were 2 per cent, and by 45.4 per cent if the rate of decrease of fertility were 3 per cent annually.

This last point—the greater growth potential of a population with a history of declining fertility than of a stable population with the same fertility and mortality—returns us to one of the early uses of stable population analysis. Lotka in his classic article "On the True Rate of Natural Increase" showed that the stable population had a rate of natural increase of only 5.47 per thousand, although the actual population had a rate of natural increase of 10.99 per thousand (white female population of the United States, 1920).[7] The primary reason for the difference was that the actual population was one with a history of declining fertility. Figure 4 shows the stable population in 1930, the estimated actual population, and a population with a history of constantly declining fertility at the average rate of decline, 1910–1930. We can now explain the

---

[7]Louis I. Dublin and Alfred J. Lotka, "On the True Rate of Natural Increase," *Journal of the American Statistical Association*, **20**, 1925, pp. 305–39.

approximate extent of the difference between the intrinsic and actual rates by noting the existence and average pace of a long downtrend in fertility.

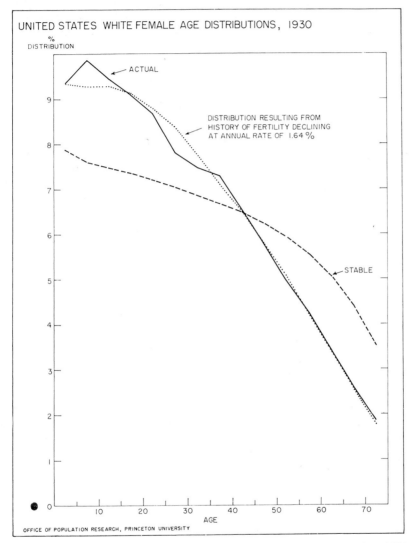

Figure 4   Age distributions for the United States white female population, 1930: actual, stable, and distribution resulting from a history of fertility declining at average rate observed in United States 1910–1930. (from Coale & Zelnick, "New Estimates of Fertility and Population in the United States")

Table 1   Birth rates, death rates, and rates of increase in stable populations at various levels of fertility and mortality, and in populations with the same fertility and mortality, but a history of a prolonged decline in fertility at 2 per cent annually.

	r_s	−0.100	0.000	0.0100	0.0200	0.0300	0.0400
$e_0^0 = 30$	r_k	−0.0003	0.0074	0.0154	0.0237	0.0322	0.0409
	b_s	0.0245	0.0333	0.0437	0.0552	0.0676	0.0808
	b_k	0.0287	0.0372	0.0468	0.0574	0.0687	0.0807
	d_s	0.0345	0.0333	0.0337	0.0352	0.0376	0.0408
	d_k	0.0290	0.0298	0.0314	0.0337	0.0366	0.0399
	GRR	1.60	2.11	2.77	3.62	4.71	6.11
$e_0^0 = 50$	r_k	0.0024	0.0098	0.0174	0.0253	0.0335	0.0420
	b_s	0.0139	0.0200	0.0275	0.0361	0.0457	0.0560
	b_k	0.0178	0.0239	0.0309	0.0389	0.0476	0.0569
	d_s	0.0239	0.0200	0.0175	0.0161	0.0157	0.0160
	d_k	0.0154	0.0141	0.0135	0.0136	0.0141	0.0149
	GRR	1.04	1.32	1.80	2.36	3.08	4.01
$e_0^0 = 70$	r_k	0.0045	0.0116	0.0189	0.0266	0.0346	0.0428
	b_s	0.0095	0.0143	0.0203	0.0276	0.0358	0.0448
	b_k	0.0131	0.0181	0.0240	0.0307	0.0382	0.0463
	d_s	0.0195	0.0143	0.0103	0.0076	0.0058	0.0048
	d_k	0.0086	0.0065	0.0051	0.0041	0.0037	0.0034
	GRR	.80	1.06	1.40	1.84	2.41	3.14

6

High Fertility Impairs Credit Worthiness of Developing Nations

STEPHEN ENKE*

General Electric Co., TEMPO, Washington, D.C.

INTRODUCTION

All major developmental assistance agencies, including the World Bank Group and US AID, should realize that continued high fertility rates in assisted countries not only inhibit their economic development but also impair their ability to service loans from abroad. Most development assistance agencies are loath, because of sensitivities, to make expanded birth control programs a condition of loans and grants. And the opportunities to make capital loans for increased contraception and possibly abortion are relatively limited. However, it is reasonable to expect assisted countries to practice self-help, and there may be no more significant manifestation of self-help practices than energetically practiced birth control programs. Moreover, major assistance agencies have always sought to evaluate the credit worthiness of loan applicants, and it can be shown that continued high fertility means credit *unworthiness*. Finally, if development assistance agencies were ever to allocate their disbursements so as to maximize future incomes

*The author is Consulting Economist to TEMPO, General Electric's Center for Academic Studies. He acknowledges with gratitude the assistance of Mr. Richard Brown of the TEMPO staff. The views expressed here are those of the author and are not necessarily shared by his employer or anyone else.

per capita, countries with high fertility would not long qualify for aid.

PRACTICAL CONSTRAINTS ON LENDING AGENCIES

Continued high fertility prevents the yearly improvements in per capita incomes to which governments and peoples of LDCs (less developed countries) aspire.[1] But traditional operations of lending institutions such as the World Bank Group do not lend themselves to promotion of birth-control programs. And lack of loans for contraception, whether in hard or soft currencies, does not appear to be the problem.

Birth-control programs do not require large investments. Clinics can be constructed (with soft currency loans) and equipped (with hard currency loans). Two or three condom-making plants are needed in the underdeveloped world. Loans for vehicles to transport women to clinics, or for mobile clinics to reach villagers, offer very limited loan opportunities. The training of doctors, paramedics, registered nurses, etc., may on occasion be considered an investment cost. But the simple truth is that most of the costs of LDC birth-control programs are recurrent operational costs and not really investment costs. Hence, lending agencies that, as a matter of policy will not fund operating budgets, are largely precluded from assisting birth-control programs directly.

Indirectly, in theory anyway, development assistance agencies could make loans and grants for traditional objects (e.g., dams, plants, education) on the condition that the receiving nations undertake specific programs having stipulated costs to facilitate contraception (and possibly abortion). But most officials of assisted and assisting countries assert that tying such strings to conventional loans and grants would be undesirable and impracticable. Bad feeling would allegedly result. The receiving government might be politically unable to accept such terms because of intense local resentments.

---

[1]"Rapid population growth not only affects parents and their families but also slows up economic and social advance in many developing countries. Countries which have not yet recognized the dimensions of their population problems should take cognizance of its impact on their development efforts and take appropriate action." *Partners in Development*, Report of the Commission on International Development. N.Y.: Praeger Publishers, 1969, p. 20.

Against this view, two points can be made.

First, it is ordinarily accepted that an assisted country should manifest "self-help." The developed nations cannot truly and indefinitely assist an LDC that will not help itself. And, as the next section demonstrates, one of the most important acts of self-help is an induced fertility reduction.

Second, any lending agency has a duty to evaluate the credit worthiness of each borrowing LDC. Such credit worthiness evaluations have long considered the ability of the debtor country to earn enough foreign exchange in excess of other needs to ensure debt service. However, its ability to save a surplus for external transfer as debt is also important; and this ability is very sensitive both to a nation's aspired yearly improvements in per capita income and projected fertility rates (see the next section).

FERTILITY AND IMPROVEMENTS IN INCOME PER HEAD

One highly significant indicator of true economic development is a continued improvement in income per head. GNP/population is obviously greater if population *can* be made to grow less rapidly without slowing GNP growth. Demographic-economic models, of the kind used below, suggest that this in fact is the case.[2]

A smaller than otherwise population certainly means a smaller-than-otherwise labor force. However, as an offset, the nation's capital stock grows more rapidly than otherwise because more is saved from a given GNP with fewer people consuming. Thus the smaller-than-otherwise labor force is more fully employed and more productive because it is combined with a larger capital stock.

Moreover, some fraction of a nation's annual per capita income improvement comes from the application of a more productive technology, and this yearly improvement in the "state of art" is probably independent of labor force and population size.

The TEMPO model has been described elsewhere.[3] The main

---

[2] A pioneer and now famous work in this area was that of Professor Edgar M. Hoover with Professor Ansley J. Coale in 1958 (*Population Growth and Economic Development in Low Income Countries: A Case Study of India's Prospects*).

[3] Notably in the *Journal of Biosocial Sciences* ("Effect of Fewer Births on Average Income"), January 1969, and *SCIENCE* ("Birth Control for Economic Development"), 16 May 1969.

interactions involved are shown in Figure 1. Briefly, GNP (or V) depends on employment (E), stock of Capital (K), and state of art or technology (T). E depends on K and the labor force size (L). L is a function of population size and age distribution. K depends on annual domestic saving (S), which in turn increases with V and decreases with population (P), except insofar as there are external borrowing additions or repayment subtractions from S. Population changes result from age-specific fertility and mortality rates. No international migration is assumed.

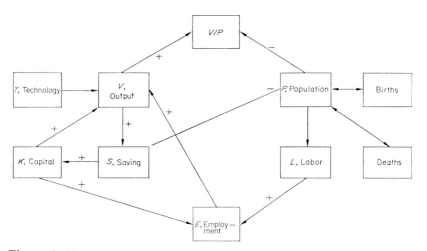

Figure 1 Determinants of output per head. N.B. A plus indicates a positive monotonic relation, etc.

For each projected set of specific fertility rates, year by year calculations are made of population size and distribution, labor force size, employment, savings, stock of capital, marginal productivity of capital and labor, GNP, and output per head (GNP/population). Such calculations can be made for real or hypothetical countries if their initial demographic and economic situation is known or assumed, respectively. Thus, the economic incidence of birth control programs, as reflected in age-specific fertility changes in future years, can be projected.

An additional feature of this model is that a sustained and constant annual improvement in per capita income can be stipulated. If this stipulated annual improvement (X%) in income per head

(V/P) is not attainable from domestic resources, it is supposed that domestic saving is augmented by inflows of foreign exchange capital that increase the national capital stock just enough to produce the GNP needed to achieve the stipulated (X%) yearly improvement in V/P. In this scheme of things, the lenders are passive, lending no more and no less than this required amount. Repayment occurs when and to the extent that domestic savings exceed the annual domestic investment necessary to maintain the X% improvement. Thus, there is an implicit and variable "grace" period on principal and interest payments.

If the stipulated (X%) value is incompatibly high, in relation to projected fertility, there will never be enough domestic savings to provide debt repayment (quite apart from foreign exchange availability), and external assistance has to increase each year to impossible magnitudes. For too modest values of (X%), where fertility projections are so low as to be compatible, no loan assistance will be necessary and hence there are no credit worthiness problems. In between are (X%) values that require loans than can in time be completely serviced—and these are the interesting cases.

TYPICAL RESULTS OF COMPUTER MODEL

Table 1 is based on calculations for a representative nation called Developa, which has an initial population of 10 million and an initial income per head of $200 a year. For *each* of several *constant* annual improvements in income per head there are shown (1) the number of years before the international capital flow reverses, (2) the total debt including accrued interest at the date of reversal, and (3) the number of years before all debt service is completed. The essential contrast is between Developa with "high" fertility (which means no change in the present gross reproduction rate of 3.025) and with "low" fertility (which means a reduction in the gross reproduction rate from 3.025 to 1.479 during the initial twenty-five years).

In all cases, a higher rate of V/P improvement means more assistance and a longer delay in completing debt service when feasible.

The relations summarized in Table 1 are for a so-called "standard" case. Developa is assumed to have a labor output elasticity of 0.6 (so that 10 per cent more employed labor occasions 6 per cent

Table 1 Number of years until principle repayment begins and ends, and maximum debt outstanding, for different required rates of GNP *per capita* growth.

Required annual growth in GNP per capita (per cent)	Year when repayment of principle begins		Year when loans completely repaid		Maximum debt when repayment begins (c) (Millions)	
	Fertility		*Fertility*		*Fertility*	
	High	*Low*	*High*	*Low*	*High*	*Low*
1.2	3	(b)	5	(b)	$12	$(b)
1.5	8	3	12	5	98	16
1.8	18	6	23	9	506	100
2.0	32	7	45	11	2038	174
2.2	(a)	9	(a)	14	(a)	300
2.5	(a)	13	(a)	20	(a)	674
2.8	(a)	18	(a)	28	(a)	1502
3.0	(a)	22	(a)	40	(a)	2680
3.2	(a)	(a)	(a)	(a)	(a)	(a)

(a) Debt never repaid
(b) No foreign debt required
(c) As compared with an initial GNP of $2000 million

more GNP) and a capital output elasticity of 0.35 (so that 10 per cent more capital stock means 3.5 per cent more GNP). The productivity of labor and capital increase by 1.5 per cent a year because of exogenous improvements in technology. The nation's annual savings equal 20 per cent of its GNP less $30 per head of population. Interest on outstanding foreign loans is at 4 per cent compounded yearly. At time zero, there is no foreign indebtedness. All the proceeds of foreign loan debts are translated into domestic capital investment. There is a variable and implicit grace period in that loans are repaid exactly to the extent that domestic saving exceeds the necessary domestic investment to maintain the stipulated annual improvement in per capita income.

Table 2 indicates the maximum constant V/P annual improvement possible without debt service default, using different key parameter values, for two projected "high" and "low" fertilities.

It also shows that calculated outcomes are not especially sensitive to variations in certain of the model's parameters from their "standard case" values. Predictably, a lower rate of technological

Table 2 Sensitivities of the maximum sustainable annual improvements in output per head (V/P) to key parameters

Cases	Maximum change in V/P in percent/yr		Year when repayment of foreign loans begins		Year when loans are completely repaid		Maximum Debt* (millions of dollars)	
	Fertility		*Fertility*		*Fertility*		*Fertility*	
	High	*Low*	*High*	*Low*	*High*	*Low*	*High*	*Low*
1 Standard case	2.0	3.0	24	19	45	30	2038	2680
2a Savings function high (0.3V–$50P)	2.4	3.4	19	16	34	29	1036	2027
2b Savings function low (0.1V–$10P)	1.4	2.4	23	20	43	46	1299	2445
3a Technical change high (2%/year)	2.7	3.7	22	18	38	37	1897	2991
3b Technical change low (1%/year)	1.2	2.2	23	16	45	25	1166	1815
4a High output elasticities: labor 0.6, capital 0.4	2.3	3.4	20	19	37	41	1537	3002
4b Low output elasticities: labor 0.5, capital 0.35	1.5	2.5	25	17	49	36	1897	2361

* As compared with an initial year GNP of $2000 millions.

improvement increases the relative desirability of low fertility, as does a low savings function or a low labor-output elasticity when combined with a high capital-output elasticity. As against "high" fertility, almost regardless of the other parameter values assumed, the sustainable constant annual improvement in income per head is higher by about one percentile with "low" fertility.[4]

Developa's economic growth, at five-year intervals, is shown in Table 3 for the standard combination of parameter values. The

[4]The mean *differences* between the high and low fertility cases, averaging the seven sets of assumptions shown in Table 2, are one percentile annual growth in V/P, 4.5 years before payments reverse their flow, ten years before debt service is completed, and maximum debt attained equal to initial GNP. The maximum outstanding debt is higher in the low fertility case because the country has more savings to service the debt. It also needs to borrow more in early years to sustain the higher required annual improvement in GNP per head.

Table 3 A comparison of high and low fertility countries, in which both maintain a growth rate in GNP/P of 2.8 per cent per year with foreign loans

Year	Population (thousands)		GNP (millions of $)		GNP/P ($)	Foreign loans outstanding(c) (millions of $)	
	Fertility		*Fertility*		*Same for both Cases* (a)	*Fertility*	
	High	*Low*	*High*	*Low*		*High*	*Low*
1970	10000	10000	2000	2000	200	96	82
1975	11637	11493	2672	2638	230	826	614
1980	13576	12970	3578	3419	263	2224	1170
1985	15872	14442	4803	4370	302	4619	1496
1990	18594	15904	6460	5525	347	8444	1303
1995	21823	17322	8705	6909	399	14410	322
2000	25668	18762	11755	8592	458	23698	—1593(b)
2005	30265	20292	15912	10667	526	38223	—4539(b)
2010	35778	21863	21596	13196	604	61039	—8696(b)

a) Increasing at 2.8% a year compound.
b) Country can maintain a growth rate in GNP/P of 2.8% *and* be a net exporter of capital after 30 years.
c) As compared with an initial year GNP of $2000 millions.

stipulated annual improvement is 2.8 per cent. The purpose of this table is to contrast debt service performance with "high" fertility as against "low" fertility. With low fertility, there is full repayment of debt and interest, after which GNP per head can increase more rapidly than stipulated. With high fertility, there is an eventual default, and, without continued borrowings from abroad, the LDC eventually cannot make the stipulated annual gain in GNP per head.

RELATIVE UNIMPORTANCE OF INTEREST COST

The interest cost to an LDC of borrowing has a relatively minor affect on the relations described above. Even an 8 per cent as compared with a 1 per cent interest charge on outstanding balances changes the sustainable GNP/P improvement by under 0.1, the number of years before completed debt service (when feasible) by about 0.15 and maximum indebtedness by about 2.0. Whether a nation can or cannot finally repay with interest depends far more on fertility differences than on loan interest rates (see Table 4).

Table 4 Maximum feasible constant annual improvements in GNP/P as a function of fertility and interest rates

Loan interest rate (percent/yr)	Maximum constant change in GNP/P (percent/yr)		Year when repayment of foreign loans begins		Year when loans are completely repaid		Maximum debt balance* (millions of $)	
	Fertility		*Fertility*		*Fertility*		*Fertility*	
	High	*Low*	*High*	*Low*	*High*	*Low*	*High*	*Low*
1.0	2.0	3.0	24	19	39	32	1131	1786
2.5	2.0	3.0	24	19	41	35	1470	2167
4.0	2.0	3.0	24	19	45	40	2038	2680
6.0	2.0	2.9	24	16	52	37	3942	2789
8.0	1.9	2.8	19	16	46	38	2834	3010

* As compared with an initial year GNP of $2000 millions.

ALLOCATING LOANS TO MAXIMIZE INCREASES IN GNP OR GNP/POPULATION?

Major development assistance agencies do not formally allocate loans (or grants) in a manner calculated to maximize anything. To do so might be neither practical nor desirable. But even so, it is conceptually informative to imagine that a development assistance institution lends money to maximize *either* collective increases in GNP, *or* collective increases in GNP per *head*.

Imagine a continuing high-fertility North Developa and a declining-fertility South Developa, both with 10 million population in 1970, both with the "standard" set of parameter values, but both with very different futures because of their contrasting fertility projections.

Suppose there is a development assistance consortium that determines the net magnitude of external capital flows for each of these two Developas.[5] The consortium has indefinitely $100 million a year to "invest" in one or the other or both of these two countries. What is the consequence of adopting either the combined maximization of combined GNP or combined GNP/population as the criterion?

---

[5]For simplicity's sake, there are no external capital flows except those related to the consortium loans, and no outstanding debt balances at time zero.

If $100 million is allocated each year to maximize the combined increase in GNP of these two Developas, regardless of which nation has the most GNP increase or receives the most loans, these capital transfers should be allocated so that the marginal return on capital is the same for both countries in any year. High-fertility North Developa will have a lower ratio of capital to labor than low-fertility South Developa in the absence of borrowings from abroad. Hence, high-fertility North Developa will, apart from borrowings, have a higher rate of return on capital. If rates of return are to be kept the same, as a means of maximizing *combined* GNP growth, an increasing share of the annual $100 million of loans will go to high-fertility North Developa. Table 5 shows that the country that is poorer in per capita income terms, because of its

Table 5   Maximizing combined GNP: The annual allocation of $100 million in loans.

Year	GNP (millions of $)		Population (thousands)		GNP/P ($)		Annual allocation of loans (millions of $)	
	Fertility		*Fertility*		*Fertility*		*Fertility*	
	High	*Low*	*High*	*Low*	*High*	*Low*	*High*	*Low*
0	2000	2000	10000	10000	200	200	50	50
2	2186	2186	10625	10572	206	207	50	50
4	2399	2400	11289	11177	212	215	51	49
6	2642	2645	12001	11774	220	225	52	48
8	2917	2925	12764	12358	228	237	53	47
10	3230	3242	13576	12970	237	250	54	46
12	3581	3602	14452	13540	247	266	57	43
14	3977	4008	15384	14135	259	284	65	35
16	4422	4462	16383	14723	269	303	80	20
18	4924	4964	17453	15302	282	325	100	0
20	5491	5517	18594	15904	295	347	100	0

unwillingness or inability to reduce its fertility, is rewarded with more assistance.

After eighteen years, all the $100 million will be allocated yearly to high fertility North Developa. At that date, GNP/Population is about 16 per cent higher in low-fertility South Developa. The latter's demonstrated self-help has penalized it so far as loans are concerned.

Alternatively, the consortium might allocate the $100 million a year so as to maximize GNP per *head* improvements in the two countries combined. In this case, after allowing for increases in national capital stocks from domestic savings each year, the consortium should allocate so as to maintain equality between the *ratio* of rate of return on capital to population in the two countries. If the rate of return on capital before the year's external loans was 10 per cent in high-fertility Developa and 7 per cent in low-fertility Developa, but the ratio of population was higher than 10:7, then a larger share of the year's lending should be to low-fertility South Developa. Hence, one might expect that allocating loans to maximize continued increases in GNP/population would favor the low-fertility country. Calculations indicate, using standard parameters, that after eight years, all the $100 million loaned yearly will go to low-fertility South Developa.[6]

The policy choice for major assistance agencies is suggested by a comparison of these two policies. After ten years, the choice between maximizing combined GNP versus combined GNP/Population, means respectively an allocation of $54 and $46 million as against $10 and $90 million to the high- and low-fertility Developas. By 20 years, GNP maximizing means all the $100 million is annually allocated to North Developa, while GNP/Population maximizing gives all these annual loans and grants to South Developa.

It has often been argued that assistance loans and grants, if they are to be more than partially wasted charity, can best be extended to nations that most help themselves. A willingness and ability to reduce fertility by contraception and/or abortion would seem to be one of the more significant measures of self-help. Allocating "loans" to maximize GNP increases in two or more LDCs may be an exercise in charity. But allocating repayable loans to maximize GNP/population improvements may be a requirement for development. Which is the proper objective?

DANGERS OF DEFAULT ON LOANS

In abstract terms, without citing debt statistics for individual nations, enough has been presented above to suggest that wide-

---

[6]It is conceptually possible however that, if extra consumption per head of population is rather high, low-fertility South Developa will save and invest so much more that its rate of return on extra capital will be low even in proportion to its lower population.

spread defaults on development loans are a very real prospect for the 1970s.

To maintain annual improvements in GNP/population, even *below* those often announced as national goals, high-fertility countries with economic parameters not too different from those of Developa will have to borrow increasing sums each year. Repayment without reductions in fertility will often be impossible. Otherwise, unless euphemized as drastic "rescheduling" of principal and interest payments, default appears almost inevitable for several LDCs.

Within LDC's, there are always strong political demands to reschedule debt service. Poor non-white nations are often unprepared to "sacrifice" themselves for rich white nations. That they have usually done so to date may be explained in part by the fact that, so far, annual loans and grants received are in excess of annual debt service for most LDCs. For some limited time to come, taxpayer-financed grants may indirectly pay the debt service owed the financial communities of the developed Western world. But when the international development assistance game ceases to be rewarding for most LDCs, with debt service more than offsetting annual assistance in loans and grants, some of the numerous LDC debtors will cease to play according to bankers' rules.

The inevitability of default or rescheduling by some LDCs is underlined by the fact that some capital loans have not resulted in equivalent net domestic capital investment. The legal indebtedness occasioned by some loan may be, say, $10 million, the transfer of funds may have been $10 million, funded disbursements for some capital project such as a harbor may have been $10 million, but the net indirect effect could be, say, $7 million extra investment and $3 million extra consumption for the recipient nation. Economic resources are substitutable and money is fungible. Because of a loan, an LDC government may release foreign exchange for the import of more consumer goods, or may have recourse to less forced saving and investment through inflation, than it otherwise would. Such unrecognised leakages of "investment" loans into current consumption are chronic.

A related problem is that many of the earlier hard loans at market interest rates may have provided excessive production capacity rather prematurely. The investments that resulted were probably not always as productive as the debt service burdens assumed. However, because some of the largest loans were for projects yielding "external economies" not captured as receipts, the extent to which resources have been wasted in non-commercial public sector projects will never be known.

Even more fundamental, debt service and income per capita improvement are in conflict. The conflict is more agonizing when fertility rates remain high because then realized annual improvements in GNP/population must be lower. Thus, other things equal, higher-fertility LDCs are less likely to be creditworthy than low-fertility LDCs.

Perhaps the major assistance agencies should lend only to those countries that increase their credit worthiness and demonstrate their self-help sincerities by expanding effective birth control programs as promptly as possible.

SUMMARY

Application of the TEMPO economic-demographic model to a hypothetical LDC having either continued high fertility *or* significantly decliningn fertility, suggests the following tentative connclusions:

1. The sustainable rate of constant annual improvement in a typical LDC's ratio of GNP to population is sensitive to its projected gross reproduction rates. This is so for different sets of economic performance parameters. The low-fertility country can generally improve its GNP/population ratio about half as fast again as can a high-fertility country.

2. The ability of an LDC to borrow from abroad to maintain a desired rate of GNP/population improvement annually, and eventually repay all principal with interest, can be very sensitive to projected fertilities (but not to interest rates on outstanding balances).

3. An LDC's willingness and ability to expand effective birth-control programs soon is not only a demonstration of "self-help" but also a significant indication of credit worthiness.

4. If development-assistance agencies were collectively to lend so as to maximize GNP increases in LDCs, they might apportion their loans very differently than if they were seeking to maximize their increases in GNP/population. In the first case, the high-fertility countries would receive an increasing share of

K

such total loans, but in the latter case, the lower-fertility countries ordinarily would. To some extent the choice is between charity and development, between quantity and quality of life.

5.   Taxpayer financed grants to LDCs may continue for some years to pay indirectly part of presently required debt service. But eventually, some LDC governments will surely default or enforce drastic rescheduling of debt service payments. The 1970s may yet prove to be the Decade of Default for LDCs that have not lowered their fertility rates.

7

Thünen, Weber and the Spatial Structure of the Nineteenth Century City

RAYMOND L. FALES and LEON N. MOSES*†

*Northwestern University, Evanston, Ill., and Livingston College,
Rutgers University, New Brunswick, New Jersey*

Economists, geographers, and a number of theoretically inclined
planners have developed models to explain patterns of urban land
use and rent.[1] Many of these models are adaptations of J. H. Von
Thünen's theory of agricultural location.[2] The more rigorous of

---

*This paper evaluates urban land use models that are based on J. H.
Von Thünen's theory of agricultural location. An alternative approach is
formulated that combines Thünen-type reasoning with A. Weber's theory
of industrial location. This approach is used to explain the distribution of
households and industry in Chicago in the 1870's.

†The authors wish to express their gratitude to the Center for Urban
Affairs, Northwestern University which provided financial assistance for the
research involved in this paper, and to H. F. Williamson, Jr., Charles Leven
and N. E. Savin whose critical comments in a number of stages of the
manuscript's development were extremely helpful. We also wish to acknowledge the assistance received from the Chicago Historical Society which
provided much of the information employed in this study.

[1]Some of the principal contributors to the theory have been:
  William Alonso. *Location and Land Use.* Cambridge, Mass.: Harvard
    Univ. Press, 1964.
  Richard F. Muth. *Cities and Housing.* Chicago, Ill.: Univ. of Chicago
    Press, 1969.
  Richard F. Muth. *Cities and Housing.* Chicago, Ill.: Univ. of Chicago
    sions." *Econometrica.* 29, January 1961.
  Lowdon Wingo, Jr. *Transportation and Urban Land.* Washington,
    D.C.: Resources for the Future, Inc., 1961.

[2]Johann Heinrich van Thünen, *Von Thünen's Isolated State.* Carla M.
Wartenberg, trans., Peter Hall, ed. Edinburgh: Pergamon Press, 1966.

them assume a central area in which all production and employment take place, and through which all imports and exports move. The land pattern is depicted as a series of concentric zones of exclusive and progressively less intensive use. The models replicate what is taken to be the usual order of urban land use. The business area is followed by a manufacturing zone and the latter by one devoted to residences. Finally, there is an agricultural zone. Land rents *fall continuously* with distance from the center of the city.

This essay grows out of some dissatisfaction with these models which seem designed to explain land use in a stereotype of the large, densely settled city of the 19th century. They provide little insight into the spatial structure of places like Phoenix, Albuquerque, and Los Angeles which experienced their major growth in the present century. In these cities, population densities are low and rather uniform. Industry, including banking and other services that are often assumed to be core oriented, tends to be broadly dispersed. Even if such cities have an area that can be identified as the core, it is surely not the focus of all economic, recreational, and other activity. Similarly, Thünen-type models do not seem capable of explaining the massive rearrangements of population and employment that are taking place in urban areas such as Chicago, Boston, and Philadelphia. These are examples of cities that took form and experienced their major growth in the nineteenth and the first two decades of the present century. However, powerful forces have been causing a dispersal and *intermixing* of households and firms over the metropolitan areas of which they are part. These forces are gradually making places like Chicago resemble the decentralized cities mentioned earlier. Finally, and most important so far as this paper is concerned, we are not satisfied that the currently accepted theory of urban land use even adequately explains the locational structure of large nineteenth century cities.

The paper is divided into two parts. The first contains an evaluation of Thünen-type models. Their assumptions and empirical implications are examined. In Part Two, an alternative approach that incorporates certain critical aspects of nineteenth century technology in a modified Weberian framework is formulated and tested. Alfred Weber's theory of industrial location is explained briefly there.[3] For the moment, we simply comment that his

---

[3] Alfred Weber, *Theory of the Location of Industries.* By Carl J. Friedrich, trans. Chicago: University of Chicago Press, 1929.

reasoning has not been made a part of urban land use models because its central components were viewed as not relevant for the problem or so analytically weak as to be unusable. We believe that these judgements are incorrect and that Weber's theory can provide a great deal of insight into the spatial structure of cities that developed in the nineteenth century.

Both parts of the paper employ data on the locational patterns of firms and households in Chicago during the early 1870's. This city was selected for study because it grew rapidly in size and complexity in the last century but had essentially established its spatial form by the 1870's. Its population increased from 29,963 in 1850 to 306,605 in 1870.[4] Basic street, water, and other municipal service systems had been constructed by the latter year. There were three principal and a number of feeder horsecar lines that provided regular service to large portions of the city. Chicago had a variety of linkages to its own agricultural hinterland and to the rest of the nation and the world, being served by eleven railroads as well as river and lake transport. The telegraph provided information linkages to major money and other markets. By 1870, Chicago's industries included heavy materials processors such as blast furnaces and foundries and such light manufacturing as textiles, clothing, and leather products. There was also a variety of service industries, including a large number of banks. Finally, Chicago was chosen for study because the Great Fire of October, 1871, provides a situation in which one of the serious obstacles to testing the implications of urban land use models was largely eliminated.

This obstacle arises because these models place a good deal of emphasis on price relationships of products with respect to each other and to the inputs they require. These relationships are constantly changing. However, patterns of land use change slowly since the buildings and other fixed investments made by firms are expensive, long lived, and often designed for specialized use. If the researcher who wishes to test the models' predictions is unwilling to assume perfect foresight on the part of firms, he is left with an extremely difficult task. In order to explain the current pattern of land use, he must identify the price relationships that

---

[4]Chicago Board of Education. *Census of the City of Chicago.* Report submitted to the board, Oct. 15, 1872.

existed at various times in the past when different investment decisions were made.

The Great Fire removed this difficulty for Chicago. It destroyed the industrial-commercial districts of the city and thereby eliminated much of the fixed capital commitment to the past. Those firms that survived the catastrophe were left relatively free to relocate. This freedom was enhanced by a very active land market, the absence of zoning restrictions,[5] and considerable availability of capital, the latter because the period was one of economic boom. It is this relative freedom from prior locational commitments that permits us to test *some* of the implications of urban land use models without information on relative prices.

1. EVALUATION OF THÜNEN-TYPE MODELS

The main idea of a Thünen-type model is that alternative uses compete (perfectly) for space and thereby allocate it efficiently. The competitive process is explained in terms of bid rent curves. These show the maximum rent that can be paid by economic units, such as industry or households, in a given land use category, as distance from the center of a city increases. The center is treated as a point and assumed to be the economic focus of all production and marketing activities.

The models generally assume that transport cost from any point to the center is a function of distance between them but is unaffected by the radial on which such a point is located. Therefore, the net price received by the producer of a product is strictly a function of the distance of his site from the center. The prices of material and other intermediate inputs are usually assumed to be the same everywhere, implying that they move at zero transport cost. In these circumstances, all bid rent curves peak at the center. They decline continuously with distance from the center, and in the same way, in all directions around it. A condition necessary for spatial equilibrium is that the profit rate of all firms in an industry is identical, regardless of location. Otherwise, equilibrium is not attained since some firms will wish to change their locations. Similar reasoning is applied to the household sector:

---

[5]Chicago Zoning Commission, *Tentative Report and a Proposed Zoning Ordinance for the City of Chicago.* Jan. 5, 1923.

transport cost is the cost of commuting to the center for work; the equality condition is that the level of utility achieved by all (identical) households must be the same.

The intersections of various bid rent curves establish boundaries between uses and represent the optimum allocation of space. Each segment is occupied by the use with the highest bid rent curve there. The overall rent gradient is the envelope of the individual bid curves. The derived land pattern is a series of concentric zones, one for each type of use. There is no intermixing of uses within any given concentric zone.

The rigorously formulated versions of the Thünen model make assumptions or adopt procedures that result in each industry or land use exclusively occupying one concentric zone. Otherwise, the analysis involves severe theoretical difficulties. One such procedure is to ignore the influence of scale economies in individual enterprises or to assume them away. Such economies might easily result in a situation in which large and small firms within a given industry or land use locate quite differently. Muth is very explicit on this point. He assumes that the firms in his industries have identical production functions and that these functions are homogenous of degree one.[6] There are then no scale economies and no differences in location due to differences in technology within an industry.

The exclusive zone result is also achieved by ignoring urbanization economies: i.e., reductions in the cost of such things as streets and water mains due to the massing of many users in a compact area. The linkages that exist between firms because they have buying and selling relationships with one another are also ignored. This is essentially accomplished by the assumption, mentioned earlier, that intermediate inputs move at zero transport cost. In this situation, there is no need for firms in different industries to cluster closely in order to minimize the cost of their interindustry purchases. If transport costs on such inputs are important, the locational preferences of firms from different industries become interdependent. It has been shown that there is then no set of rents that will cause individual decision-making to result in the optimal spatial allocation.[7] We now turn to some empirical issues.

---

[6]Muth, Richard. "Economic Change and Rural-Urban Land Conversion," p. 9.

[7]Tjalling Koopmans and Martin J. Beckman, "Assignment Problems and the Location of Economic Activities." *Econometrica*, 1957, pp. 53–76.

Testing Thünen-type Models

We could not test the models by actually using them to explain locational patterns of individual industries. Such tests would have required estimation of production functions and input and output prices. Instead, some of the broad implications of their assumptions and conclusions were examined. One such implication is that the intensity of land use declines with distance from the center of a city. This is implied by the negatively-sloped rent gradient. A second implication is that this decline in intensity is uniform in all directions from the center. This follows from the assumption that transport costs are radically identical. The final implication is the exclusive zone concept noted above.

To test these implications, the addresses and number of employees of 659 Chicago manufacturing firms were obtained for 1873.[8, 9] As a preliminary test of the declining intensity of land use hypothesis, firms were grouped into one-half-mile rings by their distance from the commercial center of the city (the intersection of State and Madison Streets). The percentage of total employment in each ring was then plotted. Employment was used as the measure of intensity because data on output and space used by individual firms were not available. The result is shown in Figure 1. As expected from the model, employment is highest in the center and falls off steadily, at least through the fourth ring. The data do reveal two smaller satellite peaks—one in the fifth ring and the other in the eighth.

The declining intensity hypothesis was tested by a regression technique. A one-half-mile grid pattern was imposed on the city that divided the area into 129 grid squares, most of which were one-quarter square mile in area.[10] Firms were allocated to these squares by their addresses, and the total number of employees in each square was determined. An equation was estimated in which percent of total employment per grid square was the dependent variable. The log of distance from the commercial center of the city to the mid-point of each square was the independent

---

[8]S. S. Schoff. *The Industrial Interests of Chicago.* Chicago, Ill.: Knight and Leonard Book and Job Printers, 1873.

[9]A comparison of this data with that found in Alfred T. Andreas—*History of Chicago.* 3 (1871–1875), p. 714—suggests that there was some bias toward larger firms in our sample since it covered 46 per cent of manufacturing firms but 75 per cent of manufacturing employment.

[10]The zones that border the lake vary in size.

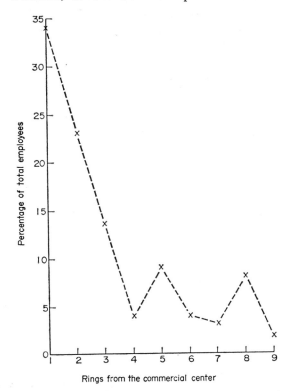

Figure 1   Percentage distribution of employees per ring (All Firms)

variable.[11] The results are shown in Equation 1 (column 1), Table 1. For this and subsequent equations, we present the constant, the coefficients, and their standard errors and significance. The coefficient of determination, corrected for degrees of freedom, and its significance are also shown. In Equation 1 the latter value is 0.434. It is significant at the 1 per cent level which, given the historical nature of the data, seems a good result. The distance coefficient has the same level of significance and has the expected negative sign. It anticipates results described in Part Two of the paper, but it is worth commenting that *the significance of distance*

---

[11]The log form used implies congestion or, in other words, that the cost of travelling a unit of distance increases as the center of the city is approached. This is a reasonable assumption. The log form was also used because it gave better results in the regressions presented here and below than did the linear form.

Table 1   Predicting the percentage of employment per grid square

	Equation Number	1	2	3	4
	Firm size	All	Small	Medium	Large*
	Squares with firms	61	42	46	28
Constant	Coefficient	13.93	15.87	13.00	8.892
	Standard error	1.329	1.507	1.309	1.422
	Significance	0.01	0.01	0.01	0.01
Log Distance from the Commercial Center	Coefficient	−4.007	−4.597	−3.721	−2.470
	Standard error	.4022	.4560	.3960	.4302
	Significance	0.01	0.01	0.01	0.01
	$\bar{R}^2$ (corrected) Significance	0.434 0.01	0.440 0.01	0.405 0.01	0.200 0.01

* Clothing firms were excluded in order to provide consistency with the logic and results in Table 3.

is reduced and its sign sometimes found to be positive when other, more meaningful variables are included in such regressions.

The transport cost assumptions of Thünen models imply radial uniformity in the intensity of land use. We did not wish to place too narrow an interpretation on this, or for that matter, any of the other implications. However, we were interested in determining the extent to which channelization of transport routes and the natural geography of the area would cause departures from radial uniformity. The city was therefore divided into quadrants by the North-South and East-West axes through its commercial center. The percentage of a given quadrant's total employment located within each ring in that quadrant was determined. The results for three of the four quadrants are presented in Figure 2,[12] which shows that the effect of distance is quite different in various portions of the city. The Southeast quadrant has three peaks, and those in the third and fifth rings are almost as great as that in the first. The Southwest quadrant has its major peak in the second ring and peaks again in the eighth. The three quadrants are

[12]The Northeast quadrant is omitted because it is much smaller than the other three due to the configuration of Lake Michigan.

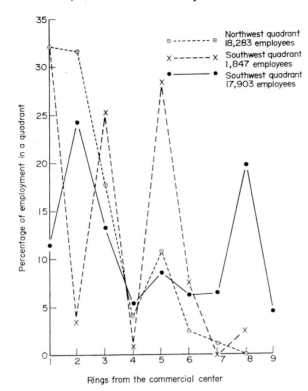

Figure 2   Percentage distribution of employees per quadrant (All Firms)

similar in that they each have something of a peak in the fifth ring, but its importance varies considerably between them.

As mentioned earlier, most Thünen-type models conclude that the urban land pattern is a series of concentric, exclusive zones. Three aspects of this hypothesis were investigated, beginning with the under-lying assumption that scale differences have no effect on location. The results described below are only suggestive be-cause there were not enough observations to investigate the in-fluence of distance on the locational patterns of different size firms *within* given industries.

All firms were classified into three size groups.[13] The earlier

---

[13]Small   —   2 to 19 employees.
  Medium   —   20 to 99 employees.
  Large   —   100 or more employees.

regression was then rerun for each group. The results are shown in Equations 2 through 4 in Table 1. Again, the regressions and coefficients are significant at the 1 per cent level. While the distance coefficient has the expected sign in each case, it varies consistently with firm size. It is smallest (absolutely) for large firms and largest for small firms. These results are not unexpected if one believes, contrary to the assumptions of Thünen models, that scale economies are important: that small firms tend to cluster more closely to the center of the city to achieve certain agglomeration economies that large firms can provide for themselves.

The exclusive land use concept was also investigated by studying the ring distribution of employees in thirteen industries. They were selected because our sample contained at least ten firms in each of them. The data appear in Table 2. A few industries, such as clothing and shoes, were relatively concentrated in the first ring, while brick manufacturing was largely conducted at the periphery. However, nine of them were dispersed across a band of five or more rings, which is impressive since all firms in the sample were within nine rings of the city's center. The above results suggest that land use tended to be quite mixed rather than exclusive in nineteenth century Chicago and that linkages between firms may have been very important.

The exclusive zone concept is also involved in the allocation of space between business and households. In Thünen-type models, there is an inner zone that is devoted to business use; it is followed by a residential zone. On this issue, a comparison of Maps 1 and 2 is revealing. The former shows the number of employees in each grid square and the latter the population in the various wards of the city in 1870.[14] As expected, few people lived in the ward that cut across the grid square in which the commercial center of the city was found. In Map 1, this square is shaded and contains a star.[15] In addition, over the city at large, population was more dispersed than employment. However, contrary to the logic of Thünen-type models there was a significant amount of employment in almost every ward of the city. Moreover, the difference in dispersion between population and employment was less, or

---

[14]Population is only available by these irregularly shaped geometric divisions.

[15]A fuller explanation of the shading and marking in this and the other squares is given later.

Table 2 Percentage of employees per industry per ring. Rings from the Commercial center (rings are $\frac{1}{2}$ mile wide)

Ring	1	2	3	4	5	6	7	8	9	Total No. Employees
Breweries 2082		4.55	13.3	3.27	22.7	56.1				308
Cigars 2121	72.2	17.5	7.61	2.69						223
Clothing 2311	97.78	.065	2.16							9246
Planing Mill 2421		47.2		14.0	32.3	6.46				464
Millwork 2431		15.4	33.8	17.6	30.4	2.94				3163
Wood Furn. 2511		30.4	39.9	12.9	2.81		14.1			1850
Uph. Furn. 2512	9.15	74.3	12.9	1.31	.56	1.68				535
Shoes 3141	92.1	5.73	1.43		.72					1395
Misc. Leather 3199	54.5	23.1	18.6	3.85						156
Bricks 3251						28.5	41.9	29.7		1147
Cut Stone 3281	16.3	64.3	9.64	2.08	2.34	5.22				2987
Foundries 3321		54.2	37.4	4.80		13.7				1461
Wagons 3799	7.50	52.3	32.7	4.12	2.11	1.48				947
13 Industries	46.8	21.2	13.3	4.44	5.59	4.27	3.10	1.42		23882
All Firms	34.0	23.0	13.6	3.84	8.97	3.86	1.33	7.98	1.78	45112

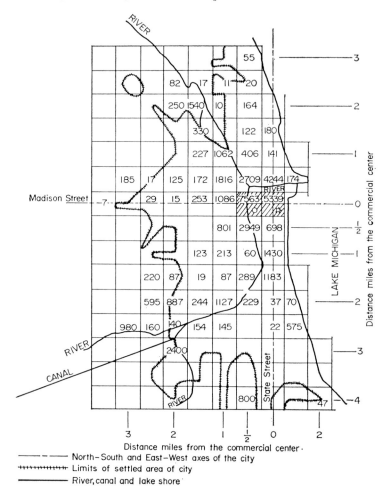

Map 1   1873 Chicago. Manufacturing employees per grid square.

alternatively, the extent of intermixing was even greater, if the comparison is based on the settled area of the city. This is the area, according to Homer Hoyt, within which most of the city's population was found in the early 1870's.[16] The boundary of this area is marked off with a crossed line in Maps 1 and 2.

[16]Homer Hoyt. *One Hundred Years of Land Values in Chicago.* Chicago, Ill.: Univ. of Chicago Press, 1933, p. 106.

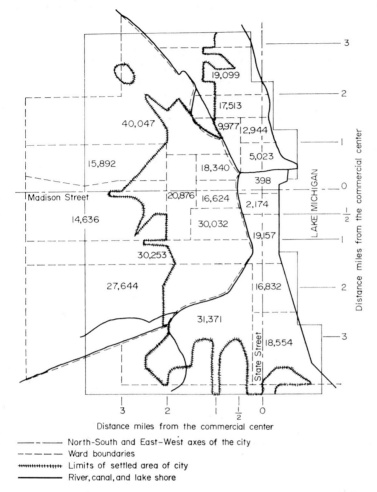

Map 2   1872–1873 Chicago. Ward boundaries and ward population.

In summary, the central idea of Thünen models that activities compete for space and thereby allocate it efficiently is one that we accept. Our disagreement with these models grows out of the highly simplified view they take toward the city and its techno-logy. The simplifications have been necessary because the scholars who have worked on land use models have been interested in de-veloping formal analytical models. They have therefore tended to ignore such things as channelization of transportation routes;

transport costs for intermediate inputs and resulting linkages between firms in different industries; and scale economies within individual firms. Perhaps most important, they have ignored the very basis for the existence of cities and the concentration of economic activity within them: the agglomerative and broad urbanization economies that are achieved when numerous firms cluster closely.

Unfortunately, the above assumptions and procedures yield a model that offers almost no help to physical planners who must think in terms of such policy variables as the location of transport routes.[17] In addition, we have seen that the model is quite limited in its ability to explain the actual distribution of population and industry in Chicago of the 1870s. Thus, our data revealed significant variations in the intensity of land use between radial sectors of the city. (Part Two of this paper provides a fuller explanation of these variations.) The data also indicated considerable intermixing of industries with each other and with households so that, in the city as a whole, the exclusive zone concept was not even roughly approximated. There is clear evidence of the existence of satellite employment centers in the city. On the other hand, it does appear that the intensity of land use declined fairly regularly with distance.

2. WEBER AND THE ROLE OF TECHNOLOGY

We begin this section with a brief statement of Weber's theory. Some modifications are then suggested that make its relevance for urban analysis more apparent. Certain critical aspects of nineteenth century technology are then considered and incorporated into an empirical model that is essentially an extension of the Weberian framework. The cost of transmitting information, the material intensity of production functions, and the cost of transporting people and goods enter importantly into this model.

---

[17]This is seen in a recent volume of urban planning. The volume contains a chapter in which the contributions of Alonso and Wingo to land use theory are listed in a footnote. However, the procedures described in the chapter do not draw on the theory. See *Principles and Practices of Urban Planning.* William I. Goodman, ed., Washington, D.C.: Institute for Training in Municipal Administration by the International City Managers' Association, 4th ed. 1968.

Weber defined a location factor as a cost advantage that is gained when an activity is conducted in one place rather than others.[18] He divided such factors into two groups: those that determine the broad regional distribution of industry, and those that cause agglomeration or deglomeration of industry within the regional distribution. He began his analysis of the former by assuming that processing costs were the same everywhere and by examining the influence of transportation cost. The location of the market in which a product was sold and the locations of the materials required to produce it were taken as given. He assumed a fixed-coefficient production function, which eliminated the influence of scale economies and input substitution on location.[19] The optimal location was therefore defined as the place where the total cost of bringing together enough of the raw materials to produce a unit of the product and delivering it to the market was a minimum.

Weber devised the concept of a system of isodopanes to illustrate the determination of the least cost location. Each isodopane is a mapping in space of locations that have the same total transportation cost. The least cost location is (often but not always) within the lowest valued isodopane. Weber also developed a classification of materials that he felt provided clues as to whether a given process would tend to be materials or market oriented.

Materials were either ubiquities, meaning that they were everywhere present (presumably at equal price), or localized. Weber reasoned that firms whose processes required ubiquities would tend to locate in the markets where they sold their products. Such locations would eliminate the need to ship that portion of the weight of ubiquities that entered into the final product. Localized materials were classified as pure or weight-losing, the distinction between the two being that the former impart all and the latter only a portion or none of their weight to that of the product. Because he reasoned in terms of fixed coefficient production functions

---

[18]He did not take demand and monopoly elements into consideration. On this see Melvin L. Greenhut. *Microeconomics and the Space Economy.* Chicago, Ill.: Scott-Foresman, 1963.

[19]On these issues see: Leon Moses. "Location and the Theory of Production." *Quart. J. Econ.,* May 1958. William Alonso. "A Reformulation of Classical Location Theory and its Relation to Rent Theory." *Regional Science Association Papers,* **19**, 1967.

L

and transport rate structures which, if they had discriminatory elements in them, involved higher charges for finished products than inputs, Weber concluded that pure materials would not bind production to their sites. Weight-losing materials could do so because the total weight to be transported and therefore total transport cost would be reduced. Overall, Weber felt that the ratio of the weight of localized materials to final product weight provided the basic answer as to whether a product would tend to be market or materials oriented.

In the second part of his theory of the regional distribution of industry, Weber introduced differences in production cost. He ascribed these to regional variations in labor cost. The system of isodopanes was used to show that location would be moved from the point of minimum transport cost to a cheap labor site if the labor cost saving exceeded the increased transport cost.

Weber considered all factors other than labor and transport as causing industry to agglomerate or deglomerate within the regional distribution. Among the agglomerating forces, he placed such things as scale economies of individual plants, despite the fact that he reasoned in terms of fixed coefficient production functions; linkages between firms, which he described as advantages due to nearness to auxiliary trades; more effective marketing situations, found in places where there are many firms; and reductions in the cost of general overhead items such as streets, and water mains that occur when there are large concentrations of industry. He believed that all the deglomerative factors followed from the rise in land values caused by large concentrations of industry. In a third part of his theory, the total orientation, Weber dealt with the influence of a number of different interrelationships between industries.

Economic theory was not Weber's strong suit, and there is much that can be criticised in his volume. Yet the basic framework he laid out together with the additions and refinements made by Hoover,[20] Isard,[21] Greenhut,[22] Alonso[23] and others, is still part of the accepted body of location theory. It is therefore interesting to

---

[20] Edgar M. Hoover. *Location Theory and the Shoe and Leather Industries.* Cambridge: Harvard Univ. Press, 1937.

[21] Walter Isard. *Location and Space Economy.* Cambridge: The Technology Press of Massachusetts Institute of Technology and New York: John Wiley & Sons, Inc. 1956.

[22] Melvin Greenhut. *Microeconomics and the Space Economy.*

[23] William Alonso. "Reformulation of Classical Location Theory."

inquire why theorists who were concerned with the internal spatial structure of cities largely ignored his reasoning and turned to Thünen.

One explanation may be that households occupy a large part of the area of a city, but Weber really had no theory of their locations. Population concentrations enter his model as markets or as cheap labor sites, but the locations of such concentrations were treated as given in the more analytical portions of his work. A second explanation for the failure to include Weberian reasoning in intra-urban models may be that he did not treat land as an input in his production functions. He did stress that increasing concentration of industry in an area would cause land values to increase and that these were the most important deglomerative economy. Nevertheless, his failure to determine rents may have made it appear that his approach was incapable of dealing with the central issue of intra-urban models, the optimal allocation of space. However, there is nothing to prevent the inclusion of land in Weber's model and the derivation of bid rent functions that are in some ways richer and more meaningful than those that are derived in a simple, Thünen-type model.

Bid rent functions in a **Weberian Model**

Consider the simple case of a product that is available to an urban area from national sources of supply at a constant price, $\bar{P}$. Its delivered price, P' is the sum of $\bar{P}$ and transport cost, which is a function of distance D_{oj}, from the center of the city to a site j:

$$P'_j = \bar{P} + f(D_{oj}). \tag{1}$$

The product can also be fabricated locally. Its production requires weight a_1 of one raw material and a_2 of a second. It also requires a_3 of labor and a_4 of land per unit of output. Suppose, to use one of a variety of possible cases, that the first raw material is imported. The second is available at a site k in the urban area or its environs. The cost of a_1 of the first raw material at the center of the city is $\bar{c}_1$. The delivered cost, c_{1j}', of this quantity at site j is the sum of $\bar{c}_1$ and transport cost, the latter being a function of distance from the center to the site:

$$c'_{1j} = \bar{c}_1 + f_1(D_{oj}). \tag{2}$$

The cost of a_2 at the site k of its production is c_2 and its delivered cost is:

$$c'_{2j} = \bar{c}_2 + f_2(D_{kj}). \tag{3}$$

Since commuting requires both time and money expenditure, the wage rate a producer pays at site j, c'_{3j}, may also vary with the wage rate at the center, $\bar{c}_3$, and distance:

$$c'_{3j} = f_3 (\bar{c}_3, D_{oj}).^{24}$$ (4)

The cost of producing a unit of the product at site j is the sum of equations (2), (3), and (4):

$$C_j = \sum_{i=1}^{3} c'_{ij}.$$ (5)

The maximum rent that local producers of the product could pay per unit area for site j is:

$$R_j = [P'_j - C_j]\frac{1}{a_4}.$$ (6)

Equation (6) can be expressed in Weberian graphics. C_j represents the system of isodopanes. Each isodopane is made up of points for which the total cost (the sum of production cost and transport cost for obtaining all inputs, including labor) to produce a unit of the product is the same. P'_j represents the system of isotims. Each isotim is made up of points where the delivered price of the imported product is the same. Each intersection of an isotim and an isodopane yields the rent for a site at that location. Rent can be computed in this way for all sites and a bid rent curve generated. Such a curve may peak at the center of the city, at the site of the local raw material, or at an intermediate site. If labor costs decline with distance from the center, it could peak at a site that is beyond that of the local raw material. Bid rent curves for other uses can also be generated and competition for space thereby introduced.

These bid rent curves differ from the usual ones in that they rest in part on the introduction of alternative sources of supply and, therefore spatial competition. Thus, the delivered price of the imported product could be less than production costs everywhere in the urban area. In this case Equation (6) would yield negative rents, and space would not be allocated to the activity unless it received a subsidy. Alternatively, the rents yielded by Equation (6) might be negative at the center, the negative value could decrease (absolutely) as the source of the local raw material was approached, then turn positive and achieve its maximum

[24]Leon N. Moses. "Towards a Theory of Intra-Urban Wage Differentials and Their Influence on Travel Patterns." *Regional Science Association Papers.* 9, 1962, pp. 53–63.

positive value at the site of that material. Further away, it might decline and turn negative again. The above reasoning involves a number of modifications of the Weberian framework but does not violate its basic logic. The real issue is whether Weberian-type reasoning can help explain intra-urban location.

Examples of Transport Orientation

The manufacture of bricks in Chicago in 1873 provides an example of the theory's usefulness. This industry was very important after the Fire because a tremendous amount of rebuilding was necessary. In addition, an ordinance had been adopted that required brick construction in the burned-out district. Bricks were made by forming clay and baking the forms in kilns. Clay is weight-losing since it contains water that is driven off in the heating process. It can be found all over the city of Chicago, but is located most abundantly along the South Branch of the Chicago River.[25] The coal used to heat the kilns is an example of a fully weight-losing input. Because coal came into the city from the East by water transportation,[26] so far as the city was concerned, the "site" of the coal was the land along the river. While bricks were undoubtedly sold all over the city, it does not seem unreasonable to treat the burned-out district as the major market.

Weber's theory would lead us to expect that brick manufacture would take place along the river, it being the "site" of the coal. This was the case for the twenty-four brickyards whose locations we were able to establish. Each of them is found in one of the half-mile grid squares that bordered the river or had a canal slip. Twenty of the brickyards were located along the South Branch of the river, where the most abundant supplies of clay were found. This area is about three-and-one-half miles from the burned-out district. In other words, the industry was oriented to transport, particularly to materials.

The locational patterns of other industries also demonstrate the relevance of Weberian reasoning. Beer production took place along the lake. The large amount of ice, a fully weight-losing input, necessary for cooling was presumably cut from the lake. Blast furnaces were located along the river, the "site" of the two weight-losing inputs, coal and ore. Foundries were also located along the

[25]Alfred T. Andreas, **1**, *op. cit.*, p. 570.
[26]*Ibid*, **3**, pp. 386–89.

river. However, they tended to concentrate along those segments that passed through the major manufacturing district rather than the squares in which the blast furnaces were located. If these districts are viewed as the major markets for metal products, the locational pattern of foundries can also be explained in Weberian terms: i.e., the industry located with reference to the weight-losing input—coal—and the market, rather than the pure material —pig iron—obtained from the blast furnaces. Slaughtering was concentrated near the rail facility that was constructed for bringing animals into the city.

Further details for the above and other industries will not be presented because our primary goal is to extend the Weberian model in ways that can help explain the distribution of all industries rather than individual ones. This extension is based on our understanding of nineteenth century methods of production, transport, and communication. This understanding can be put forward as a series of straightforward propositions. They lead, in turn, to the identification of variables that are then included in an empirical model of intra-urban location.

1. *Scale economies in interregional transport were very great.*

The two principal means of interregional or long-distance transportation in the latter half of the nineteenth century were rail and water. Except for those rivers and lakes that were capable of being used without improvement, the rights-of-way of these modes were extremely expensive to construct. Once constructed, they had great capacity and were capable of carrying large quantities of freight before on-line congestion was encountered. As a result of the above factors, relatively few routes were constructed; and there was a channelization and concentration of traffic on them. This concentration permitted the carriers to achieve very great economies of scale in line-haul operations.

Scale economies, particularly in rail transportation, went beyond the line-haul and included terminal operations. Many shipments were in less-than-carload lots. The combining of individual shipments in cars for given destinations, and the assembly of a train according to the destinations of the cars that comprised it, required time and expensive equipment. As a result, freight handling and train assembly tended to be concentrated at relatively few points. It seems likely that barge transport also required such concentration. We judge this from the fact that there tended to be a massing of large firms in the heavy materials processing industries along the river during our period. Barge transportation is not now, and probably was not then, well adapted for handling small-lot shipments.

In summary, concentration of traffic along relatively few routes and at relatively few terminals permitted the two interregional forms of transport to achieve very great economies of scale, low carrier costs, and relatively low shipping rates. These rates encouraged considerable regional specialization in production and interregional trade in raw materials and semi- and fully-fabricated products. Chicago, for example, received large quantities of coal and ore that were converted into pig iron which was then used to manufacture a wide variety of metal products. Some of these were consumed locally, others were shipped to the city's own agricultural hinterland and to regional and national markets. An important leather products industry grew up on the basis of the hides available from local slaughtering operations and those that were imported. Cloth was imported and clothing manufactured for local consumption and export. A few of these clothing firms employed more than 1,000 people each.

2. *Intra-urban freight transport was less technologically developed.*

Within cities, freight moved largely by horse and wagon, a mode that had not experienced any significant technological change in hundreds of years. It was characterized by smallness of scale because the tractive power of horses, operating as they did on ordinary city streets, was not very great. At best, the streets were cobbled, but often they were badly rutted or impassable because of mud or snow and ice. Thus, intra-urban freight transport tended to be slow, undependable, and costly. J. L. Ringwalt's data for 1873 indicate that railroads operating east of Chicago had average rates across commodities that ranged from 1.135 to 1.958 cents per ton-mile. The comparable rate for New York canals was 0.887 cents per ton-mile. Wagon rates ranged from 20 to 30 cents per ton-mile.[27]

The number of miles that a horse could pull a loaded wagon in a day was also quite limited. In these circumstances, we would

---

[27]John L. Ringwalt. *Development of Transportation Systems in the United States*. Philadelphia, Pa.: Author, 1888, pp. 241–47.

expect the locational patterns of industries to exhibit a good deal of transport orientation, namely an orientation that would mini- mize the cost of moving materials and products within cities. Industries requiring weight-losing materials that were brought in from outside, or producing products that were largely sold in export trade, would tend to cluster closely to railroad freight- handling facilities and along the river. Processes requiring large amounts of weight-losing materials that were available locally would tend to be drawn to the sites of these materials.

3. *Materials orientation may have been more important than market orientation.*

Transport cost minimization may involve orientation to markets, either local or export, or to materials. The locational patterns of industries in nineteenth century cities may well have exhibited more of the latter than the former because production functions were highly materials intensive. They involved a great deal of weight loss, much more than comparable products and processes today. This reasoning leads to the expectation that, other things constant, industries requiring the greatest amounts of materials per ton of product would bid more than others for land along the river and closest to rail terminals.

4. *Intra-urban person transport was efficient relative to freight transport.*

A curious division existed in the technology of nineteenth cen- tury urban transportation. Horse railways came into use quite early for the movement of people. Chicago had its first line in 1859. By 1873, there were three main lines and a number of feeders. A horse pulling a vehicle that is mounted on a rail is six to eighteen times more efficient than one operating on ordinary city streets.[23] The cost of moving labor inputs tended therefore to be low relative to the cost of moving material inputs and outputs by horse and wagon. As a result, industry largely oriented itself to the river and the various rail terminals; and households located with reference to the horsecar lines that fed into major employ- ment districts.

The arguments involved in the present and the preceding pro- position can be clarified by asking what might have happened if

---

[23]*Ibid,* p. 39.

intra-urban person transport had been as inefficient and costly as freight transport. In that case, there would have been a tendency for households to concentrate in the areas where firms were located along the river and around each rail terminal. The city would, in other words, have been made up of a number of relatively isolated production areas, each with its own local labor market. However, Part One of the paper showed that this was not the case. Households were found to be relatively dispersed compared to employment.

5. A gap existed in the technology of information flow.

Between cities, information was transmitted with relative ease and at relatively low cost by telegraph. The telegraph was not extensively used for intra-urban information flow, probably because it did not lend itself to switchboard-type operation and therefore had limited capacity. Within cities, business information was largely carried by messengers. Firms that were closely tied because their need for one another's inputs were important and changed frequently, or because the prices of these inputs did so, tended to agglomerate. Firms that were highly dependent on quick access to information on such things as prices in regional and national markets tended to cluster closely to telegraph terminals. Later, an explanation is offered for the locational pattern of commercial banks that involves these ideas.

Selection of Variables for the Empirical Model

The above propositions led us to select a number of variables for inclusion in two regression models that were designed to explain the distribution of employment and households. We will deal with the employment model first. The data on manufacturing employees and the grid-square division of the city used in the regression are the same as those in Part One of the paper.

Railroad Freight Terminals

Terminals were expected to draw manufacturing firms because of the high cost of intra-urban goods movement. In order to express this effect properly it was necessary to take into account the fact that eleven railroads entered Chicago, and that these railroads served different sections of the country. Access to a large number of terminals was therefore important for firms that traded with several regions. A variable, Terminals, was constructed that summed the number of terminals within a grid square and the squares that adjoined it. This specification of the variable implies that the economic limit of a round-trip by horse and wagon within Chicago's congested industrial districts was approximately three miles. The Terminal variable was expected to have a positive sign.

River

Chicago's waterways were also expected to attract industry. A dummy variable, River, was entered which took the value one if the North or South Branches of the Chicago River or a canal slip from it passed through a square. This specification of the variable means that the power of the river to attract industry was permitted to extend only one zone, while railroad terminals were treated as extending their influence two zones. The two modes of transport and the sites near them were treated differently because lower valued freight tended to move on the waterways. This freight could be expected to exhibit even less intra-urban mobility than the commodities that entered or left the city by rail. The River variable was expected to have a positive sign.

Horsecar Lines

A dummy variable, Horsecar, was entered which was unity for squares through which a horse rail line passed and zero for others. This variable was included in the employment regression as a test of one of the parts of the theory presented above. According to the theory, industry tended to be more strongly influenced by the cost of moving materials and products than labor because intra-urban freight transport was inefficient, relative to person transport. This reasoning suggests that the Horsecar dummy should *not* have significantly positive effect on employment in most grid squares, but should have such an effect in the regression that explains the spatial distribution of household.

Core Zone

Most urban economists are likely to concede that agglomeration and other scale economies should lie at the very heart of an explanation of city size and form, despite the fact that such economies are ignored in Thünen-type models. We defined agglomeration effects as the attraction of more firms to an area than could be accounted for by the above variables separately. We reasoned that such combined effects would be exhibited by a few squares that had the following characteristics: 1) they had the greatest access to all of the city's rail terminals; 2) they were close to the River; 3) they had the best access to all of the city's labor force, as distinct from access to particular concentrations of labor.

The center of gravity of all rail terminals was determined. It was found to occur in the shaded square that contains a circle in Map 1. The South Branch of the Chicago River, which is part of the waterway system that connects the Great Lakes to the Mississippi River, passes through this square. This square (happily) adjoins the one in which the three principal horsecar lines came together. That square is shaded and contains a star. The two shaded squares were called the Core Zone. A variable was entered which took the value one if a square was in the Core and zero if it was not. Our expectation was that this variable would have a strongly positive effect.

Distance

Distance was the only explanatory variable included in the regressions described in Part One of the paper. A distance variable was also entered in the present employment regressions. We wished to demonstrate that it had served as something of a surrogate for other, more theoretically meaningful variables, and that its effect and significance would decline when these were included. Distance was measured from the center of the Core Zone to the mid-point of each square.

The Regression Results

The results of the estimation appear as Equation (5) in Table 3. As shown by the last two entries, the equation explains 78 per cent of the variance and is significant at the 0.01 level. The Thünen-type regressions described in Part One explained 43 per cent of the variance. *The distance coefficient does have a negative sign, but it is not statistically significant in the present regression.* The Horsecar variable has a positive effect, but its coefficient is statistically insignificant, which is also in keeping with the theory. The remaining variables have the expected signs and their coefficients are significant at the 0.01 level.[29]

To test for the effect of scale, similar regressions were run for the three sizes of plants described in Part One. The results appear as Equations (6) through (8) in Table 3. All the regressions are significant at the 0.01 level, but the large firm regression has lower explanatory value. This may be due to an incorrect assumption that is implicit in it: namely, that large city firms used the regular public rail terminals. In fact, many of them generated enough freight to support a private siding. This permitted them to select sites on the outskirts of the city and avoid the congestion and high land values of the principal industrial districts. Unfortunately, information on private sidings was not readily available. We therefore proceeded as if large firms used the public terminals, despite the fact that many of them had their own sidings and occupied sites that were relatively distant from these terminals.

There are also some interesting differences in the coefficients of the three regressions. The coefficient for River is negative for small firms but not significant. It is positive and significant at the

---

[29]In order to determine whether River squares that were nearer the center of the city attracted more firms, Richard Muth suggested that an interaction variable, Distance x River dummy be entered into Equation (5). This amounts to entering distance from the center of the Core Zone to River squares as a variable. We decided to enter a second variable as well, distance to non-river squares. The results for all firms follow:

	Constant	Distance to River Squares (In Logs)	Distance to Non-River Squares (In Logs)	Terminals	Horsecar	Core Zone
Coefficient	2.340	−0.4945	−0.6966	0.4366	0.02113	9.378
Stand. Error	2.731	0.7955	0.8015	0.09796	0.2194	0.8970
Significance				0.01		0.01

$\overline{R}^2$ (corrected) = 0.772   significance 0.01

The same coefficients are significant in this Equation as in Equation (5). The two distance variables have the expected negative sign. In addition, the relationship between them is as expected since density of employment falls off more rapidly for squares that are not on the river. However, neither of the coefficients is statistically significant. This result led us to retain the original form of the River variable, which implies that all land along the river was equivalent.

Table 3   Predicting the Percentage of Employment per Grid Square

Independent Variables					
	Equation Number	5	6	7	8
	Firm Size	All Firms	Small	Medium	Large*
	Squares with Firms	61	42	46	28
Constant	Coefficient	2.286	4.416	4.120	−0.4164
	Standard error	2.701	2.869	2.346	4.021
	Significance		0.10	0.10	
River	Coefficient	0.7407	−0.2333	0.5830	0.9544
	Standard error	0.2160	0.2294	0.1876	0.3215
	Significance	0.01		0.01	0.01
Terminal	Coefficient	0.4203	0.4561	0.5033	0.4093
	Standard error	0.09766	0.1037	0.08482	0.1453
	Significance	0.01	0.01	0.01	0.01
Horsecar	Coefficient	0.02837	−0.01321	−0.2132	0.2443
	Standard error	0.2175	0.2310	0.1889	0.3237
	Significance				
Core Zone	Coefficient	9.407	11.61	7.292	3.521
	Standard error	0.8888	0.9442	0.7720	1.323
	Significance	0.01	0.01	0.01	0.01
Log Distance from Core Zone	Coefficient	−0.6846	−1.265	−1.208	0.1220
	Standard error	0.7923	0.8417	0.6882	1.179
	Significance		0.10	0.10	
	$\bar{R}^2$ (corrected)	0.777	0.806	0.817	0.388
	Significance	0.01	0.01	0.01	0.01

* Clothing firms were excluded since their particular production function tended to be labor rather than materials intensive.

.01 level in the regressions for medium and large firms. The explanation given earlier for this difference is that the barge industry was not well suited for handling small-lot shipments. A riverfront location would therefore tend to have relatively little value for small firms and they would be unable to bid successfully for such sites. The Core Zone variable is positive and significant in all of the regressions, but its size falls off as size of firm increases. In addition, the Distance variable while not significant, is *positive* for large firms. These results suggest that there were differences in production techniques open to different sizes of firms. As mentioned above, those that generated large quantities of freight probably had their own rail sidings. This amounts to saying that they used a different production technique.[30]

Relative prices in inputs and outputs *at the center of a city* are very important in Thünen-type models. The results described above were obtained without such information. They suggest that underlying technological relationships and the structure of the city's transport network may have been more important determinants of intra-urban land use than such prices. This conclusion is based on three suppositions and some facts. The first supposition is that firms that survived the Fire were relatively free to adjust their locations because buildings and other fixed capital had been destroyed. The second is that while the Fire may have destroyed such things as freight houses, it did not lead to changes in the rights-of-way of the various modes: it certainly did not alter the position of the river. The third is that there had been significant changes in the relative prices of inputs and outputs over the eight years before the Fire, this being the median age of the firms in our sample. The facts are that a comparison by ring and quadrant of

---

[30]We were interested in determining the variables that explained the differences in the coefficients of the three regressions, and in establishing the statistical significance of the explanation. Therefore, the three equations were re-estimated using absolute levels of employment as the dependent variables. The equations for large and small firms differed at the 0.05 significance level. This result was found to be due to the different effects of the River and Terminal variables in the equations. The test method used was an extension of Sheffé's S-Method. On this, see Henry Sheffé. *The Analysis of Variance.* New York: John Wiley & Sons, 1959, pp. 66–72, and Carlos Toro-Viscarrondo and T. D. Wallace. "A Test of the Mean Square Error Criterion for Restrictions in Linear Regression." *Journal of the American Statistical Association.* June 1968, pp. 558–72.

the location pattern of all firms, as well as the patterns of individual industries, before and after the Great Fire revealed that there was very little change.[31] We now turn to the population regression.

Explaining the Distribution of Population

Three variables were included in the basic equation to explain the distribution of population: Core Zone, Horsecar, and Distance.

A negative sign was expected for the first variable because sites within the Core Zone were so valuable for firms that households would be unable to bid effectively for them. The coefficient for the Horsecar dummy was expected to have a positive sign since squares through which these lines passed had good access to the principal employment areas. Distance was interpreted somewhat differently in the population than in the employment regressions. It was viewed as a good measure of commuting time. Of several zones on a given Horsecar line, those that were closer to principal employment areas would involve less travel time. Households would bid higher prices for sites in such zones and occupy less space. Therefore, the coefficient for distance was expected to be negative and significant. The results of the regression are shown in Equation (9), Table 4. The equation explains 54 per cent of the variance. The regression and the coefficients are significant at the 0.01 level, and the coefficients have the expected signs.

An additional regression was carried out to test the hypothesis that the locational pattern of firms was strongly influenced by access to the interregional modes of transportation, while population located with reference to horsecar lines. The three basic variables discussed above were included in this regression. In addition, a type of gravity variable was included for employment. This variable was the sum of employment in a square and those surrounding it. The results are shown in Equation (10), Table 4. The three basic variables have the expected signs and are significant at the 0.01 level. The Employment variable is also somewhat

---

[31]An equation was estimated for all firms that utilized 1873 employment levels and 1871 plant locations. The former were used because employment was not known for 1871. The coefficients of this equation have the same signs and significance levels as those in Equation 5, Table 3. Except for Core Zone, which was substantially larger in Equation 5, the coefficients of the variables in the two equations do not differ by one standard error. These results suggest that the Fire did not cause a major change in the locational pattern of industry.

significant, but it is *negative*.[32] The interpretation of this result is similar to the one given for the negative sign of the Core Zone dummy: households either could not or, because horsecar lines provided them with good access to employment areas, had no need to compete effectively for sites that were valuable to firms.

The Location of Banking

Earlier, the point was made that Chicago was a service as well as a manufacturing center. It is therefore interesting to examine the locational pattern of an industry, such as commercial banking, in which the weight of material inputs was trivial, and the output was a service rather than a physical product, subject to high costs of wagon transport. The theory developed above suggests that such industries, as contrasted to manufacturing, would exhibit elements of labor orientation. To test this idea, the addresses of thirty-six commercial banks were determined. Twenty-nine of them were located in the shaded and starred square of Map 1. This was the square in which the three horsecar lines came together and which therefore had the best access to the city's entire labor force. Locations with such access permit firms and industries that employ large numbers of people to acquire labor at lower wage rates.

---

[32]The two principal methods of personal transport in the eighteenth century were walking and riding horsecars. John F. Kain suggested that the effect of these modes on population density be investigated. This was done by using two Distance variables: 1) distance from the Core Zone to squares on Horsecar lines; 2) distance to squares not on such lines. The following results were obtained:

	Constant	Core zone	Distance to Horsecar Squares in Logs	Distance to non-Horsecar Squares in Logs	Employment
Coefficient	10.57	−2.251	−2.873	−3.002	−0.01629
Stand. Error	1.579	0.4968	0.4768	0.4578	0.00936
Significance	0.01	0.01	0.01	0.01	0.10

$\overline{R}^2$ (corrected) = 0.552   Significance level 0.01

All the coefficients are significant. The two interaction variables have the expected relationship: population density declines somewhat less rapidly with distance in Horsecar corridors.

Commercial banking may also have exhibited elements of market orientation, but of a type that involved the cost of transmitting information. Manufacturing firms were the market since they were probably the major customers for loans. The relationship of a bank and its customers rests on a closeness of contact that was best achieved by physical proximity in nineteenth century cities. Proximity was required because the transmission of business information rested on the transport of people. The lack of a more efficient method of intra-urban communication may help explain why the square in which most commercial banks were found adjoined those in which the density of manufacturing firms was highest. It should also be noted that many firms whose manufacturing facilities were near the outskirts of the city maintained a central office in or near the banking center.

Conclusion and Implications

The currently accepted theory of urban land use is based on J. H. Von Thünen's model of agricultural location and land rent. The urban versions of this model appear to have been designed to replicate the spatial structure of large cities of the nineteenth century. However, in this paper we have shown that their ability to explain the actual distribution of population and industry in one such city—Chicago in the 1870's—was quite limited.

We presented an alternative approach which combined the essential element of Thünen-type models, the allocation of space according to the rent-paying ability of alternative uses, and A. Weber's theory of transport orientation. The technologies and relative costs of transmitting information, and transporting people and goods were important components of this approach. In brief, the position taken was that the cost of moving goods was very high, relative to the cost of moving people in nineteenth century cities. Therefore, they evolved in a way that tended to minimize goods transport: manufacturing tended to orient itself to interregional transport (railroad terminals and the river); and population was dispersed relative to employment and oriented to horsecar lines. Our investigation of banking suggested that the location of at least this important component of the service sector was strongly influenced by the distribution of manufacturing firms and households.

The technology that formed the nineteenth century city is not

M

the technology of our age. The motor truck, freeway, and Interstate Highway have reduced the cost of intra-urban goods transport. They have reduced the need for physical proximity between manufacturing firms that use each other's products as inputs and have given them greater freedom in location. It is true that the service sector is much more important in today's cities than it was in the last century. However, there is a real question as to whether such industries as finance, insurance, and advertising will continue to be concentrated within the central areas of such cities as Chicago, Boston, and New York. Continued rapid improvements in communication and in the storage and transmission of information are expected. There may reduce the effects of the agglomerative economies that have been achieved by having the various parts of the business service sector in close physical proximity to one another. In this case, such things as finance and insurance may follow manufacturing, retailing, and wholesaling to the suburbs. The inner portions of existing nineteenth century cities may then be little more than monuments to past technology.

8

Directions for Metropolitan Policy

JOSEPH L. FISHER and LOWDON WINGO*

Resources for the Future, Inc. Washington, D.C.

INTRODUCTION

It is commonly thought that our metropolitan regions are in a mess. Population growth has been concentrating in the 233 metropolitan regions of the country, until by now they account for two-thirds of the nation's population. Industries, jobs, and the resulting incomes are even more concentrated in these places. At the same time, the most severe social problems of the times are to be found in these great settlements, almost in proportion to their size, including violent crime, delinquency, concentrations of poverty, hazardous and unsanitary housing, traffic congestion, air pollution, solid waste disposal problems, chronic breakdowns of key public services, and racial and ethnic conflicts.

In recent years the growth of population, employment, and income within metropolitan areas has been concentrated in the suburban hinterland outside the central cities. Indeed, between 1960 and 1970 many of the great central cities of the country lost population, as did many rural areas. While three-fourths of the national growth in population has taken place within metropolitan regions, 85 per cent of that fraction has located in jurisdictions outside of the central city. Jobs, purchasing power, talent and leadership, strength of tax base, good schools and housing, and relatively

---

*Revised March 5, 1971

liberal endowments of open space generally distinguish the suburbs from the central cities.[1]

These well-known trends are set against a background of a confused and fragmented political milieu. The three largest metropolitan areas—New York, Chicago, and Los Angeles—have well over 1,000 units of local government each. With smaller cities following the same pattern, the number of local governmental units per 100,000 of population is large for cities at any level of population size. Efforts to reduce the number of local governments and to streamline those retained have been successful in few instances. As the economic and social elements of the American metropolis have become more interrelated, political jurisdictions have remained divided, competitive, and largely incapable of joint response to emerging problems. Restoring congruence between the economic and social dimensions of the American metropolis and the capacity to plan, manage, and govern it, is an issue high on the list of natural priorities for the 1970s.

In counterpoint to these trends is the desperate need of urban people to find the personal satisfactions that come from living in communities and neighborhoods where social exchange can be on a reasonably intimate and trustful scale enabling men, women, and children to deal with one another as whole persons. The great challenge for the future, it seems to us, is to fashion the processes and institutions for the governance of the metropolis in such a way that individual citizens will find these deep personal satisfactions within a total urban complex, many of whose problems can only be dealt with on a large and impersonal scale.

This paper will broadly assess some features of appropriate next steps in the governance of metropolitan regions. While metropolitan America has been growing and transforming itself for a long time, only in the last decade has any considerable number of American scholars focused their attention on the analysis of the ways governmental institutions respond to these deep-seated changes. The growing literature of research on the subject constitutes a rich intellectual resource, but at this moment, a report and appraisal from the development front, where politics, analysis, planning, and innovation are shaping tomorrow's system of metropolitan governance would be especially useful. Accordingly, this

---

[1] Ironically, the school desegregation decision handed down some sixteen years ago, along with other factors, has rapidly increased the concentration of minority groups in central cities and whites in the suburbs.

is not primarily a scholarly and detached paper, although it respects those qualities; it seeks instead to sense and describe opportunities for improving governmental institutions that emerge from the welter of policies and problems that characterize the American metropolis. Its raw material, then, consists of an intimate contact with research and thinking in the urban field as well as experience in the difficult task of shaping and giving content to new institutions of local government. Its point of view derives in part from the role of scholar and, in part, from the role of metropolitan politician.[2]

The modern American metropolis is a large and dense aggregation of people and activities groping for a reconciliation of the large scale, metropolitan-wide approaches necessary to deal with such matters as transportation, basic public services, and industrial location, with the restoration of personal dignity and fulfillment that comes only through involvement with smaller groups. Our attention will be directed principally to the metropolitan-wide aspects. First, as a matter of exposition, we shall take a two-way view of metropolitan areas looking at major problems such as transportation and housing, and then at several political-organizational alternatives for dealing with them. From this, we shall move to a delineation of some criteria for dealing with them. We shall then move to a delineation of some criteria for judging metropolitan policies. Finally, we shall discuss some of the features of a preferred policy strategy for the future.

METROPOLITAN "PROBLEM CLUSTERS"

The strategy followed by this paper is to juxtapose specific substantive metropolitan problems against general institutional arrangements which have been proposed or tested at one time or another to deal with them. Clearly, problems are not solved by rearranging organizational structures, but it is equally clear that institutional arrangements can expedite or retard the formulation and execution of well-conceived policies addressed to these prob-

---

[2]Specifically, one of the authors has been president and board chairman of a major metropolitan council of governments, as well as an elected official in a suburban jurisdiction, while the other has been directing a research program on regional and urban problems and himself doing research in this field.

lems. We shall concern ourselves with these institutional arrangements in terms of their potential contribution to the effectiveness of specific kinds of metropolitan policies. Ideally, we should like, first, to test an array of institutional arrangements against the requirements of each general problem in terms of historical experience, policy analysis, and judgment, and then to synthesize from these tests the characteristics of that set of governmental institutions which would best serve a region, given its unique problem set. In reality, our purpose is served by a less rigorous examination that will permit the extraction of what seem to us to be basic principles or criteria for metropolitan reform.

The analysis of metropolitan problems is gravely complicated by two considerations: in these massive, dense concentrations of people, activities, and institutions, everything affects everything else; and a configuration of events constitutes a problem only when enough people perceive it to be one. Thus, we are inclined to talk about problem clusters instead of single problems simply because the interests of many groups typically are tied up with the public role involved, perhaps in a multitude of different ways.

The following substantive problem clusters would have high priority on any metropolitan policy maker's list of issues for metropolitan policy: poverty-employment-training; transportation-utilities-location of activities; pollution and waste; amenities-parks-open space; social welfare-health-housing; schools-community control-neighborhood services; and crime-delinquency-drugs-public safety. Numerous difficulties will be confronted in orchestrating governmental processes to bring about "solutions" to these substantive issues. This orchestration will involve mobilizing the resources of the metropolitan community, allocating them among the high-priority tasks and maximizing the managerial and administrative effectiveness of the institutions in carrying out their assigned functional responsibilities. Dealing successfully with any one of the substantive problem clusters will involve modification of the arrangements for planning, financing, and administering the constituent programs in the metropolitan development process.

The metropolitan dimensions of the poverty-employment-training cluster of problems derive from the fact that the metropolitan region is generally a self-contained labor market—the great bulk of the labor force both lives in the region and works there. In large degree, this congruence stems from the fact that the real costs of the journey to work rise quite sharply beyond the one hour door-to-door daily trip and return—a fact which brings most of the region's jobs within reach of most of the region's inhabitants and excludes all but the nearest of those outside the region's limits. Within the metropolitan region, the labor market is intricately structured by the economic processes which have differentiated the parts of the region by economic specialization and the socio-economic characteristics of residents.

Metropolitan poverty tends to be concentrated in the inner city where low-cost housing units are clustered. While a good part of this poverty can be attributed to the concentration of the aged and the very young, it also includes large numbers of low-income persons of working age who have been unable to find an employment niche in the local economy because of economic discrimination, lack of appropriate skills, or lack of access to appropriate jobs. New job formation, however, takes place in a more diffuse manner throughout the metropolitan region with a bias in favor of suburban jurisdictions. The problem, hence, of upgrading these persons and relating them to emerging job opportunities is neither one for local jurisdictions, which are unable to intervene effectively in the full labor market, nor for state or federal jurisdictions, the attention of which is necessarily riveted on more aggregate perspectives of labor force-employment relationships. It is pre-eminently a metropolitan problem, where programs transcending local jurisdictions can provide for effective human resource policies relating to that particular labor market.

The problem cluster which embraces the quality of transportation and utility services and the location of economic and residential activities has clear metropolitan-wide dimensions. While not all metropolitan regions are growing, all are changing in their economic features: Old firms disappear, while new ones are being born, and still others are growing or changing their technology or their locations among the various parts of the region. The composition of economic activity in any locality in the region moves in response to economic change in the region as a whole. The same thing can be said of the socio-economic characteristics of its population. How well a local jurisdiction fares in this process of intra-regional change depends on a number of things—its current stock of commercial facilities, private services, industries, households, and governmental institutions; the quality of the public services it offers its citizens and enterprises compared to those offered by other local jurisdictions; and, perhaps more important, its accessibility to other activities in the region. On the whole, it seems easy to accept the proposition that new business investment in the region seeks out the more profitable locations, while families and households seek locations also rich in social and physical amenities.

It is also easy to agree that the qualities of access and amenity are unequally distributed throughout the region at any point in time so that the impacts of these change processes are felt in very different ways by the various jurisdictions. Demands for public services are transformed too, while the financial capacities of the region's jurisdictions change in contrasting ways. Thus, some local communities find themselves increasingly hard put to meet emerging demands for public services, with demands growing and tax resources shrinking. Other communities can find their tax bases growing rapidly through new business investment at a time when the rates of growth of demand for expensive public services, such as education, are falling off. In general, these processes tend toward an increasing maldistribution of tax burdens and service qualities within the region.

Key elements in these processes of business and household location are the networks of transportation and utility services. The transportation network as the key allocator of access qualities around the metropolitan region exerts a powerful effect on the flow of new investment among local jurisdictions. In recent years, the provision of metropolitan transportation services has been the source of severe interjurisdictional and interclass conflict in which central cities, with their concentration of poverty groups, have been fiercely resisting the construction of new freeways to connect the auto-dependent suburbanites with their center city jobs. The major public utilities, especially water and sewerage, but also gas, telephone, and electricity, determine the relative service qualities among the various alternative growth sites in the region. The utilities, too, have become the source of metropolitan crises. Major service failures in New York's power supplies and distribution systems have become a chronic threat, while the quality of its telephone system has deteriorated disastrously. New national concern with water and air quality is forcing metropolitan communities to review the effectiveness of their institutions and processes for handling the growing volume of effluents. Both the utilities and the transportation system share important metropolitan-wide features. First, while they can be modified and extended at acceptable levels of cost, the core, or first-stage investment to make them operable is very large; second, the parts of the various systems are highly interdependent—that is, conditions in one part of the network can exert very strong effects on the quality of service rendered at other, even distant, parts of the system. In short, no single jurisdiction can exert full control over the quality of transportation or utility services within its jurisdiction, and it may contribute to the social costs of other jurisdictions. Furthermore, the way in which the region is growing and changing is a matter of concern for the entire region, and to the extent that changes in transportation and utility services, as well as the way in which land is regulated, affect the character of these changes, some greater-than-local controlling mechanisms seem to be required.

Maintaining the quality of the physical environment in metropolitan areas is a comparatively new member of the metropolitan problem clusters. We are just becoming aware that the production of goods and services which people want is accompanied by unwanted products that pollute the air and the water, and clutter up the landscape. Two aspects of these residual products make them appropriate matter for metropolitan regulation and policy. First, they tend to spill over the boundaries of the jurisdictions in which they are produced. Residuals ending up in the air or water are carried to other jurisdictions in the air- or watershed, and the receiving jurisdictions fall victim to the impacts. Residuals classified as solid wastes can be converted by incineration into air or water pollutants, or they can be disposed of in solid form as "fill." In the latter case, the policy problem for the region is created by the simple fact that surrounding jurisdictions can intercept the residual at jurisdictional boundaries and forbid its disposal within them. Central cities, hence, with no open land area for fill can be prisoners of the surrounding jurisdictions and can be compelled to go to incineration as a way of exporting their solid wastes.

These interlocality effects are accompanied by large-scale regional effects as the metropolitan areas grow larger. The San Francisco Bay area has been contemplating a plan to haul solid wastes by train to unpopulated areas in the northern part of the state, while New York is giving consideration to a plan that would use railroad-borne solid wastes to fill up old mining excavations in northeast Pennsylvania. The sheer scale of the problem for large metropolitan areas transcends the capabilities of local jurisdictions acting on their own, for such a decentralized approach will increasingly compound costs and environmental damage.

Strong interdependencies are also found among the forms of residuals. The interrelationship between solid wastes and air pollution via incineration is one. As a further example, industrial water pollutants can be converted to solid waste by settling, precipitation, or flotation and have to be disposed of on land. Electrostatic precipitation of particulate air pollutants produces a solid waste which then needs to be disposed of in the environment. Other interrelations readily come to mind. Thus, a key policy problem for the metropolitan region is to achieve some mix of residuals for disposal in the air, the water, or on the land; this represents a "good" solution for the region as a whole, given the unit costs of the various forms of disposal, the composition of the residual products generated by the metropolitan economy, and the amount and incidence of damage. These complex physical-economic relationships and the complexity of jurisdictional structures lead to the conclusion that the metropolitan level is the appropriate focus for residuals management.

Parks, open spaces, and landscape amenities constitute a metropolitan problem cluster simply because the natural endowments of a region are unequally distributed among parts of the region in a manner which tends to bear little relationship to the wants and needs of the metropolitan citizenry at large. The high density of population that characterizes the inner city carries with it a highly intensive use of space, which makes open, recreational, or amenity use of land extremely costly. The poor who are confined to these high-density areas would be largely barred from enjoyment of such places were it not for the intervention of government. The converse of this observation is that the great supply of potentially public open space is to be found in the metropolitan hinterlands beyond the development front and at distances accessible to inner city residents only on rare occasions. Hence, there is a metropolitan interest in the distribution and accessibility of these natural amenities.

Furthermore, it can be argued that since these kinds of facilities produce pure public goods, their enjoyment cannot be confined to a particular clientele; each jurisdiction, hence, will tend to produce less of them than would be the case if the beneficiaries bore their costs in some proportion to their enjoyment. "Free riding" jurisdictions will produce none of these goods, while the producing jurisdictions will produce less than they would if the free riders were willing to remunerate them for the value of these zero-priced goods. In short, *local* production of these goods may result in a *regional* output that is considerably less than people would be willing to pay for on a metropolitan scale.

Finally, some landscape resources uniquely belong to the region —Washington's C&O Canal, San Francisco Bay, Central Park— so that the extent and form of their development is a matter of interest to everyone in the region. Hence, it is clear that resolution of the many issues bound up in parks-open space-amenities problem cluster can only be effected satisfactorily at the metropolitan-wide scale.

The social welfare-health-housing problem cluster has crucial policy interfaces with the poverty-employment-training cluster as well as with the transportation-utilities-location of activities cluster, but its main issue is the impact of the slum or ghetto environment on the lives and well-being of the poor, who find there the only housing supply available to them. The issue has been dramatized around two polar strategies for coping with the ghetto problem. In the long run, liberal dogma has called for progressive racial and economic integration, which in practical terms means a gradual absorption of the poor in the ghettos by neighborhoods throughout the region as their economic status and social characteristics change. Such an objective requires integration of the metropolitan housing stock, which can only be achieved by a metropolitan-wide policy focus.

Oppressed by pessimistic estimates of the time horizons involved, many have argued that an integration strategy means little for the great majority of the poor and the black and have stated that the only way to benefit from the current drift of public policy within a reasonable future is to concentrate attention on upgrading the ghettos and slums to provide a better environment for poor families. This doctrine of "gilding the ghetto" has been the subject of a continuing debate among urbanists for several years, but its main import is that there is no way in which any acceptable policy in this area can be implemented through independent policy-making by individual—and independent—political jurisdictions. The metropolitan level, on the other hand, commands the means to achieve the main policy options in this problem cluster.

Related to this is the schools-community control, neighborhood services cluster. Clearly the social response to the desegregation of public school systems has played a large role in recent metropolitan social ecology. The effective intensification of racial segregation brought about by the white flight to the suburbs and the barriers subsequently erected against the poor and the black made them the heirs to—and the captives of—the massive, inert, and unresponsive public service bureaucracies of the central city. The growing dissatisfaction of the poor and the black with the patronizing and patriarchial political decision processes has taken the form of militant campaigns for community control of decision-making in key public services, especially schools. While the courts and higher levels of government seek methods to expand effective integration within and among jurisdictions by "busing," inter-jurisdictional school consolidations, and in more effective housing desegregation in the suburbs, inner city groups press for neighborhood control of schools, of police activities, of recreation programs, and of social services to make them more responsive to local needs. Hence, this cluster of problems ranges from the metropolitan focus necessary to provide effective educational opportunities to all the region's children to the neighborhood of the inner city that is struggling to make governmental institutions respond to neighborhood needs and wants in the way of public goods and services.

That the public safety problem cluster has metropolitan-wide dimensions is also easily shown. It is not enough however to point out that criminals do not recognize jurisdictional boundaries. Actually, criminal behavior has close correlates in the social ecology of the region as a whole. Environments that favor or encourage such behavour show up in many different ways in the city. Ghettos whose size and concentration surpass some critical social threshold, interface areas between the central business district and the ghettos, areas in which social transition or disorganization is proceeding too rapidly for adjustment, all of these provide opportunities to satisfy anti-social impulses that offer incentive and temptation to criminal behavior. The forces producing these situations are region-wide in scope.

Furthermore, vast differentials in the criminal statutes, in their enforcement, in the administration of justice, in the resources available for crime prevention as well as prosecution can only have the effect of providing differential incentives to criminal behavior by allowing the crime payoff to vary with jurisdiction. Not every metropolitan area has a counterpart to Chicago's notorious Cicero, but they can certainly be found in many of the larger ones.

Thus, both the phenomenology of urban crime and the institutional structure through which it can be attacked argue for a metropolitan framework for public safety services. Present levels and distribution of criminal activities are in part attributable to the incapacity of existing institutions to work at the proper governmental level.

ORGANIZATIONAL GAMBITS IN METROPOLITAN GOVERNANCE

Now for the second dimension—What are the principal organizational approaches to the problems? While these range across a broad conceptual spectrum, there has been practical experience with special-purpose authorities metropolitan-wide planning, city-county consolidation, interjurisdictional compacts, annexation, voluntary councils of government, metropolitan government, and increased roles for federal or state governments in metropolitan affairs. Special-purpose authorities have been widely used in metropolitan areas for the discharge of functions that are technologically region-wide, largely self-financing, and involve the planning and management of large engineering systems. The New York Port Authority, the Washington Metropolitan Area Transportation Authority, and Detroit's metropolitan park system are well-known examples. Metropolitan-wide planning is now widespread in the U.S. as a result of federal stimulation provided for in Section 701 of the National Housing Act of 1954. Not only have matching funds been made available but the federal government has offered substantial inducements for some programs in the form of higher matching ratios in government programs to those areas that have metropolitan planning agencies with powers to review local programs that have region-wide impacts. And, finally, in accordance with Section 204 of the Housing Act of 1966 and with Budget Circular A-95 of 1969, local government applications for federal grants are required to be reviewed by an appropriate area-wide planning body.

City-county consolidation continues to be a favored way of attacking the metropolitan problems of middle-size intrastate metropolitan areas not only because, once voted, it is the simplest way to institute but also because it does the least damage to the existing tissue of government. Indianapolis, Jacksonville, and

Nashville have all chosen this route in the recent past. Interjurisdictional compacts are the principal means for creating metrowide institutions in those situations where the metropolitan area falls in more than one state. New York City, Philadelphia, and Washington have resorted to this device on more than one occasion to bring about regional institutions for particular purposes and give authority to regional programs. Annexation is the device favored in a few states to bring about political consolidation of metropolitan areas. The principal of annexation is simple—the extension of the city limits of the central city to bring residents and enterprises in adjacent areas under the laws and policies of the municipal corporation—but the means by which this can be achieved under state constitutions varies widely. For Texas cities, which have produced some spectacular acts of annexation in recent years, the State permits annexation by simple ordinance of the City Council. In Virginia annexation is primarily a matter of judicial determination. All in all, annexation has limitations as a means of governance in that it has a kind of imperialistic quality about it, which frequently ignores the interests and sentiments of the annexed. Usually it can be fought off successfully.

Outside of city-county consolidations and large-scale annexations, Miami has the only multi-purpose metropolitan government (Dade County) that has been voted into being in the U.S. in the post-war period. The governmental institutions in this case were created anew rather than merely by modifications of preceding ones. The political and institutional difficulties of creating acceptable new government structures are such that Miami's example has not been duplicated.

Voluntary councils of government can be considered the wave of the present. Also supported and encouraged by 701 funds and other federal programs, the number of Council of Governments (COGs) has grown from a handful in 1960 to well over a hundred in 1970, with Texas again leading the parade. Basically, COGs are a device by which local jurisdictions can come together to study and discuss regional problems, propose guidelines, and undertake region-wide functions about which there is a high degree of political consensus throughout the region. Distrusted at first both by suburbs and central city, they have now achieved generally high levels of acceptability within metropolitan regions, largely by doing some useful things and avoiding controversial ones. The most advanced case is that of the Twin Cities Metropolitan

Council, which has received from the Minnesota legislature not only strong powers of planning review but also authority to plan and manage region-wide services. It also has the power to levy a one and one-half mills property tax.

Finally, state and the federal government have been assuming new responsibilities for the nation's metropolitan areas. New York's Urban Development Corporation has been designed to provide an effective, mobile, and large-scale institution, specializing in land development, which can help cities seek out and launch solutions to their problems of physical growth. California's Bay Area Conservation and Development Commission is assuming increasing responsibility in the name of the state for the physical development of the Bay Area. Other such examples can be found across the country. Federal programs to aid metropolitan institutions have already been alluded to; others have been proposed, e.g., the Nixon administration's family assistance plan, under which, a major part of local welfare costs would be taken over by the federal government. Proposals have been advanced for state assumption of elementary and high school programs. The federal role in the model city, urban renewal, and public housing programs is large and crucial, especially in financing them.

The framework relating problem clusters to types of solutions suggests that many of the problems are best dealt with on a metropolitan scale, certainly in their major aspects. The transportation-utilities-location of activities problem cluster and pollution, for example, most certainly have to be tackled on a metropolitan basis if progress is to be made. This does not necessarily argue for a special-purpose authority for transportation or air pollution, although such a solution would be logical. These two problem clusters could also be handled by means of a compact, through consolidation or annexation, or by turning the whole matter over to the states or the federal government.

The two clusters most definitely concerned with human resources—poverty-employment-training and social-welfare-health-housing—probably require metro-wide general planning and perhaps finance to some extent, but in many particulars can be handled at the level of the local jurisdiction or at some newer and smaller level such as the model city, urban renewal, or neighborhood area. A realistic approach to assigning each problem cluster to one particular line of solution would examine each problem carefully so as to separate the parts that are best approached through a metro-wide agency (e.g., overall planning or basic transportation) and which parts are best approached at the neighborhood level (e.g., delivery of certain welfare or adult education services). We shall concentrate chiefly on metropolitan solutions, although we are clear that certain problems can be dealt with more effectively at the local or neighborhood level, and virtually all problems can be broken down so that certain aspects can be handled effectively at this level.

CRITERIA FOR METROPOLITAN POLICY

These various lines of solution to major metropolitan problems suggest some broad criteria for good metropolitan policy which are prerequisite for coherence and direction among the numerous possible policies. They are not necessarily listed in order of importance; each one seems relevant and useful by itself.

The first criterion should be obvious; but it seems frequently to be disregarded in fact—Problems should be dealt with on the geographic, social, and economic scale on which they occur. Minimizing interjurisdictonal "spillovers" would carry us a long way toward the problem-by-problem rationalization of metropolitan policies. For example, planning and operating the basic transportation network needs the perspective of the whole metropolitan region. No smaller area will encompass the problem, and any larger area will blur the focus unnecessarily. Similarly, the pollution "airshed," which, with respect to most air pollutants, tends to be roughly congruent with the metropolitan region, is the logical geographical unit for dealing with air pollution.

Social welfare policies require a nation-wide focus for the income maintenance functions and for basic planning and financing of general social welfare services, whose administration, however, can be effectively discharged through existing local political jurisdictions under the national umbrella of a common set of guidelines. However, within the separate jurisdictions, there is much to be said for further decentralization of administration and case work to preserve a more direct and personal relationship between social workers and clients. Some kinds of social services may be best discharged at a neighborhood level.

The characteristics of other problem clusters suggest a broad strategy of setting general planning and operations at a metropolitan scale while allowing special aspects of programs to be dealt with on other appropriate bases. For example, in the parks-open space-amenities cluster, the basic approach, especially to planning, can be carried out most efficiently at the regional level; but parks and other facilities will more nearly meet the particular needs if neighborhood and community variations are built into implementation and administration: One neighborhood may need athletic playing fields while another will be more satisfied with a nature park, a garden, or a playground for little children.

Relative efficiency in the use of public resources is a second criterion for good metropolitan policy. It requires that the investments and expenditures accompanying a policy produce outcomes that are more desirable than any rejected alternative. Explicit cost-utility evaluations can provide strong policy guidance in this respect; for example, the benefit/cost ratio is particularly useful in selecting among alternative projects for achieving the same objective—a park in this location compared to one nearby, or one scheme for collecting solid waste against another. Of course, this is only one of a number of criteria, and care must be taken that it is not allowed to override others. Decisions should rest on a broader base than simply a calculation of those benefits and costs that can be measured in dollars. Ideally, those who decide policy should have other kinds of information in addition to estimates of non-monetary benefits and costs, including appraisal of the impacts of program to be expected on health, on the environment, on social problems, on the regions' comparative advantage in the national economy and on aesthetic qualities.

A third criterion, stemming from this broader view of benefits and costs, requires that implementation of a particular metropolitan policy not only contribute to the solution of the immediate problem to which it is addressed but also ameliorate the broader array of social and economic difficulties in the region. Proposed metropolitan policy should be evaluated in terms of effects on such matters as the status and prospects for minority groups; the distribution of income among groups, with special attention to poorer people; the capacity and willingness of people to take part in their local government; and the general morale of the citizenry.

A fourth criterion may be stated in the form of a question. Will the proposed policy gain the acceptance and support of the citizens to the degree necessary for its success? Assessment of citizen acceptance and support will depend on skillful political examination;

N

presumably, experienced metropolitan politicians will be able to gauge political receptivity accurately enough to avoid measures doomed to failure from the beginning for lack of adequate popular support. Nothing is more frustrating to citizens than policies or programs that are ineffective because the citizens themselves, not understanding them, withhold necessary support in the form of votes, taxes, or cooperation. A greater role for policy sensitivity, however, needs to be complemented by an enrichment of political leadership in persuading citizens about what is needed and can be made acceptable. The schools, the various adult groups, and local media afford opportunities for exercising this leadership-information role with respect to citizen attitudes.

A fifth criterion for metropolitan policy calls for built-in mechanisms for improving the policy as it unfolds through a variety of programs and activities. Periodic reviews and evaluations of progress are essential. It is, of course, possible to err in the direction of too much flexibility: A given metropolitan policy, carefully and deliberately settled upon, must not be subjected to so much reconsideration that citizens become confused and their desires for specific policy outcomes become frustrated by those who may not have liked the policy from the beginning. The ideal is an appropriate blend of stability and flexibility in policy. Furthermore, new forms of political participation need to be tried if urban people are to have a wholesome attitude toward urban government and policies that will determine to a large degree how they will live. For example, the conventional forms of public hearings on cut-and-dried proposals put forward by technicians are no longer politically acceptable. Just as the citizens should participate in the formulation of policy in appropriate ways, they should also have the opportunity to take some part in its review and improvement from time to time.

Finally, new policies should be tested against the feasibility of administering them in an orderly and efficient manner. A necessary condition for any policy should be a capability for translating it into action, consistent with the canons of good administration.

There is no perfect way to state or to order general criteria for metropolitan policy. The essential point is that metropolitan policies designed to provide solutions to problems be tested against reasonable criteria. Such an analytical exercise is a strong safeguard against inconsistency among policies and against policies that are not well designed for achieving the intended objectives.

Furthermore, the mere statement of criteria on this broad and basic level will be instructive and will help citizens decide what they really want and have a right to expect from those who ultimately will decide most policy questions in their behalf.

ELEMENTS OF A METROPOLITAN STRATEGY

The principal function of a metropolitan policy is to provide the framework, within which, progress can be made toward desired objectives. Elements of this framework include incentives that lead agencies and individuals to move in the desired direction, regulations and penalties to discourage inappropriate actions, direct intervention by public authority when this seems to be required, and frequently a restructuring of relationships among the various governmental units involved. Metropolitan areas now represent such a complex set of activities and organizations that the first requirement is to view the metropolitan area as an organic whole. This view can be attained only through a carefully designed research and planning process, which can expedite "social learning" in the region with respect to its problems and potentials. What is the economic base of the region, its export products and services, its employment pattern, the required job skills, the income levels and distribution? What are the social characteristics of the population—the educational levels, health, racial and ethnic makeup, cultural characteristics, and the like? What capital equipment does the region have to work with; what technology; what transportation and communication networks? Without some depth of understanding of these matters, it will not be possible to understand what development objectives are attainable, much less to develop the plans and policies through which change can be directed.

Research into these questions is a prerequisite to more specific plans and policies for a metropolitan area in such matters as land use, transportation, public investments in facilities, utility systems, open space, and parks. Skeleton plans for each of these major areas are necessary elements of a basic strategy for metropolitan development. An early step in the strategy involves identification of those items that, for technical reasons, have to be planned on a metrowide basis. Of the several mentioned above, two types seem to be essential: the "connectors" (transportation lines, sewer and water systems, and perhaps other communications) and "spacers" (principally parks, open spaces, natural buffer zones, and the like). If skeleton systems are provided for the principal connectors and spacers, and to this is added a degree of planning for density or concentration of land occupancy and activities, then it is likely that the other elements in the total metropolitan system will fall into place. Connectors, spacers, and density form the skeleton of the modern metropolis; they can only be approached on a metropolitan scale, and without them, coherence of structure and performance of a metropolitan region will be impossible to achieve. Within this framework, great degrees of freedom for local action and initiative can be maintained.

Regional planning organizations frequently start off by following such a framework strategy but soon are drawn away into detailed planning activities simply because particular problems seem to be necessary or because funds or personnel happen to be available. Concentration on such detail diverts attention from the need to treat exceedingly well the planning of the strategic elements, such as transportation, land use, and open space. Federal and state programs, using financial and other kinds of assistance as lures for particular activities, magnify this problem, although regional planning groups have been known to fall into this trap without any outside assistance.

A central capability for planning the essential elements in a metropolitan framework does not assure that development will actually happen along the lines indicated in the planning. Implementing institutions and mechanisms are required. Hence, special regional authorities are sometimes established to handle the detailed planning, construction, and operation of particular public service systems in metropolitan regions such as rapid transit, water supply, air pollution abatement, and outdoor recreation. This approach seems to have worked best where the service can be sold or the physical and geographic case for a metro-wide agency is overwhelmingly persuasive. However, the special-purpose authorities can dilute the effectiveness of local governments by preempting both their revenues and functions and, at the same time, increasing the difficulties of achieving a coordinated approach to metropolitan problems across functional lines. In short, two or three functional authorities may present only modest problems, but eight or ten or more will not only come close to destroying local government but also may foreclose the development of more comprehensive approaches to regional problems. Nevertheless, a restrained use of special authorities offers significant benefits to the region, among them, getting some things done efficiently and providing an example and encouragement to local governments to increase effectiveness in all their programs.

Another institutional strategy for dealing with metropolitan problems would transfer particular functional programs away from local and even metropolitan jurisdiction to the state or federal levels. It is now argued, for example, that the financing and administration of income maintenance ought to be a direct federal program, not only because state and local programs have produced great disparities across the nation but because the number of welfare recipients has become very large (more than a million in New York City alone) and the costs have risen much more rapidly than the financial capacity of local and state governments. Similarly, there are advantages in transferring education, long a prerogative of local government, to the state level with its larger financial resources. Such a step might improve the effectiveness of direct federal aid to education and expedite the reduction of the disparities in the quality of educational services throughout the state.

Any serious consideration of metropolitan problem clusters quickly converges on the financial dependence of local government on property tax revenues, which respond sluggishly to changes in the economy and are more regressive than most citizens would like. A consensus is growing that one practical resolution of this problem is to be found in the direction of the income tax, either levied at the local or metropolitan level or rebated from the federal government, probably through the states. In fact, a bill submitted to Congress by the current administration provides a rebate to the states which would build up to $5.3 billion annually at the end of five years, nearly $24 per person per year on the average, about two-thirds of which would go to local governments. Hence, a metropolitan area of one million persons would receive around $17 million per year in rebated funds. Coupled with this revenue-sharing approach, is a program of block grants (or "special" revenue sharing) from the federal government covering wide ranges of related assistance categories. Actually, block grants could be directed to any problem cluster: regional transportation by whatever means (highways, bus lines, rail rapid transit, and perhaps other means); regional pollution abatement and management (water, air solid waste, and perhaps other types); and comprehensive crime prevention and control (drug abuse, delinquency, high speed police communications programs, etc.). Such grants would approach the general-purpose rebate in their usefulness to local or metropolitan units of government.

How many and which metro-wide programs are undertaken will depend ultimately on the resolution of the central problem—how to find the financial resources to carry on the programs at efficient levels. The problem confronting local jurisdictions is eased to the extent that federal and state governments provide funds. Experience has indicated however that local governments rely on these two sources at the price of program discontinuity and instability. Additional local sources of revenue for financing metro-wide facilities and services offer only limited possibilities.

Where possible, service charges may be levied to settle a major proportion of costs, current and capital, on users. While water and sewer charges can be expected to carry virtually all the costs of providing these services, in most instances, bus and rapid transit fares will not be sufficient to carry the full costs of those services. Depending on revenue policies, the fare box can be expected to defray a significant part of operating and maintenance costs. Because transit systems appear to exhibit long-run decreasing costs, and because they have to compete with the private auto, there is much to be said for low "developmental" fares to attract riders away from private automobiles. If successful, the costs of such a policy would be offset substantially by the benefits of reduced congestion in the densely traveled part of the region, in addition to those reaped by the transit riders. Hence, benefits would be broadly spread around the region, while the impact of the cases would depend on the source of the subsidy. How successful such a policy is likely to be will depend on the extent to which a particular transit system will be able to afford effective competition to the private auto, especially in the face of the continuing decentralization of trip origins and destinations.

Many metropolitan facilities or services do not lend themselves to user charge financing. Education, health, recreation, and public safety will have to be paid for, in large degree, out of general tax revenues. Shifting the responsibility for any one of these functions from the local jurisdiction to metro-wide operation will require new methods of financng. An obvious course is direct contribution to the metro-wide agency or agencies from the local jurisdictions. Another is through assignment of taxing power by state and local legislative bodies to the metro-wide organization. Another interesting possibility came to light last year in the Twin City experience: recently a bill advanced quite far in the Minnesota state legislature, under which, local jurisdictions would assign a large share of the increase in real property values from non-residential land zoned for more intensive use to a regional "pool" for reducing inter-jurisdictional disparities in fiscal capacity. A rough kind of justice is apparent here: the increase in property values resulting from rezoning is due partly to the economic growth and governmental decisions in the local jurisdiction where the property is located and partly to the general growth and rearrangement in the full metropolitan region.

However the financial details of metro-wide activities are worked out, the effectiveness of any metropolitan program will depend on the availability of adequate and predictable financial sources. A more metropolitanized approach to metro-wide problems would provide for some kind of favored treatment in federal and state financial assistance to programs undertaken on a metropolitan scale rather than a local jurisdictional scale. The federal open space acquisition program, as well as the recreational land acquisition program carried out with the federal land and water conservation fund, offer appropriate precedents.

In fact, any federal or state programs that are predicted on the establishment of a "workable program" at the local level could be treated in the same manner by favoring workable programs planned and carried out at the regional level. In such a carrot-and-stick approach, the federal or state government provides inducements favoring metro-wide workable programs, metropolitan regions in tax sharing, or review of local programs by a metropolitan planning and review agency. Where federal programs are administered through parallel state and local agencies as is the case in law enforcement, public health, and water pollution abatement, state agencies will have to be persuaded to favor metropolitan over strictly local approaches. The intense loyalty that most state legislators have to the traditional localities they represent will make this difficult: State legislators from the metropolitan suburbs tend to guard jealously what they call the "integrity" of their local areas, while a fair number of blacks and inner city patriots fear a takeover by clever, fast-talking politicians from the suburbs.

What then happens to the personal need for a feeling of neighborhood and small community, which was identified earlier as the other tier in metropolitan government that needed to be established more clearly? Progress in this direction will be made more difficult by movement toward metropolitanization that may reduce the scope and authority of the existing transitional local governments. A continuing initiative will be required from government and community groups to review government programs at whatever level they are administered or whatever the source of their finances, to see which program elements can be managed by community or neighborhood groups or in response to their needs. These will tend to be in the recreational and cultural areas of concern, at least in the beginning. To some extent educational, public health, informational, and other programs can also be decentralized to the neighborhood level. Means for coordination will be required at this level if full potential benefits are to be realized by the citizens. Many communities are experimenting along these lines by establishing neighborhood city halls or information centers. The essence of the model cities program is the focusing of as many separate programs as possible on selected poverty areas in major cities.

In cities with well developed local civic associations, experiments can be tried to increase citizen participation not only in local affairs but also in all metropolitan affairs that have a neighborhood application. Modest general purpose grants-in-aid to civic associations may trigger large returns in citizen participation and understanding. The City of Dayton is trying this kind of approach. An obvious candidate for new and creative administration at the neighborhood level is in the growing and vexing field of public welfare. As finance and overall management move away from the traditional cities and county level toward the state and federal level, it will be important that the administration of programs in many of their aspects be shifted in the other direction to neighborhoods and communities within existing jurisdictions. Unless the latter can be arranged, there is danger that welfare programs will become entirely disconnected from real-life situations and even more insensitive to neighborhood variations.

The general direction of coherent metropolitan policy is clear. Those urban functions that are clearly metro-wide in scope and interrelation should be shifted to an appropriate metropolitan agency with administration established at that level and, to the extent feasible, finance as well. The expectation is that as more special functions are undertaken at the metropolitan level, it will become increasingly apparent that some suitable instrument will have to be established to provide for direction and coordination. The existing voluntary councils of government, made up of elected officials from component jurisdictions, hold some promise of evolving into general government for metropolitan regions. Ultimately, the direct election of metropolitan legislators based on effective party politics will probably have to be instituted if the citizens of the metropolis are to exercise responsible control over their governance. This development can be pushed only at the risk of having such councils dismantled by the local politicians who comprise them and who are not ready to stand before their own electorates as advocates of metropolitan government—a term which has become a code word in many places for heedless, insensitive denial of the birthright of sovereignty of the citizens of whatever local jurisdiction one has in mind. However, powerful geographic, technological, economic and demographic forces are making the case for an enlargement of metropolitan government difficult to overthrow. The real issue is how to accommodate those forces, move with them, and create the metropolitan forms that can be sustained politically and financially.

Progress in the other direction, toward enhancement of neighborhood-level activities and approaches, may prove more difficult. People move frequently from one neighborhood to another; it is difficult to draw lines separating one neighborhood from another without exaggerating differences of income, race, and life styles. Decentralized administration, while it can be more sensitive to personal and local needs, is frequently more expensive. These are among the obstacles that come to mind. The strategy here seems to be one of constant search and pressure in the direction of placing as much responsibility for programs at neighborhood levels as can be done without too great a sacrifice of efficiency, financial adequacy, and common standards.

9

Externalities and Urban Decision-Making

BRITTON HARRIS

Professor of City and Regional Planning
University of Pennsylvania

There are a number of aspects of urban planning and policy-making which are of major interest to the social sciences and to Operations Research if the latter is considered in very general terms as a systematic search for better solutions to problems. In this discussion, I shall deal with two important issues while neglecting many others. These issues are embedded in the process of planning. First, the most simple-minded views of policy-making require some sort of prediction of the outcomes that will eventuate from the application of selected measures. Second, the search for improved policies is in general a problem of optimization—one which for large and complex systems is quite difficult. It is the modest purpose of this paper to examine, in a non-rigorous way, the impacts on these two processes of urban economies and diseconomies of scale and agglomeration. The results of this examination, while perhaps not intrinsically very surprising, may provide a somewhat better insight into the nature and some of the pitfalls of policy-making.

Economists and operations researchers are well aware of the fact that there is a duality between equilibrium and optimality. In well-conditioned situations, it is a primary principle of economics that a general market equilibrium can be identified with an optimal allocation of resources. This identification can be verified by reference to the elementary properties of the extreme values of a function. By extension, similar ideas may be applied to dynamic systems that are viewed as tending toward an equilibrium and therefore in the process of correcting any existing non-optimal conditions. A great deal of the energy of economists in developing theory and policy recommendations has been directed toward guaranteeing that these systems are in fact well behaved and that impediments to a rapid approach to the equilibrium are removed. In a slightly different context, Operations Research workers and economists have both been concerned at the micro-level with facilitating the types of rational behavior by the firm that would fit into this grand rationale and contribute towards its expeditious achievement.

Conversely, it is well understood that certain widely prevalent conditions militate against the identification of equilibrium and optimality. Amongst the most important of these are monopolies, decreasing cost industries, and externalities or spill-overs. These correspond in urban and locational affairs to a certain extent with ideas of indivisibility, increasing returns to scale, and the economies and diseconomies of agglomeration. There seem to be in general three principal routes for dealing with these difficulties. One is to levy charges for the external impacts of public and private actions. This recourse includes, on occasion, changing certain rules of interaction or organizational self-regulation. A second approach has to do with the regulation or public ownership of actual monopolies that arise as the result of decreasing costs. A variation on this is anti-trust regulation, which is probably the principal factor in keeping General Motors from being the only automobile manufacturer in the United States. A third recourse, which is perhaps a variation on the first, lies in the realm of game theory. This branch of analysis is ideally suited to analyzing certain types of cases that arise in this general context; and the analysis will often suggest possible changes in the rules and rewards, which may improve the outcomes of an otherwise pejorative situation.

My principal concern here, however, is not with this important aspect of economic theory but with another and equally troublesome one. Even assuming for the moment that an equilibrium situation is indeed optimal, in the situation we are discussing, this optimality may be purely local. The term "local" is being used in the mathematical sense, and implies that while small changes in prices, wages, factor allocations, and the location of facilities may in every direction lead to a situation that is no better, still there may be other combinations of factors whch likewise give the best available results in the immediate region—but results which may indeed be better than the first case.

The problem of local optimality in mathematical programming terms is the problem of non-convexity. Most of our rules for mathematical programming have been developed for continuous variables and convex response surfaces (or objective functions), as in the case of linear and quadratic programming. When the inter-actions between variables become more complex, even though the decision variables are continuous, this desirable property of con-vexity may disappear. The situation is even more difficult in the case of discontinuous variables. These lead rapidly into large-scale combinatorial problems formally similar to those which are en-countered, for example, in integer programming. Such problems are more resistant to solution for an *optimum optimorum* and are the subject of the development of many new techniques such as branch-and-bound methods and various types of heuristic pro-gramming. Characteristically, these methods are very closely re-lated to a particular problem and very much lacking in generality.

It seems to me that these concepts of non-convexity, multiple local optima, and search arising out of interacting ideas of dis-creteness and externalities have two principal applications in urban planning and analysis. The first and most natural application of these thoughts is to the economic problem of prediction. It is fre-quently assumed, and indeed I concur, that most people, insofar as their information, judgment, and resources permit, will act to optimize some utilities or profitabilities. I would even contend that in many important cases, the interaction of these strivings for optimality tend to drive a system to equilibrium and also in most cases to an over-all optimum of a Pareto type. But externalities may limit the scope of the system in finding paths and patterns of development and may lead to an equilibrium which is locally but not globally optimal. I shall provide below several examples of this situation.

As a corollary of this first point, we may see some justification for the insistence of some urban analysts on the importance of stochastic events. If these events are sufficiently large and carry with them sufficient externalities or non-linearities, they may change the direction of development and lead to a different local optimum which may be more or less rewarding. The second implication of this type of economic difficulty has to do with the selection of policies that will produce optimal results. Economists are accustomed to deal with optimizing problems in much less complex situations than are planners in the urban field, and it is not uncommon for them to arrive at a single figure such as a rate of interest or a price which satisfies certain very limited conditions of optimality. Where decisions are interacting in the complex ways that I have suggested, where they are frequently discrete in nature, and where there is a very large number of them, this charming simplicity of economic theory disappears completely.

My first example related to these problems has to do with the prediction of the location of retail trade. This may be done in a variety of ways, using a variety of models among which models with gravity-type distribution concepts are quite common and, I believe, relatively sound. Such models have been developed or used by Huff, Lowry, Lakshmanan and Hansen, Fidler, and myself [9, Huff, 1966; 11, Lowry, 1964; 10, Lakshmanan and Hansen, 1965, pp. 134–43; 3, Fidler, 1967; 6, Harris, 1964]. A somewhat less commonly used but equally relevant type of model is based directly rather than indirectly on central place theory, as typified by the descriptive approach of Berry's *Commercial Structure and Commercial Blight* [2, Berry, 1963].

Some of these models to a considerable extent evade problems of optimality and economies of agglomeration in the larger setting. For example, the shopping centers located in the Lakshmanan-Hansen model and the Berry model have more or less predetermined sizes. In the first of these, adjustments of size are made within a small range; and there is basically an all-or-none decision as to whether a particular shopping center would or would not be efficient. I imagine that if the Berry model were used to attempt to define an equilibrium, the size of shopping centers would have to be input on the basis of assumption—even though these assumptions are economically based and determined by analysis.

Models which, like my own, Fidler's, and Lowry's, have more or less continuous volumes of shopping located in metropolitan sub-areas rather than discrete units of predefined sizes need, if they are to be realistic, to embody some mechanism for creating clusters and concentrations of business activity. There are various mechanisms which move in this direction. One of these is the historical condition of the transportation system, such as the locaton of expressways, arterials, and mass transit facilities. This factor plays a decisive role in the clustering which takes place in Schneider's recent land use and transportation model [12, Schneider, 1968, pp. 164–77]. This model does not deal individually with different activities such as retail trade, but it is a continuous general equilibrium locational model that produces concentrations of activity. A second factor pushing retail trade in the direction of forming clusters is the location of demand. This in itself is already clustered, perhaps owing to the types of interaction posited by Schneider. Similar interactions appear in my retail trade model, which identifies all non-manufacturing employment as a source of demand for the services of retail trade. But there appears to be also a natural tendency for minor clusters to appear at regular intervals in a gravity model with a smooth distribution of demand and without any explicit factors pushing in the direction of agglomeration. This might be taken as a mild confirmation of some of the basic ideas of central place theory.

It appears, however, that partial equilibrium models of total location may not result in sufficiently peaked concentrations. A tendency to flatten out retail trade distributions appears to be inherent, therefore, in models such as EMPIRIC [8, Hill, 1965, pp. 111–20]. The nature of additional mechanisms seems to take two principal forms. One of these is a minimum size of cluster, which leads us directly back into central place theory and to procedures for shopping center location. This minimum size of cluster was applied by Lowry in his "Model of a Metropolis" [11] but the clusters were not really explicitly defined. The effect of a minimum size constraint on uniform square mile sub-areas is fairly clear, but their application to irregular shopping areas is much more obscure.

In my own model of retail trade location [6], the matter was dealt with in an equally unsatisfactory fashion from the functional point of view. It was assumed that the attractiveness of areas for shopping variety is a function of the density of opportunities in that area. This concept is preferable to one that makes attractiveness depend on the *number* of opportunities, except in the unusual case where all sub-areas are defined to be the same size. In these concepts, density might have an exponent ranging from zero to about two with the expectation (which was verified with actual data) that more specialized goods would have the higher exponent —that is to say, that in common with central place theory, this model predicts that some specialized goods will be found principally in larger and denser shopping clusters. These concepts are not wholly satisfactory because a large area with low overall density may contain a large, dense, and attractive shopping center whose attractive power would then be underestimated.

The preceding remarks demonstrate how a practical and realistic consideration of some simple and well-known locational patterns leads directly into considerations of economies of agglomeration and hence to non-linearities and local optima which complicate questions of equilibrium and global optimality. Not only is the gravity model itself nonlinear (possibly a trivial consideration), but any model which contains one or more of three features discussed above creates an intrinsically nonlinear programming or optimizing problem. These three conditions are: a minimum size constraint, a scale effect on attractiveness, and in the larger context, the interaction of supply and demand in influencing each other's location.

In a prediction context, the results of the equilibrium tendencies are clouded in two or three different senses. First, if we try to predict general equilibrium *de novo,* we find that the solution may be indeterminate. Thus, if the location of the central business district (CBD) is shifted, it may remain shifted—that is to say, from a locational point of view, any particular choice within a limited range for a high concentration of retail activity is locally optimal. In policy-making, the name of this phenomenon is sometimes the "self-fulfilling prophecy." The solution may even depend on the method of decision-making within the model, as appears to be the case to a limited extent with the application of Lowry's minimum size constraint. This objection applies also to central place models, where a rotation or translation of the pattern may be equally feasible.

If, in a slightly different case, the method takes as its starting point an existing pattern and makes incremental predictions, the situation may be somewhat more controlled. But insofar as developments are made discrete within the model, as with the procedures suggested by Fidler for locating new shopping centers, then each discrete decision affects the future development path of the prediction. Thus, in the first instance, the procedures employed are of critical importance. In addition, in the real world or in the stochastic model, mistaken decisions or decisions less than optimal have to be admitted, and these are influential in defining the outcomes. Finally, what is optimal for a small locator may not be so for a large one. Most particularly, a large-scale investor or group of investors may be able to open up a new territory and to create a subcenter within a metropolitan area which could not be created by a concatenation of small decisions.

All the difficulties that arise in projection (and quite possibly others) also arise in the development of planning policy. This line of development might be typified by reference to the Lakshmanan-Hansen model [10] which purports to optimize a plan by using equilibrium concepts applied to a preselected set of possible shopping center locations. In this case and within limits, a substantial virtue of the model is that it permits a selecton of shopping center sites without a large and costly combinatorial search. This, however, depends in a considerable measure on the restrictive assumptions of the model and on the limited number of sites which are input as possible locations. Characteristically we may regard planning as a means of removing some of these restrictions, and once the problem is thus enlarged, the search and optimizing methods become sensitive to all the considerations just discussed with regard to prediction. The way in which combinations and options are excluded in the planning and optimizng process can lead to prejudgng the solution in a less than optimal fashion.

Another example of important externalities in locational behavior has often been discussed, but its implications for theory and practice have been inadequately explored. This is the idea, well supported by conventional wisdom, that the choice of residential location reflects social preference as well as preferences determined by the need to travel and by the physical qualities of the neighborhood and the residence. Recent research that we have conducted has demonstrated the existence of these preferences in a remarkable and very interesting fashion. Since about 1960, there has been substantial interest in the potential of the Herbert-Stevens model [7, Herbert and Stevens, 1960] for reproducing residential behavior. This model, with modifications suggested by me [5, Harris, 1962; 4, Harris, 1966], represents a linear programming solution to the market allocation problem defined by Alonso [1, Alonso, 1964]. We have implemented various parts of the programming solution with no serious difficulty, but the

o

model formulation requires the prediction of bid rents; and this prediction, in turn, requires an understanding of the complete preference structures of households as they affect these bid rents. Our principal research was directed toward specifying these structures and their parameters, and in the course of conducting it, we encountered several very interesting phenomena.

In the Alonso and the Herbert-Stevens models, an observed rent surface over the metropolitan area should be regarded as the envelope of individual rent offer surfaces for families and households in various socioeconomic situations. While this concept is theoretically strong, it is to an extent statistically weak. The reason for this weakness is that we desire to predict a large portion of the rent offer surfaces of various types of households; but in any given market situation, only a small portion of those surfaces is directly revealed. The question at interest then becomes the behavior of the estimated rent offer outside of the range of observed behavior.

We succeeded in deriving well-defined and seemingly reasonable preference structures for up to seventy segments of the population, using census tract and other auxiliary data for the New York metropolitan region. When we projected outside of the range of observation, we found however that the higher-income households were given an imputed behavior that would lead them to offer excessively high bids for inferior housing. This finding illustrated amongst other things that we were not making any statistical use of the fact that high income groups did *not* locate in areas of inferior housing and that consequently their bids in these areas should be indeed lower than the going rates. We conducted many experiments for dealing with this problem, but the only satisfactory solution for the highest-income groups was to introduce variables measuring the accessibility to other high-income families, to low-income families, and to non-white families.

It is in principle possible that this explanation, offered by social preferences, could, in fact, be equally well measured by data on obsolescence, size of dwelling units, and selected unspecified neighborhood characteristics that did not appear amongst our variables. Since, however, density, age of structure, type of structure, and number of rooms were included, it seems doubtful that this direction of explanation would be satisfactory.[1]

---

[1] The results of this study are being prepared for publication.

It is quite obvious that the Alonso model and its basic modifications cannot deal with the externalities of social preferences in an equilibrium framework. The bid rents depend on the locational pattern, and the locational pattern depends on the bid rents. From any particular starting point, or test pattern, it probably is possible iteratively to reassign the population until an equilibrium is achieved; but this equilibrium is not unique. Remarks similar to those above about retail trade could also be made about growth model applications of the Alonso/Herbert-Stevens models. Not only do the outcomes depend n the starting point, but it also may be that the solutions are sensitive to stochastic events or to the algorithm employed by the model.

In a planning and policy-making context, the effects of these externalities are greatly to enlarge and complicate the problem of choice. Let us, for example, examine briefly a typical planning problem in different settings. We can imagine a debate regarding the feasibility of a particular urban redevelopment project designed to serve a specified clientele. Such a project, illustrating the present difficulties, might be the Society Hill Project in Philadelphia. This is designed to attract upper-middle-income residents and to serve a number of additional purposes, such as the preservation of an historical milieu and the enlargement of the participation of middle-class groups in the life of downtown Philadephia. The critical issue in such a redevelopment project might, in the first instance, be the feasibility of a particular pattern of offerings of new and rehabilitated housing. In a general sense, this represents a housing market study of a fairly conventional type, and the problems that it poses can easily be tackled through more or less standard economic analysis methods that have been elaborated and implemented over the last ten to twenty years. For studies of this kind, it must be recognized, however, that the ideas expressed in the present discussion imply that the size, location, and layout of any redevelopment project may critically affect its marketability and its success.

Now let us consider this same problem in the slightly larger context. One or more planning agencies and private developers in the larger region may be considering jointly a number of different projects for different income levels in different locations and employing different types of resources. The public agencies can influence private development directly through programs of rehabilitation and renewal. Decision-making is now made much more complex by the fact that each project influences every other project both directly and indirectly. For example, a low-income housing project will directly influence the desirability of a nearby upper-income redevelopment project through the kinds of social preferences that we have described. Indirectly, different groups compete with each other for housing space, and different housing developments or submarkets compete with each other for occupants. In this situation, the outcome of any particular decision will depend upon the other decisions already taken or to be taken. Any large number of determinations with regard to housing must be taken jointly.

The interaction of decisions in any one field such as retail trade or housing provides a sufficient basis in itself for identifying difficulties in prediction and optimization. When we expand our view to include a number of such issues jointly, matters become even more difficult. The combined consideration of issues is in part the basis for a "plan." Public agencies in particular have a very large number of options open to them in terms of zoning patterns, the location of redevelopment, rehabilitation, and public housing, the location of schools, libraries, and other public facilities, and the disposition of transportation routes, stations, and interchanges. Owing to interactions or spread effects, each of these decisions will affect all other decisions; and in the total context, particular parts of the plan may become inefficient or substantially infeasible.

This general sketch suggesting some of the roles of externalities in urban growth and equilibrium and in optimality in urban arrangements leads us into a consideration of the differences between planning and economic analysis that depend on these features. The first of these has to do with a slight but non-trivial divergence of views about continuity in development. The second, and perhaps more significant difference, has to do with the systematic treatment of optimality. I shall briefly explore each of these.

One cannot fail to be impressed by what appears to be a pervasive temperamental contrast between many planners, architects, and designers on the one hand and many economists on the other. One expression of this difference is a distinction between normative guidance of human behavior through regulation and public actions and reliance on more general structural rule-making with market interactions guiding behavior. In the second case, the economist would argue that there is more freedom for the individual without any necessary impairment of the goals of society—

always provided that the rules are appropriately framed.

There are a number of reasons for this difference in attitude, some of which are peripheral to our present concerns. There is, for example, a role for the designer and planner as a maker or initiator of new concepts in life style, taste, and aesthetics. In this role, his normative conduct might be considered as an effort to persuade, and the adoption of his norms in construction or legislation, as either an extension of or an acquiescence in that persuasion. Frequently the designer or planner focuses upon imperfections in the market or on particularly serious cases where monopolies or externalities lead to non-optimal outcomes, and here, the economist might agree with his judgment. On issues such as this, a much wider discourse would be desirable.

The important case for present purposes, however, is a question regarding the paths to alternate futures. It appears clear that both the economist and the planner can and do frequently accept the possibility that there are many alternative futures in urban development and that national and local policies can help determine our choice of these futures. In general, it would appear that the economist is more apt to be a gradualist and an evolutionist toward the selection of these futures, while the planner appears to be more willful and perhaps revolutionary—at least in the sense of desiring abrupt changes. Basically, this issue contains two related sub-issues. The first of these concerns continuity versus discreteness, and the second concerns the reachability of various possible new configurations.

I shall touch only briefly on the first of these sub-issues. Economic thinking is full of ideas of continuity in the mathematical sense, and I believe in the present context that these ideas of continuity across variables such as capital, labor, rates of interest, etc. tend to lead into concepts of continuity across time. There exists a strong presumption, however, that large-scale public works such as highways and dams, and large-scale public decisions affecting educational policy, welfare policy, or housing policy may be lumpy and discontinuous and thereby affect this continuity. At a larger scale, with wars, revolutions, and shifts in governmental power, these discontinuities are even more apparent. These ideas are not foreign to economic thinking, especially regarding public policy; but their interaction with externalities and with the planning process has not perhaps been adequately explored.

The second sub-issue concerns the possibility of reaching alternative futures. Some illustrations of how this arises in the context of externalities may be useful. It could be argued, for example, that our large metropolitan areas are improperly organized, in that some very large sub-centers should be established independently of the central city but connected with it, so as to provide for some of the amenities and economies of scale associated with the city center itself, but so as to avoid the diseconomies of great congestion and long travel times. Such an alternative metropolitan development pattern would require large-scale positive action to establish the outlying centers, but currently for most business locators the economies of scale which might inhere in such sub-centers do not yet exist and cannot be anticipated with certainty. Another example may be found in the probable need for the development of a new intra-urban transportation mode that could combine the advantages of public transit and the private automobile. Not only is the initial development of such a system a major undertaking but its capability of replacing the automobile system is problematical. This is because the automobile system has preempted a huge variety of facilities and arrangements devoted to it. There are great economies of scale in a single ubiquitous system, and this preemption would be very hard to overthrow.

I have purposely chosen two very large-scale examples of the way in which externalities and economies of scale tend to keep development on a single track. This is equivalent to saying that where all decisions are small ones relative to the size of the problem, the best progress that may be anticipated is to the nearest local optimum. If any alternative configuration offers a higher level of optimality, it cannot be reached by decentralized decision-making because such decisions would be individually counterproductive. This is an essential reason that planners and designers frequently maintain that substantial progress can only be made by an innovative jump, and that the economists' preoccupation with evolutionary adjustments leads into a dead end.

Of course, is it not at all obvious that any particular alternative that may be proposed to present circumstances is necessarily optimal or even desirable. I have so far only attempted to establish that in a world full of externalities, a revolutionary innovative approach is perfectly rational and perhaps necessary. I now turn to the question of the search for optimality, where there is once again a major difference between planners and economists.

The economist is accustomed to optimum-seeking under extremely favorable conditions. In the continuous case, he examines the appropriate conditions for equilibrium and optimality and, hopefully, is able to prove that his function is unimodal or convex. In this case, there is also frequently an explicit solution for the appropriate values of selected control variables. The constrained case may be somewhat more difficult, but as long as it is unimodal, solution methods may exist. These methods include Lagrangian multipliers, linear programming, and quadratic programming. It is rapidly becoming apparent, however, that the favorable and easily-solved cases for economic optimization represent a very limited subset of all possible cases. There exist, in the first instance, cases that are continuous but not unimodal. An example of this might be the generalized Weber problem with certain particular forms of the transportation cost function or of the location of demand or both. Discrete problems lead very naturally into multiple optima, and countless cases of these have been adduced. Most particularly, problems that lead to an integer programming or a dynamic programming formulation are apt to be in this class. It may be observed that, not infrequently, problems which are essentially continuous (such as route location for a highway) are formulated in discontinuous form to take advantage of specific known solution methods.

In general, there is a strong thrust in the various decision sciences and particularly in Operations Research to find ways of dealing more effectively with these discrete programming problems. It is distressing to note that most general solution methods are largely ineffective until they have been given a coloration due to the specific nature of the problem. Thus, for example, "branch-and-bound" refers to a general approach to the solution of this class of problems, but it is largely a vacuous method until the particular problem at hand has been analyzed and specific methods for its solutions have been developed.

There is, however, another aspect of these problems that may be perhaps still more distressing to the economist. It is the fact that, in most cases, the number of combinations to be explored increases explosively (exponentially or factorially) with the number of decisions to be made. In practice, this means that the elegant and complete methods which the mathematically-minded researcher is apt to focus upon will be effective principally for small problems. In the case of larger problems, a complete exploration of possible decisions is impossible; and some form of "bounded rationality" must be developed. The approximate search methods ("heuristics") which are used in these circumstances open the door wide for intuition and skill, and thus also for normative concepts and personal judgment. These the economist is apt to find disturbing, at least when engaged in by others.

In principle, the number of ways in which it is possible to deal with our incapacity to find a strictly optimal solution to complex problems is somewhat limited. A systematic exploration of these possibilities is perhaps the subject for a major research work. At this point, I can only sketch a few of the available options with a view to distinguishing various roles of economists in this planning activity.

The easiest path with respect to difficult economic problem-solving is to identify the complexity of the problem and to fall back upon judgmental and heuristic methods in much the same fashion as a planner or designer. This type of retreat from unbounded rationality is, in my view, quite respectable if freely acknowledged since it is the method by which human beings have been attacking the most difficult decisions for many millenia. No one blames a chess player for failure to conduct an absolutely optimal game, and indeed, despite centuries of experience, no one knows what an optimal game is; a win is patently only locally optimal. In these situations, the professional acts as a pure expert, and his rationality may be somewhat privileged or private. Having recourse to this stance is not particularly popular with economists because it lays them open to the same type of criticism and argument as might be directed against a less trained or more political proponent of particular ideas.

As a second possibility, therefore, the analyst may attempt to use certain formal methods for reducing the complexity of the problem. These methods include, for example, partitioning and hierarchical structuring. Partitioning suggests that several sets of decisions are mutually independent; this approach is bureaucratically popular since it is organizationally simple. A hierarchial structure implies that certain decisions dominate others; this expresses a mode of (possibly misplaced) rationality. One could easily expand this list of options designed to reduce complexity. The important point is that only to a limited extent do they actually express a superior rationality on the part of their users. More frequently, while they succeed in simplifying the manipulation of a problem, they do so at the expense of injecting a bias of the user —a bias which is often largely unconscious and hence perhaps more dangerous.

A third tactic that probably forms an important part of every designer's repertoire is to sample widely amongst all possible solutions. In problems of high dimensionality (that is, involving many decisions), the number of samples which may effectively be drawn is a minute proportion of the total space. In order for sampling to be effective, therefore, several additional conditions are helpful. If, for example, it is feasible to hill-climb rapidly to the nearest local optimum, comparisons between samples are facilitated. In this case, the structure of the problem may permit some degree of confidence that it is more probable that higher optima will be more likely to be reached. Similarly, the intuitions of the knowledgable expert can be used not to determine the solutions but rather to select sample points from which solutions may be developed. Techniques of this type are widely used in architecture and city planning under the heading of sketch planning, and in other situations, under the heading of brain-storming. Their use in economics is less widely acknowledged but probably quite prevalent.

Still a fourth approach would be to strive for a conscious and rationalistic merger of the earlier approaches. Utilizing this strategy entails a number of requisites. The nature of the decisions and their interactions must be clearly understood. The types of bias introduced by different search methods must be explored not just in general, but in relation to the structure of the problems. There must, in particular, be a clear understanding of the fact that no true optimality can be sought and that perfection must be sacrificed in the interests of abbreviating the search. Once this recognition is present, it is possible rationally to attempt to decide in what form this sacrifice may best be made.

In the process of trying to satisfy these strictures, it seems likely that a way will be opened for the gradual development of a meta-rationality—that is, for a rationality of incompletely rational search procedures. We are beginning to see the development of such a field through heuristic programming and through explicit considerations of the design process. It is my view that the distance between design and optimizing procedures is much narrower than the users of each set of methods would be apt currently to concede. It is my further view that progress is most likely to be made by

starting from a consideration of the inherent logical and mathematical nature of problems of optimality and of search procedures.
The so-called "protocols" used by designers for organizing their
work are not necessarily the best models for understanding
bounded rationality, although they may prove to be a fruitful
source of suggestions. This is because new developments in
mathematics are often counter-intuitive and because some aspects
of computers and computation may make feasible approaches that
could not previously have been considered.

Starting from very simple but widely understood ideas in economics, I have moved a long way into problems of planning and
design, and I have tried to show that these problems arise largely
because of the widespread violation of limiting assumptions of
classical economics and general equilibrium theory. These in particular have to do with monopoly and with economics and diseconomies of scale and agglomeration. Such features are particularly common in spatially distributed economic phenomena and
even mre particularly in urban economic phenomena. The situation is further aggravated by the pronounced discontinuities or
lumpiness that apply to many public decisions and public works.
I have tried to show in a largely descriptive and intuitive way that
these two features of urban public life lead to the possibility of
multiple local optima in the policy space. The recognition of these
multiple local optima leads planners and designers to adopt procedures which, at first gance, appear to be less rational than those
of the economists. It is apparent however that it will be necessary to develop systematic approaches to bounded rationality. In
this event, if other differences can be resolved, there is room for
a substantial cooperation and interplay of methods between concepts of planning and of economics.

REFERENCES

(1) Alonso, William. *Location and Land Use—Toward a General Theory of Land Rent.* Cambridge: Harvard Univ. Press, 1964.
(2) Berry, Brian J. L. *Commercial Structure and Commercial Blight.* Research Paper No. 85. Chicago: Univ. of Chicago, 1963.
(3) Fidler, Jere. *Commercial Activity Location Model.* Publication TP00–332–01. Albany: Subdivision of Transportation Planning and Pro-gramming, New York State Department of Public Works, Jan. 1967.
(4) Harris, Britton. "Basic Assumptions for a Simulation of the Urban Residential Housing and Land Market." Philadelphia: Institute for

Environmental Studies, University of Pennsylvania, July 1966. (Mimeographed.)

(5) Harris, Britton. *Linear Programming and the Projection of Land Uses.* Penn Jersey Transportation Study Paper No. 20. Harrisburg, Pa: Pennsylvania State Department of Highways, 1962.

(6) Harris, Britton. "A Model of Locational Equilibrium for Retail Trade." Paper presented at a seminar on Models of Land Use Development, Institute for Urban Studies, Univ. of Pennsylvania, Oct. 1964. Mimeographed.)

(7) Herbert, John and Stevens, Benjamin H. "A Model for the Distribution of Residential Activities in Urban Areas." *Journal of Regional Science.* 1960, 2 (2).

(8) Hill, Donald M. "A Growth Allocation Model for the Boston Region." *Journal of the American Institute of Planners.* May 1965, 31 (2), pp. 111–20.

(9) Huff, David L. *Determination of Intra-Urban Retail Trade Areas.* Los Angeles: Real Estate Research Program, Univ. of California, 1966.

(10) Lakshmanan, T.R. and Hansen, Walter G. "A Retail Market Potential Model." *Journal of American Institute of Planners.* May 1965, 31 (2), pp. 134–43.

(11) Lowry, Ira S. *A Model of Metropolis.* Memorandum RM-4035-RC. Santa Monica: The RAND Corporation, August 1964.

(12) Schneider, Morton. "Access and Land Development." *Urban Development Models.* Special Report No. 97. Washington: Highway Research Board, 1968, pp. 164–77.

Policy Location Games: Some Applications of Location Theory to Political Decision Making[*]

WALTER ISARD and TONY E. SMITH

Department of Regional Science, University of Pennsylvania

INTRODUCTION

Historically, an important branch of location theory has developed from analysis of a political policy problem. This problem, first studied by Hotelling, concerns competing political leaders, each of whom must choose a location (take a stand) along a continuum of possible policy positions on an issue. This approach, which is usually designated as the problem of location along a line, has been cultivated by economists and regional scientists concerned with the location behavior of competing economic firms in a linear market.[1]

Recently, we [(6) Chapter 9] have had occasion to extend this approach to the problem of moving from an inefficient stable equilibrium set of competitive locations along a line to an efficient set of locations along the line through the use of cooperative procedures. We have also had occasion to synthesize this approach with elements of Weberian location and agglomeration theory.

In the pursuit of cooperative solutions to reach efficient sets of location patterns involving more than one locator, which may involve location at several sites or at a single site of agglomeration, we have come to see how the Hotelling approach, in conjunction with the use of relevant cooperative procedures, can be extended and put to more effective use in attacking the political location problem for

[*]Part of the research of this manuscript was supported by a grant from the National Center for Air Pollution Control, Grant No. AP00842.

[1]See literature cited in Isard [(2) Chapter 7] and in Stevens and Brackett [(8)].

N.B. In Figures 2–10 for example, p corresponds to **p** in the text.

which it was originally designed. Since the analysis of this problem is of utmost importance to urban and regional analysts, we now wish to develop it further. That is, we wish to develop political location theory for the insight that it can provide into decision-making at the urban-regional level. (Incidentally, as we develop such theory, we may well move into new ground, which in turn, will allow considerable advance in the current location and agglomeration theory of economics and regional science.)

Generally speaking, the classes of urban problems that concern us are those in which local political leaders are confronted with one or more key metropolitan issues on which they must each establish some policy position. If we designate the set of all relevant policy positions as a *policy space*, then such decision situations for political leaders may be characterized as a *location problem* in policy spaces.

In choosing a location or policy position, we assume that each leader is motivated to maximize his own political support within the metropolitan area. The most interesting problems that arise in this context are those in which the political support accruing to any political leader depends not only on his own policy position but also on the policy positions taken by the other leaders. We designate such situations as *interdependent location problems* in policy spaces, or more simply as *policy location games*.

Probably the simplest form of interdependency which can arise in such contexts is direct competition for political support by the leaders. This is precisely the situation analyzed by Hotelling for the case of two political parties (or leaders) competing with respect to a single policy issue. Such "one-dimensional" policy location games are particularly simple in that the full structure of the problem may be depicted graphically. Hence, in order to illustrate the basic concepts and methods of analysis we shall first consider in Section 2 a one-dimensional policy location game for two metropolitan political leaders. We shall then examine, in Section 3, the more complex situation of two-dimensional policy location games, in which tradeoffs between two issues are possible. Moreover, this analysis will be seen to be easily extendable to any numbers of issues, i.e., to n-dimensional policy location games.

Since the equilibrium solutions reached in the situations of Sections 2 and 3 are inefficient, we then illustrate in Section 4 how the use of cooperative procedures may lead each political leader to an improved position—that is, a position characterized by a larger percentage of voter support.

Finally in Section 5, we suggest some further useful extensions and reformulations of the Hotelling approach and conclude with a few general remarks.

ONE-DIMENSIONAL EXAMPLE: A SCHOOL TAX PROBLEM

Consider a situation where two candidates (an Incumbent and his Opposition) are campaigning for mayor in a major Eastern city. Suppose this city's school system is old and needs major improvement. School bonds have been judged to be inadequate as a sole source of revenue. Hence, to meet costs, an increase in property taxes is being considered. But this potentiality has led to much resistance among the city property owners and has become the major campaign issue of the coming election. Both the Incumbent and the Opposition candidate recognize they must take an explicit stand on this issue.

For simplicity, assume that each possible position on this issue can be characterized in terms of the percent of the school improvement budget which should be financed out of additional property taxes. If we designate each such percentage as a campaign *policy*, p, and designate the continuum of possible policies $(0 \leqslant p \leqslant 100)$ as the relevant *policy space*, P, then the problem of choosing a campaign platform for these two candidates can be characterized as a location problem in the policy space P.

Consider the possible voter support which each candidate can derive from various policy positions. First, assume that the candidates each recognize from past elections that a certain percentage of the voters can be counted on to vote for one candidate or the other, for reasons totally independent of the current issues. Some always vote along party lines; others always vote for the incumbent, etc. Hence, these voters can be excluded from consideration in choosing a campaign platform. But we assume that a sizable majority of the voting population is attuned to the issues and is willing to vote for either candidate, depending on the candidates' relative positions on the issues. These voters, whom we designate as *issue-oriented voters*, form the main focus for the campaign strategies of each candidate.

Given a choice between the campaign policies of each candidate, who will an issue-oriented voter support? To answer this question, we assume that each issue-oriented voter has formed his own most preferred position on the current tax issue and is only willing to vote for that candidate whose policy position is closest to his own position. Hence, if we let V denote the set of issue-oriented voters and let p_v denote the most preferred position of voter v in V, then for any policies p_I and p_o of the Incumbent and Opposition candidates respectively, v will support the one closest to p_v. If we measure closeness between two policies p and p' in terms of Euclidean distance, say $d(p,p')$, then v will support p_I only if $d(p_I,p_v) \leqslant d(p_o,p_v)$ and p_o only if $d(p_o,p_v) \leqslant d(p_I,p_v)$.[2] Now, if we were to follow Hotelling's assumptions to the letter, we would assume further that v *always* votes for the policy closest to his own. But this assumption requires that each issue-oriented voter vote, regardless of how far the campaign policies of all candidates are from his own policy. In reality, such voters may refuse to vote, and at times, rally together behind some third candidate. Hence, to recognize these possibilities, we follow Smithies' generalization [(7)] of Hotelling's assumptions, originally formulated in terms of "elastic demand" behavior in spatial economics markets. We assume: 1) that the Hotelling assumption of full voter support holds only when some candidate's policy coincides exactly with that of the voter; 2) that when this is not the case, then as the distance from the closest campaign policy to any voter position p increases, a larger and larger percentage of the voters holding position p will refuse to vote for any candidate at all; 3) that this percentage increases *linearly* with distance; and 4) that no voter v in V will support any position p which differs from his own position by 50 percent or more (i.e. for which $d(p,p_v) \geqslant 50$).

With these assumptions, the support percentages for each possible pair of campaign policies p_I and p_o can be determined. We illustrate this in Figure 1. There we depict a situation where the Incumbent chooses a campaign policy advocating that 50 percent of the school budget be collected from property taxes ($p_I = 50$), and where the Opposition advocates that 70 percent come from property taxes ($p_o = 70$). Observe that all voters with policy positions closer to p_I than p_o (i.e., to the left of the policy $\bar{p} = 60$ percent) will support only p_I. Hence, in this range of policies, we have plotted the percentage of voters holding a given policy position p expected to

---

[2] For a discussion of the special case in which $d(p_I,p_v) = d(p_o,p_v)$ see footnote 3 below.

support p_I given p_o. For example, we see that 50 percent of the voters holding policy position $p = 25$ can be expected to support p_I, and that none can be expected to support p_o. Similarly, for each policy position to the right of $\bar{p} = 60$, we have plotted the support percentage for p_o given p_I.[3]

Finally, if we can determine the numbers of voters holding each possible policy position, we can then compute the total percentages of issue-oriented voters who will support p_I and p_o. To do so, we assume for simplicity that the distribution of voter positions over the policy space P is fairly even and that it can be approximated by a *uniform density* on P. This implies that the total percentage of voters supporting p_I is always proportional to the area under the curve of support percentages for p_I given p_o, as shown in Figure 1.[4] Hence, if we let $s_I(p_I/p_o)$ denote the total percent support for p_I given p_o, and observe that our assumption allows us to compute this percentage for each possible pair of policies p_I and p_o, we see that $s_I(p_I/p_o)$ defines a function s_I over policy pairs, which we designate as the Incumbent's *policy support function*.[5] In Figure 2 we plot this function[6] in the *joint policy space* **P** defined as **P** $= \{$**p** $= (p_I,p_o) \mid p_I,p_o \varepsilon P\}$. For example, if we denote by the point **p** $= (50, 70)$ the joint policy choices for the two candidates as depicted in Figure 1, and if we compute the incumbent's percentage support for this situation, we obtain $s_I(50/70) = 34$. Hence, we see that the locus of

---

[3]Note that our assumptions have not specified the percentage of voters holding policy position $\bar{p} = 60$ who will support either candidate. We assume below that the density of voters' most preferred positions is *continuously* distributed over the policy space, which implies that the set of voters equidistant from any two given policy positions is only a set of "measure zero" in the population V. Hence, the behavior of these exceptional voters can never influence the total support levels for the candidates, which are defined in terms of an integral over this density. But for sake of completeness, we assume that of those voters who choose to vote at all in such situations, half will support each candidate. In the case of Figure 1, where 80 percent of the voters with position $\bar{p} = 60$ are willing to support either candidate, we assume that 40 per cent supports each.

[4]For a demonstration of this result see Isard, Smith, *et al.*, [(6) p. 455, footnote 49].

[5]It is important to emphasize that while the above assumptions help to simplify the computations and graphical presentations, they are in no way essential for the analysis. We could, with the aid of computers and numerical methods, analyze problems with *any* well-defined distribution of most-preferred positions and support percentages. However, all the major ideas can be depicted within the context of these simplifying assumptions, and hence, we view them as illustrative devices rather than essential behavioral postulates.

[6]For an explicit definition of this function see footnote 50 Isard, Smith, *et al.*, [(6) p. 456].

P

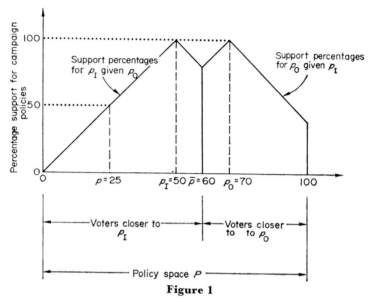

Figure 1

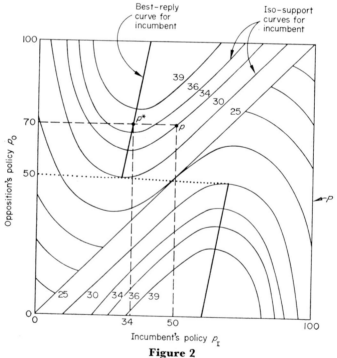

Figure 2

joint policies yielding the Incumbent a 34 percent level of support, i.e., his 34 percent *iso-support curve*, passes through the point **p** in Figure 2.

Next, observe that given an Opposition policy of $p_o = 70$, the Incumbent can actually do better than choosing a policy of $p_I = 50$. From Figure 2, we see that if he shifts his policy to the left, he can increase his percent support. Given this particular support position, his percent support is maximized if he shifts his policy to $p_I = 34$, corresponding to the point $\mathbf{p}^* = (34, 70)$ in Figure 2. At this position, his percent support $s_I(34/70)$ increases to 37.2. We designate this optimal policy position for any given p_o as the Incumbent's *best-reply* to p_o and designate the locus of joint policies involving a best-reply by the Incumbent as the Incumbent's *best-reply curve*. This curve is the discontinuous bold line in Figure 2.

Similarly, we may compute the Opposition's policy support function $s_I(p_o/p_I)$ and determine his best-reply curve. This curve is the discontinuous bold dashed curve in Figure 3, where we have

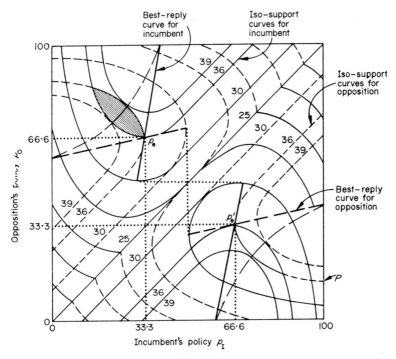

Figure 3

superimposed both candidates' policy support functions—the Opposition's support function being described by the dashed iso-support curves. From Figure 3, we observe that the Opposition's best-reply curve intersects the Incumbent's best-reply curve at two positions, denoted by $\mathbf{p}_e = (33.3,\ 66.6)$ and $\mathbf{p}_e' = (66.6,\ 33.3)$. These two joint policy positions, which correspond to mutual best replies for the candidates, have the unique property that once either of them is chosen, neither candidate is independently motivated to shift his policy position. Hence, these joint policies are designated as *equilibrium positions* for the candidates.[7] Note also than *any* sequence of best-reply policy adjustments by the candidates must converge to one of these two positions. In game-theoretic terms, this set of equilibrium positions is *globally stable*. Hence, if the candidates are able to estimate their own policy support functions, and if we assume that each candidate responds to the other's present campaign policy in a best-reply manner, we may then conclude that the campaign policy positions for the candidates will eventually stabilize in some small region about either $\mathbf{p}_e$ or $\mathbf{p}_e'$.[8]

Because of the obvious symmetry of these policy positions, we may focus on either one without loss of generality. To do so, assume that the Incumbent has in the past counted quite heavily on the support of community property owners and, hence, is quite sensitive to their demands. We might then expect him to start from some initial campaign position, advocating only a minimal additional property tax, or even no tax at all. On the other hand, we may suppose that the Opposition is out to win the support of the non-property owners in the community and advocates that required school funds be raised almost entirely by additional property taxes. In either case, we can expect that the best-reply process initiated by such campaign policies will converge eventually to the equilibrium position $\mathbf{p}_e$.

[7]Note that this pattern of equilibrium positions is in accord with Smithie's generalization of Hotelling. Under Hotelling's assumption of full support, the only possible equilibrium position is the center point (50,50). However, Smithies [(7)] observes that by introducing elasticity into the demand function, the equilibrium positions of spatial competitors need not coincide. In the context of our simplified example, we conclude that the more elastic the constituent's political support functions, the farther apart will their equilibrium campaign positions be.

[8]Note that such best-reply behavior by each candidate requires no knowledge of the other candidate besides his announced policy positions. For further discussion of this point see Isard and Smith *et al.* [(6) Chapter 6].

Given the position $\mathbf{p}_e$, however, observe that there exist joint policy positions which would yield both candidates higher levels of support, namely those in the shaded area of Figure 3. Hence, if both candidates are motivated to maximize their individual levels of political support, the equilibrium position $\mathbf{p}_e$ may then be considered as *inefficient* in the sense that there exist other positions which both candidates would prefer. However, such positions cannot be achieved independently by either candidate. The candidates must *coordinate* their campaign policies in order to do so, and thus, engage in cooperative as well as competitive efforts.

Before exploring such cooperative possibilities, we wish to extend this "one-dimensional" campaign problem to a multidimensional context. Such an extension leads to a range of more complex situations in which it is not possible to display geographically the full structure of either the patterns of equilibria or the regions of potential cooperation in the joint policy space. However, with the structure of the one-dimensional case in mind, it is relatively easy to see what such an extension involves. In the following section, we restrict ourselves to a two-dimensional extension, in order that at least the most important properties of the equilibria and the regions of cooperation can still be graphically depicted.

.

A TWO-DIMENSIONAL EXAMPLE: LAW-AND-ORDER AND POLLUTION

Suppose that in the mayorality campaign of the previous example the major issues are two-fold. First, in response to recent rises in the level of street crimes and violence, City Hall is presently considering the possibility of a major increase in the size of the city police force. Moreover, we suppose that general public controversy over "law-and-order" versus "police repression" has focused on this specific policy question and has escalated it into a major campaign issue.

Second, suppose that in response to recent increases in the level of air pollution, City Hall has, during the past year, imposed a system of taxation and penalties on air polluting activities to discourage pollution. However, the tax levels and penalties have proved to be too low to curb pollution significantly; hence, City Hall is presently considering an across-the-board increase in these impositions to render them more effective. But those groups most directly affected by the potential increase have succeeded in mounting a strong body of public opposition, which neither candidate can afford to ignore.

We therefore assume that both the Incumbent and Opposition have focused their campaign platforms in general on the two issues of law-and-order, and environmental management; and in particular, on the size of police force, and level of air pollution taxes (and penalties). They wish to form policy positions on each that will maximize their own support. To analyze the possible policies they may choose, we assume that each position on the police-force issue can be characterized by an advocated percentage change p^1 in police manpower, and that each position on the pollution-tax issue can be characterized by an advocated percentage change p^2 in the existing tax level. We may thus represent the set of all possible *policies* $\mathbf{p} = (p^1, p^2)$ for the candidates by the *policy space* $\mathbf{P}$ shown in Figure 4.

Now consider the possible voter support that the candidates can obtain from various locations in this policy space. We again focus on the issue-oriented voting population V, and consider the support behavior for a representative voter v in V. As in the one-dimensional case, we assume that each voter v establishes a most-preferred policy position $\mathbf{p}_v$ in $\mathbf{P}$, and that the density of these policy positions is continuously distributed over $\mathbf{P}$. However, we now drop the

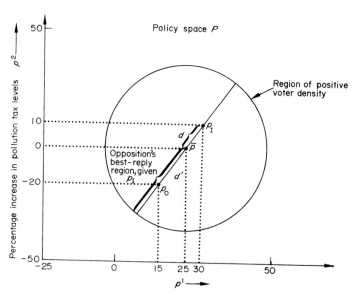

Figure 4 Percentage increase in police force Manpower.

assumption of uniformity, and assume that the density of voter positions falls off symmetrically in all directions about the *average* policy position of voters in V.[9]

Specifically, we posit that on average, voters in V favor a 25 percent increase in the size of the police force but no increase in the pollution tax level. If we designate this average position by the point $\bar{\mathbf{p}} = (25, 0)$ in Figure 4, we are positing that the density of voter positions clusters symmetrically about this position and falls off with distance from $\bar{\mathbf{p}}$. We take the rate of fall-off in density to be quite gradual in the region around $\bar{\mathbf{p}}$ and to increase sharply outside this region—as shown in Figure 5.[10]

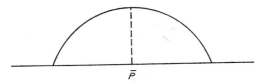

Figure 5 Diameter cross section of density function of most-preferred policy positions in P.

Turning to the voting behavior of individual voters v in V, we assume, as in the one-dimensional case, that v will only support that candidate whose policy is closest to his own position $\mathbf{p}_v$. We also assume for simplicity that each voter v's perception of "closeness" in the policy space $\mathbf{P}$ can be represented solely as a function of Euclidean distance d in $\mathbf{P}$. Hence, given policies $\mathbf{p}_I$ and $\mathbf{p}_o$ by the candidates, we posit that v will support $\mathbf{p}_I$ only if $d(\mathbf{p}_I, \mathbf{p}_v) \leqslant d(\mathbf{p}_o, \mathbf{p}_v)$ and will support $\mathbf{p}_o$ only if $d(\mathbf{p}_o, \mathbf{p}_v) \leqslant d(\mathbf{p}_I, \mathbf{p}_v)$.[11] Finally, we assume that the percentage of voters holding any policy position $\mathbf{p}$ who will support either candidate falls off from 100 per cent as the distance from $\mathbf{p}$ to the closest candidate's position increases from zero—falling off gradually in the near vicinity of $\mathbf{p}$ and more rapidly at greater distances from $\mathbf{p}$. For example, the function shown in Figure 6[12] may be taken to depict a portion of

---

[9]For a statistical interpretation of these assumptions, see footnote 12 in W. Isard and T. E. Smith [(5)].

[10]For an explicit formulation and analysis of this density function, see forthcoming manuscript by T. Smith.

[11]We continue to employ the assumption of footnote 3 for the case in which $d(\mathbf{p}_I, \mathbf{p}_v) = d(\mathbf{p}_o, \mathbf{p}_v)$.

[12]For a more explicit formulation and analysis of this function, see forthcoming manuscript by T. Smith.

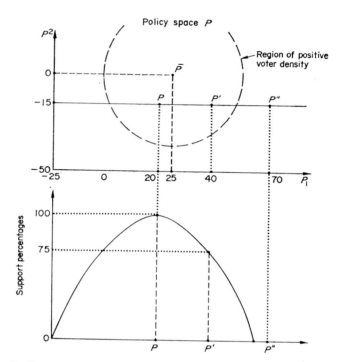

Figure 6 Support percentages for voters holding policy position **P** (for the subset of policies constrained by $p^2 = -15$)

the "support profile" of those voters most preferring a 20 percent increase in the police force and a 15 percent reduction in the pollution tax, *i.e.*, for those voters holding position $\mathbf{p} = (20, -15)$. Here we have plotted the percent of such voters who would be willing to support each possible policy in the subset of policies advocating a 15 percent reduction in pollution taxes. For example, we see that 75 percent of these voters would be willing to support, in that subset, a policy which also advocates a 40 percent increase in the police force, i.e., $\mathbf{p}' = (40, -15)$, but that none would go so far as to support, in that subset, a policy which also advocates a 70 percent increase in the police force, i.e., $\mathbf{p}'' = (70, -15)$.

   We may now imagine that each candidate can estimate these voter-support percentages together with the density of voter policy positions and that each can employ these estimates to calculate the percent support he would receive for each possible pair of policies that he and his opponent might choose.[13] For example, suppose that the Incumbent advocates a 30 percent increase in the police force and a 10 percent increase in the pollution tax, i.e., chooses policy $\mathbf{p}_I = (30, 10)$ as shown in Figure 4. Then if the Opposition assumes that only those voters with policy positions closer to his own policy position than to $\mathbf{p}_I$ will support him, he may use the above estimates to compute the total percent support he could receive from any announced policy position $\mathbf{p}_o$, given $\mathbf{p}_I$. As in the one-dimensional case, the Opposition could compute his *policy support function* $s_o(\mathbf{p}_o/\mathbf{p}_I)$.[14] Similarly, we also assume that the Incumbent can compute his *policy support function* $s_I(\mathbf{p}_I/\mathbf{p}_o)$.

As in the one-dimensional case, we may now ask: What is a given candidate's *best-reply* policy choice for any policy announced by the other? Given our specific functional forms, it can be shown that this best-reply policy for, say, the Opposition, given a policy $\mathbf{p}_I$ of the Incumbent, must always lie on the line (diameter) in Figure 4 coursing through $\bar{\mathbf{p}}$ and $\mathbf{p}_I$. Moreover, this policy response must always lie in the region of positive voter density on the side of $\bar{\mathbf{p}}$ opposite $\mathbf{p}_I$.[15] This locus of possible policy responses is designated in Figure 4 as the Opposition's *best-reply region*, given $\mathbf{p}_I$. Hence, we may conclude that given any policy of the other candidate, each candidate need only consider those policy responses which lie in his best-reply region—given that policy.

Now we consider more specifically the support levels which the Opposition can achieve, given the Incumbent's policy choice $\mathbf{p}_I = (30, 10)$ as shown in Figure 4. These support levels can be depicted as in Figure 7. On the vertical axis of Figure 7 we measure the distance from $\bar{\mathbf{p}}$ of any policy position of the Incumbent along the radius above $\bar{\mathbf{p}}$ in Figure 4. For example, the policy $\mathbf{p}_I = (30, 10)$ of Figure 4 is shown on Figure 7 to be a distance d from $\bar{\mathbf{p}}$. Along the horizontal axis of Figure 7, we measure the distance from $\bar{\mathbf{p}}$

---

[13]For a detailed development of one possible method of estimation and computation, see forthcoming manuscript by T. Smith.

[14]The discussion of footnote 5 is also pertinent to the assumptions used in constructing this policy support function.

[15]The fact that the optimal response to $\mathbf{p}_I$ lies on this diameter follows basically from the symmetry conditions postulated in the density and support functions. This fact is important for illustrative purposes since it permits the relevant policy space to be reduced to one dimension (and hence permits joint policy choices to be illustrated in two dimensions). The fact that the optimal response always lies on the other side of $\bar{\mathbf{p}}$ from $\mathbf{p}_I$ is a very special property of the functions chosen. For a more detailed discussion, see forthcoming manuscript by T. Smith.

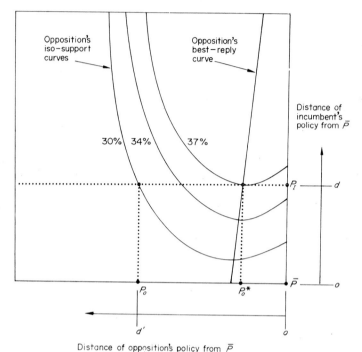

Figure 7

of any policy that the Opposition might choose in the best-reply region shown in Figure 4. For example, suppose that given policy $\mathbf{p}_I = (30, 10)$, the Opposition candidate responds by choosing a policy advocating a 15 percent increase in the police force and a 20 percent decrease in the pollution tax level, i.e., $\mathbf{p}_o = (15, -20)$ as shown in Figure 4. Then this policy is depicted in Figure 7 at a distance d' from $\bar{\mathbf{p}}$. Now suppose that the Opposition computes his estimated support level for this choice of $\mathbf{p}_o$, given $\mathbf{p}_I$, to be 30 percent. Then we may plot the joint policy $(\mathbf{p}_o, \mathbf{p}_I)$ as a point on his 30 percent iso-support curve, shown in Figure 7. Similarly, we assume that the Opposition can estimate his support for a number of other policy choices, given $\mathbf{p}_I$, and thereby (approximately) determine his best-reply policy to be $\mathbf{p}_o^*$ as shown in Figure 7. Moreover, we assume that for a wide range of possible policy choices by the Incumbent along the radius of Figure 4, the Opposition can also determine his support for a range of possible policy responses in his best-reply region. He may then plot out (by inter-polation) his iso-support curves and best-reply curve, as shown in Figure 7. Finally, observing that our symmetry assumptions imply that the form of these curves is independent of the diameter through $\bar{\mathbf{p}}$ which we choose to analyze, we see that Figure 7 effectively represents the Opposition's *entire* policy support function $s_o(\mathbf{p}_o/\mathbf{p}_I)$.

Similarly, we assume that the Incumbent can estimate his policy support function $s_I(\mathbf{p}_I/\mathbf{p}_o)$ and hence (approximately) determine his best reply to any policy choice $\mathbf{p}_o$ by the Opposition. If we then assume that the candidates always respond to one another in a best-reply manner, and observe that, given any initial policy position, the resulting sequence of best-reply responses must always lie on the diameter through $\bar{\mathbf{p}}$, we may effectively restrict our analysis to any representative diameter through $\bar{\mathbf{p}}$.

To do so, we superimpose the policy support functions for the candidates along a common diameter through $\bar{\mathbf{p}}$, as shown in Figure 8.[16] Here we have plotted the Opposition's iso-support

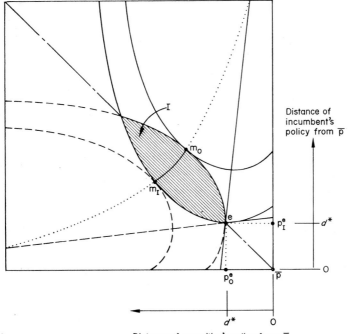

Figure 8

and best-reply curves as solid lines and the Incumbent's as dashed lines.[17] Now comparing Figure 8 with Figure 3, we see that this two-dimensional case has been effectively reduced to a one-dimensional case, which is in fact, very similar to the case we have already developed. In particular, we see that any sequence of best-reply responses must converge eventually to the joint policy position $\mathbf{e} = (\mathbf{p}_o^e, \mathbf{p}_I^e)$. Hence $\mathbf{e}$ is the unique equilibrium joint policy[18] for the candidates, and represents a *globally stable equilibrium position*.[19] Moreover, if we assume that both candidates are motivated solely to maximize their own voter support, then the equilibrium position $\mathbf{e}$ is *inefficient* in the sense that there exist joint policy positions that both candidates would prefer to $\mathbf{e}$; namely, those in the shaded area of Figure 8. But, as in the school-tax example, the achievement of such policies is only possible if the candidates can coordinate their policies through some form of *cooperation*.

POSSIBLE COOPERATIVE PROCEDURES

Let us now designate the set of joint policies yielding each candidate a higher support than $\mathbf{e}$ (i.e., the shaded area in Figure 8) as the *improvement set* $\mathbf{I}$ for this policy location game.[20] As an initial basis for any cooperation, we assume that neither candidate will consider agreements that reduce his support relative to $\mathbf{e}$, i.e., that each considers only those joint policies in $\mathbf{I}$ as potential agreement positions. But observe from Figure 8, that within this set, the joint

---

[16]Since the best-reply regions for each candidate are always on opposite sides of $\bar{\mathbf{p}}$, we have only shown the relevant radius for each candidate.

[17]Observe that our symmetry assumptions imply that these two functions are reflectively symmetric, as shown in Figure 8.

[18]To be more precise we should say that $\mathbf{e}$ is the unique equilibrium position on the particular diameter we have chosen to analyze. In other words, $\mathbf{e}$ is unique up to the choice of an initial policy position for the sequence of best-reply policy responses.

[19]More precisely, the set of equilibrium policies corresponding to all possible initial policy proposals forms a *globally stable set* of equilibrium policies. From our symmetry assumptions this set is easily seen to be the set of all policy pairs $(\mathbf{p}_I, \mathbf{p}_o)$ satisfying $d(\mathbf{p}_I, \bar{\mathbf{p}}) = d(\mathbf{p}_o, \bar{\mathbf{p}}) = d^*$ and $d(\mathbf{p}_I, \mathbf{p}_o) = 2d^*$ such as the pair $(\mathbf{p}_I^e, \mathbf{p}_o^e)$ in Figure 8.

[20]More formally,

$$\mathbf{I} = \{(\mathbf{p}_I, \mathbf{p}_o) \, \epsilon \, \mathbf{P} \times \mathbf{P} \mid s_\alpha \, (\mathbf{p}_\alpha \mid \mathbf{p}_\beta) \geq s_\alpha(\mathbf{p}_\alpha^e \mid \mathbf{p}_\beta^e) \}, \, \alpha \neq \beta\} \quad \alpha, \beta = I, o.$$

policy yielding the Incumbent a maximum support level is $\mathbf{m}_I$, while the maximum support position for the Opposition candidate is $\mathbf{m}_o$. Hence, there exists a basic conflict of interests regarding a joint policy. It is this conflict which must be resolved if any joint policy agreement is to be reached.

Elsewhere we have developed a number of cooperative procedures that might be utilized in resolving this conflict.[21] Hence, we shall illustrate only a few possibilities at this time. To begin, recall that in individually determining their best-reply policy responses to one another, each candidate need consider only his potential support from among the issue-oriented voting population V. However, in entering into a possible mutual agreement (implicitly or explicitly), each candidate may well wish to consider relative support from the *total* voting population. Suppose that past voting histories indicate that about 75 percent of the voters tend to be *issue-oriented*. From among the remaining 25 percent, the Incumbent has always enjoyed a slight edge in support—perhaps reflecting a tendency of nonissue-oriented voters to persist in voting for the party in power. In particular then, history suggests that the Incumbent can expect to win about 14 percent from this 25 percent; and the Opposition, the remaining 11 percent. Using these percentage figures, we can then determine the Incumbent's *total percent support*, t_I, as follows: $t_I(\mathbf{p}_I/\mathbf{p}_o) = 14.0 + (.75)s_I(\mathbf{p}_I/\mathbf{p}_o)$. Similarly, the Opposition' s*total percent support*, t_o, is given by $t_o(\mathbf{p}_o/\mathbf{p}_I) = 11.0 + (.75)s_o(\mathbf{p}_o/\mathbf{p}_I)$. On the enlarged portion of Figure 8, shown in Figure 9, we have plotted the total percent support for each candidate.

If the candidates take these total percentage figures to be fully comparable, we may consider as a first possibility that neither candidate is willing to agree to any joint policy position that yields the other candidate a higher total support level than his own. In this case, the only agreement possibilities remaining in the improvement set $\mathbf{I}$ are those joint policies $(\mathbf{p}_I, \mathbf{p}_o)$ for which $t_I(\mathbf{p}_I/\mathbf{p}_o) = t_o(\mathbf{p}_o/\mathbf{p}_I)$. The joint policies satisfying this condition are those which lie on the dashed curve inside $\mathbf{I}$ in Figure 9. From among these joint policy positions, the unique position yielding each candidate a maximum level of total support is defined by point $\mathbf{s}_1$ in $\mathbf{I}$. Thus, the candidates might be willing to settle on $\mathbf{s}_1$ as a *maximum equal-support solution* to their policy location game.

---

[21]For example see Isard, Smith, *et al.* [(6), Chapters 6 and 7], and Isard and Smith, [(3) and (4)].

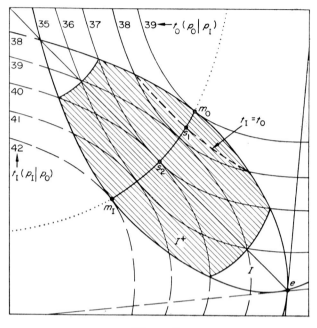

Figure 9

As a second possibility, observe that the Incumbent may consider $\mathbf{s}_1$ unacceptable for the following reason. At the equilibrium position $\mathbf{e}$, he enjoys a 3 percent edge in support over the Opposition. So, while his total support is increased at $\mathbf{s}_1$, he loses his position of relative advantage over the Opposition. Hence, if for any joint policy $(\mathbf{p}_I, \mathbf{p}_o)$, we designate the difference between the total supports $t_I(\mathbf{p}_I/\mathbf{p}_o)$ and $t_o(\mathbf{p}_o/\mathbf{p}_I)$ for the candidates as their *strategic positions relative to* $(\mathbf{p}_I, \mathbf{p}_o)$, then the candidates may wish to consider only those joint policies in $\mathbf{I}$ that preserve their strategic positions relative to $\mathbf{e}$. The set of joint policies in $\mathbf{I}$ that satisfy this condition are those that lie on the solid diagonal line through $\mathbf{e}$ in Figure 9. From among these joint policy positions, the unique position yielding each candidate a maximum total support level is the point $\mathbf{s}_2$ in $\mathbf{I}$. Thus the candidates may be willing to agree on $\mathbf{s}_2$ as a *maximum equal-support-increments solution* to their policy location game.

Observe, however, that in both the above solution procedures, we have assumed implicitly that those issue-oriented voters who choose not to support either candidate do not vote at all, and hence can be ignored. But suppose that these "abstaining voters" throw their support behind some third candidate who more adequately represents their views. If there is a sufficiently large number of abstainers, this third candidate can pose a serious threat to both the Incumbent and the Opposition candidates. Hence, the Incumbent and Opposition candidates may also be motivated to reach an agreement in order to minimize the percent of abstainers and the potential threat of a third candidate. Specifically, suppose that past voting experience has shown that the likelihood of a third candidate emerging rises sharply as the level of abstention increases beyond 25 percent of the voting population. Then, the Incumbent and Opposition candidates might both be motivated to ensure that, together, they control at least 75 percent of the possible votes. In this case, we may observe from Figure 9 that since $t_I(\mathbf{p}_I^e/\mathbf{p}_o^e) = 38$ and $t_o(\mathbf{p}_o^e/\mathbf{p}_I^e) = 35$, the two major candidates together capture only 73 percent of the possible votes at their equilibrium position $\mathbf{e}$. Hence, the candidates might be motivated to restrict their consideration to that subset of possible policy combinations in the improvement set $\mathbf{I}$ which permits them together to capture at least 75 percent of the votes. This subset, the shaded area of $\mathbf{I}$ in Figure 9, is denoted by $\mathbf{I}^+$.[22] From Figure 9, this restriction to $\mathbf{I}^+$ does not alter the above solution procedures since $\mathbf{s}_1$ and $\mathbf{s}_2$ are both elements of $\mathbf{I}^+$. In general, however, such additional constraints may exclude many possible solutions from consideration.[23]

To motivate one final class of procedures, observe that our two previous solutions both yield easily identifiable solution points ($\mathbf{s}_1$ and $\mathbf{s}_2$, respectively). But since the Incumbent surely prefers $\mathbf{s}_2$ to $\mathbf{s}_1$ and since the Opposition surely prefers $\mathbf{s}_1$ to $\mathbf{s}_2$, we see that any joint consideration of such cooperative solution procedures may, in fact, dissolve into a conflict over which cooperative procedure to use. We have discussed this problem at length elsewhere. We have sought to construct procedures which, while guaranteeing both candidates some degree of mutual improvement, would at the same time permit the candidates to determine the final agreement position only through a sequence of small incremental agreements, whose final outcome cannot be predicted beforehand.[24]

---

[22]More precisely, $\mathbf{1}^+ = \{(\mathbf{p}_I , \mathbf{p}_o) \; \epsilon \; \mathbf{I} \mid t_I(\mathbf{p}_I/\mathbf{p}_o) + t_o(\mathbf{p}_o/\mathbf{p}_I) \geq 75\}$.

[23]Moreover, such restrictions may in fact leave no feasible solutions at all. This would be the case if, say, 80 percent rather than 75 percent was the cutoff level. For this stronger restriction, $\mathbf{I}^+$ is empty.

[24]See Isard, Smith, *et al.* [(6) pp. 309–25].

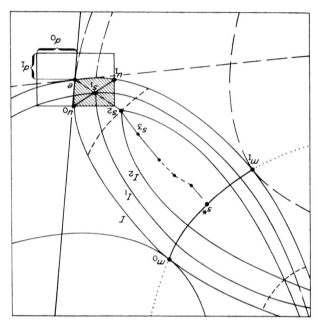

Figure 10

One possible "incremax" procedure is depicted in Figure 10. Here we suppose that in considering an incremental movement from their present stalemate position **e**, each candidate is willing to consider only those policy positions for himself which are within some small distance of his present policy. Hence, if these "distance limits" for the Incumbent and Opposition candidates are designated by d_I and d_o respectively, the set of joint policies that the candidates might consider is depicted by the box around **e** in Figure 10. Here we see that $d_o > d_I$, indicating that the Opposition candidate is—at least initially—willing to consider slightly larger shifts in his policy position from **e** than is the Incumbent. Once these limits are established, it is clear that the only policies open for consideration on the first round of bargaining are those in the intersection of this box with the improvement set **I**, as shown by the shaded area of Figure 10. But within this set of policies, the Incumbent can achieve his highest support at position $\mathbf{u}_I$, while the Opposition achieves his highest support at $\mathbf{u}_o$. Hence, even within this small range of policies, there is a conflict of interest. As one possible resolution of this difficulty, we may suppose that the candidates are each willing to go "half-way" in resolving their small policy differences and hence to settle on the policy s_1 which is midway between u_l and u_o. Hence, this "split-the-difference" procedure yields s_1 as a first-round agreement in the improvement set I. But relative to s_1, there is still a range of jointly preferred policies, namely those in the improvement set I_1 of Figure 10. Hence, the candidates may be motivated to consider a second round of incremental bargaining, leading say to the position s_2 in I_1. But again we see that further improvement is possible relative to s_2, namely those policies in the improvement set I_2, and so on. Given our assumptions, this series of bargaining rounds must lead eventually to some position, such as s^*, on the locus of (Pareto) efficient policies between m_l and m_o. Moreover, since the exact nature of this sequence depends on the policy restrictions at each step, the final position s^* cannot be predicted beforehand.

CONCLUDING REMARKS

We now have treated two types of situations in which we have extended the Hotelling approach to political location problems involving elements of cooperation as well as conflict. In Section 2, we restated the Hotelling approach, as modified by Smithies for the problem where two political leaders are competing in one dimension for political support. In Section 3 we examined their competitive behavior in a two-dimensional policy space. In Section 4, we demonstrated how cooperative procedures can be effectively used in the competitive location problem of Section 3, and where they, in fact, may be employed to reach an efficient, or at least a better location (policy position) for each participant. Since Figures 8 and 3 are parallel in basic structure, the discussion of the cooperative procedures that might be relevant for the political situation of Section 3 is applicable to the political situation of Section 2.

There is a rich variety of other political-type and nonpolitical-type situations to which the reformulation and extension of the Hotelling approach can be fruitfully employed, in conjunction with the use of cooperative procedures and related analysis. Elsewhere, we have already demonstrated [(5)] for another important type of political situation how leaders, having reached—via independent actions—a deadlock situation involving inconsistent (incompatible) policy proposals, can be motivated (or induced) to adopt a *common*

Q

policy. The adoption of a common policy, based on the use of a cooperative procedure, such as those mentioned in Section 4, is equivalent to *political agglomeration.*

A number of other types of situations are of interest and relevance; for example, those that arise when three or more political leaders are involved in choosing a location in political space, and where coalitions are possible.[25] These, too, are beyond the scope of this essay.

In conclusion then, the main purpose of this paper is to illustrate the kinds of contributions that the location theory of economics and regional science—as developed by Professor Edgar M. Hoover and others—can now make to the analyses of basic problems in the political and policy arenas. And, as already suggested, explorations and analyses of situations in such arenas will undoubtedly stimulate the more effective development of location theory in economics and regional science.

REFERENCES

(1)   Hotelling, H. "Stability in Competition" in G. J. Stigler and K. E. Boulding, eds, *Readings in Price Theory*. Chicago: Irwin, 1952, pp. 467–84, and *Economic Journal*, March 1929, *39*, pp. 41–57.

(2)   Isard, Walter. *Location and Space-Economy*. Cambridge, Massachusetts: M. I. T. Press, 1956.

(3)   Isard, Walter and Smith, Tony E. "On Political Conflict Resolution in Policy Spaces". *Papers, Peace Research Society, International, 14*, 1970.

(4)   Isard, Walter and Smith, Tony E. "On Social Decision Procedures for Conflict Situations." *Papers, Peace Research Society, International, 8*, 1968.

(5)   Isard, Walter and Smith, Tony E. "The Major Power Confrontation in the Middle East: Some Analysis of Short-Run, Middle-Run, and Long-Run Considerations." *Papers, Peace Research Society, International, 15*, 1971.

(6)   Isard, Walter and Smith, Tony E., *et al. General Theory: Social, Political, Economic and Regional.* Cambridge, Massachusetts: M.I.T. Press, 1969.

(7)   Smithies, Arthur. "Optimum Location in Spatial Competition." *Journal of Political Economy*. June 1941, *44*, pp. 423–39.

(8)   Stevens, Benjamin H. and Brackett, Carolyn A. *Industrial Location*. Bibliography Series No. 3, Regional Science Research Institute. U.S. Government Printing Office.

---

[25]For example, see Isard, Smith, *et al.* [(6) Chapters 8, 9, and 16] for suggestions of relevant directions.

Population Policy, Welfare, and Regional Development

IRA S. LOWRY*

The RAND Corporation, Santa Monica, California

INTRODUCTION

An agency of government charged with planning regional development can hardly avoid a triple perspective on the population of
the region over which it has jurisdiction. First, this population is
the agency's clientele, whose welfare is the object of planning.
Second, as a labor force, this same population is a primary resource
for the creation of wealth. Third, the population consumes scarce
resources which might otherwise be used to increase the productive
capacity of the economy. For wealthy regions, the implicit conflict
among these perspectives is attenuated by the general abundance
of means. For poor regions, the conflict is more evident.

From the welfare perspective, the generally accepted objective
of development planning is to raise real income per capita. (There

*Any views expressed in this paper are those of the author. They should
not be interpreted as reflecting the views of the Rand Corporation or the
official opinion or policy of any of its governmental sponsors.

This paper was prepared for the Conference on Regional Development
Planning organized by Cornell University and the University of Puerto Rico
and held in Rio Piedras, Puerto Rico, March 29–31, 1967. It was prepared
while the author was on leave from the Rand Corporation as a visiting
lecturer in the Department of City and Regional Planning, Massachusetts
Institute of Technology. The author gratefully acknowledges financial support provided by that Department, by the Harvard-M.I.T. Joint Center for
Urban Studies, and by the sponsors of the conference.

D. Gordon Bagby, Department of City Planning, Harvard University, greatly
assisted in the research for this paper (which was written in 1968).

is no general agreement as to the appropriate distribution of this income among components of the population, although there seems to be a consensus that extreme inequalities are "bad.") But there are two ways to increase the magnitude, "income per capita." One is to increase the numerator, income. The other is to decrease the denominator, population.

Since World War II, most development economists have designed their models of national and regional development in a way that emphasizes the factors that might be manipulated so as to increase the aggregate income of the community—factors such as the stock of capital, the technology of production, the organization of markets. Taking the rapid growth of population in poorest regions as a troublesome "given," they have sought solutions in measures designed to achieve an even more rapid growth in aggregate income. To date, this strategy has relatively few successes to its credit.

A plausible account of the failure of income-increasing measures to result in higher incomes per capita is provided by models of the "low-income trap" developed independently by Nelson and Liebenstein in the middle 1950s [(13), Nelson, 1956; (9), Liebenstein, 1957]. These models begin with the assumption that both the rate of capital accumulation and the rate of population growth are themselves functions of the level of per capita income (given the pattern of income distribution). As per capita income increases above subsistence, so does the propensity to save, hence the possibility of capital accumulation which, in turn, increases aggregate output. On the other hand, as consumption rises above subsistence, the death rate is assumed to fall; and the rate of population growth consequently increases. If per capita incomes rise substantially and the higher level of living is sustained over a considerable time, it is assumed that the birth rate will eventually decline as it has done in industrially advanced regions. The likelihood of entrapment at a "low-level equilibrium" results from the more immediate response of the death rate to rising incomes. In the short run, the rapid increase in population is likely to offset the conceivable increments of output due to capital accumulation, and per capita income returns to the subsistence level, halting further capital accumulation.

This model suggests two complementary programs to escape from the low-income trap. One is the massive importation of capital, so that the region's ability to increase output does not depend on the ability of its citizens to save out of low per capita incomes. To be effective, such a program would have to persist certainly for a generation, in view of the observed lags in fertility-response to rising income. The other policy is one that addresses itself to reducing the rate of population growth and is generally conceived in terms of publicly-sponsored programs to popularize both the techniques and values of "family planning," i.e., of reducing the birth rate.

Most economists feel a bit out of their depth on the topic of birth control. Beyond widespread agreement that it would be a good idea, there is much uncertainty about the means, costs, and effectiveness of such programs. But according to one serious estimate, $5 spent on birth control in a developing country with a per capita income of $200 would have the same economic benefit as capital investment of $200 [(2), Coale, 1967].

This essay explores both the rational objectives and the alternative methods of population control as an instrument of regional development—bearing in mind the conflicting perspectives indicated in its first paragraph. The ideas presented would require considerable quantification before they could be applied to any concrete case, but it seems to me that they illuminate a dimension of regional development policy which is much in need of light.

THE CONCEPT OF OPTIMUM POPULATION

The theory of optimum size for the population of a nation or region was discussed at considerable length by economists, sociologists, and demographers from the early 1920s to the end of World War II. It has since almost dropped out of the literature.[1]

---

[1] I have not made a thorough search of the extensive postwar literature in development economics, but it is safe to say that in general the population problem is perceived in terms of a given rate of growth with respect to which other variables (e.g., the rate of capital accumulation) must be optimized. One exception is a brief exposition of the theory of optimum population size in Enke's *Economics for Development* [(4), 1963].

For a spirited review o fthe earlier controversy, see Gottlieb [(7), 1945]. Among the other participants in the discussion were Edwin Cannan, Lionel Robbins, Knut Wicksell, Alva and Gunnar Myrdal, A. B. Wolfe, P. Sargent Florence, A. M. Carr-Saunders, and Warren H. Thompson.

Professor Spengler, at least, has kept the torch burning. See his Presidential Address to the 78th Annual Meeting of the American Economic Association [(15), Spengler, 1966].

The optimalists took the view that a steady increase in population, given a fixed supply of arable land and other natural resources, implied eventual diminishing returns to labor in agriculture and extractive industries—the classical Malthusian view. The anti-optimalists saw in manufacturing a mode of production with constant returns to scale and indefinite possibilities of balanced growth through capital accumulation. Those regions threatened with diminishing returns in essential resource-intensive activities could specialize in manufacturing and import food and raw materials.

By 1940, the impact of the Great Depression and of Keynes's *General Theory* was apparent in the literature. The question was then posed whether a stationary population in a capitalist economy would provide enough investment opportunities to maintain full employment. If not, the "optimum" population can only be defined as one that is growing rapidly, thus creating demands for capital-intensive infrastructure as well as offering expanded consumer markets for all industry [(8), Hansen, 1939]. Today, there are few who would take this view.

I propose to resuscitate and develop the earlier but still pertinent concept of optimality. I will do this in two steps, first by defining the optimum size of labor force for a nation or region, then by defining the optimum size of the population from which this labor force is drawn. The criterion of optimality in both cases is maximum income per capita (without regard for distribution). My model is based on the following assumptions.

Aggregate regional output is a function of the resource endowment of the region, its inherited stock of capital, the size of its labor force, and the state of technology. Each of the three factors of production—resources, capital, and labor—is homogeneous,[2] having only the dimension of quantity. The production function offers increasing returns to scale over some part of this range; thereafter, returns to scale may be either constant or decreasing. Holding inputs of any two factors fixed, there exists a level of input for the third, beyond which, increments of input yield diminishing returns.

At any particular time, the state of technology, the stock of

---

[2]This is a difficult assumption to maintain in any extended discussion of macro-economic problems. I am occasionally conscious of fudging it in the pages that follow.

capital, and the quantity of resources of the region are "fixed" in this sense. If we vary the quantity of labor inputs, the marginal product of labor first increases, then decreases. (See Figure 1.) Our object is to select that quantity of labor which yields the largest average product. Under the assumptions of the preceding paragraph, such a maximum exists at L_0, and it will be an interior maximum.

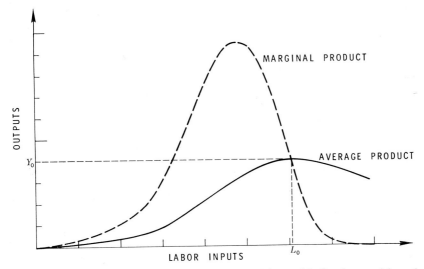

Figure 1 Marginal and average products of labor with fixed quantities of capital and other resources

At low levels of labor input, marginal product is small and increases but slowly, despite the relative ubiquity of capital and natural resources. This is because a small number of workers cannot take advantage of the efficiencies that come from specialization and division of labor. Nor can they use capital equipment whose efficiency is premised on large production runs for single-commodity outputs. As the size of the labor force is increased, the marginal product grows until increasing returns to scale are offset by diminishing ratios of capital and resources to labor. We then encounter the full force of the law of variable proportions; each further unit of labor adds less to output than its predecessor.

We need not specify that the given endowments of capital and natural resources are large enough to encompass all known economies of scale. It is possible that if these endowments were increased, the optimal size of the labor force would also increase. Our optimum is therefore defined not only by the *mix* of factors but by the *absolute quantities* of the nonhuman factors and the state of technology. But given the latter, the optimum is well-defined. It occurs at that size of labor force (L_0), at which the declining curve of marginal product intersects the curve of average product, i.e., at maximum average product.[3]

Although the principle is clear, its application to a concrete case is obviously difficult. We lack sufficient knowledge of empirical production functions to identify the optimum with any precision. However, it is quite obvious that many nations and regions of nations—including some parts of the United States—are well past that optimum. The marginal product of labor in such regions is close to zero.

I now define the optimum population as the smallest one that will yield the optimum labor force. This definition follows from the criterion of optimality, maximum income per capita. In the short run, such a population is one which consists entirely of able-bodied workers, i.e., is identical with the labor force. However, such a population is not self-maintaining. Its membership will decline over time as age and mortality take their tolls. A self-sustaining population must have a positive birthrate and will certainly include children too young for productive labor as well as able-bodied workers.

Assuming no change over time in the available quantities of nonhuman factors of production or in the state of technology, the desired labor force is constant in size; and our optimum population should also be constant in size. It has been demonstrated that a population with an invariant number of annual births and an invarient schedule of age/sex-specific annual death rates will eventually achieve a stable age-distribution and a zero rate of natural increase [(10), Lotka, 1939]. If labor-force participation is assumed to be an invariant function of age and sex, the manpower yield of such a stationary population is also determined. Our optimum

---

[3]Enke's exposition [(4), 1963, p. 346] distinguishes between 1) the average product of labor "in the sense that the money value of this output is attributable to no other factor such as land or capital" and 2) total product per laborer "without any attempt to to suggest how much income is attributable to one or another factor." I am unable to follow this distinction; it apparently implies that, with zero labor, output would be greater than zero—and this is indeed the case illustrated in Enke's Fig. 18–3.

population is therefore a member of this family of stationary populations. How small it can be in total numbers depends on two sets of parameters:

1) The mortality schedule, which determines the age/sex distribution of the population.

2) The labor-force participation schedule, which determines the manpower yield of any given age/sex distribution.

Given these two schedules, we can select an annual number of births that will give rise to a population with a zero rate of natural increase and the desired manpower yield. The optimum population is then defined as to total numbers, age/sex distribution, and crude rates of birth and death (which are of course equal).

Suppose that this optimum population and the corresponding maximum per capita income were achieved. How stable would the optimum be thereafter? The question is difficult to answer in the abstract because displacement of the optimum might occur either positively or negatively in response to several factors whose relative strength cannot be easily specified *a priori*, and because a shift in the optimum population might be associated with either an increase or decrease in the corresponding maximum per capita income. However, we can list the most relevant sources of change.[4]

Some natural resources, e.g., mineral ores—are nonrenewable. As these are exhausted over time, the ratio of resources to labor declines, and the optimum size of the labor force is negatively displaced from L_0. If this displacement moves the production function from the range of constant returns to the range of increasing returns, the maximum per capita income may decline as well.

At maximum per capita income, capital accumulation may be both feasible and in accord with community preferences. If additional capital permits the achievement of further economies of scale, the optimum labor force will be positively displaced from L_0; average product and per capita income will be larger at the new optimum than at the old. Even if all known economies of scale have been achieved, further additions to the stock of capital imply a range of labor inputs for which the marginal product of

---

[4]The following discussion takes no account of the institutional problems of factor-rewards, inducements to invest, etc., which loom so large in the literature of Keynesian economics. Unlike the technical input-output relationships discussed below, the structure of rewards is subject to adjustment by public policy.

labor is constant and the average is rising—given proportional increases in the inputs of natural resources. The optimal labor force is positively displaced from L_0, per capita income rises, and the rate of resource depletion increases.

Alternatively it may be the case that at maximum per capita income, the community is consuming rather than accumulating capital. Such an economy is not viable. Over time, both the capital stock and the optimum population will shrink at accelerating rates.

Inventions that improve the efficiency of productive processes often, but not necessarily, require larger scales of production to effect their economies. If so, the optimum size of labor force is displaced positively. However, such inventions may instead (or also) increase the substitutability of factors of production. For example, replacement of manually-operated by automatic machinery without expansion of the stock of capital causes the marginal product of labor to decline more steeply than before. Technological change may thus actually reduce the optimum population while increasing per capita income at that optimum.

Finally, inventions that permit the substitution of capital for depletable natural resources, or the substitution of abundant for scarce natural resources permit a given optimum to persist for a longer period than would otherwise be possible.

AN EMPIRICAL APPROXIMATION TO THE OPTIMAL POPULATION

For a region in which resources are fixed and the rate of capital accumulation is zero, I have defined in principle the size and characteristics of the optimum population. Because its characteristics may be decidedly different from those of observed populations in more ways than size alone, it is worthwhile to construct a crude numerical example for closer scrutiny and comparison. I first examine the difficulties of such a project and describe my way of resolving (or evading) them.

The first problem is that of determining the parameters of a regional production-function with enough accuracy to allow specification of the optimum size of the labor force. We know that underdeveloped regions often have labor forces so much greater than optimum size that the marginal product of labor is virtually zero. We do not know, for any particular region, how much the labor force would have to be reduced to reach the optimum; and such an investigation is beyond the scope of this essay. I will simply evade the issue by assuming that the optimum size of the labor force is known. This variable may then be treated as a scalar in describing the corresponding optimum population.

The second problem is that of selecting an appropriate mortality schedule. Some attempts have been made in the literature of economic development and of demography to establish a relationship between the mortality schedule and per capita income [(1), Adelman, 1963]. If such a relationship exists, we should have to solve simultaneously for the morality schedule and the population size, corresponding to the desired labor force. This is because the mortality schedule determines the minimum population which will yield the necessary manpower, while the size of the population enters into the denominator of per capita income and is thus a determinant of the mortality schedule.

The hypothesized relationship, however, is not established for the relevant range of per capita income, i.e., the neighborhood of the maximum possible under the constraints of resource endowment, the stock of capital, and the state of technology. Indeed, there is much evidence that, above the subsistence or famine level of consumption, the mortality schedule can be reduced to a level and a pattern very near to that of the most advanced industrial nations by simple and inexpensive programs of public health and sanitation. Thus the crude death rate of Ceylon was reduced from 20 to 14 per thousand persons in a single year (1946–1947) simply by broadcasting DDT [(14), Political and Economic Planning, 1955, p. 12]—a remarkable achievement even if longer-term consequences turn out to be less salutary. Although per capita income in Puerto Rico is one-fourth that of the United States, the respective crude death rates are 6.7 and 9.1 per thousand persons—a tribute to the Commonwealth's program of public health.[5] Consequently, I will assume that the empirically relevant mortality schedules for the near future in underdeveloped regions are approximately those of the United States in 1960.

---

[5]Puerto Rico's exceptionally low crude death rate is partly accountable to the age structure of the island's population which is considerably "younger" than that of the United States. But United Nations demographers estimated that Puerto Rican expectation of life at birth (both sexes) was over 65 years in 1955–1958, as compared to 69 years for the United States in 1957. These estimates are given in [(16), United Nations, 1963, pp. 28 and 34].

Statistical analysis of recorded annual death rates from many nations—some with historical records covering the past century—reveals a rather regular pattern of component detail. Age-specific death rates for each sex corresponding to any given expectation of life at birth are similar, regardless of the place and time for which they were recorded. In the past few years, several groups of demographers have exploited this regularity to construct model-life

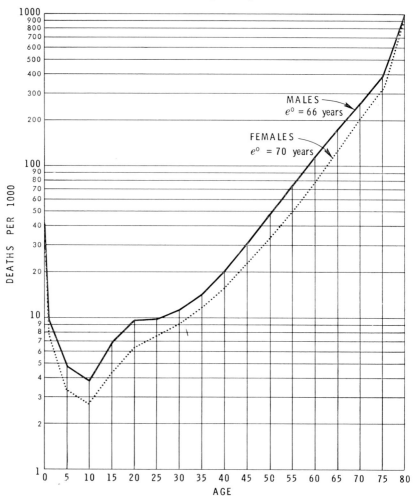

Figure 2 Annual Deaths per thousand persons by age and sex: Model mortality schedules for optimum populations. **Source:** Coale and Demeny [(3), 1966, p. 22].

tables keyed to expectation of life at birth. Rather than selecting a life table based on recorded death rates for the United States, I find it convenient to use a synthetic table of this type.

Specifically, I have adopted as the age/sex specific death rates of my optimal population those given in model life tables prepared by Ansley Coale and Paul Demeny, keyed to a life expectancy at birth for males of 66 years; for females, 70 years [(3), Coale and Demeny, 1966, Model West, Level 21]. Annual age/sex-specifis death rates corresponding to these parameters are shown in Figure 2.

The third problem is selection of an empirically relevant schedule of labor-force participation by age and sex. In this matter, I am guided by the conviction that economists have become prisoners of a makeshift statistical measure. In order to avoid uncomfortable problems of imputed value, we count as output only those commodities which enter the market, and count as labor only that work which is remunerated. If our wives did each other's housework instead of their own, the labor force would increase by perhaps 30 per cent. In agricultural production, where family employment and self-employment is the rule, the informality of arrangements is reflected in nonsensical estimates of labor-force participation even for males.

I therefore choose to err in the other direction by assuming that the labor force consists of everyone between ages 15 and 60. Such persons are certainly capable of productive labor (with due allowance for the sick and the handicapped), whether or not under present institutional arrangements they are so occupied. We can even regard those engaged in child-care and those still in school as producing human capital to offset the depreciation and obsolescence of such capital among the elderly.

Under these empirical assumptions, the optimal population is completely defined except for the scalar which is required to match its manpower yield to the desired size of labor force. Even without this scalar, we can nonetheless examine the age-distribution and dependency rate of this population and compare them to those of several contemporary regional populations.

The center bar of Figure 3 shows the age-distribution of an optimum population as defined above. Note that the age-distribution is nearly rectangular, with about 20 per cent of the total in each fifteen-year age-bracket. Sixty per cent of the total is thus included in the employable age-bracket, 15–59 years. For every thousand employable persons, there are 682 dependents.

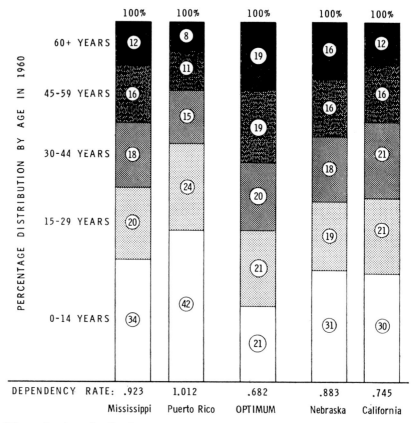

Figure 3   Age-distributions and dependency rates: Comparison of optimum population with selected actual populations in 1960. **Source:** U.S. Bureau of the Census [(18), 1963. Table 17].

The figure shows similar distributions for the 1960 populations of Mississippi, Puerto Rico, Nebraska, and California. Notice that the dependency rate is in every case higher than for the optimum population. Mississippi and Nebraska have similar dependency rates, but a larger proportion of Nebraska's dependents are elderly. California's dependency rate is closest to the optimum, but a much larger proportion of the dependents are children. Puerto Rico's population is strikingly handicapped by its age-distribution: even if jobs were available for all employables, each employable person would have to support at least one dependent.

Since the income of the entire population is produced by that portion in the labor force, these variations in dependency rates reflect in per capita incomes. For example, if the average annual product of labor in each place were $3,000, per capita incomes would vary as follows:

Mississippi	$1,560
Puerto Rico	1,491
OPTIMUM	1,783
Nebraska	1,593
California	1,719

Of course, the average product of labor, as well as the dependency rate, varies among these places because each has a more or less advantageous mix of capital and natural resources to combine with its labor. Usually (though not necessarily), a place with high dependency rate is also overpopulated in the sense that its labor force it too large for its capital stock, if not also for its natural resources.[6] It is thus doubly disadvantaged, with a low average product of labor and a high dependency rate.

But Figure 3 shows that even if the labor force were of optimum size, the demographic structure of the population would have a significant impact on the level of per capita income. Thus, even under the best of circumstances with respect to the mix of labor, capital, and resources, per capita income for a population with Puerto Rico's present demographic structure would be about 83 percent of the attainable optimum.

---

[6]Because of the weaknesses noted earlier in our methods of accounting for income and employment, one cannot be very precise about variations in the average product of labor. The best available index is the typical earnings of those who are gainfully employed. In 1960, median earnings varied among the four places named above as follows:

Mississippi	$2,197
Puerto Rico	819
Nebraska	3,891
California	5,495

Although four cases hardly constitute a significant sample, these values exhibit a striking inverse correlation with the dependency rates shown in Figure 3.

POPULATION POLICY FOR REGIONAL DEVELOPMENT

In the preceding sections of this essay, I have shown that there exists an optimum population for any region and have described the properties of this population. It is apparent that many regions have populations far in excess of their respective optima. I now turn to two relevant questions. What measures of population control would enable a region to reach such an optimum from above? Can such measures be reconciled with the planner's triple perception of a population as simultaneously client, resource, and burden?

Three instrumental variables operate directly on the size of a human population, jointly determining its change over time: the incidence of deaths, births, and migration. Any program of population control must operate through one or more of these three variables. But each relates differently to the triple perception mentioned above. I will consider the relevant policies in turn.

Regulation of the Death Rate

The simplest and cheapest way to reduce the size of a population is to raise the death rate. This can be done, for instance, by reducing budgets for public health and sanitation, thus actually freeing resources for other uses. And in most poor regions, the level of popular understanding and political participation is low enough that such a policy is politically feasible if quietly endorsed by the political elite.

From the planner's point of view, however, there are certain drawbacks to such a program. One drawback is that it collides directly and obviously with his perception of the population as a clientele whose welfare is the object of planning. One suspects that there are public officials in some overpopulated nations who wish, in retrospect, that DDT and preventive medicine had never been introduced; and for the future, they may be reluctant to place a high priority on as-yet-unexploited public health measures. But a forthright reversal of public health programs is an unlikely event even in the most crowded nations.

Another drawback is the difficulty of designing a politically feasible mortality program that is efficient in its incidence on various population components. Elimination of public health and sanitation programs would raise the incidence of death for all age/sex groups but most dramatically for small children. It would be least effective against the elderly. Nonetheless, a population exposed for a long time to high death rates develops a younger age structure than one exposed to low death rates. This is illustrated in Figure 4, which compares the age distributions of two stationary

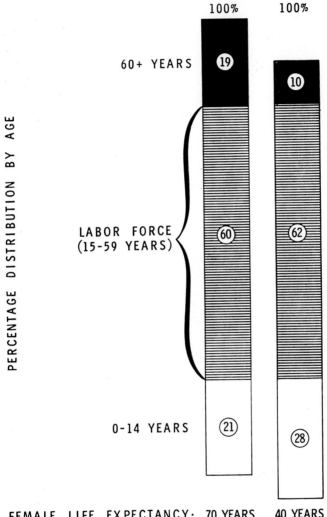

Figure 4 Age-distributions for two stable populations with different expectations of life at birth scaled to produce the same number of labor force participants. **Source:** Computed from data in Coale and Demeny [(3), 1966, pp. 114 and 162].

R

populations (zero growth rate), one with female life expectancy of 70 years and male life expectancy of 66 years, another with female life expectancy of 40 years and male life expectancy of 37 years. The second population need be only slightly larger than the first to provide the same number of persons of labor-force age, but it requires a much greater expenditure on child-care and education than the first. In other words, a high-mortality population has a lesser yield on investment in human resources than does a low-mortality population.

A third drawback to a high-mortality program is that the measures indicated also have side-effects that reduce the productivity of the labor force. Elimination of public health and sanitation programs not only increases the incidence of death, but also increases the incidence of illness and chronic debility in the entire population.

Regulation of the Birth Rate

It is much easier for the planner to refuse responsibility for the welfare of those not yet born than to refuse responsibility for the welfare of persons already living. This is the principal reason that birth control is such an appealing instrument of population policy. Moreover, as compared to a high-mortality program, birth control is efficient in the sense that no resources are wasted on the maintenance of the redundant population.

In contrast to a high-mortality program, however, the implementation of birth control requires the expenditure of public funds—probably more for persuasion than for supplies. Current estimates of these costs indicate that they are very small as compared with alternative measures for maintaining a given level of per capita income.[7] In most poor regions, however, public advocacy of limitations on family size involves a direct attack on long-established social norms and religious convictions.

---

[7]Stephen Enke estimates that the prevention of 24 million births in India over a ten-year period would cost about Rs 150 million in resources for supplies and administration. (Transfer payments to induce birth control might run 50 to 100 times that sum.) The associated ten-year "saving" in consumption requirements would amount to Rs 7,500 million, or 50 times the resource costs. He concludes, "As regards per capita consumption, resources devoted to population control would . . . be 500 times as rewarding as resources of equivalent value invested in traditional development projects such as industry, transportation, or irrigation" [(5), Enke, 1960].

In all human populations, female fertility is negligible below age 15 and above age 44. Within the fertile age-interval, the incidence of births typically rises smoothly to a peak somewhere between 20 and 30 years of age and declines smoothly thereafter. The mean age of the fertility schedule varies among populations according to customs of marriage and cohabitation and with the availability of employment for women outside the home. While an anti-natal program could possibly operate on the shape of the fertility function, it seems more feasible to offer generalized inducements to contraception which tend to shift the whole schedule up or down, perhaps with some displacement of the mean toward the younger years.

For any given schedule of death rates, we can shift a model fertility schedule up or down to achieve, within limits, any desired rate of population growth—positive, negative, or zero. The positive limit is imposed by human biology; a certain interval must elapse between conceptions. The negative limit is reached wth zero fertility; the rate at which the population decreases is then determined by the given schedule of age/sex-specific death rates and the initial age/sex distribution of the population.

Figure 5 shows four alternative fertility schedules, all designed so that the mean age of the schedule is 27 years. This particular choice of mean age is arbitrary but empirically relevant. The lowest fertility schedule, in combination with the model mortality schedule described earlier ($e^0 = 70$ years for females, 66 years for males), would yield an annual crop of babies just equal to the annual crude death rate for a stable population. In other words, this fertility schedule is consistent with a zero rate of natural increase in a population subject to the indicated incidence of death.

The other schedules of fertility shown in Figure 5 are scalar transformations of the first. Under the identical mortality conditions, they would yield, respectively, annual rates of natural increases of 1, 2, and 3 per cent. Note that these successive 1-per cent increments to the rate of natural increase require progressively greater upward shifts of the fertility schedule. This is because the four populations differ in age-structure, as shown in Figure 6. The required fertility changes cannot easily be inferred from that figure because the period of peak fertility (ages 20–29) happens to contain the pivot of the shifting age-distribution.

From the standpoint of our interest in birth-control programs, one possible interpretation of Figure 5 is that it would be more difficult to reduce a 3-per cent rate of growth to 2 per cent than to reduce a 1-per cent rate of growth to zero: The first step is the hardest! But the implication is not clear because the fertility schedules shown in Figure 5 result in the indicated rates of growth only for "stable" populations, i.e., populations that have been subjected to invariant age/sex-specific death rates and an invariant crude birth rate for many years, so that the age-distribution stabilizes. These age-distributions do not correspond with those that would emerge at stages in the evolution of a single population

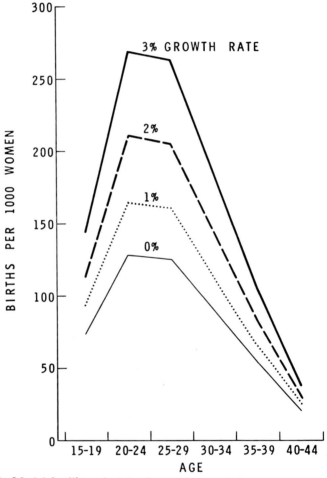

Figure 5 Model fertility schedules for stable populations with selected rates of growth. **Source:** Computed from data in Coale and Demeny [(3), 1966, p. 30].

under a regimen of falling birth rates. Nor is it clear whether public resistance to birth control measures would increase or diminish as the actual birth rate fell.

Returning to Figure 6, we can see obvious economic advantages to the age-distribution of the stationary population as compared

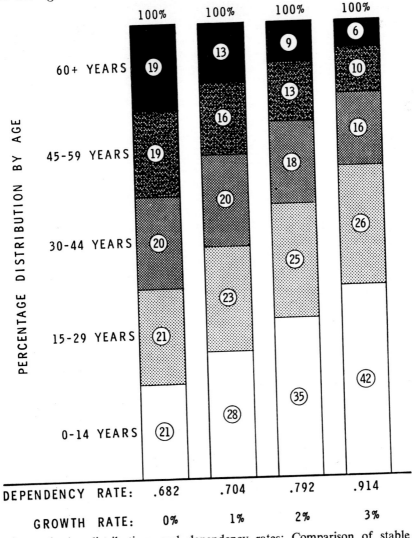

Figure 6 Age-distributions and dependency rates: Comparison of stable populations with selected rates of growth. **Source:** Computed from data in Coale and Demeny [(3), 1966, pp. 114 and 162].

to those of populations with positive growth rates. For example, the stationary population (zero growth rate) contains only 682 dependents per 1,000 persons of employable age. The population growing at three per cent per annum contains 914 dependents per 1,000 employables. To yield the same absolute number of employables, the size of the growing population must be 114 per cent of the size of the stationary population. Assuming the same *aggregate* income for the two cases, *per capita* income for the growing population would be 88 per cent of that for the stationary population.

Regulation of Migration

Although large-scale emigration is common enough in human history, it is seldom taken seriously as a feasible method of population control for poor regions of the contemporary world. One reason is that the contemporary world is rather thoroughly nationalized, and nations have by custom the right to refuse admittance to outsiders. Unless there happen to coexist nations wanting immigrants as well as nations with surplus population, the possibilities for the latter of sponsored emigration as a means of population control are indeed limited. Even so, we tend to overlook some quite substantial international population movements that have occurred since the end of World War II. Italy, for example, exported 1.7 million nationals (net of returnees) between 1956 and 1961—mostly to Switzerland and West Germany [(17), United Nations, 1962, Tables 25 and 26].

It is also easy to forget that not all regional development policies are formulated at the national level, and there are few barriers to movement among regions within a single nation. For generations, the southern region of the United States has exported population to the northern and western regions. Some 578,000 persons left Puerto Rico between 1940 and 1962—a number amounting to nearly one-fourth of the Commonwealth's 1950 population.

For the regional development planner, a program of publicly sponsored emigration may be in some circumstances a ponderable alternative or supplement to birth control as a means of reducing the rate of population growth. If a resident can be induced to leave "of his own free will" by the prospect of greater prosperity elsewhere, or by subsidy, he is painlessly eliminated from the client-group for whose welfare the planner feels responsible.

But there are drawbacks over and above the direct costs of inducements to emigration. Mobility in all populations varies with age. Those most likely to take the opportunity to emigrate are young adults—persons in whom society has invested fifteen to twenty years of sustenance, education, and training, without economic return. Moreover, they are likely to be the more enterprising and imaginative members of their cohorts. An emigration program tends to skim the cream of a region's population.

Yet if a region is so badly overpopulated that the marginal product of labor is close to zero, even the loss of the best can result in a better life for those who stay behind. And there is an additional benefit from emigration in that it removes disproportionate numbers of highly-fertile females from the population. Stanley Friedlander concludes that the 578,000 emigrants from Puerto Rico between 1940–1962 would have added more than 700,000 children to the island's population had they remained in residence. In other words, without emigration, the population of Puerto Rico would have been half again as large as it was in 1962 [(6), Friedlander, 1965, pp. 49–59].

Because of the complex age-structure of migratory movements, and concurrent changes in the crude fertility of remaining residents, it is difficult to envisage the longer-run consequences of population control by means of emigration inducements. In order to explore these consequences, I have simulated a twenty-five-year program of population control which relies entirely on emigration as a means of preventing growth.

This simulation was performed for each of three stable populations described earlier, those with rates of natural increase of 1, 2, and 3 per cent per annum, respectively. Each year, just enough emigration is scheduled so that the size of the labor force remains unchanged despite the excess of births over deaths.[8]

---

[8]The simulation was performed on M.I.T.'s IBM 7094, using a special adaption of GPOP, a generalized population projection model programmed by the author [(11), Lowry, 1964]. The algorithm works with five-year age-cohorts, printing out complete tables of population composition and vital statistics at five-year intervals. During each interval, the given initial population is aged and subjected to user-selected age/sex-specific death rates and user-selected age-specific fertility rates for females. For this occasion, an added subroutine performed the computations necessary to select an emigration schedule which would just offset natural increase in the labor force during each quinquennium. The emigrants are subtracted from the population prior to each reporting date, and the nonemigrants become the initial population for the succeeding time interval.

Given the age/sex distribution of a population at the beginning of each year, an age/sex-specific mortality schedule, and a female age-specific fertility schedule, it is easy to determine the *number* of emigrants of labor-force age necessary to maintain a labor force of constant size. It is not so easy to decide on the appropriate age/sex composition of the full stream of emigration. Yet this composition is important because it controls the age/sex composition of the remaining population and thus the subsequent incidence of deaths and births, as well as subsequent entries to the labor force.

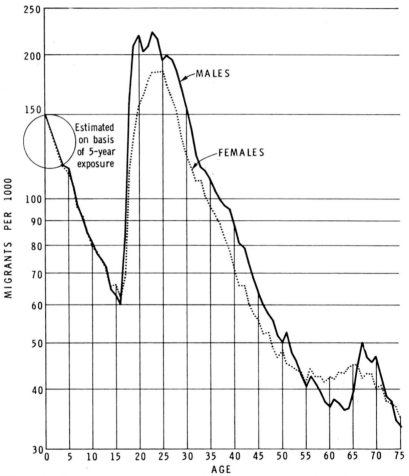

Figure 7   Interstate migration rates by age and sex: United States 1955–1960. **Source:** Computed from U.S. Bureau of the Census data [(19), 1963, Table 3].

Figure 7 shows age/sex-specific rates of interstate migration for the United States for the five-year interval, 1955–1960. Because no account is taken of intervening places of residence, these rates are only about three times as large as corresponding annual rates, but do exhibit the same age/sex pattern as the latter. Annual rates have been sampled by the Bureau of the Census since 1947, and year-to-year variations in the number of migrants per thousand population of each age/sex group have been slight as compared to the differences in rates among age-groups. Above age seventeen, males are typically more mobile than females, but sex differentials at all ages are relatively small.

The shape of this migration function is not difficult to interpret. Young adults migrate with the highest frequency because, as compared to their elders, they have fewer vested interests in property ownership or job seniority. They are physically more vigorous and usually more adventurous, and have yet to find a satisfying niche in the social system. Children, on the other hand, ordinarily move only as members of a family. Since young, mobile parents have only young children, migration rates are distinctly higher for infants than for adolescents whose parents are older and more settled.

The general pattern of age/sex-specific mobility rates shown in Figure 7 is not peculiar to the United States but is a feature of most orderly population movements.[9] For concreteness, I have chosen this pattern as the norm or model for persons fifteen years of age and over. Migration rates for persons under fifteen are assumed to reflect the mobility of their female parents.[10]

---

[9]See [(17), United Nations, 1962, Table 28] for abundant confirmation. Emergency evacuation has an altogether different pattern.

[10]Migration rates for persons under 15 years of age were calculated as follows:

$$M_y = \frac{K_y \Sigma_x [C_y{}^x M_x]}{C_y}$$

where: M_y = Migration rate for children of age y.

M_x = Migration rate for all women of age x.

C_y = Number of children of age y.

$C_y{}^x$ = Number of children of age y belonging to women of age x.

K_y = A fitted parameter.

The parameter K_y can be interpreted as an adjustment for the difference in mobility of women with children as compared to women of the same age without children. It was fitted by compiling $C_y{}^x$ from birth records for the United States, 1945–1959, and adjusting for interim mortality; directly estimating M_x and M_y from mobility surveys of the U.S. Census for the period 1955–1960; then solving the formula given above for K_y instead of M_y.

While an emigration program could be designed to offer special inducements to particular components of the population, I have chosen an equally reasonable assumption: that the program takes the form of a generalized inducement (say, a per capita migration subsidy) whose value is increased or decreased according to the desired amount of emigration. The effect of such variations in inducements is assumed to be a scalar shift of the migration schedule shown in Figure 7, with all rates increasing or decreasing in the same proportion. For my simulation, inducements are manipulated—i.e., the migration schedule is shifted—so that annual emigration of persons fifteen–fifty-nine years of age exactly equals natural increase of this group.

Table 1 summarizes the simulation results for each of the three model populations, whose rates of natural increase are 1, 2, and 3 per cent per annum, respectively, and whose age-distributions vary accordingly. For 1960, the nominal base-year, each population contains approximately one million persons.

The first column of the table shows how these populations would have grown in the absence of emigration. Column 2 shows how they grew under the emigration policy described above, with the differences (Column 1 minus Column 2) noted in Column 3. Column 4 shows the number of emigrants of all ages during the preceding five years, and these quinquennial figures are cumulated in Column 5.

One striking result of the simulation is the marked decline after 1970 in the number of emigrants required to maintain a labor force of constant size (Column 4). Until 1975, the decline is primarily accountable to emigration of children born before 1960 who would otherwise have entered the labor force at fifteen years of age. Thereafter, another factor comes into play. Children born *after* the emigration of their parents are, of course, not included in the population of interest; had their parents remained, these children would also have eventually entered the labor force.

This avoided fertility is substantial and cumulative, as can be seen by comparing Columns 3 and 5. By 1985, Population B has lost 217,000 persons by emigration and avoided 47,000 births. Population C has lost 465,000 by emigration and avoided 153,000 births. Population D has lost 739,000 by emigration and avoided 340,000 births.

For each population, the total number of emigrants between ages fifteen and fifty-nine is strictly determined by the policy of

Table 1   Population control by emigration: Summary of 25-year simulations
of population changes in three model populations

Population model and Year	Numbers of persons (in thousands)				
	(1) Total without emigration	(2) Total with emigration	(3) Difference due to emigration	(4) Emigration for preceding 5 years	(5) Cumulative emigration
Population B					
1960	1,000	1,000			
1965	1,050	1,002	48	48	48
1970	1,103	1,003	100	47	95
1975	1,160	1,006	154	44	138
1980	1,219	1,011	208	40	179
1985	1,281	1,017	264	38	217
Population C					
1960	1,000	1,000			
1965	1,102	1,001	101	101	101
1970	1,216	999	217	100	202
1975	1,342	1,000	342	94	296
1980	1,482	1,008	474	87	382
1985	1,638	1,019	618	83	465
Population D					
1960	1,000	1,000			
1965	1,159	1,000	159	159	159
1970	1,344	993	351	161	320
1975	1,559	992	567	151	471
1980	1,809	1,004	805	136	607
1985	2,100	1,021	1,079	132	739

Note: Distributions may not add exactly to totals because of rounding. Population
Models B, C, and D differ in rates of natural increase, which are 1, 2, and 3 per
cent, respectively, see text for details.

maintaining a labor force of constant size. As explained above, the
policy operates through scalar shifts in the entire schedule of
emigration rates. Consequently, the numbers of emigrants under
fifteen and over fifty-nine years of age are determined endogen-
ously; and the total number of emigrants may be either larger or
smaller than necessary to maintain a population of constant size.
Yet the constant-labor-force policy turns out to be virtually
equivalent to a constant-total-population policy, a result which is
not intuitively obvious considering that children and old persons
account for more than 40 per cent of the total population in each

of the three cases. At the end of twenty-five years of emigration, each of the three populations has grown to approximately 102 per cent of its original size.

Table 2 Shows age distributions for each of these populations at five-year intervals, 1960–1985. The changes over time are surprisingly slight. In each case, there is a small decrease in the proportion of the population under age fifteen, and an increase of up to three percentage points in the proportion over age fifty-nine. In the extreme case, the dependency rate rises by only forty-one per 1,000 employables.

Table 2 Age distributions of nonemigrants for three model populations controlled by emigration, 1960–1985

Population model and age interval	Percentage distributions by age for selected years					
	1960	1965	1970	1975	1980	1985
Population B						
60+ years	13.6	13.9	14.2	14.6	15.1	15.4
45–59	15.6	16.0	16.4	16.6	16.7	16.5
30–44	19.6	19.6	19.4	18.9	18.5	18.5
15–29	23.5	22.8	22.7	22.8	22.8	22.7
0–14	27.7	27.5	27.2	27.0	26.9	26.9
Total	100.0	100.0	100.0	100.0	100.0	100.0
Population C						
60+ years	9.6	9.9	10.4	10.9	11.4	11.9
45–59	12.5	13.2	13.9	14.4	14.5	14.2
30–44	18.1	18.4	18.0	17.1	16.5	16.5
15–29	25.2	24.2	24.0	24.3	24.3	24.0
0–14	34.6	34.4	33.7	33.3	33.2	33.3
Total	100.0	100.0	100.0	100.0	100.0	100.0
Population D						
60+ years	5.8	6.3	7.0	7.7	8.4	9.0
45–59	9.6	10.6	11.5	12.1	12.4	12.0
30–44	16.3	16.7	16.3	15.2	14.4	14.4
15–29	26.3	25.0	24.8	25.3	25.2	24.7
0–14	41.9	41.4	40.4	39.6	39.6	39.8
Total	100.0	100.0	100.0	100.0	100.0	100.0

Note: Distributions may not add exactly to totals because of rounding.

Table 3 shows comparable age-distributions for the emigrants from each population, 1960–1965 to 1980–1985. As might be expected from the stability of the age-distributions of the parent populations, the emigrant age-distributions are also stable. The economic efficiency of emigration is least for Population B, in which nearly 63 per cent of the emigrants are of employable age; and greatest for Population D, in which only 53 per cent of the emigrants are of employable age.

Table 3 Age-distributions of emigrants from three model populations controlled by emigration, 1960–1985

Population model and age interval	Percentage distributions by age for selected intervals				
	1960–65	1965–70	1970–75	1975—80	1980–85
Population B					
60+ years	5.3	5.6	5.7	5.9	6.0
45–59	7.4	7.7	7.8	7.8	7.7
30–44	18.8	18.7	18.2	17.9	18.0
15–29	36.4	36.3	36.6	36.6	36.4
0–14	32.0	31.8	31.6	31.7	31.8
Total	100.0	100.0	100.0	100.0	100.0
Population C					
60+ years	3.4	3.7	3.9	4.1	4.3
45—59	5.5	5.9	6.1	6.2	6.1
30–44	16.4	16.2	15.3	14.8	15.0
15–29	36.1	36.0	36.6	36.6	36.2
0–14	38.6	38.2	38.0	38.3	38.4
Total	100.0	100.0	100.0	100.0	100.0
Population D					
60+ years	2.0	2.3	2.5	2.7	3.0
45–59	4.0	4.5	4.7	4.8	4.7
30–44	14.0	13.7	12.6	12.1	12.3
15–29	35.1	35.2	35.9	35.8	35.0
0–14	44.9	44.3	44.2	44.5	45.0
Total	100.0	100.0	100.0	100.0	100.0

Note: Distributions may not add exactly to totals because of rounding.

In summary, the simulation results suggest that large-scale emigration is a quite plausible means of reducing population pressures, in the sense that its effects on the age distribution and dependency rate of the parent population are negligible. Moreover, the net "saving" in population size is considerably greater than the actual outflow of emigrants.[11]

[11]My model does not yield nearly so great a bonus of avoided fertility as Friedlander's empirical estimates for Puerto Rican emigration [(6), Friedlander, 1965, pp. 49–59]. I have not checked his calculations.

There are several obvious qualifications to these conclusions. One is that I have not tested the sensitivity of the results to variations in mobility parameters. It may be that sponsored emigration would differ in age structure from the unsponsored population movements, on which my mobility parameters are based. Nor have I estimated either the resources or transfer payments necessary to induce migration on the desired scale.

My findings in an earlier study of internal migration in the United States [(12), Lowry, 1966] suggest certain limitations on the use of economic incentives to promote emigration from a region. Analysis of place-to-place migration flows among 90 SMSAs, 1955–1960, revealed no evidence that the rate of out-migration from an SMSA was sensitive to the local unemployment rate or to the local wage rate; indeed, the more prosperous communities tended to have higher rates of out-migration, probably because the residents of these communities were relatively concentrated in the mobile age-brackets. However, the migrants' choices among alternative destinations did show considerable sensitivity to labor-market conditions at these destinations. The high rates of out-migration from prosperous communities were offset by even higher rates of in-migration, while poor communities experienced a net outflow.

While these findings need to be tested on a wider range of data, they imply that public policies intended to alter population distribution are likely to be more successful at redirecting migratory movements than at changing the aggregate volume of such movement. Thus, for the regional development planner, faced with rural overpopulation and with a massive movement of underemployed farmers to the cities of the region—cities unprepared to cope with such a population influx—the more promising policy is not to try to keep the farmers down on the farm, but to offer them inducements to leave the region altogether.

Alternatively, inducements to emigrate from the region might be offered to city dwellers, in which case the region's cities would become way-stations and training schools for a population moving from farm to city before emigrating from the region. While in the larger national or international setting, this may be a useful social function for the cities of poor regions, it is a less beneficial policy for the region itself than is the more direct strategy of exporting the surplus rural population.

REFERENCES

(1) Adelman, Irma. "An Econometric Analysis of Population Growth." *American Economic Review.* June 1963, 53, pp. 314–39.

(2) Coale, Ansley. Reported in *Population Crisis.* Population Crisis Committee, Washington, D.C., January–February 1967, p. 5.

(3) Coale, Ansley and Demeny, Paul. *Regional Model Life Tables and Stable Populations.* Princeton, N. J.: Princeton Univ. Press, 1966.

(4) Enke, Stephen. *Economics for Development.* Englewood Cliffs, N. J.: Prentice-Hall, Inc., 1963.

(5) Enke, Stephen. "The Gain of India from Population Control: Some Money Measures and Incentive Schemes." *Review of Economics and Statistics.* May 1960, 42 (2), pp. 175–81.

(6) Friedlander, Stanley. *Labor Migration and Economic Growth. A Case Study of Puertok Rico.* Cambridge, Mass.: The M.I.T. Press, 1965.

(7) Gottlieb, Manual. "The Theory of Optimum Population for a Closed Economy." *Journal of Political Economy.* December 1945, 53, pp. 345–49.

(8) Hansen, Alvin H. "Economic Progress and Declining Population Growth." *American Economic Review.* March 1939, 29, pp. 1–5.

(9) Leibenstein, Harvey. *Economic Backwardness and Economic Growth.* New York: Wiley & Sons, 1957.

(10) Lotka, Alfred J. *Theorie analytique des associations biologiques.* Paris: Hermann et Cie., 1939.

(11) Lowry, Ira S. *Metropolitan Population to 1985: Trial Projections.* RM-4125-RC. Santa Monica, California: The RAND Corporation, 1964.

(12) Lowry, Ira S. *Migration and Metropolitan Growth: Two Analytical Models.* San Francisco: Chandler Publishing Company, for the Institute of Government and Public Affairs, UCLA, 1966.

(13) Nelson, Richard R. "A Thory of the Low-Level Equilibrium Trap." *American Economic Review.* December 1956, 46, pp. 894–908.

(14) Political and Economic Planning. *World Population and Resources.* London: George Allen & Unwin Ltd., 1955.

(15) Spengler, Joseph J, "The Economist and the Population Question." *American Eonomic Review.* March 1966, 56 (1), pp. 1–24.

(16) United Nations Department of Economic and Social Affairs. *Population Bulletin of the United Nations.* New York: United Nations, 1963.

(17) United Nations Department of Economic and Social Affairs. *Demographic Yearbook 1962.* New York: United Nations, 1962.

(18) U.S. Bureau of the Census. *U.S. Census of Population: 1960. General Population Characteristics.* Washington, D.C.: U.S. Government Printing Office, 1963.

(19) U.S. Bureau of the Census. *U.S. Census of Population: 1960. Subject Reports. Mobility for States and State Economic Areas.* Final Report PC (2 -2B. Washington, D.C.: U.S. Government Printing Office, 1963.

12

Regional and Interregional Input-Output Models: A Reappraisal

WILLIAM H. MIERNYK*

West Virginia University

It has been more than a dozen years since Tiebout wrote his well-known critique of regional and interregional input-output models [(101), Tiebout, 1957, pp. 140–47]. Tiebout made it clear in his paper that he was not criticizing input-output analysis at the conceptual level, but he was quite critical of the "operational limitations" of the empirical regional and interregional tables that had been constructed at the time he wrote. Instead of issuing the customary call for further research, he concluded that "alternative methods of attacking similar issues should be appraised" [(101), Tiebout, p. 147]. In a recent compendium which reprints Tiebout's article, the editor points out: "Tiebout's appraisal of regional input-output models was written in the infancy of the subject it examines. His warnings of the difficulties involved in constructing and interpreting regional input-output tables have

*Professor of Economics and Director, Regional Research Institute, West Virginia University. This paper was written while the author was Visiting Professor of Economics at Harvard. Helpful comments on an earlier draft by Dr. Karen Polenske and Dr. Anne Carter, of the Harvard Economic Research Project, and by Mr. James McGilvray, of the University of Sterling, are gratefully acknowledged. The author also wishes to express his appreciation for the assistance of staff members and the use of facilities at the Harvard Economic Research Project. He alone is responsible for any errors or omissions.

S

not been challenged, but neither have they prevented a proliferation of such studies since he wrote" [(85), Needleman, 1968, p. 17].

This essay was not written to "challenge" Tiebout's criticism of empirical input-output studies. Instead, the objective is to examine more recent contributions to regional and interregional input-output analysis—especially those made since 1960—to evaluate the efforts that have been made to deal with the problems which Tiebout correctly identified.

Tiebout's criticism of regional and interregional input-output studies can be summarized briefly. He objected to: (1) the use of national production coefficients in regional models, (2) the assumption of stable trade coefficients, and (3) the failure to deal with the problem of variation in regional product-mix [(101), Tiebout, 1957, pp. 143–47]. He was also critical of the use of input-output models in conjunction with location theory to analyze regional phenomena such as agglomeration. This issue will not be discussed here because it is concerned with the shortcomings of location theory for predictive purposes rather than the input-output model *per se*. The reader interested in the use of input-output in locational analysis may wish to consult Isard and Keunne [(48), Isard and Keunne, 1953] and a more recent paper by Ghosh and Chakravarti [(31), Ghosh and Chakravarti, 1970]. Although Tiebout did not distinguish sharply between regional and interregional models in his paper, the discussion that follows will do so where it is appropriate and possible to make this distinction.

NATIONAL VERSUS REGIONAL COEFFICIENTS

Most regional input-output models are simply small-scale versions of national models. Because of geographic specialization and interregional trade, however, regional tables are more "open" than their national counterparts. Exports and imports are a larger part of total transactions in the typical region than in the nation, and there is wide variation in export and import patterns from region to region. If the size of the import coefficient in a given column is quite large, other input coefficients in that column will differ from those in the national table. Thus, Tiebout was right when he questioned the use of national coefficients in regional models; there are bound to be substantial divergences.

At the time Tiebout wrote, a few regional tables had been constructed by a "backdoor" method. Regional control totals were used to estimate the total gross output of each sector, and these were multiplied by a national inverse matrix to estimate the interindustry flow of goods and services in the region. Before such an operation could be carried out, however, it was necessary to aggregate the national table to conform to regional sectors. The process of aggregation may have created the illusion that the national coefficients had been altered in some way, but in fact they had not. As Tiebout pointed out, this method implicitly assumed identity of national and regional production functions. It also ignored the statistical problems of aggregation [(29), Fisher, 1958, pp. 250–60; (25), Evans, 1963, pp. 87–95 and (28), Fei, 1956].[1] But he concluded that: "As an operational necessity, all models discussed (Moore and Petersen excepted) have used national coefficients as regional coefficients" [(101), Tiebout, 1957, p. 143]. Actually, Moore and Petersen used national coefficients, but they did not use the precedure described above to derive their table for Utah [(80), Moore and Petersen, 1955, pp. 368–81]. Instead, they used the national coefficients as *first approximations* of the region's coefficients, then adjusted the production coefficients on the basis of differential trade coefficients. This procedure was rather severely criticized by Moses [(79), Moses, 1955, pp. 149–53].

After the publication of Moore and Petersen's table, other economists used "adjusted" national coefficients to approximate regional interindustry flows. One popular technique employed location quotients to adjust production coefficients downward—the assumption being that a regional input coefficient cannot be larger than the national coefficient. This method has been criticized elsewhere, and the details will not be repeated here [(70), Miernyk, 1968, pp. 165–67]. Briefly, however, the method fails to account for differences in industry and product-mix, and this difficulty is compounded by the aggregation problem.

Economists are not always deterred by statistical difficulties, however, and some have continued to employ various short-cut methods to construct regional input-output tables. Some of these methods have been tested by comparing survey-based tables with tables derived from national coefficients [(23), Czamanski and

---

[1] An alternative method for dealing with the problems of aggregation has since been suggested [(62), Leontief, 1967, pp. 412–19].

Malizia, 1968; (95), Schaffer and Chu, 1969]. Czamanski and Malizia prepared a set of seven interindustry tables for the State of Washington, using national input-output data and a set of regional weighting matrices. Their method of deriving regional tables from national data followed that developed earlier by Shen [(99), Shen, 1960, pp. 113–19], but it was also related to a method used by Stone and Brown to adjust for temporal changes in national input-output coefficients [(100), Stone and Brown, 1965, pp. 434–36]. Each of the derived tables was then compared with the table that had been constructed for the State of Washington by Bourque, Tiebout and others, using primary data [(10), Bourque and Weeks, 1969; (103), Tiebout, 1969, pp. 334–40]. This table, it was assumed, expressed the "true" interindustry relationships in the state.

Deviations between the calculated and "true" regional coefficients were compared in terms of the mean percentage error, the standard deviation of percentage error, and an information theory approach developed by Tilanus and Theil [(105), Tilanus and Theil, 1964]. Most of the errors were far beyond acceptable levels. In only one case, and then only in terms of the information theory test, were the errors reduced to tolerable levels. And this was accomplished only by removing eight "problem" sectors from the calculated table which by then had been reduced to a 28-order matrix.

Various writers, including Tiebout and the present author, had been critical of the use of national coefficients for regional analysis; but this criticism had been based on *a priori* grounds. The Czamanski-Malizia study not only provided statistical verification of the earlier criticism, but also showed that the errors involved are quite large. The only way to reduce them is by Procrustean aggregation and the elimination of "problem" sectors. The resulting loss of sectoral detail, however, reduces the usefulness of the regional table.

Schaffer and Chu tested several methods of adjusting national coefficients to obtain estimates of regional coefficients, also using the Washington State table as the basis for their comparisons. The methods tested ranged from a simple location quotient approach to a computerized, iterative procedure that they developed to redistribute local sales which had been initially distributed by the national sales pattern. After testing the differences between their calculated state coefficients and those in the Washington table, they concluded that ". . . the nonsurvey methods may prove useful supplements to survey studies. . . . But it seems that, at the moment, there is still no substitute for a good survey-based study" [(95), Schaffer and Chu, 1969, p. 96].

An acceptable method of deriving regional input coefficients from their national counterparts has not been developed up to the present. This does not mean that it is an impossible task. The Office of Business Economics of the U.S. Department of Commerce is presently experimenting with various weighting techniques for the estimation of regional input coefficents, and a similar effort is under way at the Battelle Institute.

Within the framework of regional (as opposed to interregional) analysis, there is a workable alternative to the adjustment of national coefficients. This is the collection and processing of primary survey data on interindustry transactions for the region in question. The procedure follows that used in the construction of national tables. Instead of deriving the transactions table indirectly, the basic table is constructed directly from primary data on interindustry flows and regional control totals. This provides the basis for calculating a table of direct input coefficients and a Leontief inverse matrix for the region.

The first regional table based on primary data to be published was constructed by Hirsch for the St. Louis Metropolitan Area [(43), Hirsch, 1959; see also (44), Hirsch, 1959]. Many of the regional tables published since Hirsch's study have been developed wholly or in part from primary data. Those completed by 1969, or known to be in progress at that time, have been listed in an inventory compiled by Bourque and Cox [(9), Bourque and Cox, 1967]. A few have included details about the sampling and data-gathering methods employed [(10), Bourque and Weeks, 1969; (26), Emerson, 1969; (74), Miernyk, Bonner *et al.*, 1967; (75), Miernyk, Shellhammer *et al.*, 1970; (107), Udis, 1968]. Examination of the production coefficients calculated from primary-source regional tables reveals that they tend to depart substantially from average national coefficients, as one would expect on *a priori* grounds.

The issue of primary versus secondary regional data can be discussed in terms of the costs and benefits involved. On the cost side the matter is fairly clear. Most of the tables based on secondary sources have been low-budget studies often conducted by a single individual. The collection of sample data generally requires a team of interviewers and relatively large budgets. The critical issue, however, is the purpose for which the table is to be used. If it is to be used for illustrative purposes—to show, for example, how interindustry transactions are related to other systems of social accounts—the use of secondary data can be defended [see, for example, (4), Barnard, 1967]. If however the table is to be used to make impact studies, forecasts, or for other analyses, the benefits of secondary-source regional tables are dubious. At the same time, the cost of collecting primary data can be kept within reasonable bounds by the use of small-sample survey techniques [(73), 1970].

FIXED VERSUS CHANGING COEFFICIENTS

Early critics of input-output analysis centered much of their attack on the assumption of fixed technical coefficients. As Tiebout put it: "If their use at the national level is at all dubious, even more is left to be desired at the regional level" [(101), Tiebout, 1957, p. 143]. The assumption of fixed technical coefficients is not an essential one. If the model is to be used for a purely static analysis, the effects of technical change on production coefficients need not be considered. Increasingly, however, input-output models have been used to make long-range forecasts; and in making such forecasts, technical change cannot be ignored.

The effects of changing technology on production coefficients has been studied extensively at the national level by Anne Carter on this side of the Atlantic, and by Stone, Sevaldson and Tilanus abroad [(14), Carter, 1960; (15), 1966; (16), 1967; (17), 1970; (96), Sevaldson, 1970; (100), Stone and Brown, 1965; (104), Tilanus 1967; and (33), Gostenhofer, 1968]. Models used to make long-range national forecasts have relaxed the assumption of fixed technical coefficients. In these models, input coefficients are projected along with changes in final demand [(1), Almon, 1963; (2), 1963; (108), BLS, 1966].

The projection of national technical coefficients involves the collection of data on new technological developments on an industry basis and estimates of the rate of diffusion of technical change throughout an industry. At any given time, old and new production techniques coexist in an industry. The problem is to estimate how rapidly new developments will be adopted, and how this will affect the pattern of interindustry purchases [(17), Carter, 1970].

At the regional level, the problem of projecting input coefficients is compounded by changing trade patterns as well as changing technology. Even with constant technology, changes in scale will alter regional input patterns. At a given stage of regional development, for example, a region might import packaging materials and containers. When regional output reaches a level that will support local production of such inputs, and if it is possible to produce them locally at a profit, capital will be attracted to the region. The result is a shift from imported to locally-produced inputs. Similarly, at an early stage of its development, a region might be an exporter of raw materials. Later, these outputs can be sold to regional processors and manufacturers. Thus, in projecting regional production coefficients, it is necessary to anticipate both technological and trade pattern changes.

Two general approaches have been followed in projecting regional coefficients. One method was used by Bourque, Tiebout, and their associates at the University of Washington. To handle technological change, they assumed that the *rate of change* in regional coefficients would be the same as the rate of change in national coefficients. Using Almon's projected national coefficients [(2), Almon, 1966], they made proportionate changes in the State of Washington coefficients. The problem of changing trade patterns—or import substitution—was approached in a different way. The assumption was made that as the regional demand for a product increases, relatively more of that product will be produced within the region unless there is a supply constraint. A corollary assumption is that if region A is more highly developed than region B, B's future input coefficients will tend to resemble A's present coefficients. The Washington coefficients were compared with those for the San Francisco Bay Area, for which a 1964 table was available, and adjustments were made on a judgmental basis, sector by sector. This assumes that as the Washington economy grows, its economic structure will more closely approximate that of the more highly-developed region [(103), Tiebout, 1969, p. 337].

Another approach, which attempts to adjust for changes in technological change and trade patterns simultaneously, was followed by the present author and his associates in the Colorado River Basin and West Virginia studies [(107), Udis, 1968; (75), Miernyk, Shellhammer *et al.*, 1970]. The details have been given elsewhere, and the method will only be summarized here [(69), Miernyk, 1965, pp. 117–25; (70), 1968, pp. 169–72]. The first step is to identify a sub-sample of "best practice" establishments in each sector in terms of productivity. The inputs of the "best practice" establishments are used to calculate a new table of "projected" input coefficients. This method assumes that today's "best practice" interindustry coefficients will tend toward average sectoral coefficients in the future, and that the shifts will reflect both technological and trade pattern changes.

Both methods leave something to be desired. They probably result in reasonable adjustments for technological change. The Bourque-Tiebout method does this by assuming that regional changes will be in the same direction and at the same rate as national changes. It is interesting to note that the "best practice" approach, while independent of national projections, follows the general trends that Anne Carter has found for the national economy. Neither method however adequately adjusts for changing trade patterns, although both take such changes into account to some extent. This is an area where the paucity of data on a regional basis makes it virtually impossible to run independent checks. In the West Virginia study, further adjustments were made in selected coefficients where adequate data were available. An example is the shift from the direct export of coal to the export of electrical energy. The only real test of the accuracy of either method of projecting regional coefficients will be comparison with the realized levels of output when target dates are reached.

THE USE OF REGIONAL INPUT-OUTPUT MODELS

Why have so many regional input-output studies been conducted? One may hazard the guess that a number of such studies—particularly those based entirely on secondary sources—have been carried out as academic exercises. As Leonief has pointed out, however: "The input-output table is not merely a device for displaying or storing information; it is above all an analytical tool" [(59), Leontief, 1966, p. 43].

One of the more popular applications of regional input-output models has been in making regional impact studies. This typically involves the calculation of income and employment multipliers. One can then trace the effects on all sectors of specified exogenous changes in final demand. By closing the model with respect to households, it is possible to estimate the induced as well as the direct and indirect effects of such changes. In estimating the consumption effects of exogenous changes, earlier studies relied on national data to estimate consumption functions [(80), Moore and Petersen, 1955]. In one small area study however, consumption data were collected from a random sample of households, and these were used to estimate income multipliers. Following a suggestion by Tiebout, marginal propensities to consume were applied to the consumption patterns of established residents, and average propensities to the consumption patterns of in-migrants to estimate the differential income changes generated by the two types of households [(74), Miernyk, Bonner *et al.*, 1967, pp. 95–116]. As expected the income multipliers were much lower than those found in earlier studies.

Several regional input-output studies have been used to make long-range interindustry projections; and in at least three of these, the input coefficients were projected [(103), Tiebout, 1969; (75), Miernyk, Shellhammer *et al.*, 1970; and (107), Udis, 1968]. In the Colorado River Basin study, water quantity and quality constraints were introduced in the forecasting model. The details have been given in a voluminous mimeographed report edited by Udis [(107), 1968], and a brief description of the method is included in a recent paper by the author [(72), 1970, especially Figure 1].

Carter and his associates at the University of California have used input-output techniques in the analysis of water problems [(19), Carter and Ireri, 1970; (24), Davis, 1968]. Carter has also investigated agricultural problems within the framework of input-output analysis [(18), Carter, 1965]. The West Virginia model was used to analyze the process of regional development by simulating structural changes in the economy [(75), 1970]. Bergmann has suggested a method for integrating an input-output system with other social and economic data to analyze urban problems [(6), Bergmann, 1969], and Hirsch has demonstrated that input-output techniques can be applied to a variety of urban decision problems [(45), Hirsch, 1968]. Bahl and Shellhammer used input-output analysis to evaluate the tax structure of a region [(3), Bahl and Shellhammer, 1969]. This brief list does not exhaust the analytical uses of regional input-output models, but it indicates the versatility of the basic model and its actual or potential applicability to a wide range of social and economic problems.

Most of the advanced industrial nations of the world have continuing input-output programs, and tables have been published for some of the less-developed countries. Although of fairly recent origin, there also appears to be a growing interest in regional and interregional tables abroad. Regional or interregional tables have been constructed for southern Italy, Wales, and the eastern provinces of Canada [(20), Chenery and Clark, 1959, pp. 314–18; (21), Chenery *et al.*, 1953, pp. 97–116; (86), Nevin *et al.*, 1966; (38), Hartwick, 1969]. Krengel has constructed a table for West Berlin, which is fully compatible with the table for the Federal Republic of Germany [(55), Krengel, 1969; (54), Krengel *et al.*, 1969]. For several years, Russian economists have been interested in regional input-output analysis; and an interregional table is reported to exist in the Soviet Union. The Ministry of International Trade and Industry has published a ten-sector, nine-region table for Japan [(88), Polenske, 1970; (90), Polenske, 1969; (110), Yamada and Ihara, 1967]. And Brodersohn has constructed multiregional tables for Argentina [(11), 1969]. Regional studies in other countries are listed in the most recent input-output bibliography published by the United Nations [(109), U.N., 1967].

INTERREGIONAL MODELS

In his 1957 critique of input-output tables, Tiebout did not distinguish between regional and interregional models. Relatively few interregional models existed at that time, and the completed work was largely exploratory. Interregional models are far more complex than the smaller-scale regional models, and this helps explain the lag in their statistical implementation.

The analytical framework of interregional input-output analysis had been developed as early as 1951 [(47), Isard, 1951; (58), Leontief, 1953], but empirical implementation came slowly. Moses constructed the first interregional model to be published. This was an eleven-sector, three region model based on a highly restrictive set of assumptions. By assuming fixed supply patterns, he was able to derive a set of trade coefficients, which are sectoral ratios of imports to total consumption. He assumed fixed technical and trade coefficients, stable trade relationships, and uniform production functions among regions. Had the model been used for making projections, it would have been necessary to assume excess capacity in all sectors, in the entire transport network, and in the labor force in each region to obtain a solution. In spite of these restrictive assumptions, Moses was able to show how changes in final demand in one region generate differential changes in output in all regions. Because of the high degree of aggregation—both regional and industrial—and its restrictive assumptions, this model was limited in terms of application [(82), Moses, 1955].

The same technique was used independently by Chenery to develop an interregional model for Italy [(21), Chenery *et al.,* 1953] and is now customary to refer to this as the Chenery-Moses model. It has been used by Reifler to analyze linkages between the States of California and Washington [(94), Reifler, 1966] and by Brodersohn in his detailed interindustry analysis of Argentina [(11), Brodersohn, 1965]. An excellent summary and comparison of the Leontief, Isard, and Chenery-Moses models are given by Davis [(24), 1968, pp. 78–83].

Moses later developed a more elaborate model consisting of the nine Census regions and sixteen manufacturing sectors. This model is a blend of linear programming and input-output analysis designed to allow for substitution in an effort to obtain optimal trade patterns [(83), Moses, 1960]. Unlike the conventional linear programming transportation model, the Moses model does not assume trade patterns as given. Along with regional outputs and requirements, they are determined by the system. The model allows only for substitution among regions, but Moses felt that it could "be adapted to permit substitution between industries and between different technological layers of the same industry" [(83), Moses, 1960, p. 373].

Moses recognized the weakness of the assumption of uniform production functions among regions, and in his theoretical model he assumed different production coefficients for each region. As he pointed out, however, the derivation of a matrix of technical coefficients for each region "is out of the question for an individual research worker" [(83), Moses, 1960, p. 381]. As a consequence, he was forced to use national coefficients for the endogenous sectors of each region's structural matrix. He was able, however, to estimate labor coefficients for each sector in each region. This permitted him to minimize both labor and transport costs in determining "optimal" trade and location patterns.

A major weakness in linear programming interregional models was pointed out by Leontief and Strout [(59), Leontief, 1966, p. 224], and by Polenske [(88), 1970]. This is its failure to allow for cross-hauling among regions. At a relatively high level of aggregation, different products will be included in the same industrial classification; and a realistic model must be able to allow for the shipment of these products from region to region. Even in a highly disaggregated model there can be seasonal cross-hauling of food products, recreational services, and other *identical* goods and services. Since Moses worked at the highly aggregated two-digit level of industrial classification, and since his empirical findings did not allow for cross-hauling, his results are not highly plausible.

To allow for cross-hauling, where it occurs, Leontief and Strout developed an interregional input-output gravity model [(66), Leontief and Strout, 1963; see also (111), Yan, 1969, pp. 117–20]. To implement their model empirically, Leontief and Strout used only four goods: coal, cement, soybean oil, and steel shapes. For shipments of coal, they divided the United States into thirteen regions, and for the other products into nine regions. Their estimates of the cost of shipping coal were revisions of earlier estimates made by Henderson [(41), Henderson, 1958; (42), 1956]. To estimate the cost of shipping the other products, they used weighted average distances between two regions [(59), Leontief, 1966, pp. 252–55].

Empirical implementation of a complete Leontief-Strout gravity model is a major statistical undertaking in the absence of input-output data on a regional basis. Such data are available for Japan for 1960 and 1963. The 1960 data were collected on an *inter-regional* basis for nine regions and twenty-five sectors, although in the published version of this model, the industrial data were aggregated to ten sectors. Data were collected on a *regional* basis for the nine regions and more than forty sectors for 1963. Using the Japanese data for 1960 and the Leontief-Strout model, Polenske estimated interregional trade flows and regional levels of output by sector for 1963 [(88), Polenske, 1970; (90), 1969]. Since actual output figures were available for 1963 on a regional basis, she was able to compare projected with realized results. In the aggregate, projected output exceeded actual levels by 3.6 per cent. The largest errors for specific sectors were 22.2 per cent for mining and 20.6 per cent for agriculture. Polenske was able to explain these errors to some extent by shifts in crop patterns and weather conditions in the case of agriculture, and by a major mining disaster in one of the principal coal-producing regions. To some extent, however, the errors were due to differences in methods of data assembly for the 1960 interregional table and the set of nine *intra*regional tables compiled for 1963 [(88), Polenske, 1970, pp. 143–45].

The results of the Japanese study were sufficiently encouraging to stimulate a large-scale effort to implement the Leontief-Strout model for the United States. Data have been collected for thirty-three industries and fifty-one states (with Washington D.C. treated as a state), and "internal consistency being maintained between the state figures and the national aggregates" [(89), Polenske, p. 14]. A general, or multi-purpose, model is being developed. Since the data are being assembled on a state basis, various regional combinations of states can be made, and "as the need arises, adjustments can be made to the data to reflect different relationships among the economic variables" [(89), Polenske, p. 16].

The assumption of fixed coefficients and uniform regional production functions has been relaxed in this model. Separate coefficients have been calculated, by state, for agriculture, mining, and new construction. In the manufacturing sectors, national coefficients have been adjusted to allow for differences in product mix. The detailed (370 sector) national table for 1963 was used to develop weights for the adjustment of state coefficients, and the results were later aggregated to the thirty-three basic sectors. Unadjusted national coefficients were used for the trade and service sectors.

To project state coefficients, the assumption was made that regional changes will occur at the same rate as national changes. Essentially, this is the assumption that Tiebout made in projecting coefficients for the State of Washington [(103), Tiebout, 1969, p. 337]. Independent projections of final demand have been made for each state. These projections are consistent with those made for the nation by the Bureau of Labor Statistics [(108), BLS, 1966].

Compared with earlier interregional input-output systems, the Polenske version of the Leontief-Strout model is very large. This raises the question of computational problems. Although the final decision has not been made, it is likely that the result will be a thirty-three region, fifty-nine industry model. This will involve the inversion of a nearly 2000-order matrix. The cost of inverting a matrix by conventional methods is roughly proportional to the cube of the order of the matrix [(67), Luft, 1969, p. 4]. There is also the problem that errors in the original data are greatly magnified in the inverse, and the effects of such error can only be determined after the inversion has been completed. Luft has experimented with the method of partitioned bordering which simplifies the computational routine and reduces the cost of inversion. Applied to this model, each submatrix would be only of fifty-nine-order, and the complete solution would be obtained by a "sequence of matrix multiplications, additions, and inversions of the basic submatrices" [(67), Luft, 1969, p. 3]. Using the Japanese data, others at the Harvard Economic Research Project also experimented with a variety of methods to detect the transmission of error from the original data to the final inverse. They hope to develop an "early warning" system that will identify the transmission of error before the inversion is completed.

The Leontief-Strout model has been used by others in a variety of contexts. Davis employed the gravity approach to estimate trade flows in an interregional model which includes eleven Western states [(24), Davis, 1968, pp. 92–109]. He used the model to demonstrate interregional water dependencies and to compute water withdrawal multipliers. Brodersohn implemented separate Chenery-Moses and Leontief-Strout models for five regions and twelve sectors in Argentina. One of his objectives was to compare forecasts made by the two models with those obtained from two "naive" models and to test all forecasts against observed data. Both the CM and LS models yielded better forecasts than did the naive models, although there was little difference in the magnitude of errors between the projections of the two input-output models. Data constraints forced the assumption of uniform regional production functions, and this "evidently affects the performance of the input-output technique." [(11), Brodersohn, 1965, p. 159].

Another approach to interregional analysis was followed by Leontief and several associates in investigating the industrial and regional economic impact of a compensated cut in defense spending [(65), Leontief *et al.*, 1965; (64), Leontief, 1967]. Interindustry data for this study were taken from the 1958 national table. The economy was divided into nineteen regions and fifty-eight industrial sectors. Of these, forty-one were defined as *national* and the remaining seventeen (including the two dummy sectors in the 1958 table) as *local* sectors. A twenty percent reduction in the military bill of goods was assumed with a proportional increase in the non-military components of final demand.

The national matrix of technical coefficients was aggregated to the desired number of sectors and partitioned into national and local sectors. The first step was to determine the direct and indirect effects of the hypothesized shift from military to non-military spending on the total output of all sectors. Next, the increase or decrease in output in each national sector was allocated on a regional basis by assuming a uniform percentage change in all regions. The absolute change in each region depends, of course, on the relative size of that sector in the region. Finally, changes in the levels of activity of local sectors were estimated by treating deliveries of local sectors to final consumers within the region *plus* deliveries to national industries located in the region as a given bill of goods [(65), Leontief *et al.*, 1965, p. 218].

Two refinements were suggested by the authors of this study for future applications. First, the restrictive assumption of a uniform percentage change in the national sectors of each region could be relaxed, and a "relative share" or shift analysis could be substituted. National industries in some regions could increase their output as the result of increased non-military expenditures, while the same industries in other regions could experience a decline in output due to the cut in defense spending. The second modification would divide the regions into sub-regions to allow for deliveries of *local* goods across sub-regional boundaries, although not across the original regional boundaries. Both of these modifications would require additional rounds of computations, but neither would alter the basic analytical scheme.

A more recent study by Boulanger used the model to estimate the effects of Vietnam de-escalation on the economy of Massachusetts [(7), Boulanger, 1969]. Boulanger used the 1967 Leontief Vietnam study for his sub-regional analysis. He assumed four sets of alternative percentage changes in sectoral output, and estimated the impacts of a $19 billion compensated reduction in military spending on the nation, New England, and finally on the state of Massachusetts.

Another approach to interregional analysis has been followed by Harris at the University of Maryland. His objective is to forecast output, population, income, the labor force, and unemployment at the county level. The Harris model is linked to Almon's national model [(2), Almon, 1966], and his regional forecasts will sum to the national projections [(36), Harris, 1969].

Harris plans to use linear programming, but not to determine optimal location patterns or trade flows. It will be used to obtain shadow prices which will then be introduced as independent variables in a set of equations designed to explain the location of industry. The model does not use trade coefficients; and by using small geographic areas, Harris hopes to minimize the problem of cross-hauling. He plans to implement the model for 3,112 counties and 100 industrial sectors. Much of the county data has already been compiled for 1965 and 1966, the base years from which projections will be made [(37), Harris, 1969].

As part of a larger project dealing with water pollution, Stillson has developed an interregional model which he hopes to use to analyze some of the economic aspects of pollution abatement [(99), Stillson, 1970]. The region to be analyzed is the Western Basin of Lake Erie, but interindustry linkages with other regions are to be included. The object, briefly, is to identify the present regional allocation of tradeable commodities, then to estimate the effects on costs of various abatement programs, and to determine a new regional distribution of production. This model is still in the early stages of development. As it now stands, the model will require input-output coefficients for each region.

In spite of the availability of regional input-output data in Japan, there has been relatively little analysis of the Japanese economy. As noted earlier, Polenske has used the Japanese data to test the Leontief-Strout gravity model. Yamada and Ihara have used the same data with a different object in mind. They note that the typical interregional model is designed to show the *total* effects on all regions of exogenous changes but that one cannot "draw any information on the partial interreactions among two or three regions" [(110), Yamade and Ihara, 1967, p. 3]. They have developed a model which will permit this to be done, by generalizing Miyazawa's earlier two-region model [(64), Miyazawa, 1966]. They do this, essentially, by using Miyazawa's "internal" and "external" matrix multipliers in conjunction with what they have called "augmented input coefficients" [(110), Yamada and Ihara, 1967, p. 3].

The internal matrix multiplier for a region is the Leontief inverse matrix for that region. The external matrix multiplier is the Leontief inverse of a matrix showing the direct and indirect input requirements from regions 1 and 2, for example, with an initial increase in production in region 1. The matrix of augmented input coefficients extends the external matrix multiplier to two *or more* regions. Since any number, and any combination, of regions may be considered at one time, the Yamada-Ihara model permits the analyst to focus attention on only the regions in which he is interested. It is not necessary to solve the entire interregional system, for example, if one is interested in examining the effects of a given exogenous change on sets of two, three, or four regions.

Horiba has tested the Heckscher-Ohlin hypothesis at the interregional level using the twenty-five-sector Japanese data [(46), Horiba, 1969]. He used the same formulation which led to the Leontief Paradox in international trade [(59), Leontief, 1966, pp. 68–133]. The test was made for the four regions where relative factor intensities stand out clearly. In five of the six possible paired regions, Horiba's test did not contradict the Heckscher-Ohlin hypothesis. In the sixth test, the pair of regions exchanged mutually capital intensive for mutually labor intensive goods. Horiba attributed this factor intensity reversal to differences in structural relations in the two regional economies.

A number of experimental studies, using interregional models, have been conducted by A. Ghosh [(30), Ghosh, 1968]. Much of his work is theoretical, but some of Ghosh's models have been tested with Indian regional data. Ghosh developed an interindustry programming model which was tested empirically with data aggregated to five regions and six sectors. He found large differences between actual and "optimal" interregional flows. This is not surprising since with such large regions, and at such a high level of industrial aggregation, his model could not handle the problem of cross-hauling [(30), Ghosh, 1968, p. 124]. If nothing else, his work corroborates earlier findings that the linear programming technique will not yield meaningful trade patterns when applied to large regions and highly-aggregated industrial classifications.

Ghosh has also examined the effects of price changes on interregional flows in a model which allow for substitution either between regions or sectors; his model does not distinguish between the two types of substitution. The empirical results were far from satisfactory, but this may be largely the result of inadequate data. Ghosh also pointed out, however, that: "Models of this type may work better in more stable situations where more or less unlimited amounts may be made available at certain prices in the different regions. But in an area where capacities are limited, and where new industries are growing, capacity limits are changing all the time and models of this type are not adequate to describe the drastic revisions taking place continuously" [(30), Ghosh, 1968, pp. 101–02].

T

Relatively few studies have taken interregional feedback effects into account in the calculation of regional multipliers [see, for example (48), Isard and Kuenne, 1953, p. 296]. The first studies to consider feedback effects explicitly were conducted by Miller [(76), 1966; (77), 1969]. Miller developed a method for calculating feedback effects in an interregional model, but because of the nature of his data, he labeled his empirical results "experimental." His data came from a variety of sources which could not be expected to show actual interregional linkages.[2] His findings suggested that feedback effects are negligible and that little error will result from ignoring interregional linkages entirely [(76), Miller, 1966, p. 118; (77), Miller, 1969, pp. 41–50].

Greytak has applied Miller's method to an eight-region, twenty-three-sector model of the United States in which interregional commodity flows were obtained from various sources and, in which, a gravity model was used to estimate flows for the trade and service sectors [(34), Greytak, 1969]. He calculated separate regional multipliers without feedback as well as interregional multipliers which include the feedback effects. His results differed markedly from those obtained earlier by Miller. Greytak found that neglect of interregional feedback effects results in an average difference of more than twenty percent between his two sets of multipliers and that more than one-fourth of the total impact on the aggregate level of a region's output, with a given change in final demand, is due to interregional feedback effects.

DYNAMIC MODELS AND REGIONAL DEVELOPMENT

The theory of dynamic input-output analysis was well-developed by the late 1940s, and the two leading essays in *Studies in the Structure of the American Economy* dealt with this subject [(56), Leontief, 1953, pp. 17–52; (57), pp. 53–90; see also (59), Leontief, 1966, pp. 145–52; (81), Morishima and Murata, 1968, pp. 71–92, and (30), Ghosh, 1968, pp. 85–89]. During the theoretical phase, there was a debate about the stability of dynamic input-output

---

[2]Miller used a hypothetical "regional" table which was the 1958 national table aggregated to ten sectors; a ten-sector table for Kalamazoo County, Michigan, and an eleven-sector table for India, also aggregated to ten sectors [(76), Miller, 1966, pp. 121–23].

systems [(60), Leontief and Sargan, 1961], but stable solutions have been obtained, and a dynamic model has been used to make long-range national interindustry forecasts [(2), Almon, 1966]. More recently, Leontief has developed the concept of the "dynamic inverse" which can be used to analyze investment behavior historically [(63), Leontief, 1970; see also (13), Byrd, 1969]. With minor modifications, it can also be used to project interindustry investment requirements and for development planning [(53), Koti, 1969].

There has been relatively little dynamic analysis at the regional level. The Colorado River Basin study [(107), Udis, 1968] allowed for the effects of technical change (and changing trade patterns) on input coefficients, but this was a comparative static rather than dynamic model. The first dynamic regional model known to the present author is the West Virginia model [(74), Miernyk, Shellhammer *et al.,* 1970].

One of the requirements of a dynamic model is a matrix of capital coefficients relating investment to changes in capacity. Typically, the capital coefficients relate to expansion investment only with replacement investment, treated as one of the components of final demand. The West Virginia model, however, has a separate matrix of replacement capital coefficients, in which replacement investment is related to changes in output, as well as the conventional matrix of expansion capital coefficients. A modification of the Leontief dynamic inverse was used to project capital requirements. The advantage of a dynamic model has been succinctly stated by Leontief: ". . . in a static formulation, investment in additional productive capacity is treated as a component part of the given final demand, from a point of view of dynamic analysis these magnitudes have to be explained rather than considered as having been fixed beforehand" [(59), Leontief, 1966, p. 147].

The Harris interregional model mentioned earlier will be linked to a dynamic national model, and the regional projections will be consistent with national projections. The Harris model is dynamic in another sense: ". . . the static model fails to account for the shifting location of industries" [(36), Harris, 1969, p. 2]. His system of location equations will allow for such shifts. Although these equations assume uniform production and price functions among regions, they will allow for changing shares in regional production largely as the result of changes in transportation costs. Polenske's interregional model does not assume uniform regional production functions, except in the trade and service sectors. Since both technical coefficients and final demand will be projected by region, her model will allow for regional shifts in production, consumption, and trade.

Regional input-output analysts have shown little inclination to date to relate their work to linear models of economic growth such as the Leontief models referred to above or the one developed by Brody [(12), Brody, 1965]. It has become almost conventional to compute one or more sets of static multipliers [see, for example, Bourque (8), 1969 and Peterson (87), 1968]. There has been little interest, however, in experimenting with such elementary dynamic multipliers as the one suggested by Goodwin more than two decades ago [(32), Goodwin, 1949, pp. 545–55]. Multipliers of the Goodwin type could be used, for example, to investigate lags in regional adjustment to exogenous change. Also, to this author's knowledge, no one has engaged in experimental work with the Turnpike Theorem at the regional level, although it should be possible to estimate efficient growth paths for regions in the same way this has been done for national economics.[3] Growth models of the type developed by Morishima and others are highly abstract, but their use at the regional level might provide additional understanding of the process of regional development.

A number of regional input-output models have been used in a development context [for example, Chenery *et al.*, (21), 1953; (20), Chenery and Clark, 1959, pp. 314–18; (26), Emerson, 1969; (74), Miernyk, Shellhammer *et al.*, 1970]. But relatively little has been done at the regional level to parallel the work of Leontief in terms of comparative input-output analysis [(61), Leontief, 1963]. By contrasting the interindustry structures of industrialized and less-developed economies, Leontief has shown how the technique of input-output analysis can be used to help understand the process of development. It is also possible to project structural changes in a developing economy in terms of the interindustry transactions, investment, and trade patterns of industrialized economies.

Comparative analysis is greatly facilitated if the input-output tables are triangularized, that is, arranged in decreasing order of interdependence on the input side from the left to the right side of the table [(39), Helmstädter, 1962; (40), 1962]. In the inter-

---

[3]For a lucid discussion of linear growth models, see Jorgensen [(52), 1968].

national comparisons, this has been done both in terms of transactions tables [(61), Leontief, 1963] and tables of technical coefficients [(98), Simpson and Tsukui, 1965]. Most regional input-
output tables published to date have followed the conventional
ordering of agricultural, mining, manufacturing, and service
sectors. Thus, they fail to reveal the "dependence and independence, hierarchy and circularity," which are at the heart of structural analysis [(59), Leontief, 1963, p. 46].

THE DATA PROBLEM

From an analytical point of view, most regional and interregional
studies must be considered as fairly elementary. Perhaps one reason
for this is that so much time has had to be devoted to the collection,
assembly, and interpretation of data. Individuals working alone
have had to rely entirely on secondary sources with all their limitations for regional analysis. A growing number of regional tables
are based on primary data, but these data are of uneven quality.
The data required for a regional transactions table are fairly complex, and any attempt to collect such data by mail questionnaire
cannot completely avoid the problem of sample bias. One alternative is to use field interviewers, but this can be done only at a
substantial increase in cost.

At the conclusion of their study of the regional effects of a
compensated cut in defense spending, Leontief and his associates
stressed the need for improved regional data: ". . . highest priority
should be assigned to improvement of the basic data. For statistics
which are collected on a national level, a systematic, regional
breakdown becomes more and more important. On the other hand,
most data collected by local and state organizations . . . are limited
in their usefulness because of lack of comparability with other
regional and national statistics. This needs to be remedied by
agreement on and compliance with certain common classifications
and standards" [(65), Leontief *et al.*, 1965, p. 228].

The Colorado River Basin study [(107), Udis, 1968], demonstrated that it is feasible to collect interregional data on an input-
output basis. While this study covered only a limited geographic
area, it was basically an interregional model. Six separate transactions tables were constructed, one for each sub-basin of the
broader region, and these were linked together through disaggre-

gated export columns and import rows. While it was not always a simple matter for the respondents to provide input and sales data on a geographic basis, they found it could be done. Interestingly, when the tables were completed, the provisional interregional balances of imports and exports by sector were very close. Only a modest amount of reconciliation was required to achieve the necessary exact balances.

The purchasing and sales departments of large establishments generally keep records on the origin and destination of purchases and sales, and it would not be unduly burdensome for them to report them on a state basis to the Bureau of the Census. Smaller establishments might object since they rarely keep such records, at least not in the required detail. But such establishments usually deal with a relatively small number of suppliers, and retail establishments would typically report all their sales as "local." Thus, the added burden for them would not be great. As an alternative, the Bureau of the Census and other statistical agencies could require detailed reporting by large establishments and collect the same data from smaller establishments on a sample basis. This would still result in uniform procedures and *consistent* estimates of interindustry transactions and would represent a major advance for the producers and consumers of interregional studies.

CONCLUSIONS

This survey of developments in regional and interregional input-output analysis over the past dozen years has been selective, of necessity, because of the author's limited knowledge of studies currently underway and because of space limitations. The selected studies which have been discussed briefly show that there have been important advances since Tiebout wrote his 1957 article. Not all the problems that he discussed have been completely solved; but at the regional level, his major objections have been overcome. Despite the growing sophistication of interregional models, most still assume uniformity of regional production functions. The Polenske model is a notable exception, however, and other regional researchers, as well as the Office of Business Economics of the Department of Commerce, are attempting to develop state or regional input coefficients. There is also a need for improved regional estimates of final demand, and additional data on interstate commodity flows as well as service transactions are needed to provide better estimates of trade coefficients.

A casual reading of Needleman's introduction to Tiebout's 1957 essay leaves the impression that the situation remains unchanged today [(85), Needleman, 1968, p. 17]. There has been no "quantum leap forward" in empirical regional and interregional input-output analysis; and at times, progress has appeared to be at the pace of a glacial drift. Over the past dozen years, however, there have been marked improvements in technique and an increasing number of applications. With a growing interest in regional and interregional models, both in this country and abroad, it is not unreasonable to expect further major advances in methods, data, and applications.

REFERENCES

(1) Almon, Clopper, Jr. "Consistent Forecasting in a Dynamic Multi-Sector Model," *Review of Economics and Statistics,* 1963, **45** (2), pp. 148–161.

(2) Almon, Clopper, Jr. *The American Economy to 1975.* New York: Harper & Row, 1966.

(3) Bahl, Roy W. and Shellhammer, Kenneth L. "Evaluating the State Business Tax Structure: An Application of Input-Output Analysis," *National Tax Journal,* 1969, **22** (2), pp. 203–16.

(4) Barnard, Jerald S. *Design and Use of Social Accounting Systems in State Development Planning.* Iowa City, Iowa: Bureau of Business and Economic Research, The Univ. of Iowa, 1967.

(5) Bergmann, Barbara R. "Economic Projections for the Region as a While" in Bergmann, Barbara R.; Chinitz, Benjamin and Hoover, Edgar M., *Projection of a Metropolis.* Technical Supplement to the New York Metropolitan Region Study, Cambridge, Mass.: Harvard University Press, 1961.

(6) Bergmann, Barbara R. "The Urban Economy and the 'Urban Crisis'," *American Economic Review,* 1969, **59** (4), Part I, pp. 639–45.

(7) Boulanger, Donald R. *The Implication of Vietnam De-Escalation for the Commonwealth of Massachusetts.* Harvard Economic Research Project, Report No. 15, August 1969.

(8) Bourque, Philip J. "Income Multipliers for the Washington Economy," *University of Washington Business Review.* Winter 1969, pp. 5–15.

(9) Bourque, Philip J. and Cox, Millicent. *An Inventory of Regional Input-Output Studies in the United States.* Occasional Paper No. 22, Graduate School of Business Administration. Seattle: Univ. of Washington, 1970.

(10) Bourque, Philip J. and Weeks, Eldon E. *Detailed Input-Output Tables for Washington State, 1963.* Washington Agricultural Experiment Station Circular 508, September 1969.

(11) Brodersohn, Mario S. *A Multiregional Input-Output Analysis of the Argentine Economy.* Instituto Torcuato Di Tella, Centro de Investigaciones Económicas, October 1965.

(12) Brody, Andrew. *A Simplified Growth Model.* Harvard Economic Research Project (Mimeo), March 1965.

(13) Byrd, Brookes. *The Crude Oil Industry and the Leontief Dynamic Model.* Harvard Economic Research Project. Research Papers, 1 (5). September 1969.

(14) Carter, Anne P. "Investment, Capacity Utlization, and Changes in Input Structure in the Tin Can Industry," *Review of Economics and Statistics,* 1960, **42** (3), Part I, pp. 283–91.

(15) Carter, Anne P. "The Economics of Technological Change," *Scientific American,* 1966, **214** (4), pp. 25–31.

(16) Carter, Anne P. "Changes in the Structure of the American Economy, 1947 to 1958 and 1962," *Review of Economics and Statistics,* 1967, **49** (2), pp. 209–24.

(17) Carter, Anne P. *Structural Change in the American Economy.* Cambridge, Mass.: Harvard Univ. Press, 1970.

(18) Carter, Harold O. *Input-Output Analysis as a Research Technique in Agricultural Economics.* Harvard Economic Research Project (mimeo), March 1965.

(19) Carter, Harold O. and Ireri, D. "Linkages of California–Arizona Input-Output Models to Analyze Water Transfer Patterns" in A. P. Carter and A. Brody, eds. *Applications of Input-Output Analysis.* Amsterdam: North-Holland, 1970, pp. 139–67.

(20) Chenery, Hollis B., and Clark, Paul G. *Interindustry Economics.* New York: John Wiley & Sons, Inc., 1959.

(21) Chenery, Hollis B; Clark, Paul G., and Cao Pinna, Vera. *The Structure and Growth of the Italian Economy.* Rome: United States Mutual Security Agency, 1953.

(22) CONSAD Research Corporation. *Impact Studies: Northeast Corridor Transportation Project.* US Department of Transportation, September 1967.

(23) Czamanski, Stanislaw and Malizia, Emil E. "Applicability and Limitations in the Use of National Input-Output Tables for Regional Studies," *Papers,* Regional Science Association, 1969, **23,** pp. 65–77.

(24) Davis H. Craig. *Multiregional Input-Output Techniques and Western Water Resources Development, Economic Evaluation of Water.* Part 5. Contribution No. 125. Berkeley: College of Engineering and School of Public Health, Water Resources Center, 1968.

(25) Evans, W. Duane. "Input-Output Computations" in Tibor Barna, ed. *Inter-Dependence of the Economy.* New York: John Wiley & Sons, Inc., 1963, pp. 53–102.

(26) Emerson, M. Jarvin. *The Interindustry Structure of the Kansas Economy.* Kansas Department of Economic Development, Economic Analysis and Planning Division, Report No. 21, 1969.

(27) Faucett, Jack G. "Data Requirements for Multiregional Input-Output Models" in *Input-Output Analysis and Transportation Planning.* Papers presented to an economics seminar conducted by the Office of Economics and Systems Analysis. Washington, D.C.: U.S. Department of Transportation, January 1969, pp. 50–59.

(28) Fei, John C. H. "A Fundamental Theorem for the Aggregation Problem of Input-Output Analysis." *Econometrica,* 1956, 24 (4) pp. 400–12.

(29) Fisher, Walter D. "Criteria for Aggregation in Input-Output Analysis." *Review of Economics and Statistics,* 1958, 40 (3) pp. 250–60.

(30) Ghosh, A. *Planning, Programming and Input-Output Models: Selected Papers on Indian Planning.* London: Cambridge Univ. Press, 1968.

(31) Ghosh, A. and Chakravarti, A. "The Problem of Location of an Industrial Complex" in A. P. Carter and A. Brody, eds. *Applications of Input-Output Analysis.* Amsterdam: North-Holland Publishing Company, 1970, pp. 148–63.

(32) Goodwin, R. M. "The Multiplier as Matrix." *Economic Journal,* 1949, No. 236, pp. 537–55.

(33) Gostenhofer, George. *Annual Report on Coefficent Projection: Projection of Coefficients for the Paper and Allied Products Industry to 1980.* Harvard Economic Research Project (mimeo), July 1968.

(34) Greytak, David. "The Regional Impact of Interregional Trade in Input-Output Analysis." Presented to the Annual Meeting, Regional Science Association, 1969.

(35) Harmston, Floyd K. *An Inter-Sectoral Analysis of the Missouri Economy, 1963.* Columbia, Missouri: Univ. of Missouri Research Center, School of Business and Public Administration, 1968.

(36) Harris, Curtis C., Jr. "A Multi-Regional, Multi-Industry Forecasting Model." Presented to the Annual Meeting, Regional Science Association, 1969.

(37) Harris, Curtis, Jr. *State and County Projections: A Progress Report of the Regional Forecasting Project.* College Park, Maryland: Univ. of Maryland, Bureau of Business and Economic Research, 2969.

(38) Hartwick, John M. *An Interregional Input-Output Analysis of the Eastern Canadian Economies.* Kingston, Ontario: Queen's Univ. Center for Economic Research, Discussion Paper No. 2 (mimeo), 1969.

(39) Helmstädter, E. "Die Drieksform der Input-Output matirx und ihre moeglichen Wandlungen in Wachstumprozess" Presented to the Wirtschaftswissenschafteliche Tagung der Gellschaftspolitik fuer Wirtschaftsund Socialwissenschafter, 1962.

(40) Helmstädter, E. "Die geordnete Input-Output Struktor." *Jarbucher fuer Nationaloekonomie,* 1962, 174 pp. 322–61.

(41) Henderson, James M. *The Efficiency of the Coal Industry.* Cambridge, Mass.: Harvard Univ. Press, 1958.

(42) Henderson, James M. "Efficiency and Pricing in the Coal Industry." *Review of Economics and Statistics,* 1956, 38 (1), pp. 50–60.

(43) Hirsch, Werner Z. "Interindustry Relations of a Metropolitan Area." *Review of Economics and Statistics,* 1959, **41** (3), pp. 360–69.

(44) Hirsch, Werner Z. "An Application of Area Input-Output Analysis." *Papers and Proceedings, Regional Science Association,* 1959, **5** pp. 79–2.

(45) Hirsch, Werner Z. "Input-Output Techniques for Urban Government Decisions." *American Economic Review, Papers and Proceedings,* 1968, **58**, pp. 162–70.

(46) Horiba, Y. "Testing the Heckscher-Ohlin Trade Model: An Input-Output Approach." Presented to the Annual Meeting of the Econometric Society, 1969.

(47) Isard, Walter. "Interregional and Regional Input-Output Analysis: A Model of a Space-Economy." *Review of Economics and Statistics,* 1951, **33** (4) pp. 318–28.

(48) Isard, Walter and Kuenne, Robert F. "The Impact of Steel Upon the Greater New York-Philadelphia Industrial Region." *Review of Economics and Statistics,* 1953, **35** (4), pp. 289–301.

(49) Isard, Walter. "Some Empirical Results and Problems of Regional Input-Output Analysis" in Wassily Leontief *et. al. Studies in the Structure of the American Economy.* Oxford Univ. Press, 1953, pp. 116–81.

(50) Isard, Walter. *Methods of Regional Analysis.* Cambridge, Mass.: M.I.T. Press, 1960.

(51) Isard, Walter; Langford, Thomas W., and Romanoff, Eliahu. *Philadelphia Region Input-Output Study.* Regional Science Research Institute, 2 vols., 1966.

(52) Jorgenson, Dale W. "Linear Models of Economic Growth." *International Economic Review,* 1968, **9** (1), pp. 1–13.

(53) Koti, Raghunath. *Application of the Dynamic Inverse in Economic Development Planning.* Research Papers, **1** (6). Harvard Economic Research Project, 1969.

(54) Krengel, Rolf; Stäglin, Reiner; Weisz, Jorg-Peter and Wessels, Hans. *Input-Output Relationships for the Federal Republic of Germany, 1954–1960.* Berlin: German Institute of Economic Research, 1969.

(55) Krengel, Rolf. *Input-Output Rechnung für Berlin (West) 1962.* Berlin: Duncker & Humblot, Heft 9, 1969.

(56) Leontief, Wassily. "Structural Change." *Studies in the Structure of the American Economy.* New York: Oxford Univ. Press, 1953. pp. 17–52.

(57) Leontief, Wassily. "Dynamic Analysis." *Studies in the Structure of the American Economy.* New York: Oxford Univ. Press, 1953, pp. 53–90.

(58) Leontief, Wassily. "Interregional Theory." *Studies in the Structure of the American Economy.* New York: Oxford Univ. Press, 1953, pp. 93–115.

(59) Leontief, Wassily. *Input-Output Economics.* New York: Oxford Univ. Press, 1966.

(60) Leontief, Wassily. "Lags and the Stability of Dynamic Systems," with A Reply by J. D. Sargan and a Rejoinder by Leontief, *Econometrica*, 1961, **29** (4), pp. 659–75.

(61) Leontief, Wassily. "The Structure of Development." *Scientific American*, 1963. Reprinted in *Input-Output Economics*, 1966, pp. 41–47.

(62) Leontief, Wassily. "An Alternative to Aggregation in Input-Output Analysis and National Accounts." *Review of Economics and Statistics*, 1967, **49**, pp. 412–19.

(63) Leontief, Wassily. "The Dynamic Inverse" in A. P. Carter and A. Brody, eds. *Contributions to Input-Output Analysis*. Amsterdam: North-Holland Publishing Company, 1970.

(64) Leontief, Wassily. Statement before the Joint Economic Committee, 90th Congress, 1st Session. *Statements of Witnesses and Supporting Materials*. 1. Washington, D.C.: U.S. Government Printing Office, 1967, pp. 237–63.

65) Leontief, Wassily; Morgan, Allison; Polenske, Karen; Simpson, David and Tower, Edward. "The Economic Impact—Industrial and Regional—of an Arms Cut." *Review of Economics and Statistics*, 1965, **47**, pp. 217–41.

(66) Leontief, Wassily and Strout, Alan. "Multiregional Input-Output Analysis" in Tibor Barna, ed. *Structural Interdependence and Economic Development*. New York: St. Martin's Press, reprinted in Leontief, Wassily. *Input-Output Economics*. 1966, pp. 223–57.

(67) Luft, Harold S. *Computational Procedure for the Multiregional Model*. Harvard Economic Research Project, Report No. 16, 1969.

(68) Middlehoek, A. J. "Tests of the Marginal Stability of Input-Output Coefficients" in A. P. Carter and A. Brody, eds. *Applications of Input-Output Analysis*. Amsterdam: North-Holland Publishing Company, 1970, pp. 261–75.

(69) Miernyk, William H. *The Elements of Input-Output Analysis*. New York: Random House, 1965.

(70) Miernyk, William H. "Long-Range Forecasting with an Input-Output Model." *Western Economic Journal*, 1968, **6**, pp. 165–76.

(71) Miernyk, William H. "The West Virginia Dynamic Model and its Implications." *Growth & Change*. 1, 1970.

(72) Miernyk, William H. "An Interindustry Forecasting Model with Water Quantity and Quality Constraints." *Proceedings*. Fourth Annual Symposium on Water Resources Research, The Ohio State University, 1970.

(73) Miernyk, William H. "Sampling Techniques in Making Regional Industry Forecasts" in A. P. Carter and A. Brody, eds. *Applications of Input-Ouput Analysis*. Amsterdam: North-Holland Publishing Company, 1970, pp. 305–21.

(74) Miernyk, William H.; Bonner, Ernest R.; Chapman, John H., Jr.; and Shellhammer, Keneth. *Impact of the Space Program on a Local Economy*. Morganstown W. Va.: West Virginia Univ. Library, 1967.

(75) Miernyk, William H.; Shellhammer, Kenneth L.; Brown, Douglas M.; Coccari, Ronald L.; Gallagher, Charles J. and Wineman, Wesley H. *Simulating Regional Economic Development.* Lexington, Mass.: D. C. Heath and Company, 1970.

(76) Miller, Ronald E. "Interregional Feedback Effects in Input-Output Models: Some Preliminary Results." *Proceedings.* Regional Science Association, 1966, **17**, pp. 105–25.

(77) Miller, Ronald E. "Interregional Feedbacks in Input-Output Models: Some Experimental Results." *Western Economic Journal,* 1969, **7**, pp. 41–50.

(78) Miyazawa, K. "Internal and External Matrix Multiplier in the Input-Output Model." *Hitotsubashi Journal of Economics.* June 1966.

(79) Moore, Frederick T. "Regional Economic Reaction Paths." *American Economic Review,* 1955, **45**, pp. 133–48. Discussions by Phillip Neff and Leon Moses, pp. 149–53.

(80) Moore, Frederick T. and Petersen, James W. "Regional Analysis: An Interindustry Model of Utah." Review of Economics and Statistics, 1955, **37**, pp. 368–81.

(81) Morishima, Michio and Murata Yasuo. "An Input-Output System Involving Nontransferable Goods." *Econometrica,* 1968, **36** (1), pp. 71–92.

(82) Moses, Leon N. "The Stability of Interregional Trading Patterns and Input-Output Analysis." *American Economic Review,* 1955, **45**, pp. 803–32.

(83) Moses, Leon, N. "A General Equilibrium Model of Production Interregional Trade and Location of Industry." *Review of Economics and Statistics,* 1966, **42**, pp. 373–97.

(84) National Planning Association. *Interindustry Studies and Model Development.* Vol. 4 of the Central Economic and Demographic Study for the State of New York, September 1968.

(85) Needleman, L., ed. *Regional Analysis.* Baltimore, Maryland: Penguin Books, 1968.

(86) Nevin, Edward; Roe, A. R.; and Round, J. I. *The Structure of the Welsh Economy.* Cardiff: Univ. Press, 1966.

(87) Peterson, R. D. *Economic Structure of Idaho: A Provisional Input-Output Study.* Moscow, Idaho: Univ. of Idaho, Bureau of Business and Economic Research, 1968.

(88) Polenske, Karen R. "Empirical Implementation of a Multiregional Input-Output Gravity Trade Model" in A. P. Carter and A. Brody, eds. *Contributions to Input-Output Analysis.* Amsterdam: North-Holland Publishing Company, 1970, pp. 127–47.

(89) Polenske, Karen R. *Interim Report: A Multi-Regional Input-Output Model—Concepts and Results.* Harvard Economic Research Project. Prepared for the Economic Development Administration, U.S. Department of Commerce, 1969.

(90) Polenske, Karen R. *An Empirical Test of Interregional Input-Output Models: Estimation of 1963 Japanese Production.* Eighty-second Annual Meeting, American Economic Association, 1969.

(91) Polenske, Karen R. *A Case Study of Transportation Models Used in Multiregional Analysis.* Unpublished Ph.D. dissertation, Harvard University, 1966.

(92) Polenske, Karen R. "A Multiregional Input-Output Model—Concepts and Results." *Input-Output Analysis and Transportation Planning.* Papers presented to an economics seminar conducted by the Office of Economics and Systems Analysis, Washington, D.C.: U.S. Department of Transportation, 1969, pp. 60–75.

(93) Polenske, Karen R., ed. *Techniques of Multiregional Input-Output Research.* 5 volumes. Lexington, Mass.: D. C. Heath and Company, 1971.

(94) Riefler, Roger F. *Interregional Input-Output: Washington and California.* Unpublished Ph.D. dissertation. Seattle: Univ. of Washington, 1966.

(95) Schaffer, William A., and Chu, Kong. "Nonsurvey Techniques for Constructing Regional Interindustry Models." *Papers.* Regional Science Association, 1969, **23**, pp. 83–101.

(96) Sevaldson, Per. "The Stability of Input-Output Coefficients" in A. P. Carter and A. Brody, eds. *Applications of Input-Output Analysis.* Amsterdam: North-Holland Publishing Company, 1970, pp. 207–337.

(97) Shen, T. Y. "An Input-Output Table with Regional Weights." *Papers and Proceedings of The Regional Science Association,* 1960, **6**, pp. 113–19.

(98) Simpson, David and Jinkichi, Tsukui. "The Fundamental Structure of Input-Output Tables, an International Comparison." *Review of Economics and Statistics.* 1965, **47**, pp. 434–46.

(99) Stillson, Richard. "Regional Trade and Structure Model for Pollution Abatement Study." *Proceedings.* Fourth Annual Symposium on Water Resources Research, Ohio State University, 1970.

(100) Stone, Richard, and Brown, Alan. "Behavorial and Technical Change in Economic E.A.G.." Robinson, ed. *Problems in Economic Development.* London: Macmillan and Company, 1965, pp. 434–36.

(101) Tiebout, Charles M. "Regional and Interregional Input-Output Models: An Appraisal." *Southern Economic Journal,* 1957, **24**, pp. 140–47.

(102) Tiebout, Charles M. *The Community Economic Base Study.* Supplementary Paper No. 16. Committee for Economic Development, 1962.

(103) Tiebout, Charles M. "An Empirical Regional Input-Output Projection Model: The State of Washington, 1980." *Review of Economics and Statistics,* 1969, **51**, pp. 334–40.

(104) Tilanus, C. B. "Marginal Versus Average Impact Coefficients in Input-Output Forecasting." *Quarterly Journal of Economics,* 1967, **81**, pp. 140–45.

(105) Tilanus, C. B. and Theil, H. *The Information Theory Approach to the Evaluation of Input-Output Forecasts.* Econometric Institute of the Netherlands School of Economics, 1964.

(106) Udis, Bernard. "Regional Input-Output Analysis and Water Quality Management." *Journal of the Rocky Mountain Social Science Association*, 1965, pp. 34–41.

(107) Udis, Bernard, ed. *An Interindustry Analysis of the Colorado River Basin in 1960 with Projections to 1980 and 2010*. (mimeo), Bureau of Economic Research, Univ. of Colorado, 1968.

(108) U.S. Department of Labor. Bureau of Labor Statistics, *Projection 1970*. Bulletin No. 1536, 1966.

(109) United Nations. *Input-Output Bibliography*, 1963–1966, Statistical Papers, Series M, No. 46, 1967.

(110) Yamada, Hiroyuki and Ihara, Takeo. "Input-Output Analysis of Interregional Repercussion." *Proceedings* Third Far East Conference, Regional Science Association, 1967, pp. 3–31.

(111) Yan, Chiou-shuang. *Introduction to Input-Output Economics*. New York: Holt, Rinehart and Winston, 1969.

13

On Health, Population Change, and Economic Development

MARK PERLMAN

University of Pittsburgh

This essay reflects a summary of my perception of the present interface between what we "know" from the deductive and from the empirical standpoints about demographic and economic relationships and the policy questions with which we seem to be concerning ourselves. Obviously, it is impossible to present within the confines of a single essay a comprehensive survey of either our stock of knowledge (including "conventional wisdom") or a discussion of the spectrum of population and economic growth problems of our time. Thus, what I attempt to do is simply to identify where we are and to suggest some of the more logical as well as likely next steps. This discussion of the interface can be summarized in a very few sentences which I pose at the outset to reinforce the thrust of what I wish later to expand.

SUMMARY OF THE ARGUMENT

1. Demographic analysis was long hampered by lack of data. One consequence was reliance upon *a priori* conclusions which failed to pass the most simple empirical tests.
2. The second consequence was to identify empirically mensurable entities and to try to link them by probabilistic relationships. These relationships sometimes, but not always, proved stable.

3. Purportedly empirical general theories of demographic transition (relating industrialization to lengthened life and, after a lag, to diminished fertility) have been pretty thoroughly exploded; they did not measure up to later empirical experience.

4. I contend that the empirical theory of demographic transition suffered from two unnecessary specification errors, really mistakes which showed in the measuring of the "wrong" things— (i) an implicit agreement upon per capita economic growth as *the* high-priority social goal and (ii) reductions in mortality, having both a positive and proportional relationship to reductions in morbidity.

5. As we lack much statistical information about individual health patterns in rich, developed nations, it is unlikely that it will appear in less developed countries—areas where its presence seems even more needed.

6. Nonetheless, as it is likely that the capacity of the adult population to produce (whether it be that which is included in the Gross National Product, as I prefer, on all goods and services) is what affects fertility patterns, there is a logic to implementing public policies designed at turning chronologically (prematurely, incapacitated adults from "sometimes" workers into regular workers. This end can be achieved by "spotting medical program shots," that is, by organizing and stressing medical care programs to affect certain age and industrial groups.

7. Even the foregoing element may be insufficient. A small labor force, made so by low birth rates in some past quinquennium, may be so sought after by employers that its scarcity results in unusually large wage increases which really represent increases in productivity. These increases, in other historical situations, would more correctly be attributable to efficiency improvements in the other factors of production, to improvements in distribution, or to general increases in specialization associated with changes in the political boundaries of the product or factor markets. The great *real* U.S. wage prosperity 1946–1965 seems to me to be explained in good part by the relative smallness of the cohorts of the 1920's and the 1930's.

8. Thus, investment in the efficiency of the labor force, be it by the way of better health (which I discuss somewhat at length) or by education (which I do not discuss), is only one element of

the productivity-demographic response relationship. In impoverished economies, the usually high-fertility response to any sign of economic prosperity may reflect the need for workers physically able to work regularly—families count not the mouths to be fed so much as they count the hands capable of production. In all societies (but particularly in industrially advanced societies), when labor (for reasons of low birth rates two decades earlier) is scarce, large wage rate increases may lead to periods of larger numbers of children because families can afford them. In the first instance, medical programs are the obvious answer to encouraging demographic transition to occur. In the second instance, a once depressed birth rate has an implicit self-correcting factor—higher wages lead to larger families—larger families, to larger numbers of workers—larger numbers of workers, to the ultimate dampening of wage rate increases.

9. The real immediate need, for analytical purposes, thus, is data collection, particularly on the health inventory side so that we can determine whether it is the "counting of hands capable of production" that leads to reduced family size and the trade-off of babies for the larger consumption of real goods and services.

THE SETTING

Models

In my opinion, one of the principal obstacles to improving the quality of the demographic economic understanding is an unwillingness to assess the limitations of the various analytical methods used. Over the years, there have been two.[1] Although, one is far more deductive than it is inductive, and the other is the other way around, neither is entirely deductive nor inductive. For purposes of semantic clarity, I choose to refer to the products of the approach which leans heavily on deductive reasoning as models and products of the approach leaning heavily on observation of data as "principles" or even as "laws." These are somewhat arbitrary choices of terms, but in the absence of any convention accepting Marshall's usage, this choice seems to me to be as good as any other. The initial step in this essay is to identify the two principal models that form the intellectual heritage of the topic.

---

[1]Marshall's *Principles* . . . should still be "must" reading not only for graduate students but also for forgetful professors. [cf. 23, pp. 29–37].

U

Each was rather simple and made sense principally when considered in very special circumstances.

The first model, popularly, but to an extent erroneously, identified with Thomas R. Malthus, claimed that the population growth was checked by the growth of necessary food supply. Malthus, in the earliest editions of his *Essay on Population* [21], formulated a model which explicitly specified that the population grew at a geometric rate while the food supply expanded only at an arithmetic rate. While it is clearly obvious that Malthus' view was a product of some actual observation, what he *stressed* was the tendency towards divergence of two abstract mathematical series. It seemed "logical" to him to expect sexual reproduction to proceed at a geometric rate; similarly, it seems reasonable under the prevalent perception of the nature of agricultural production to assume that the rate of increased output would be, at best, arithmetically constant. Putting the two together, Malthus deduced that population levels could increase only after agricultural output grew. Hence, in the Malthusian model, agricultural output (really a proxy for all economic output) was the independent variable; population growth was the dependent variable.

For reasons of intellectual accuracy, it is worth noting that Francesco Botero, well over a century prior to 1799, when the initial edition of Malthus' *Essay on Population* was written, actually phrased the model in a somewhat more sophisticated way. Writing of cities [4], Botero suggested that the actual sizes of cities were a balance between the desires of individuals to migrate to the urban center and the average cost of food, as the latter had to be transported from farther and farther fields (or villages). Again, phrased formally, the size of the population of cities is a function of the price of food delivered to the city. The price of food is itself a dependent function of the productivity of the soil and climate and the costs of transportation. Botero's formulation is more sophisticated than Malthus' because Botero neither tied his model to any supposed constant proclivity to sexual reproduction nor did he assume any specified supply schedule for foods; each could be one thing at one time and something else at another period. Finally, Botero's model explicitly included migration as an alternative to natural population increase for population growth.

I refer to the Botero-Malthus model as the "demographic-dependent function" model; it makes demographic performance dependent upon economic well-being.

The second model, commonly used by economists, was derived from some intuitive views Adam Smith entertained about the comparatively greater welfare (compared to Western Europe) that artisans in the American colonies apparently enjoyed. Smith suggested that, under certain conditions, growing populations encourage the development of specialization because of market expansion [33, 34]. In these ways, population growth could be said to lead to increases in economic output and per capita economic prosperity. In the case of Smith's model, population growth occurs first and is the independent variable. Economic growth or prosperity follow and is, therefore, the dependent variable. Smith, certainly among the more canny of writers, did not advance his conclusions as a generally applicable model, but the relationships, both in specification and in direction of relationships, have relevance to other situations as well; and the model has been a tool of widespread analytical significance. In recent decades, Professor Kuznets of Harvard University has stressed the kind of reasoning which Smith had in mind [17].

I term the "Smith model," the "economic dependent function" model of demographic change; it makes economic performance the result of population change.

Both models were initially advanced in fairly formal and vigorous terms, but they were advanced largely "in the abstract" and dependent for their "proof" on rather unspecified conditions and/or on their inherent consistency. In all instances, the constraining assumptions were unarticulated (much less examined for relevance), and, most probably, were not really considered at all. Smith's model may have had the virtue of containing some dynamic elements—after all, market expansion and specialization in production do represent modifications of the institutional *status quo ante*. But, the era of more or less careful mensuration of socio-economic factors was still a long time off.

The Laws and the Evidence

In the meantime, a substantial body of literature developed that combined more analytical insight into demographic relationships with the collection of data necessary for formulation of "laws" or "generalizations." The demographic change of nations was, as a result of examination of census and vital statistics data collection, seen to be quite clearly dependent upon the initial age and sex composition of the basic population, cyclical and secular changes in mortality patterns, cyclical and secular changes in fertility patterns, and cyclical and secular changes in migration patterns.

Demographic characteristics   Strangely enough, the importance of the role of the initial age and sex composition of population did not receive as much attention from academic demographers early in the evolution of the demographic discipline as it has in the last three or four decades [3, pp. 8–25]. Just why this situation prevailed, I know not. But it may well be that mathematics- and equilibrium-conscious "ivy tower demographers" are rather recent breeds, and concepts such as "achieving population stability" meant rather little, even in spite of Malthus' influence, until about the end of World War I.[2]

Mortality   Instead, what seems to have attracted many scholars' attention as much as anything were changes in mortality patterns. While I shall have much more to say about this subject later in this essay, the important point is that the increase in life expectancy of newborn babies, to say nothing of adolescents, was noticed as one of the great marked changes in those countries that "industrialized" during the nineteenth century. Data pertaining to changes in life expectancy and causes of death for other than infants for the nineteenth century still are far less available than most scholars seem to realize. But the varieties of, particularly the uniform certainty of, explanations emerged and are there for anyone who cares to read to see. The important point is that scholars like G. T. Griffith [12] and T. H. Marshall [24] did identify the changes and proceeded to give what seemed to be a perfectly logical explanation, namely the spread of scientific or modern medicine. Again, once more, the "logic of explanation" was the method they employed: it was *a priori* rather than empirical. Professor Thomas McKeown has recently succeeded in exploding their tightly reasoned arguments pertaining to the mortality changes and the historical impact medical discovery had on life expectancy in the nineteenth century [25, 26, and 27].

Fertility   Within the past two decades, there has developed a new interest in patterns of fertility change. Perhaps one explanation

---

[2]Actually, Malthus, himself, retreated from the extreme pessimism of the first edition of his *Essay on Population* [21]; for proof see a later edition [21] and his *Principles of Political Economy* [22, Chap. 23].

for this recent focusing of interest was the fact of the unexpected "baby boom" after World War II. Another reason may well be a recent conviction that the newer methods of fertility control make it likely that a measure of social planning can be extended to the area of popoulation growth [10, Chap. 18].

Migration Interest in migration has not been consistently present. During the nineteenth century, there were vast migrations from Europe to the new world and Australasia. This migratory pattern was interrupted during the First World War and really did not resume thereafter on a large scale except in the case of Australia, Israel, Taiwan, and West Germany—and then only after the Second World War. Migration from rural to urban areas, however, seems to have been a consistent pattern throughout the last century and a half in those places where we have reasonably good demographic data. Theories explaining the reasons for migration are, themselves, relatively new. Perhaps the major difficulty is the problem of mensuration of migration. Certainly without data and data processing, one cannot speculate very assuredly about causes.

The putting together of the theories relating to the implications of basic population age and sex composition, theories relating to mortality change, theories relating to fertility change, and theories relating to the cause of migration ebbs and flows, has become increasingly "unpopular," only because two predictions, based on what seemed at one point statistically stable, failed in their predictive performance. The famous Pearl-Reed growth pattern [31], which suggested that an area's population growth started slowly, gained speed, and then leveled off, does not seem to have had empirical verification in most of the areas where the validity (stability) of its effects had been proclaimed. At the time that Professors Raymond Pearl and Carol Reed promulgated their proposition, it looked very much as though the American population level were approaching an asymptote. Whatever conviction the Pearl-Reed argument generally induced was exploded by the baby boom following the Second World War.

The other "law," the principle of demographic transition, advanced in the early 1930s originally in France [19], suggested that there was an inherent behavorial relationship between a decline in the mortality rates of the younger age groups (0–15) and the fertility rates of the parental generation (18–38) [2, 5, 7, 11, 29, and 35]. The claim was that although declining fertility rates lagged and the mortality rate declines, the casual relationship could be depended upon regularly to occur. Again, the neatness of this formulation (family desire for replenishment of its members) was exploded by the behavior of the American population immediately following the Second World War, by the fertility patterns in Latin America at all times, and most recently by the resurgence of fertility increases in Taiwan and Korea (areas where "demographic transition" seemed to be occurring).

INTERACTION EFFECTS

There are several unarticulated assumptions which modern demographic economists would do well to specify. First, most all of them believe economic growth is generally accepted as *the* high-priority social goal. Certainly *they* accept it as a high-priority social goal. Whether impecunious Latin Americans or the formally uneducated Moslems of the Middle East accept it as *a* (much less *the*) high-priority social goal seems to me to be a matter worth careful empirical investigation. My suspicion is that it is far less appreciated as *the* high-priority social goal than most economists believe it to be.

Second, foreign aid from industrially advanced nations, particularly the United States, was expected to have an apparent visible effect on the physical capacity of poor people to work and to produce marketable goods and services. The sad history is that American foreign aid did not seem to have a visible per capita capacity to produce. Instead, foreign aid meant food, and food meant greater numbers of people—particularly of the economically dependent ages. The failure of aid to enrich the poor or to augment production dampened the friendship between the donor nation and the recipients, which was supposed to result as a by-product. Appreciation of America's generosity, which could have generated even more foreign aid, was generally not apparent. At present, the American foreign aid program is much in decline; and the foreign aid programs of other companies, the British Commonwealth, West Germany, and even tiny Israel, are dominated by military and tactical political considerations rather than the kind of economic reasoning which most economists believe was originally the prime purpose.

The important reason that foreign aid programs did not have

the expected "full impact" was because in certain areas, particularly Latin America and the Moslem countries of the Middle East, there was no apparent reduction—even a lagged reduction—in fertility rates. Mortality rates for the younger age groups fell as Western medicine and improved nutrition had their expected effects. However, for a variety of reasons, some of which I wish to discuss later, fertility rates did not fall. In other words, demographic transition did not take place. The public health impact was, thus, confined to reduction in mortality. True, production rose somewhat, but the production growth rate was at about the same rate as growth in population. People were, therefore, on the average, no better off. Moreover, there was some reason to believe that the maldistribution (unequal distribution) of the product was increasing rather than diminishing. Because there seemed thus to be a lack of improvement in per capita living standards, by the beginning of the second Eisenhower Administration, there was increased reluctance in spending in foreign aid programs of any American funds on public health.

After 1960, the discovery of the "pill," consciousness of the increasing problem of too great a growth of population and, finally, some effective lobbying by individuals associated with the Planned Parenthood Federation, the Population Council, and a group of respected economists, resulted in the development of American government support for national population control programs in those countries where they were acceptable. Perhaps no individual has had a greater impact on national planners' thinking about the matter than Dr. Stephen Enke, who stressed rather convincingly (again on an *a priori* basis) that a dollar invested in population control programs probably did more (by a large factor) to improve per capita living standards in poor countries of the world than a dollar invested in any other kind of socio-economic reform program [9]. Dr. Enke, whose analysis of the theory of the economic effects of population control is universally acknowledged, published a most provocative article in a 1966 issue of the *Economic Journal,* identifying the nub of his thinking [10 and 31]. In it, he proposed several kinds of contraceptive programs and suggested how the mix might be adjusted to maximize the return on expenditure.

During this recent period, there have been several relatively important contributions by economists which stressed, again largely from an *a priori* base, the usefulness of the population control programs. Perhaps the most influential was the Coale-Hoover model appearing in their study of the Indian and Mexican economic growth and demographic problems [6]. Professor Hoover, for whom this volume is a testimonial, also worked on a study pertaining to Pakistan [15]. It drew heavily on some advice by Dr. Enke. In general, the Hoover contribution has been to stress the importance of controlling population growth because the investment process in a poor country has to be divided between investment goods and investment in human capital. If one can slow down the rate of growth of population, the need to invest relatively heavily on the human capital side is diminished, the effectiveness of investment in plant is perforce increased, or a combination of both results occurs. The Pakistan study demonstrated that if a country did not really accept as its major goal increasing per capita consumption, but was willing to trade off an increase in per capita consumption for greater economic nationalism, a population control program could logically serve that purpose as well.

Even earlier than the Coale-Hoover study, there was an important study by Professor Harvey Leibenstein, then of the University of California at Berkeley. Leibenstein tried to explain why economic development was not occurring in many poor countries in spite of the infusions of American and other foreign aid [20]. One thrust of Leibenstein's argument was that the working population lacked sufficient physical strength to sustain the physical efforts necessary to achieve production levels that would yield real economic breaks through. Professor Leibenstein's argument depended to a large degree upon his perception of the importance of caloric intake on the capacity of individuals to produce market products.

Food input, however, has not been the only variable considered. There have also been several studies undertaken, particularly at the University of Michigan, trying to tie together the impact of malaria control on demographic and economic conditions. Their intellectual antecedent was an international program initiated by Dr. Fred Soper, then of the Pan-American Health Organization, popularizing a program for malaria control under the impressively promising title of "Malaria Eradication." If and when malaria control could be achieved, Soper believed that economic progress would result. I have commented elsewhere about a few places where economic activity was generated once the malaria peril was eliminated; at times and in certain places the "plan" really worked [32]. This result, however, is not new. Many areas of the

United States and Europe, to say nothing of Israel, have had historic problems with malaria control, as well as other similar diseases, and have managed to eliminate virtually all malarial and comparable infection. Such success, however, did not occur in all the areas where Dr. Soper had had hopes that progress could be achieved. Professor Peter Newman wrote a provocative book on malaria control in Ceylon [28]. His colleague at the University of Michigan, Professor Robin Barlow, has done a good deal more to specify the results and to try to link them to causes [1]. One of Newman's contributions was to try to identify the existence of malaria on an individual basis. While his comparative intellectual advantage is not in the area of clinical medicine, what he set out to do seems to me to have been an absolutely essential element in the kind of a study he wanted to make.

In any event, all these studies have tried to show how the health factor was related to investment in human capital and how investment in human capital was, itself, significantly affected by the rate of fertility and of the rate of general population growth.

CRITICISMS OF THE INTERACTIONS

Even though many economists have alleged, if not overtly suggested, that population growth and economic development are incompatible, the two are not. Insofar as their reasoning has an *a priori* flavor their reasoning has as its "grandparent" Malthus' famous first *Essay on Population*. On the other hand, Adam Smith and more recently Simon Kuznets, have tried to indicate either on an *a priori* basis or, in the case of Kuznets, with reference to some empirical evidence [16 and 18], that population growth and economic development are compatible under a great many conditions.

I think that the recent record is all too clear that investment in human capital as well as investment in infra-structure institutions is, in the case of most poor nations, so slow in "paying off" that if a foreign aid donor demands that the trees it waters bear fruit within five years, those advocating large-scale foreign aid programs, as earlier discussed, are likely to be disappointed.

But, to my mind the major point that has to be made and one that has not been sufficiently realized, is that there had been a confusion of the role of mortality and the role of morbidity as they affect fertility rates. The introduction of modern and public health techniques probably has had a great impact on reducing mortality without necessarily reducing morbidity. We have few morbidity statistics in industrially advanced nations; we have virtually no morbidity statistics in industrially disadvantaged nations. However, my own observation has been that many of the diseases that permeate the environment of industrially backward nations are chronically debilitating; and although modern medicine has succeeded in preventing death from these diseases, it has not succeeded in eliminating the debilitating qualities. Consequently, although lives are preserved and the size of the labor force is somewhat increased, the productivity of these workers is low, and total output is not sufficiently increased.

I am told that any disease which carries with it periods of high fevers (febrile conditions in excess of 100°F.) are protein-depriving diseases. Irrespective of the amount of proteins given to the victims of these diseases, and irrespective of the amount of protein he has had prior to the infection of the fever, he will lose much, if not most, of his protein reserve during a period of prolonged high fever [18]. Similarly, I am told that individuals suffering from intestinal parasitic diseases, as well as other kinds of parasitic diseases, will not benefit from increased caloric consumption noticeably [18]. Apparently, the "worms" are fed first; whatever is "left over" goes to the host human-being.

Many of the febrile diseases as well as the parasitic diseases were present at one time in industrially advanced countries like the United States. However, countries in the temperate temperature belt have an advantage because many of the parasitic diseases are transmitted by individuals walking barefoot. In temperate climates, the temptation to walk barefoot year-round is perforce less than in tropical climates. Thus, it is easier in cooler areas to control parasitic diseases simply because the population has a "comfort-incentive" to wear shoes. It is also highly probable that infection and reinfection in a temperate climate occurs most frequently during the warmer months; during the colder months, the bacteria, worms, or viruses causing the disease may be less active. This climatic factor helps both directly and indirectly in the elimination of the disease.

Nonetheless, the elimination of malaria from many parts of the United States and many parts of Europe and Israel (to cite recent examples), was accompanied by a heavy investment in education. I venture that it was the interaction of the two, the draining of swamps, and the heavy investment on individual education (particularly the education of children) which "solved the malaria problem." Education took the form of not only teaching of the modern equivalents of the *trivium* and *quadrivium* but of also providing a basis for understanding the importance of screens and other preventive medical techniques.

The South American statistics, insofar as we have them, suggest that reduction in mortality rates has not led to reduction in fertility rates. One of the first of my comments, thus, is to suggest that one topic that needs considerable empirical investigation is the impact of the reduction of morbidity, rather than mortality, on fertility rates. I believe that those who conclude that the mission of public health is simply to reduce mortality are short-sighted. Expenditure in public health in reduction of disease, again on *a priori* grounds, can be even more important than the reduction of mortality. The reasoning goes as follows: (a) the size of a family is determined by the number of individuals who can be counted on to earn income for a family; (b) if illness abounds, it is mandatory for the family to remain large in order to insure itself of the bare necessities to maintain life; (c) if family size increases by virtue of public health measures, but the proportion of dependents (by virtue of age or illness) is not reduced, there is need for more labor force participants rather than fewer, and these should be expected to be no motivation to reduce family size; (d) consequently, the immediate purpose for those seeking to enrich the poor and less developed nations is to improve the health of those in or likely to join the labor force so that they may become regularly more productive; and (e) then it seems reasonable to expect fertility rates to fall according to the patterns set in industrialized nations during most periods.

COHORT SIZE, WAGE PRESSURES, AND POPULATION POLICY

I have already indicated earlier that there has been a strange delay in studying the impact of age and sex sizes of different cohorts on the labor force as well as on later fertility rates. Professor R. E. Easterlin in his truly insightful studies has presented several hypotheses (not necessarily completely consistent with each other) relating to the impact of wage rates on the willingness of cohorts to increase or diminish their own fertility as they approach the more usual high-fertility years of their life [8].

Easterlin's conclusion, which seems to me to be eminently sound, is that a small cohort, when it reaches the labor market, if it is not threatened by the prospect of immigration, will tend to be prosperous and enjoy this prosperity by speeding up family formation, by having more children, or by a combination of both of these factors. By the same token, a large cohort when it reaches the period of normal family formation, will find the competitive pressures of the labor market such that it chooses to delay family formation, have fewer children, or a combination of both. Thus, according to Easterlin's conclusions (all of which are quite empirical), there is an equilibrating factor in deviations from "some usual norm" of cohort size—"too small a cohort" will lead to larger families, when that cohort gets to the family formation; and "too small a cohort" will ultimately lead to correction in the other direction. I believe these points, consistent with the original Malthusian formulation (and even more consistent with the Botero formulation), tend to make *a priori* sense as well as being empirically borne out.

However, Easterlin's position views childbearing essentially as a consumer-operation. Presumably parents' feelings of wealth or poverty (security or insecurity) lead them to make decisions regarding the timing and number of births. It is, it seems to me on the face of things, quite logical to expect families also to consider children from a "producer-standpoint." I do not mean by this inference to suggest that parents look to their children to "support them in their old age"; rather, I infer that parents, particularly in many less-developed societies, tend to look upon children as part of an extended family system, and make their decisions regarding spacing and number of births according to their perception of the need to provide an assured source of wage flow into the extended family. It is at this point, I believe, that the perception of the toll of disease and premature withdrawal from the labor force is so terribly significant.

The situation is further complicated by one factor that I think has become very significant in our own time. During any quinquennium when the labor force is made unnaturally small because of the creation of small cohorts some two decades before, there is a natural tendency not only to raise real wages per worker (because of the inherent bargaining superiority of the unusually small additions to the labor force) but also a consequent tendency to shift to other agents of production—namely investment in capital equipment. Smallness in labor force, associated with low increments to the labor force, tends to speed up career advancement and further to lower the quality of worker-associated productivity. In other words, smallness of cohorts encourages disproportionately high increments in real wages and discourages maintenance of normal rates of productivity increase. The resulting effect of high wages, introduced by virtue of the unusually small cohorts entering the labor force, tends to prevent wage rates from "slipping downward" as the cohorts entering the labor force become more normal in size. Reliance upon technology tends to cause unemployment, particularly among the entrants into the labor force as the newer, larger cohorts attain working age. Any institutional factors serving to increase wage rates, be they collective bargaining, high minimum wage rates, and particularly taxes based upon payrolls but not upon capital equipment that replaces laborers, all serve to exacerbate the unemployment situation.

My general conclusion, then, is that while families look to a steady flow of individuals entering the labor force, in order to assure the family of continued wage income, there can be by virtue of such demographic events as unusually small cohorts and the ultimate economic consequences of these small cohorts, factors which exacerbate high unemployment levels.

It seems to me, writing as I am in the middle part of 1970, what I am describing here is a phenomenon known not only to less developed countries like Brazil and India, but a phenomenon known to depressed enclaves within such developed societies and economies as the United States and Great Britain.

While the purpose of this essay is not to set out the bench marks for wise policy decisions, there is one point which, in my opinion, deserves particular stress. Insofar as my contention regarding the importance of health as it pertains to labor force participation is the key, I believe it is extraordinarily important to determine empirically what the facts are. If the health of the labor force is impaired, if debilitating diseases, be they parasitical, bacteria- or virus-originated, or be they the products of patterns of living (e.g., cardio-vascular disease, circulatory disease, or even digestive in symptom), it is wise to know the degree of universality of the situation. It is also obviously wise to be able to measure how well the nation's medical manpower is matched with the nation's needs to improve the quality of the health of its labor force. In the United

States, the National Health Survey has not proven to be a very effective instrument in this matching process. Considering the importance of the problem, it is probably clear that one of the federal government's major steps in the next few years is to improve the reporting of chronic disease, particularly in the labor force and to design a program to bring medical resources to bear on the problem.

There are other implications as well. These deal with the impact of institutions that were created to protect low-paid workers by raising their rates of pay. Insofar as their rates of pay were low because of low productivity, and insofar as the low productivity was a product of ill health (a situation dramatically noted by Eric Hoffer, the longshoreman-philosopher of the 'fifties) [14], the solution is not to be found in economic institutions and their ramifications but in better appreciation of medical needs and the alternative options available to the community in matching its medical resources with those needs.

REFERENCES

(1) Barlow, Robin. *The Economic Effects of Malaria Eradication.* Bureau of Public Health Economics, Research Series No. 15. Ann Arbor, Mich.: School of Public Health, The University of Michigan, 1968.

(2) Blacker, C. P. "Stages in Population Growth." *Eugenics Review,* Oct. 1947.

(3) Bogue, Donald J. *Principles of Demography.* New York: John Wiley, 1969.

(4) Botero, Francesco. *Delle Cause Della Grandezza del Città.* 1558.

(5) Carr-Saunders, A. M. *The Population Problem: A Study in Human Evolution.* Oxford: McClarendon Press, 1922.

(6) Coale, Ansley J. and Hoover, Edgar M. *Population Growth and Economic Development in Low-Income Countries.* Princeton, N.J.: Princeton Univ. Press, 1950.

(7) Davis, Kingsley. "The Theory of Change and Response in Modern Demographic History." *Population Index, 29,* Oct. 1963, pp. 345–66.

(8) Easterlin, Richard A. *Population, Labor Force, and Long Swings in Economic Growth.* New York: Columbia Univ. Press for the National Bureau of Economic Research, 1968.

(9) Enke, Stephen. "The Economic Aspects of Slowing Population Growth." *Economic Journal, 76,* 1966, pp. 44–56.

(10) Enke, Stephen. *Economics for Development.* Englewood Cliffs, N.J.: Prentice-Hall, 1963.

(11) Glass, David V. "Population Growth and Population Policy" in Mindel C. Sheps and Jeanne Clare Ridley. eds. *Public Health and Population Change: Current Research Issues*. Pittsburgh: Univ. of Pittsburgh Press, 1965, pp. 1–11.

(12) Griffith, G. T. *Population Problems of the Age of Malthus*. Cambridge, 1926.

(13) Habakkuk, H. J. "English Population in the Eighteenth Century." *Economic History Review*, Second Series, 6, 1953, pp. 117–33.

(14) Hoffer, Eric. *The Ordeal of Change*. New York: Harper and Row, 1963.

(15) Hoover, Edgar M. and Perlman, Mark. "Measuring the Effects of Population Control on Economic Development: Pakistan as a Case Study." *Pakistan Development Review*, 6, 1966, pp. 168–76.

(16) Kuznets, Simon. "Economic Capacity and Population Growth" in Richard N. Farmer, John D. Long, and George J. Stolnitz, eds. *World Population—The View Ahead*. Proceedings of a Conference on World Population Problems held at Indiana University on May 3–6, 1967. Bloomington, Ind.: Graduate School of Business, Bureau of Business Research, Indiana Univ., 1968, pp. 51–97.

(17) Kuznets, Simon. *Economic Growth and Structure: Selected Essays*. New York: W. W. Norton, 1965.

(18) Kuznets, Simon. "Population Change and Aggregate Output" in Universities-National Bureau Committee for Economic Research. *Demographic and Economic Change in Developed Countries*. Princeton, N.J.: Princeton Univ. Press for the National Bureau of Economic Research, 1960, pp. 324–51.

(19) Landry, A. *La Revolution Demographique*. Paris, 1934.

(20) Leibenstein, Harvey. *Economic Backwardness and Economic Growth*. New York: John Wiley, 1963.

(21) Malthus, Thomas R. *First Essay on Population*. London, 1798, reprinted by Macmillan, London, 1966. A second and much enlarged edition appeared in 1803. The full title of the original first edition was "An Essay on the Principle of Population, as it Affects the Future Improvement of Society, with Remarks on the Speculations of Mr. Goodwin, M. Condorcet, and Other Writers." The fifth or best-known (today) edition was published in 1817.

(22) Malthus, Thomas R. *Principles of Political Economy*. London: First edition 1820, second edition 1836; reprinted in New York by Augustus M. Kelley.

(23) Marshall, Alfred *Principles of Economics: An Introductory Volume*. 8th ed. London: Macmillan and Company, 1920.

(24) Marshall, T. H. "The Population Problem During the Industrial Revolution." *Economic History* (Supplement to *Economic Journal*, 1, Jan. 1929, pp. 429–56.

(25) McKeown, Thomas and Brown, Archie. "Medical Evidence Related to English Population Changes in the Eighteenth Century" *Population Studies*, 9, Nov. 1955, pp. 119–41.

(26) McKeown, Thomas and Record, R. G. "Reasons for the Decline of Mortality in England and Wales During the Nineteenth Century." *Population Studies*, 14, pp. 94–122.

(27) McKeown, Thomas. "Medicine and World Population" in Mindel C. Sheps and Jeanne Clare Ridley, eds. *Public Health and Population Change: Current Research Issues.* Pittsburgh: Univ. of Pittsburgh Press, 1965, pp. 25–40.

(28) Newman, Peter. *Malaria Eradication and Population Growth, With Special Reference to Ceylon and British Guiana.* Ann Arbor: Univ. of Mich., School of Public Health, 1965.

(29) Notestein, F. W. "Population—The Long View" in T. W. Schultz, ed. *Food for the World.* Chicago, 1945.

(30) Pearl, Raymond. *The Biology of Population Growth.* New York: Knopf, 1925.

(31) Perlman, Mark Remarks made as member on Panel of World Population in *The Food-People Balance* as part of the Symposium sponsored by the National Academy of Engineers at the Sixth Annual Meeting. Washington, D.C., 1970.

(32) Perlman, Mark. "Some Economic Aspects of Public Health Programs in Underdeveloped Areas." Michigan, Bureau of Public Health Economics and Department of Economics. *The Economics of Health and Medical Care,* Proceedings of a Conference on the Economics of Health and Medical Care held May 10–12. Ann Arbor, Mich., Univ. of Michigan, 1964, pp. 286–99.

(33) Smith, Adam. *In Inquiry Into the Nature and Causes of the Wealth of Nations.* Homewood, Ill.: Irwin, 1963 (first published 1776).

(34) Spengler, J. J. "Adam Smith on Population." *Population Studies,* 24, Nov. 1970, pp. 377–88.

(35) United Nations, Population Division. "History of Population Theories." *Determinances and Consequences of Population Trends.* New York: United Nations, 1953.

14

National Urban Policy: Stage 1: Building the Foundation

HARVEY S. PERLOFF

Dean and Professor, School of Architecture and Urban Planning
U.C.L.A., Los Angeles, Calif.

If we are now more appreciative of the severity of our urban problems than we were in the past, we are still far from agreement on
the need for a basic national urban policy. One difficulty is that it
is hard to distinguish between a miscellany of federal, state and
local policies and what might appropriately be called a basic
national policy for a given area of concern. Historically, we have
arrived at a relatively coherent set of policies on various matters of
national interest by trial and error over a fairly long period of
time. Unfortunately, under current conditions in our cities, we
would pay a high price for a leisurely movement toward effective
national urban policy. The process must be compressed if at all
possible.

I want to present the following case: We will begin to cope
effectively with the difficult problems of our cities only when we
evolve *national* policy which can, on a broad front, guide urban
development toward certain equity and quality-of-life objectives
and enhance individual welfare. The urban problems are a product of our national socioeconomic system and way of doing things,
and it is to bringing about changes in the total scheme of things
to which we must initially address our efforts. Thus, the first stage
should look to the creation of a foundation on which more specific

V

policies—say, with regard to housing or new towns—might be firmly built.

EVOLVING A NATIONAL FRAMEWORK OF
POLICY AND ACTION

It is in the nature of public action that attention first be directed at the outer manifestations of pressing public problems, for it is there that the political heat is generated. Thus, it could have been expected that in the New Deal days, under the pressures of widespread and long-lasting unemployment, there would be PWAs and WPAs, and other measures established by government directly, to provide jobs. A more effectively focused policy to get at the underlying causes of unemployment could only come later, after a certain amount of experience and a learning from the past, and after certain concepts and a system of information to guide policy and programs had been developed.

In the same light, it is not surprising that in the first reaction to the building up of political pressure around certain urban problems—inadequate housing, slums, traffic congestion, and the like—the government should seek directly to provide housing for low-income families, directly to remove slums and blighted areas, and to pour tons of concrete to try to overcome traffic congestion. But we now do have a good bit of experience in coping with urban problems, and it is time we emerged from the PWA-WPA stage into one that tries to get at more basic causes and tries to overcome the problems through a well-developed and sharply-focused strategy.

There is today a vast array of federal, state, and local policies and programs concerned with the problems of the urban communities —dozens in the housing field alone and more dozens in the realms of transportation, urban planning, water and sewerage, health, welfare, training, and so on. Many of these, in spite of relatively large expenditures, seem to get at only a small corner of the problem attacked, as in the case of urban transportation, urban renewal, and public housing. They also seem to generate a great number of new problems as they go about trying to solve the ones at which they are directed. This is not only true of the urban highway and renewal programs, but also of most urban-orineted policies and programs. This has been so well documented in recent studies of the various urban programs that I need not dwell on this aspect of the question at hand. What does deserve attention is why the apparent failure and what can be done about it.

The problem is not so much that the individual programs are poorly conceived—although that is true in some instances—but rather that a *foundation* has not been laid on which successful specialized programs can be carried out. One gets a sense of what is involved when he compares the smoothly administered, relatively successful public housing programs in the Scandinavian countries with the trouble-plagued programs in the United States. One realizes that the significant differences do not relate to methods of construction and financing but rather to the fact that the programs in the United States are too overburdened with a heavy load of human pathology and social problems to be able to fulfill the housing objectives. In the same light, it should be easy to see that a large number of physical-development programs can be piled one on top of the other with only limited, marginal improvements unless greatly improved urban planning and governmental administration can be brought into being.

What we have now is a huge jumble of programs without a clear conception of what we are really trying to accomplish and without much logic as to which level of government is equipped to do what. Thus, we find the federal government deeply involved in the specifics of neighborhood programs, to the point where localities become mere agents of the federal bureaucracy. And we find local governments trying to achieve ends, as in welfare programs and in large-scale physical-development programs, that can only be achieved at the national level or at the level of the metropolitan region.

HISTORICAL PERSPECTIVE

In looking toward the development of national urban policy concerned with "fundamentals," it is instructive to review some history with regard to the evolution of national policy on matters of central concern.

Consciously directed change is not new in the United States. There is a tradition for it. (Unfortunately, there is also a tradition of serious policy lags.) Guided development, as we normally use the term, implies change in directions which promise a convergence on highly valued objectives.

The national government has taken a major role in **guiding** development, setting the broad framework for private as well as state and local decisions and activities. While this history is too well known to require much elaboration, one feature does deserve special attention. Behind the continuous struggle for power and privilege and behind the ins and outs of conservative versus progressive politics, there has been a sensible appreciation of the importance of developing and consciously channeling the basic national resources—including not only the natural resources and capital resources but the human resources and the institutional resources as well. While the official ideology was *minimum government,* the minimum generally included a strong governmental concern for rapid development and a broadening of the welfare base.

NATIONAL DEVELOPMENT AND NATIONAL POLICY: THE AGRICULTURAL AND INDUSTRIAL PHASES

The United States has gone through several major developmental phases, each with a different impact on our basic resources and each calling forth a rather large and complex set of national policies and programs that ultimately added up to a discernible national policy for that phase. A key feature in each case, as noted, was the focus on the building up of the basic capacity of the human and institutional resources. While in a short paper, it will be necessary to generalize outrageously, and to omit consideration of many significant variations and details, it is nevertheless instructive to review the types of approaches that we have used in coming to grips with the problems posed by each of the major national developmental phases.

The *agricultural development phase* was, of course, the dominant one in the earlier history of the country and, in fact, can be said to extend all the way to World War II. The natural resources that counted were land and water; and in both regards, the nation was blessed. National policy extended to distribution of public lands to farmers in a relatively orderly fashion, and the method of distribution had a great deal to do not only with the efficiency of production but with the social structure that evolved. Thus, the family-size farm was instrumental in integrating vast numbers of people, including the great flood of immigrants from Europe and elsewhere, into the mainstream of national society. In the twentieth century, increasingly the national government turned its attention to policies that helped to encourage conservation and sensible development and use of natural resources.

Human resources, too, were a major focus of public policy and expenditures, involving the federal and state governments as well as the localities. Of tremendous importance was the institution of universal free education and the establishment of land-grant colleges and extension services. It is well to remember that this was a revolutionary approach, breaking with centuries of tradition, projecting the idea that farming was not an art to be learned from one's father and grandfather but rather was to be based on the expansion of scientific knowledge and brought to the individual farmer by an elaborate system of experiment stations and extension services. Thus, at a remarkably early stage, the nation undertook to help its farmers achieve *a high level of competence* in all aspects of production, merchandizing, and farm life.

It is well to note also that throughout the agricultural era, the government was concerned with the capital needed for sound farming operations. Not only was the most important element of capital—the land—provided to individual farmers as section after section of the country was settled. But at a relatively early stage, the government concerned itself with the provision of irrigation facilities as well as farm-to-market roads and the extension of credit to meet the input and sellings needs of the farmers. While it is quite easy to be critical of the imperfections of certain aspects of the policy as implemented, it is evident that government policy and assistance were of the greatest importance in the creation of an effective agriculture.

On the institutional front, representation at the federal and state governmental levels was such that the farm interests could be guarded and promoted (although, of course, the larger farmers could generally get the best of the bargain). Direct federal expenditures and indirect federal aid to state and local governments covered the more costly investment items and gave a boost to local budgets. The rural county served the relatively simple needs of the countryside—as then perceived—at the local level, with the property tax financing the modest services that met these needs.

The *industrial development phase* overlapped the agricultural phase, covering the period from about the middle of the nineteenth century to about the middle of the twentieth. From an early stage, national efforts were directed at the discovery and exploitation of the basic industrial resources, with an increasing interest, especially after World War I, in the sound conservation, development, and use of resources needed in the industrialization processes. Concern for the caliber of human resources was reflected in the establishment of local school districts in all the industrial centers to provide a fairly high level of literacy, although some regions, particularly the Southeast and Southwest, lagged badly in this regard. In addition, state universities, with federal help, established many technical schools geared to providing the needed skills in mining and manufacturing. Many of the great technical universities of today are the products of this public policy. The government responded to capital needs through the establishment of national and state banking systems and helped provide the elaborate system of infrastructure necessary to an industrial society by massive subsidies for railroads and by direct investment in river and harbor construction, dams, and highways. Needed institutional development was reflected in the evolution of a legal structure which encouraged industrial production and which sought to prevent the more extreme business abuses by anti-monopoly laws and a host of specific business regulations. Important also for the industrial era was the establishment of labor unions and their increasing strength and scope. The nation was quite slow in appreciating the role that government might play in the development of healthy labor-management relations, but this too came with time.

The 1930's and 1940's, with the trauma of depression and war, in a very real sense, marked the culmination of both the agricultural and the industrialization phases. Public policy was directed at shoring up and filling gaps in the institutional base for the late-industrial era. First, there was need to right the balance between the encouragement of private entrepreneurship and imposing social responsibilities on business. This involved increased public regulation of banking, insurance, the stock market, and other business activities as well as public support of organized labor, as in the Wagner act. Second, it meant the acceptance of public responsibility for maintaining a floor under farm incomes to prevent a squeeze on the farmer between the prices of farm inputs and farm outputs. Third, there was need to cope with the problem of the business cycle whose severity tended to increase with the growing importance of durable-good production. The acceptance of national responsibility for full employment and price stability, on top of the other reform measures, meant the maturing of national economic policy to parallel the maturing of the industrial economy.

There is one feature of public policy during the agricultural and industrial phases that deserves particular attention because of the negative impact it was to have on the future. This was the relative indifference to equity questions as contrasted with the deep interest in efficiency issues. Governmental policy was essentially national in scope and concerned with economic growth rather than with the problems of falling behind and of depressed areas. The race was to the swift. The main thrust was promotional and developmental. A vast nation was to be opened up and developed, and those who raced ahead were encouraged. Only the most extreme abuses were prohibited. If a section of the nation or a group fell behind or was disadvantaged for one reason or another, only limited and temporary help would be provided. Thus it was that certain regions of the country could be abandoned as stagnant pools of poverty and ignorance. Not until the deep depression of the 1930's shook the nation to its foundations, did a concern for the poor and disadvantaged and for equity in general really begin to surface. But by that time, social, cultural, and economic patterns had caught the more disadvantaged in an iron vise. Thus, for example, the Southern hold on the Congressional committee structure, added to the post-reconstruction patterning of relations between whites and blacks, revealed itself as a formidable block to rapid and meaningful improvement in the lot of the Southern Negroes. Only slightly less formidable were the barriers to improvements in the other backwashes of the rapid American thrust to national development, in Appalachia, in the cutover regions of the Upper Midwest, in the Four-Corners area and other sections of the Southwest, and in isolated pockets in other regions of the country as well.

Before the New Deal effort towards greater equity could be well started, World War II intervened and speeded the nation into a new phase of development.

THE POST INDUSTRIAL PHASE

Shortly after World War II, by the mid-point of the present century, the nation was entering a new socioeconomic phase, one that has been referred to as the Post-Industrial or the Services Era. Employment in materials production—that is, in agriculture, mining and manufacturing—had stopped growing in relative terms and in the case of farming and mining in absolute terms as well. Materials production had become highly capital intensive, with automization increasingly important and with higher and higher human skills being called for. Employment growth was concentrated in the service activities—trade, professional services, business services, banking, communications, government, and the like. These "rapid growth" activities were all urban oriented so that national development ordained rapid urban expansion. This was urban growth piled on top of the extremely fast urban growth of the industrial period.

Urban evolution of the industrial period had had two major characteristics. The city had evolved as an "Americanizing," skill-upgrading mechanism, quickly turning new immigrants into workers for the factories, the railroads and the shops, and rapidly absorbing them into the American main stream. And the city had grown in a relatively compact manner, tied first to the horse carriage and then the trolley, as well as to the roalroad. The evolution of the new period was, however, to take some different forms.

One aspect of post-World War II development was to have a particularly important impact on the cities. This related to employment patterns. World War II, with its tremendous demands for military goods added to the civilian requirements, meant great pressure on industrial capacity and extremely high employment needs. With many of the men in the armed services who normally would have been in industrial employment, and with wages at an all-time high, rural workers, many of them Negroes from the South—who in normal times might have hesitated to leave the countryside for the competitive urban environment—were drawn into the cities. For example, between 1940 and 1950, the rate of migration out of agriculture ran as high as 90 per cent in some Southeastern states and of course geographic migration was closely tied to this movement. For example, during the 1940-50 decade, some 465,000 persons left farming in Alabama, amounting to a movement out of agriculture of 93.4 per cent. (This loss was more than made up by an exceedingly high rural-population replacement rate.) The war, thereby, opened up migration channels that normally would have stayed closed or would have been filling up at a very much slower pace. As it was, the movement became a virtual flood and developed a momentum quite typical of migration patterns. Thus it was that people who had been trapped in some of the most economically and culturally deprived areas of the nation began the trek to American cities.

They clustered in the older areas of the central cities, the only areas where they could find housing they could afford, and which were open to them, while the whites who had lived there earlier fled to the suburbs. Soon these areas of inmigration become giant ghettos of minority groups, in many ways effectively cut off from the remainder of the urban society.

Hardly has these new migration channels been opened up and the flow become well established than the war ended. Men—with greater skills—returned from the war and took up old and new jobs while industry very rapidly converted to modern, and often, automated plants. Once the patterns had been established, however, the migration continued—particularly of the younger people—intensified by the mechanization of cotton production and governmental restrictions on agricultural output. Jobs or no jobs, the "revolution of rising expectations," associated with the move to the cities, had touched even the most backward of the backwaters and was not to be denied. In many cases, the later moves were from town to city and from one city to another. The search for opportunity and a better life was having its repercussions in every corner of the land. But unlike the situation that had faced the European immigrant in an earlier day, the poor white and Negro migrants of the post-World War II period had few unskilled jobs readily at hand and little preparation for the more skilled jobs that were available.

It is well to note, then, that the current developmental phase of our national life—the Services phase—started with the highly distorting impact of a major world war. Actually, the full consequences were to be delayed until after the impact of the Korean War had played itself out, but the die had been cast. Millions had been drawn to greater opportunity in the cities only to find themselves unprepared to grasp such opportunity—particularly in the face of long-established racial prejudice—and forced to reside in limited areas of the city, generally far from the sections of the burgeoning metropolitan regions where the greatest growth in jobs was taking place.

Other aspects of the new era have also caught the nation unprepared. Almost all the developments have been in association with a greatly increased use of communications (in its broadest sense) in all of our socioeconomic activities: the tremendous proliferation of service activities that are essentially oriented to face-to-face contact, the increasing importance of R&D and other non-commodity aspects of production which also call for more elaborate communications, and the tendency for more and more activities to be national and often international in scope, so that rapid communications have become a critical element in overall efficiency. The city, in effect, has become something of a production "shell" or plant in itself. The efficiency of the patterns of location of various activities in relationship to each other, and movement among them, has become as important as the efficiency of the beltline in mechanized factories. The nation has not been in the habit of viewing the city as an efficient or inefficient productive environment; attention has been focused on the *individual* production units. Consequently, our institutions are not geared to the task of consciously creating efficient productive contexts for socioeconomic activities. In fact, we have permitted ourself to drift into a situation where land uses in the city tend to be, in no small part, the unplanned consequences of racial segregation and political confrontation rather than the result of rational guidance on the basis of efficiency, equity, and quality-of-life objectives.

In other respects, too, we entered the new era unprepared. The basic structure of state and local governments had been set down during the earlier agricultural phase. Certain inadequacies were becoming apparent during the latter part of the nineteenth century and the first part of the twentieth as the industrialization phase gathered momentum. The shortcomings of our state and local governments have been described so frequently in recent years that they need not be detailed here. The main point to note is that in the agricultural and industrial development phases, the states and localities were called upon to deliver only limited public services. As a general matter, the "power elite" in agriculture, mining, and industry was satisfied to keep the state and local governments weakly organized. Where certain services were deemed particularly important, as in education, special districts were established for the delivery of the services instead of strengthening the basic governmental units. Thus, we entered the post-industrial or services era with governmental units completely unequipped for positive developmental roles in the exploding metropolis which characterizes the new period. As a matter of fact, it is very much in keeping with the ideas of the previous period that local government should be at its weakest in the outlying areas of the metropolis where the new construction is going on. This fits the spirit of the former phases nicely. But the local governmental system as now organized has little relevance to the needs of today.

Not unexpectedly, state and local finance has also been geared to the governmental system of the previous phases and not to the requirements of the current phase. The property tax, which could meet the needs of local units established to deliver a certain minimum of public services, could not provide an adequate base for the much more elaborate requirements of the post-industrial era. The tremendous proliferation of categorical federal aids to states and localities reflects the inadequacies of local finance to provide for new needs—in welfare assistance, in education and health, and in the construction of airports, hospitals, institutions of higher learning, and public housing units.

One more item is needed to fill out this story of "cultural lag" and unpreparedness. This is with regard to the handling of urban land. During the agricultural and industrial phases, land became one of the most important of the development leverages. The granting of public lands to individual farmers, to corporate units, and to states had been an outstanding device for settling the land, building the railroads, encouraging education, and achieving many another developmental purpose. This, on top of an inherited common-law view of private property, had given the nation a special regard for the private use of land. Naturally enough, the prevailing view had been extended to the use of land in the building of cities. While always accepted as having certain special characteristics, the ownership and transfer of land at the edge of cities had nevertheless long been regarded as the logical way to promote urban development. The land speculators and the land developers of the modern-day city are as much a part of the national development picture as their counterparts have been in the countryside —but in a totally different developmental setting.

Coming closer to today, with a growth of concern for order in urban development and for the quality of the urban environment, a whole series of controls were superimposed on the basic structure of private property. Thus, zoning, sub-division controls, and building controls were introduced to achieve greater order and improved quality—only to be found entirely lacking in the context of traditional approaches to ownership and transfer of land. For local governments are at their weakest in precisely the zones where the controls are most needed. Organized in small enclaves, suburbanites tend to use such controls to keep "undesirables" out and to keep governmental costs down to a minimum. The needs of the metropolis as a whole rarely are a part of anyone's reckoning in the suburban communities.

All this adds up to a picture of a nation unprepared in both concepts and institutions to cope with the requirements of a quite new socioeconomic era. If we were to extrapolate current developments in a straight line, we could expect that in the decades to come, all our major cities would have three things in common. They would have a black core, they would be financially bankrupt, and they would be politically unmanageable.

THE PROBLEM AHEAD

The major problem that we face on the urban scene is not the lack of clear-cut goals with regard to the kinds of cities we want, as is often suggested. It is doubtful that we can collectively decide whether we want many giant cities or very many small ones, whether or not we want to encourage high density in central cities, whether or not our future lies in developing new towns, and the like. Rather, it is a problem of greatly increasing basic competence in certain key areas of our national life, in the same sense that key policy in the agricultural and industrial eras was concerned with the basic factor endowment of human resources, natural resources, material resources, and institutional resources.

If, today, national urban policy is to get at fundamentals, it must initially try to fulfill three basic requirements: (1) to rapidly increase the competence of individuals, particularly those in the "bottom third," (2) to rapidly increase the capacity of states and localities (as well as of the national government), to carry out needed developmental activities, (3) to rapidly increase our capacity in R&D (research and development) geared to guiding public policies and programs with urban impacts.

It should be stressed that meeting these requirements is not a panacea for solving all urban problems. Rather they are the basic ingredients for the nation to begin to cope with the uniquely urban problems, such as the problems of agglomeration and high densities, and the problems of reconciling long-lasting urban physical capital with rapidly changing tastes, social needs, and technological possibilities.

1. Increasing Human Capacity

The first requirement calls for a priority focus on human beings. The nation needs to provide a basic structure for the development of people capable of dealing with the high-skill requirements of the post-industrial era. We have to make up for decades of neglect by bringing the formerly bypassed and disadvantaged to a relatively decent level of personal competence. In a society that is overwhelmingly urban and largely affluent, poverty and prejudice can no longer be swept into isolated rural corners and in equally isolated urban ghettos. The contrasts are sharp and open and of explosive potential. The key need is to help individuals develop competence in every sphere of urban life; the capacity "to cope" must extend to the political and social sphere as well as the economic (family self-support). We cannot possibly build a satisfactory urban life when a substantial proportion of the total population is unable to amass and use political power or to achieve social and economic standing.

It is time that the nation said quite simply and openly: Humans are by far the most important resources in our post-industrial age. Every individual not only deserves to achieve the dignity that comes with being adequately prepared for a productive life but, just as important, the nation urgently needs productive individuals with skills beyond those required during earlier periods.

The key requirement for the future is a *national floor* under the basic human services, that is, for education, health, and welfare. Alvin H. Hansen and I proposed such a national minimum for human services in a book published in the early 1940's—*State and Local Finance in the National Economy* (W. W. Norton, 1944)— looking ahead to the new era that was then downing. This proposal still answers a critical requirement. Hopefully, we have reached the stage where the proposal can receive serious consideration. While we cannot say with any certainty just how much education and health care is "enough" for any one individual to achieve his or her "full" potential, we do know something of the disadvantages that are suffered by persons in, and from those urban and rural districts whose education and health services are at a low level.

The education and health care that a person receives should not be dependent on the locality where he happens to be born and grow up. People need the capability to cope with the modern era no matter where they are reared since they are likely to spend their working years in totally different communities. A national floor does not mean an equal expenditure per person but rather that expenditure needed to achieve a reasonable level of human competence and well being. Thus, the national expenditure could be expected to be higher in areas with a disproportionate number of disadvantaged persons. At the other end of the spectrum, states and localities could add as much as they desired to achieve higher levels of services where local residents were willing to tax themselves for this purpose.

By the same token, as many thoughtful persons (and study commissions) have suggested, there is much to be gained by the provision of some form of minimum income for poor families in the United States—as long as this is not employed as an excuse for cutting back on needed specialized payments and services. A guaranteed income would help to bring many presently poor families into the national mainstream. Extreme poverty—particularly in an urban setting—is an attack on human dignity that generally deprives an individual of the capacity to cope with the world around him. Thus, a minimum income financed by the federal government could be expected to substantially reduce the extent and depth of the manifest difficulties our urban communities face: the continuing strain on the body politic caused by the dead weight of a population that is unable to care for itself, is rejected by the majority group, and is often ruthlessly exploited. Again, it should be stressed that this is not a proposal to *solve* human resources problems but is a needed ingredient in programs to meet the wide range of human needs. A move by the federal government to provide an income floor at a level where all American families are taken out of debilitating poverty will be the surest, and probably the fastest, route to the improvement of the urban environment, by reducing now-severe urban problems to manageable proportions. Thus, for example, it seems logical to assume that a substantial part of the substandard housing problem would be solved by the national provision of a minimum income that brought every American family above, say, the sum suggested as the budget floor by the Bureau of Labor Statistics, in its family income-and-expenditure studies. The removal of debilitating poverty is essential, not only to greater personal capacity, but also to better relations among various social groups and to a more equitable distribution of political power among the different groups.

Until a reasonably adequate level of basic public services and of family income are provided across the whole nation, cities will find themselves in an anomalous position; the more they do to ameliorate their difficult human problems, the more these problems can intensify, since poor and disadvantaged persons will pour in to take advantage of the superior services and assistance they provide. The overall net gains from the improvement of basic human services will become much more apparent than they are today once there is a solid floor of services and income for the whole nation.

2. Increasing the Capacity of States and Localities

The second major requirement is to increase the capacity of states and localities to cope with urban-development needs.

Beyond federal government support of human services, the whole system of federal, state, and local finance must be adjusted to the era in which we live and must be employed as an instrumentality for thoroughly modernizing state and local governments. While finance is hardly the stuff around which much excitement can be generated, it turns out to be almost as much a key to the achievement of urban objectives as it is a key to the achievement of full-employment and economic-stability objectives.

Much higher levels of local public services are needed to meet the pressing problems of urban life; yet localities cannot possibly raise the money needed to finance such public services. They cannot tax beyond a certain point for fear of losing industries and higher-income families, a fear which has reality in an open and mobile society. The provision of a national floor under the basic human services would be the first and most critical step in overcoming the current dilemma. However, looking ahead over a relatively long period of time, there is also need for general-purpose federal grants to states and localities or tax-sharing arrangements to enable them to plan orderly development within the cities and on their outskirts. Cities will not undertake planned development of this kind unless they can look forward to an assured flow of funds for that purpose. Nor can they be expected to do a decent job of planned development unless their political and administrative structures and processes are thoroughly modernized.

Federal finance can be used as a powerful lever for improving states and local governments, that is, to equip them to deal more effectively with the extremely difficult problems of the present day. A sensible approach (as proposed by Representative Henry Reuss of Wisconsin) would provide for federal tax-sharing with the states contingent on the modernization of state and local governments. The objective would be to encourage the creation of more equitable and viable local governments and more representative and better equipped state governments. Just what "modernization" in today's context implies is itself a good question; it is surely a mild word for the substantial changes that are needed. If it were limited to the use of more up-to-date management methods, its payoff would probably be slight. The critical problems are clearly in the realm of politics and human relations. Minority groups and the poor must somehow acquire political and economic leverage, a real voice in decisions that directly or indirectly affect them.

Such an approach to financial assistance would put the national government in the business of up-dating state and local governments. General purpose federal grants or tax-sharing, if used specifically as a lever for modernization, would aim at bringing about a high level of state and local governmental competence in the same sense that a federal floor under human services and a guaranteed minimum family income would aim at creating a minimum level of individual competence throughout the country.

Yet another use of the federal financial lever is to promote urban development that has an inherent regional logic. While we cannot yet claim to understand fully the forces behind the present patterns of urban development over the national landscape, neither can we weigh properly all the costs and benefits of alternative forms of development. The element that has emerged most clearly is the clustering of activities around the metropolitan cores so that the commuting range has taken on a substantial significance in suburban and new-town construction as well as in the thrust of both private and public redevelopment. The very strenuous efforts that have to be made to establish independent, free-standing new towns, as contrasted with the rapid continuing expansion of suburbs and the building of new *satellite* communities, underlines the power of the metropolitan commuting element.

There is clearly need for an advanced kind of region-wide developmental planning that aims at tying together suburban and new-town construction with the layout of transportation, water, sewerage, and other utilities that have communications and developmental impact, so as to go as far as possible in achieving efficiency, equity, and quality-of-life objectives. Few states and localities can be expected to move quickly in joining forces for the achievement of this kind of planned development unless the federal government uses a very powerful financial carrot-and-stick strategy toward that end.

The establishment of a national floor of policy and expenditure supports would permit the state and local "subsystems" of our highly integrated national system to begin to function properly. This is not to suggest that they would necessarily function as models of efficiency and foresight. After all, the federal government, with much greater organizational capability, is hardly such a model. I would, however, expect them to rather quickly develop the capacity to bring key decisions into the political arena and to work out programs that bring together disparate interests around certain general, longer-range improvements.

What is proposed is in keeping with the traditional American practice of providing a national framework within which individual, local, and state activities can be carried out effectively. Actually, rather than undermining local self-government and scope for individual choices in patterns of living as is sometimes assumed, federal support would strengthen the former and greatly add to the latter. Today, local self-government has become essentially an empty slogan. Once a national floor of financial support is provided and funds for planned urban development are made available, local people would be in a far better position to control their environments.

3. R&D with an Urban Focus

There is yet a third requirement, that is, to rapidly increase our capacity in urban research and development (R&D) so as to have better guidelines for public urban policies and programs. We have seen the contribution that research has made to the various national science, health, and space programs, and also its contribution to national economic policy. It is at least as important for the evolution of urban policy—both the "foundational" kinds of policies

w

discussed here, and the more detailed and specific policies that need to follow. We do not at the present time have nearly enough knowledge to have any assurance about the detailed content of such policy. Thus, for example, the poverty program and the many experimental educational programs have served to highlight the enormous difficulty and complexity of raising the achievement levels of culturally deprived youths; the various housing programs have underlined the difficulty of getting better housing to low-income families; and, along the same lines, the limited impact of the federal 701 regional planning grants have made it evident that there is much about regional development that still has to be learned.

Unfortunately, a mere extension of present research capabilities and approaches will no more do the job that is needed than would the mere extension of present federal categorical aids. As with the first two requirements, the need now is for a major restructuring and an entirely different conception of the appropriate quantitative levels.

The question of appropriate scale and quality looms large with regard to basic data. The need for more and better data is stressed so often that everyone gets "turned off" by the mere mention of data. Somehow this problem has to be overcome and an appropriate volume of resources—multiples of what are now employed—channelled to the task. Two organizational changes deserve priority attention. One is the establishment of a mid-decade census (given the speed of urban change in the United States), with extensions into a broad range of longitudinal studies by the Census Bureau. The other is the establishment of expertly-manned data centers within every major metropolitan region of the nation, serving data-generation, clearing-house and analytical purposes. A key feature of such centers must be the availability of resources to permit them to service the data needs of scholars and research centers within their region at minimal costs to the researchers.

The consideration that gave rise to the establishment of the Urban Institute in Washington, D.C. applies also to the need for setting up strong research centers—under university and other auspices—within the various metropolitan regions; namely, the ability to achieve economies of scale and the capacity to tackle interdisciplinary problems. It should not be necessary to make a case for regional centers, as against total reliance on a single institute, given the many significant differences among the various parts of the country. One has only to compare the Los Angeles region with the San Francisco metropolis, within a single state, to make the point. The problem here, however, it should be noted, is not merely one of adequate financial resources for research but also the willingness of scholars to work with others on questions that will necessarily take many years to resolve. Academic institutions are today not well organized for inter disciplinary long-maturing research. If we are greatly to extend our research capability in the urban realm, some far-reaching changes in research organization will have to be achieved.

The "D" in R&D also deserves attention. It is all too easy to be critical of the federal government's fumbling with its so-called urban "demonstration projects" as well as other forms of experimental development efforts. Certainly, in most cases the scale has been much too small and the available resources much too limited to make for a genuine learning experience. Also, the critical evaluation component has been missing entirely or much too perfunctory to be helpful. The fact is that we urgently need fresh thinking about experimentation in the urban realm, and we need greatly to strengthen our evaluation capabilities.

It is disconcerting to note that the very R&D component expected to help provide firm, tested content to the general policy framework outlined above itself needs substantial improvement in human and organizational capacity. But this is not a surprising situation given the overall national lag with regard to the needs of the post-industrial urban world of today. It is not helpful to underestimate the scale of the problems we face in this realm as in others, any more than it is to be too impressed with the difficulties involved. We clearly have the resources needed to develop an appropriately scaled R&D capability in the relatively near future. Our job is to bring this about as quickly as we can.

To sum up, this paper stresses two key points in looking to a better urban future for the United States. First, it urges a sharply focused national policy thrust aimed directly at greatly increasing the overall competence of individuals, particularly those formerly disadvantaged, as well as the overall competence of states and localities—in both cases through the use of a highly traditional policy lever, namely, federal finance. And second, noting the complexity of the problems involved, it urges the importance of developing an R&D capability that can assist in the design of effective specific urban policies and programs.

REFERENCES

Beckman, Norman. "Our Federal System and Urban Development: The Adaptation of Form to Function." *Journal of the American Institute of Planners,* 29, August 1963, pp. 152–67.

Canty, Donald, Ed. *The New City: The National Committee on Urban Growth Policy.* New York: Praeger, 1969.

Connery, Robert and Leach, Richard. *Federal Government and Metropolitan Areas.* Cambridge: Harvard Univ. Press, 1960.

Fitch, Lyle C. "Eight Goals for an Urbanizing America." *Daedalus,* 97, No. 4, Fall 1968, pp. 1141–64.

Hansen, Alvin H. and Perloff, Harvey S. *State and Local Finance in the National Economy.* New York: W. W. Norton, 1944, Chapter 8 ("Federal Underwriting of Minimum Service Standards").

Hoover, Edgar M. (with Raymond Vernon) *Anatomy of a Metropolis.* Cambridge: Harvard Univ. Press, 1959.

———, (study director), *Economic Study of th Pittsburgh Region* 1— *Region in Transition. 2—Portrait of a Region. 3—Region with a Future.* Pittsburgh: Pittsburgh Regional Planning Association, 1964.

———, "The Evolving Form and Organization of the Metropolis" in Harvey S. Perloff and Lowden Wingo, Eds. *Issues in Urban Economics.* Baltimore: Johns Hopkins Press, 1968. pp. 237–84.

Meyerson, Martin. "Urban Policy: Reforming Reform." *Daedalus,* 97, No. 4, Fall 1968, pp. 1410–30.

Okun, Bernard and Richardson, Richard W. "Regional Income Inequality and Internal Population Migration" in John Friedmann and William Alonso, Eds. *Regional Development and Planning: A Reader.* Cambridge: M.I.T. Press, 1964, Chap. 13, pp. 303–18.

Perloff, Harvey S. "Modernizing Urban Development," *Daedalus,* 96, No. 3, Summer 1967, pp. 789–800.

Perloff, Harvey S. and Nathan, Richard P., Eds. *Revenue Sharing and the City.* Baltimore: John Hopkins Press, 1968.

Siegel, Irving H. *The Kerner Commission Report and Economic Policy.* Kalamazoo: W. E. Upjohn Inst. for Employment Research, 1969.

U.S. Advisory Commission on Intergovernmental Relations Reports: *Government in Metropolitan Areas* 1961. *Governmental Structure, Organization and Planning in Metropolitan Areas: Suggested Action by Local, State and National Government* July, 1961. *Metropolitan America: Challenge to Federalism* August, 1966. *To improve the Effectiveness of the American Federal System Through Increased Cooperation Among National, State and Local Levels of Government* 1968. *Urban and Rural America: Policies for Future Growth* April, 1968.

U.S. Chamber of Commerce. Task Force on Economic Growth and Opportunity. *Rural Poverty and Regional Progress in an Urban Society.* Washington, D.C.: Chamber of Commerce of the U.S., 1969.

U.S. Congress. Committee on Government Operations. Subcommittee on Executive Reorganization. *Federal Role in Urban Affairs:* Hearings, December 30, 1966, Appendix to Pt. I. Washington, D.C.: Government Printing Office, 1966.

U.S. Congress. Committee on Government Operations. Subcommittee on Government Research. *Full Opportunity and Social Accounting Act*, 3 pts. Hearings—June 26; July 19–20, 26, 28, 1967. Washington, D.C.: Government Printing Office, 1968. *Human Resources Development*, 2 pts. Hearings—April 8, 10, 18, 23–24, 1968. Washington, D.C.: Government Printing Office, 1968.

U.S. Department of Health, Education and Welfare. *Toward a Social Report*. Washington, D.C.: Government Printing Office, 1969.

U.S. National Commission on Urban Problems. *Building The American City*. Washington, D.C.: Government Printing Office, 1968.

U.S. President's Commission on National Goals. *Goals For Americans*. New York: Columbia Univ., The American Assembly, 1960.

U.S. White house. *"To fulfill These Rights,"* Conference—June 1–2, 1966, Washington, D.C.: Government Printing Office, 1966.

U.S. Congress. Joint Economic Committee. *Employment and Manpower Problems in the Cities: Implications of the Report of the National Advisory Commission on Civil Disorders*, Hearings—May 28–29; June 4–6, 1968. Washington, D.C.: Government Printing Office, 1968.

U.S. Congress, Subcommittee on Economy in the Government. *The Planning-Programming-Budgeting System: Progress and Potentials*, Hearings—September 14, 19–21, 1967. Washington, D.C.: Government Printing Office, 1967.

U.S. Congress, Subcommittee on Urban Affairs. *Urban America: Goals and Problems*, Hearings—September 27–28; October 2–4, 1967. Washington, D.C.: Government Printing Office, 1967.

U.S. Department of Housing and Home Finance Agency. *Metropolis in Transition: Local Government Adaptation to Changing Urban Needs* (By Roscoe C. Martin.) Washington, D.C.: Government Printing Office, September, 1963.

U.S. National Advisory Commission on Civil Disorders. *Employment and Manpower Problems in Cities*. Washington, D.C.: Government Printing Office, 1968.

15

Fertility and the Business Cycle

PINHAS SHWINGER

*School of Business Administration,
University of Tel-Aviv*

FOREWORD

This research paper is an attempt to throw light on the correlation between business cycles and birth rates in Israel.

We hope that this correlation, which can be clearly read from the results of this paper, will serve as a factor in the timing of the advancement of our family planning policies.

I would like to express my appreciation to Miss Ilana Hadida-Panner, who has been instrumental in the processing of the Data connected with this research and to the University of Tel-Aviv that sponsored this research.

THE ECONOMIST, THE BUSINESS CYCLE
AND FERTILITY

Research into the correlation between economic conditions and demographic parameters such as fertility, nuptiality and other population characteristics, is a function of the attitudes of different economists to the subject of population and its place in the study of economics. From the point of view of such classicists as Malthus and Ricardo, the population problem was an integral part of the science of economics.

But when Malthus' forecasts proved inaccurate and the focus of economic research moved into the field of micro-economics and short-term forecasting, the demographic aspect of economics took a relatively minor position in the realm of economic research.

During the Depression of the thirties the subject was revived again, this time in the form of the stagnation theory. This theory was largely a reflection of its time. It assumed population growth to be the independent variable. With the advance of statistical techniques, the availability of more reliable and detailed demographic data, and with the new techniques of electronic data-processing, research into "the population problem" has gained momentum, and several excellent research studies have been carried out in this field.

A pioneering research into the effect of business cycles on fertility has been carried out by Dorothy S. Thomas and Virginia L. Galbraith.[1] They correlated the maternity frequencies of the white population by order of birth in the U.S. with the industrial employment index for the same years. After removing the trend to avoid serial correlation, they obtained the following results:

Table 1   Measure of relationship between deviation from trend of business cycles, and birth rates 1919–1937

Independent variable	Dependent variable	Coefficient of correlation
Business Cycles	First birth	.830
	Second birth	.589
	Third birth	.723
	Fourth birth	.571
	Fifth birth	.531

Source: Galbraith, V. L. and Thomas, D. S., "Birthrates and the Interwar Business Cycles," *Journal of American Statistical Association*, **36**, Dec. 1941.

They conclude their study by saying the births of all orders are "controlled during a period of Depression."[2] In other words, they found that business fluctuations affect fertility.

It is interesting to see that according to their study, the strongest correlation exists between the business cycle indicator and the first

[1]Galbraith, V. L. and Thomas, D. S. "The Influence of the Business Cycles on Certain Social Conditions," Quarterly Publication of the American Statistical Association, 28, 1922.

[2]Galbraith, V. L. and Thomas, D. S. *op. cit.*

order birth rate, and the weakest correlation is between the cycle indicator and the fifth order birth rate.

A study which uses the same techniques as the Galbraith-Thomas paper, was carried out in 1960 by Dudley Kirk.[3] Kirk did not use the same business indicators, however. He used three indicators:

1) Real (per capita) personal income;
2) Federal Reserve Board index of industrial production;
3) Nonagricultural employment and unemployment as a percentage of the civilian labor force.[4]

Table 2 Correlation of percentage deviation from trends of fertility and economic indexes 1948–1957

Independent variable	Dependent variable	Coefficient of correlation
Per capita income	Fertility	.86
Index of industrial production	Fertility	.79
Nonagricultural unemployment	Fertility	−.65

Source: This is only part of a larger table which is in "The Influence of Business Cycles on Marriage and Birth Rates" in Kirk, D., *Demographic and Economic Change in Developed Countries*. Princeton Univ. Press 1960, p. 248.

Kirk did not break up fertility figures into birth orders. This might be the reason that his coefficients are somewhat higher than those obtained by Galbraith and Thomas. Another reason that might have caused it is, of course, his use of different business indicators. It is worth noting that Dorothy Thomas herself pointed out that the indicators chosen by Kirk are better since they are more sensitive to small changes.

Kirk's main conclusion is in accord with the findings of Galbraith and Thomas: fertility is sensitive to economic changes. However, he is not prepared to go along with the further conclusion that fertility is directly affected by economic changes. He presumes that such effects are indirect, causing important conditioning—

[3]Kirk, D. D. "The Influence of Business Cycles on Marriage and Birthrates" in *Demographic and Economic Change in Developed Countries*. Princeton Univ. Press, 1960, pp. 241–60.

[4]As Dorothy Thomas points out, the indicators that Kirk chose are preferable because of their sensitivity to small changes.

variable lag factors which influence the birth rate. Births in a modern society are not calculated on the basis of their possible marginal utility; parents do not have children because of their future economic value. The only economic influence exerted on fertility is that of *cost*. In other words, parents in modern society are more concerned with the cost of having a child than with the future economic gains that they may derive from it. Therefore, Kirk sees the correlation between the economic indicators and fertility only from the cost side and dismisses the future return factor. This distinction was not made previously by Galbraith and Thomas.

A study which does approach the relationship between economic conditions and fertility, and attacks the problem precisely from the point of view of cost utility and returns, has been done by Gary Becker.[5] Becker views children as durable goods. Children yield psychic income to their parents; fertility is determined by the income of the parents, the cost of having children and other factors such as lack of security and personal taste. Children are not viwed as "luxury goods," hence a long-run income increase would have the effect of raising the parents' expenditure on them. There are, however, two ways in which parents can increase expenditure on children. By "bettering" Becker means raising the educational and health level. Computing the cost of a child, he says, is comparatively easy. The net cost of a child "equals the present value of expected outlays plus the imputed value of the child's services."[6] If the net cost is positive, in other words, the outlays are greater than the expected income, the children must be considered as a consumer's durable goods and the "compensatory income" which is obtained from them is the psychic utility which the parents gain. On the other hand, if the net cost is negative, in other words, if the future income from the child is to be greater than the outlays, it might be considered as a "producer durable." Becker concludes his theoretical groundwork by stating that most of the cost of children is spent on "bettering" them, not having more of them.

Next he proceeds to test this theory empirically. The hypothesis

---

[5]Becker, G. S. "An Economic Analysis of Fertility" in *Demographic and Economic Change in Developed Countries.* Princeton Univ. Press, 1960, pp. 209–31.

[6]Becker, G. S. *op. cit.,* p. 213.

Table 3 Children ever born per 100 couples in Indianapolis classified by husband's income and planning status (native white protestants)

(1) Income (dollars)	(2) All couples	(3) Relatively fecund	(4) Number and spacing planners	(5) All planners
3000+ up	150	180	149	175
2000–2999	149	176	182	161
1600–1999	163	194	91	126
1200–1599	189	229	97	144
1200+ down	227	266	68	146

Source: Becker, G. S. "An Economic Analysis of Fertility." in *Demographic and Economic Change in Developed Countries*. Princeton, 1960, p. 219.

is that higher-income brackets have a higher fertility index. He uses data from the later (1955) Indianapolis survey[7] to derive Table 2, demonstrating his point that couples with higher incomes, who *practice family planning,* have more children. The reader is reminded that Becker refers to column Four of this table, which is that segment of the sample that confirms his theory. It is clear that people that do not practice family planning, and whose family grow randomly, are not a suitable subject for a study which tries to determine the influence of economic conditions on fertility. Westoff, Potter and Sagi[8] have given us a report of a very interesting study which is different from all the works previously discussed in that it concentrates on a very short period of time and derives its conclusions from a cross-sectional study of different levels in the population. The authors investigate the effect that the 1957–1958 recession had on a sample of couples who came from the major cities of the United States. The couples were asked whether the recession had had any economic effect on them and what their fertility had been in terms of pregnancies during that period.

Table 4 shows the effect of that recession and the percentage of additional pregnancies which occurred among groups who were differently affected by the recession.

[7]Whelpton, P. K. and Kisser, C. V. *Social and Psychological Factors affecting Fertility.* Milbank Memorial Fund, 1951.

[8]Westoff, C. F.; Potter, R. G., Jr. and Sagi, P. C. *The Third Child.* Princeton Univ. Press, 1963.

Table 4   Number of additional pregnancies by economic effect of the 1957–1958 economic recession in the U.S.

Effect of recession	Number of additional pregnancies (1%)			Number of couples
	0	1	2	
No effects at all	46	42	12	737
Some negative effects	47	42	11	156
No effects: White collar	47	39	14	384
Blue collar	44	46	10	342
Some effects: White collar	49	42	9	66
Blue collar	48	43	9	87
Reduced income or anxiety	57	35	9	61
Some type of unemployment	41	47	12	95
Reduced Income: White collar	53	35	12	43
Blue collar	67	33	—	18
Unemployment: White collar	39	57	4	23
Blue collar	43	45	12	69

Source: This is a combination of Tables 81/82—C. F. Westoff, R. G. Potter, Jr., and P. C. Sagi. *The Third Child*. Princeton University Press, 1963.

This study has shown two interesting things. It has shown that a recession, which causes a decline in income, reduces fertility among couples who practice family planning. This is evident from the reduction of fertility among the white collar people who were affected by the recession. The group, believed to practice little or no birth control, exhibited a higher fertility during the recession.

The blue collar workers had the highest incidence of unemployment; this was also the group that showed an actual increase in fertility during the recession. This might suggest that in the group which does not make rational economic decisions with respect to fertility, the presence of the men at home, whether because of unemployment or not, may increase fertility during that period.

Some time ago P. K. Whelpton[9] introduced a new refinement in methods of measuring fertility. This refinement, called cohort fertility, is based on the fertility experience of a cohort of women, i.e., a group of women who were all born in the same year.

[9]Whelpton, P. K. *Cohort Fertility in White American Women*. Princeton Univ. Press, 1954.

Whelpton's cohort concept permits a new approach to the study of relationship between business cycles and fertility.

First of all, it takes into account early and postponed births. The influence of economic conditions on fertility, according to Whelpton, is expressed in two ways, these being the change of timing both of marriages and of births of all birth order children. By examining the behavior of marriage rates Whelpton estimated that during the worst years of the 1930–33 Depression between 560,000 and 720,000 marriages were postponed to the late Thirties. On the other hand, the post-War prosperity advanced about 1,750,000 marriages from 1949 to 1946–47. These postponements or advancements of marriages had their effects on birth rates of those years. During a time of postponement, the birth rate goes down; and during a time of advancement it goes up.

The cohort cumulative birth rates by order of birth show that the cohorts which were in their prime child-bearing ages (15–29) during the depression had relatively low cumulative birth rates for the first and second birth orders. On the other hand, Whelpton points out that "the addition to the cumulative rates for fifth and higher order birth (combined) diminished rapidly from 1919–1923 to 1939–1943 and slowly from 1939–1943 to 1944–1948, they do not appear to have been influenced in important degree by changes in economic conditions. Intermediate trends were followed by third and fourth birth."[10]

A new study by Easterlin,[11] which appeared recently is an attempt to follow up his study of the 'baby boom,'[12] and to explain the fertility decline which started in 1957. The author points out that economic conditions since 1957 have changed and created unfavorable fertility conditions. The economic change to which he refers is mainly applicable to young people—the 15-19 and 20-24 age groups. He also points out that "the movement in unemployment rates supports the impression that in recent years the experience of younger groups has increasingly diverged in an unfavorable direction from the average."[13]

The development toward the relative deterioration in economic

[10]Whelpton, P. K., *op. cit.*

[11]Easterlin, Richard A. "On the Relationship of Economic Factors to recent and projected Fertility Changes, *Demography,* 3 *1965.*

[12]Esterlin, R. A. *The American Baby Boom in Historical Perspective.* Occasional Paper 79, National Bureau of Economic Research, 1962.

[13]Whelpton, P. K., *op. cit.,* p. 135.

conditions of the under-25 group is the first factor which Easterlin advances as contributing to the fertility decline. The second factor that he cites is a decline in the marriage rate of this group. The third and most interesting reason advanced by Easterlin is the decline of the group's income not in absolute terms, and not in relation to the average population, but in relation to their "taste" or level of desired consumption. The author points out that their "taste" in consumption had been shaped by their experience during their last few years with their parents. In other words, the young group was accustomed to the level of consumption which they had had while living with their parents. Thus the young man or woman who left home and created a new family unit is accustomed to the level of consumption which the parents can afford (having presumably a higher income than their children), but which they cannot. In essence, the author suggests measuring the desired consumption of the young group by their parents' income and not by that of the young people themselves.

Next, Easterlin suggests looking at the relationship between the desired consumption of the group and its real income. An examination of this ratio shows a decline since 1957, and the author advances this as his third reason for the decline of fertility among young people who, as previously mentioned, are the main contributors to period fertility.

Thus we have in the literature, four basic approaches to the investigation into the influence or changing economic conditions on fertility. There is the direct approach of Galbraith, Thomas and Kirk which measure the correlation between birth and the indicators of the business cycle. Then there is the short-term approach of Westoff, Potter and Sagi, which focuses the investigations on a single turning point in the business cycle. A completely different approach is represented by Whelpton's cohort fertility measurements. Here the investigator departs from the conventional fertility measurements that are periodic in nature and develops longitudinal fertility measures that permit him to measure postponements or advancements of births, and relates these to the business cycle. Finally, we have Easterlin's approach, which addresses itself to changes in relative levels of income rather than to absolute levels.

All four approaches suggest most strongly that there is a correlation between business cycles and fertility; and that fertility is itself affected by changes in income which reflect the business cycle.

ECONOMIC FLUCTUATIONS IN ISRAEL, 1949–1967

Cycle of the Economic Activity

In spite of all the work that has been done in the field of economic development in the economy, there has been as yet no systematic research into either the business cycles of the Israeli economy or into the question of whether the economic fluctuations of the last twenty years have established cycles of economic activity which can be described and fitted into the framework of the business cycle in general.

The business cycle expresses itself in a movement from prosperity to depression, in four distinct phases: depression, upswing, boom and recession.

Since the laws which govern the time-span of each phase are not known, the beginning of each phase can best be read from its by-products in the economy. For instance:

Recession shows up in a decrease of economic activity, the GNP falls, inventories rise, prices fall and unemployment goes up.

Boom periods, on the other hand, show up in full employment, rising rates of interest, prices go up and stockpiles diminish.

There have been many theories as to the reasons for the existence of the business cycle. Keynes, for example, does not attempt an explanation of the phenomenon but simply sets out to describe the correlation and mutual dependency that exist between investment, consumption and savings.

David Horowitz,[14] for example, is of the opinion that the economic development of Israel can be characterized by the total lack of any normal business cycle. "During this whole period (1954–1964) the distinctive characteristic of Israel's development has been a total lack of the ordinary business cycle, the cycle of boom and depression. At no time has it been possible to define the situation as one of depression. It has all been moving in one direction: dynamic expansion and inflational pressure, which have never been lacking in negative effects."

One should remember that Horowitz is dealing here with the '54–64 decade, so that the most pronounced recession that Israel's economy has experienced, that of 1965, 1966 and half of 1967, falls outside the scope of his study.

---

[14]Horowitz, D. "Trends and Structure in the Economy of Israel," *Massada,* Tel-Aviv, **37,** 1964 (Hebrew).

However, although there was a constant rise in economic activity during this period ('54–64), the rate of change was inconstant. In other words, the economy was not expanding at the same speed from year to year. Hence, for purposes of this investigation, I prefer to adopt the division into economic periods as made by Halevi and Klinov.[15] The division is based on changes in the rates of economic expansion. To put it another way, this investigation into the business cycle of the Israel economy will not be based on the accepted definition of the rise and fall of the GNP, which as we have seen is in any case in a state of constant expansion, but on the changes in the rate of economic expansion, which will serve as indicators as to the appearance of the different phases of the business cycle.

Changes of Rate of Expansion of Sources and Uses

The main economic development in the economy during the last twenty years can be read in the following graph, according to the periodic division of Halevi and Klinov, as mentioned above. Thus it is possible to divide the 1951–1965 period into the following phases from the point of view of economic development:

1) 1949–1951
2) 1952–1953
3) 1954–1955
4) 1956–1964
5) 1965 +

1) *The 1949–1951 period:* This period was characterized by mass immigration, which enlarged the manpower pool and, at the same time, caused a rise in the demand for consumer goods and investment. The economic integration of this mass immigration was of prime importance so that the main industrial effort was the need to feed and house these immigrants. This was the period of austerity, and although the rise in the GNP was very large in absolute terms, it was much smaller per capita because of the rapid rise in population. During this period, it is worthwhile noting a rise in imports.

---

[15]Nadav, Halevi and Klinov-Malul, Ruth. *The Economic Development of Israel.* New York: Praeger, 1968.

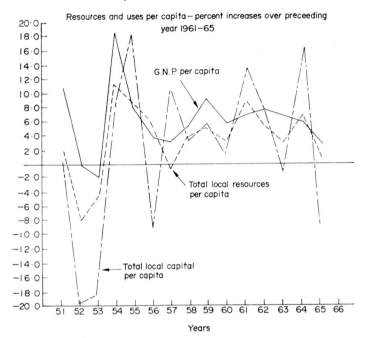

Graph 1 Source: Halevi, Nadav, Klinov-Malul and Ruth, *The Economic Development of Israel*, pp. 100–101.

2) *The 1952–1953 period:* In 1952, the government decided on deflationary measures in order to achieve a positive balance of payments. As a result the GNP started falling, and unemployment began rising. It is worthwhile to note that this period saw the end of the mass immigration.

3) *The 1954–1955 period:* This period saw the beginning of the reparation payments from Germany and the Independence Loan. Hence, there was a swift rise in sources, both in absolute terms and per capita, such as the economy had never known before. The rise in sources was almost as rapid as the rise in the GNP, which reached a peak of 21.9 percent growth, 19.2 percent per capita.

4) *The 1956–1964 period:* This is a period of an almost constant rate of growth in GNP from year to year.

5) *The 1965–1967 period:* This is a period of economic recession which started in the middle of 1965. The rate of rise of the GNP slowed to 0.6 percent in 1966 and to 1.2 percent in 1967. Consumption per capita rose by only 0.6 percent; in 1966 it even *fell*

by 1.2 percent. As we have seen, the period of recession is characterized by an almost complete cessation in the rise of the GNP, and a considerable rise in unemployment. Further, this is the first period in which one can detect a falling-off of economic activity which is an accepted part of the business cycle.

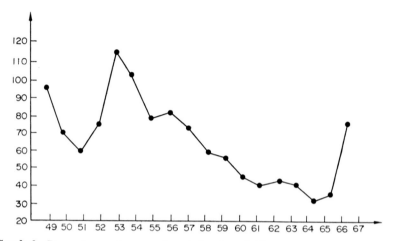

Graph 2 Percentage of unemployed in the civilian labor force. Source: Halevi, Nadev, Klinov-Malul and Ruth, *The Economic Development of Israel,* pp. 100–101.

Let us try to correlate the changes in employment that are expressed in Graph 2 with the rates of rise in the GNP and the sources as we have described them in this paper.

1) *The 1949–1951 period:* Unemployment went down from 9.5 percent to 6.1 percent. The GNP is rising, and the many immigrants that have been arriving are being absorbed into the economy that had been in need of a large labor force to answer the needs of the rising population. The correlation here is:

Rise in rate of expansion of GNP => rates of unemployment start going down.

2) *The 1952–1953 period:* There is a considerable rise in unemployment, and the percentage rises from 6.1 percent to a peak of 11.3 percent. The correlation would be:

A fall in GNP => a rise in unemployment.

---

[16]Data for 1966 were taken from *Labour Force Survey, 1964–1966.* Central Bureau of Statistics, special series No. 162. Jerusalem.

3) *The 1954–1955 period:* There is a fall in the percentage of unemployment and, at the end of the period, a percentage is reached which almost equals that at the end of the 1949–1951 period. This is a considerable drop compared with the 1953 peak. Indeed, we can see that during this period, there is a rise in the GNP. The correlation can be expressed thus:

A great rise in the GNP => great fall in the percentages of unemployment.

4) *The 1956–1964 period:* This period is marked by a slow but steady fall in unemployment, from 7.8 percent at the beginning of the period to 3.3 percent at the end. (Excluding 1956 which saw a slight rise in unemployment form 7.4 percent to 7.8 percent, possibly as a result of immigration after the Sinai Campaign.) This period is also marked by a steady and constant rise in the GNP. In other words:

A steady rise in GNP => a steady fall in unemployment.

5) *The 1966–1967 period:* This is, as I have said already, the period of recession, and unemployment rates rise from 3.6 percent to 7.4 percent. The rate of rise in the GNP falls to only 6.8 percent as against a yearly average in the former period of 10 percent. The correlation is:

A fall in the rate of expansion of GNP => a rise in unemployment. In other words, the correlation between the directions in the developments in the variables is constant over the last twenty years (throughout the various changes in the economy). The GNP, as we have seen, continues to rise year by year, but the rates of expansion change—when the rate of expansion falls, the percentage of unemployed in the labor force rises, and vice versa.

ECONOMIC FLUCTUATIONS AND FERTILITY IN ISRAEL

As I have pointed out, the purpose of this paper is to find correlations between economic changes and fertility. The hypothesis is that in periods of economic expansion, characterized by a rise in the GNP, the fertility rates will show a related rise, lagged by one year. In other words, we should find a positive correlation between the rates of rise of the GNP and their fertility rates, with a time lag of one year.

Let us review the changes in fertility and try to correlate them with the economic changes of the relevant periods.

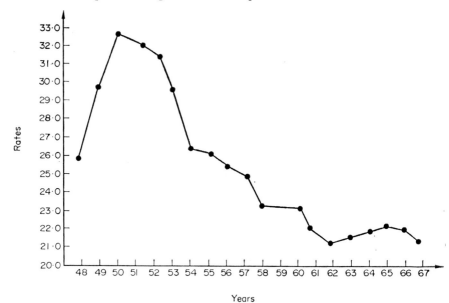

Years

Graph 3 Birth per Thousand (Jewish). Source: *Statistical Abstract of Israel*. Central Bureau of Statistics, Jerusalem, 1965. p. 54.

From this graph, it becomes clear that the general trend of births is downward. The average drop is 0.67 per cent p.a. Here too, in order to check the influence of the economic situation on the fertility rates, one must remove the influence of trend; one must pay attention to the intensity of the drop in each period (i.e., not only to the drop itself). The periodic developments according to the graph are as follows:

1) *The 1950–1952 period:* In 1950, as against 1949, there is a rise in fertility. This, by the way, is one of the few years in which a rise took place, and the only year with such a steep rise, from 30.0 percent to 33.0 percent. However, towards the end of the period the rate dropped to 31.6 percent. The overall picture is one of a rise in fertility for the '50–52 period. The corresponding period is characterized from an economic point of view by a rise in the rate of expansion of the GNP as a result of the need to absorb and house the many immigrants arriving at that time. In other words, this is a period that starts with a rise in the birth rate and ends with a falling birth rate—and rising GNP.

2) *The 1953–1954 period:* This is a period characterized by an extremely steep drop in the birth rate—from 31.6 to 27.4 per thousand—and is, in fact, the only period in which the drop in fertility exceeds the average for the whole period (1949–1967). From an economic point of view, this is the period marked by severe deflationary measures, hence, by a steep drop in the GNP.

3) *The 1955–1957 period:* During this period, the drop in birth rates is small, the yearly average drop being only 0.3 per thousand. In other words, the birth rate went down by only half the yearly average for the twenty-year period. Of course, one must take into account the fact that this drop comes after a peak period in the drop of the birth rate. Economically speaking, this is a period with a considerable rise in GNP.

4) *The 1957–1965 period:* The birth rate continues to fall out only on an average of 0.45 in the thousand, the gradient tending to flatten out, with some years having a smaller drop than that of the year preceding. The general rate of fall is smaller than the average for the whole period (1949–1966). The GNP, on the other hand, is rising steadily; and the steady rise reflects the falling birth rate.

5) *1966*—The fall in birth rates approaches the average for the twenty-year period, and exceeds it towards the end of 1966. The recession, which shows up in a slow up in the rise of the GNP, was only detectable in the birth rates in 1967. (The birth rate went down in 1967 by only 0.9 in the thousand.)

Summing up

To sum up, one may say that the economic fluctuations that we have described by means of changes in the growth of the GNP correlate well, as expected, with the changes in the birth rates. We have taken into account the fact that one must correlate the economic fluctuations of each year with the birth rate fluctuations of the year preceding.

The birth rates have a constant downward trend, which steepens abruptly in the period immediately after a slowdown in the growth of the GNP.

ASSUMPTIONS AND HYPOTHESES

Our basic assumption is that economic fluctuations affect fertility rates. In times of intensive economic activity, there is a general upward trend in birth rates; and in times of recession, birth rates tend to fall off. The effects of these economic fluctuations are different on different ethnic groups, different age groups, etc. Generally speaking, the population may be divided into "planners" and "non-planners."

The non-planners, who do not practice birth control, usually limit their use of contraception, whether because of religious scruples, tradition, lack of education or combination of these factors. Their families are consequently much larger than those of the planners.

The planners have families that are controlled by the use of contraceptive measures. The decision to add another child to the families is a least partly rational; hence, it is influenced by the economic situation in general, and, more specfically, by the free income of the family in question.

The general economic situation affects the family in various ways. We may assume that changes in the intensity of economic activity affect the amount of free income that each family has. If the wage-earner is selfemployed, he will, of course, be highly sensitive to such changes. On the other hand, a permanent employee would be almost totally unaffected. In both cases the free or disposable income will be affected. In the planner families this effect shows up, among the other things, in the decision to have or not to have another child. In times of economic recession, such families avoid enlarging the family. Times of increased economic activity appear suitable for the addition of another child.

In other words, we may assume that economic changes affect the planners first and foremost. The correlation that we may expect between economic fluctuations and the fertility rates is as follows:

A low positive correlation in the general population.

A high positive correlation among the planners.

No correlation whatsoever among the non-planners.

The high positive correlation among the planners is caused by the fact that the decision to enlarge the family in this group is affected by economic fluctuations.

Among the non-planners, not only is there no positive correlation, but there may very well be an opposite effect, as we see from the research done in this subject by Potter and Sagi.[17]

---

[17]Westoff, C. F.; Potter, R. G., Jr. and Sagi, P. C. *The Third Child.* Princeton Univ. Press, 1963.

This research shows that in times of economic depression, the birth rates of the non-planners goes up, probably because the men are at home more.

In the population as a whole, the correlation is lower than among the planner group but is still positive. The average is brought down by the presence of the non-planners. One should note that whenever one deals with the correlation between birth rates and economic fluctuations, we are looking for changes—or lack of change— in the birth rate as a result of changes in the business cycle. These changes may be expected a year after the economic cause since the cause affects the *decision* to have a child, and hence the time of conception. In a group of subjects of African and Asian extraction, who have no tradition of contraception and family planning, we may expect to find no correlation at all. On the other hand, among the subjects of European, American and Israeli extraction, who practice family planning and are less influenced by tradition, we may expect to find very strong influence in the birth rate of every kind of economic fluctuation.

RESEARCH METHOD

Generally speaking, the method of our research will be to check the correlation coefficients between indicators of economic changes and birth rates by order of birth during a certain period of time with the birth rate as the dependent variable and the economic indicators as the independent variables. We have to test the correlation coefficient between the birth rates and the economic indicators chosen, while reading into the birth rates a one-year time-lag. Thus, the economic indicators for 1960, for example, would be linked in our research with the birth rates of 1961.

The data used to indicate economic activity, as an index of the effect that such activity has on fertility, are the per capita GNP and the Industrial Productivity Index.

The first correlation checked was that between birth rates of the general population and the economic variables. Then, we divided the population up according to the mother's country of birth. This division was as follows:

1) Mothers born in Israel.
2) Mothers born in Asia or Africa.
3) Mothers born in Europe or the continent of America.

The purpose of this division into sub-groups was to make it possible to find the correlation between the birth rates of every sub-group and the economic indicators and in this way to discover the degree to which economic fluctuations affect different sectors of the population. This division will make it possible to check our basic premise (see the basic assumption two pages back) which is that people of European and American extraction—who are the main planners—are the most affected by fluctuations in the economy. Further, this division should prove the supposition that the Israeli-born, who tend to be more planners than non-planners are affected by economic fluctuations, though less so than people born in America or Europe.

A secondary check has been made in each sub-group as to the effect of economic fluctuations on birth rates according to orders of birth. In working out the data, two things had to be kept in mind:

a) Lagging the economic variable by one year compared with the birth rate;

b) Avoiding serial correlation by removing the trend.

a) The lagging variable

Since we wish to check what effect the standard of living has on the birth rate, we shall take the economic indicator which is the independent variable, as it appears on the year $t–1$; t being the year from which we take the data with regard to the number of births —i.e., the dependent variable.

Y—birth rates in the year t
X_{t-1}—economic index for the year $t - 1$ (1)
L—constant
b—Coefficient of regression
Thus: $Y_t = L + BX_{t-1}$

b) Trend removal

In trying to discover the effect of the standard of living on the number of children in the family, one must take into account the fact that there is a continuous long-term time-trend which affects each variable from the point of view of intensity and direction. Hence, the correlation or lack of correlation found between the economic variables and the number of births may be a result of correlation or lack of correlation between the trends themselves with no relation to the variables or the phenomena in question.

If, for instance, there is a rising trend in the standard of living, and on the other hand, a rising trend in the fertility rates, this may mean that each of these phenomena is merely a function of the time-sequence, and not necessarily that one phenomenon is related to the other. Hence, in searching for a correlation between fertility rates and the standard of living, one must take care that the correlation one finds may be invalid, rising as it does from the fact that both series of phenomena developed along the same time-sequence. This problem becomes especially acute when the data we use are arranged in time-series. In searching for the coefficient of regression between the economic variables and the fertility rates, one must remove the time-trend from each of the variables. This trend-removal must be carried out in three stages:

First, one must find the linear regression between the time-sequence and the fertility rates. Second, one must determine the linear regression between the time-sequence and the economic variables.

Thus: $$Y't = a_1 + a_2t \quad ; \quad X't = \beta_1 + \beta_2t \tag{2}$$

Third, one must calculate the difference between the observed values of Yt or Xt and the calculated values for the same time-sequence.

Thus: $X'' = X - X'$; $Y'' = Y - Y'$. Finally, one must correlate the values X'' and Y''; X'' being lagged by one year.

Thus: $$Y'' = L_1 + L_2X''_{t-1} \tag{3}$$

RESULTS

From a reading of the coefficient of correlation between the fertility rates (total births and according to orders of birth) and the economic variables, the effect of the economic variables can be seen on a) the total birth rates in the population and then, b) on sub-groups according to mother's country of birth.

A. The correlation between economic variables and the birth rate according to orders of birth in the population

From a reading of Table 5, it follows that:

There is a positive correlation between the GNP per capita and the birth rates, as there is between the birth rates and the Industrial Productivity Index. The highest correlation is the last—

that between the birth rates and the Industrial Productivity Index. Hence, it is feasible that the Industrial Productivity Index expresses those forces in the business cycle which have the greatest influence on the decision to enlarge the family. If we divide the population by order of birth, we find that the main

Table 5 Correlation Coefficients (r²) between economic variables and birth rates (trend removed) all births and according to orders of birth; 1965-1966.

Economic Variables by order of birth	GNP	IPI
All births	0.352	0.614
First child	0.390	0.623
Second child	0.373	0.603
Third child	0.184	0.442
Fourth child	0.083	0.162
Fifth child	−0.003	0.003
Sixth child	−0.151	−0.181

correlation is between the GNP and the IPI on the one hand, and the first, second and third order births on the other. In the higher birth orders there is no correlation.

B. Correlation between economic variables and birth rates (by birth order) according to country of birth of mother

The results dealing with the correlation between fertility and economic fluctuations, divided according to mother's extraction, are given in Table 6.

Table 6 Correlation coefficients (r²) between birth rates and economic variables (trend removed) according to mother's country of birth; 1956–1966.

Economic Variable Mother's Country of birth	GNP Per Capita	Industrial Productivity Index
Asia & Africa	−0.004	−0.013
Israel	0.383	0.482
Europe & American Continent	0.680	0.491

From these coefficients and from the ones of births according to birth-order in these population-groups (given at the end of the chapter) we see that:

Among mothers from Asia and Africa: There is no correlation between the birth rate and the economic variables. According to orders of birth (see Table 7) the coefficients (squared) are very low, the first three orders being positive and the rest negative.

Among mothers born in Israel: The coefficient of correlation between the birth rates and the GNP per capita, and between the birth rates and the Industrial Productivity Index per capita, are positive but lower than for the population in general ($r^2 = 0.383$ and $r^2 = 0.482$). These coefficients are high in the third and fifth birth orders.

Among mothers from Europe and the American continent: The coefficients in this group between the birth rates on the one hand, the GNP per capita and the IPI per capita on the other hand, are positive, and higher than the corresponding coefficients for Israeli mothers ($r^2 = 0.680$ and $r^2 = 0.491$). The clearest correlation in this group between the economic variables and the birth rate is to be found in first and second order births; in first order births, the co-efficients (squared) reach 0.678 (correlated with IPI) and 0.857 (correlated with the GNP) per capita, in all cases.

Table 7 Correlation coefficients (r^2) between economic variables and birth rates (all births, and order of births) with trend removed, according to mother's country of birth.

Economic Variables Mother's country	IPI per capita	GNP per capita
Asia & Africa		
Child No. 1	0.035	0.071
2	0.060	0.110
3	0.312	0.460
4	−0.147	−0.162
5	−0.083	−0.040
6	−0.152	−0.161
Israel		
Child No. 1	0.044	0.022
2	0.157	0.106
3	0.664	0.613
4	0.022	−0.007
5	0.690	0.583
6	0.110	0.183
Europe & America		
Child No. 1	0.678	0.857
2	0.357	0.585
3	0.002	0.007
4	0.002	−0.022
5	0.272	0.280
6	−0.346	−0.174

SUMMING UP AND EVALUATION OF RESULTS

In general, we are aware that the results tend to prove our hypothesis (given seven pages ago). We have shown how economic fluctuations affect the fertility rates. The economic indicators used to show these fluctuations were the GNP and the Industrial Productivity Index, per capita.

The effect of the business cycle on the population as a whole is most noticeable in the first and second births. On the other hand, there is hardly any effect whatsoever on higher birth orders. This may be explained by the fact that the parents of the first and second children are, on the whole, younger and their income more given to fluctuations. The older parents of the higher birth-orders tend to be more well to do and are salaried employees who have achieved permanent status in their place of employment. They are, therefore, less sensitive to economic ups and downs.

The correlation coefficients between the GNP and IPI on the one hand and the birth rates on the other, show a negative tendency which increases as the birth order rises. We may deduce from this that the effect that economic changes have on the decision to enlarge the family decreases with the rise of the birth-order.

In dividing the population according to the extraction of the subject, we are presuming that the highest percentage of planners is to be found among the mothers from Europe and the American continent. The smallest percentage of planners we may expect to find among Asian and African mothers. The percentage of planners among Israeli mothers, on the other hand, is between these two extremes. These suppositions are borne out by the results. The results show that among the planners from Europe and America there is a strong effect on the first child, a slightly weaker effect on the second (see Table 6). There is no effect on higher birth orders. Again, we can explain this by suggesting that the parents of the lower birth-orders are younger and hence, more sensitive to economic changes.

The table shows a drastic drop in the coefficients from the second child to the third in this group. Whereas the coefficients between GNP-birth rate and the IPI-birth rate are for the first child $r^2 = .678$ and $r^2 = .857$ respectively, for the third child the correlation coefficient are $r^2 = .002$ and $r^2 = .007$ respectively, but these results appear to be statistically irrelevant.

In the group from Asia and Africa no effect is apparent except in the third child, which would appear to indicate that even in this non-planning group, there is a certain degree of rational forethought once the family has passed the second child. In other words, parents who are going to add a third child to the family tend to be affected by changes in the economy; while decisions for births of the first and second child are not affected by rational considerations.

The Israeli-born group combines both the planning and non-planning qualities. Hence it is difficult to read characteristic trends of behavior in this group, as can be seen from the data given in Table 7. At any event, one may presume that Israeli mothers are not affected by economic considerations with regard to the first and second children; on the other hand they appear to be considerably influenced in their decisions with regard to the third and fifth children. We have no theories as to why the fourth child is unaffected in this way. It is really surprising.

These results support the theory that in order to raise the general fertility rate among the Israeli families, the two-child families have to be persuaded to add the third and fourth children. Now the economic incentive is operative from the third child onward, and inoperative in the case of the first two children. The desire to have two children is so strong in this group that it is unaffected by economic considerations, unlike further births.

The data presented in Table 5 deals with the correlation coefficients in the total population. They are different from those presented in Table 7, mostly because the general population is composed of immigrants from many different countries, hence, the effect of economic fluctuations on the decision to enlarge the family is uneven, each sub-group reacting in a different way according to its ethnic makeup.

The main results and conclusions may be summed up in the following points:

• There is a dfinite correlation in the total population of Israel between the birth rate and the state of the economy. This correlation falls with the rise of the birth-order.

• The strongest correlation between the birth rate and the fluctuations of the economy is in the group with mothers from America and Europe. The main influence in this group is felt in the first two children. From the third child onward, the economy has no real influence on the timing of births. The explanation is that in this group, the parents of the first two birth-orders are young and consequently sensitive to economic changes.

● Asian and African-born mothers, considered as a group, are not sensitive to economic fluctuations. A slight effect is discernable on the timing of the decision to add a third child to the family.

● In families with Israeli-born mothers, such effects are noticeable only with regard to the third and fifth children.

POLICY SUGGESTIONS

A reading of these results suggests two main conclusions: *first,* economic fluctuations as a factor influencing the decision to enlarge the family affect the American-European sub-group very strongly, and the Asian-African sub-group hardly at all: *second,* the Israeli sub-group is affected with regard to the decision to add a third and fifth child.

Hence, a policy of encouraging parents to enlarge their families will be effective in times of increased economic activity. In times of comparative recession, it will tend to have sharply decreased effectiveness. Second, such a policy should be directed towards parents of European and American extraction, although such a course would be reprehensible from a civic and moral point of view. The practical conclusion, in any event, is that fertility encouragement programs should be stepped up in times of economic prosperity, for it is during this period that they will be most effective.

Although the effect of the economy on birth-timing decisions is stronger among Western immigrants than it is among those from Asia and Africa, we can see no way to base our planning policy on racial discrimination. However, since the number of Israeli-born women of child-bearing age is rising steadily, among whom the birth-timing decision is affected by the economy only from the third child onwards, it may be worthwhile to plan our policy in such a way that it should be aimed at encouraging the third child-bearing decision and upwards.

As we have mentioned, the data show that any birth-encouragement policy would be more effective in times of economic prosperity than in times of decreased economic activity. Thus, the main result of this research relates to the *timing* of any such policy on the part of the Government. Generally speaking, one may deduce that it will produce better results if it is phased in with periods of increased economic activity.

BIBLIOGRAPHY

Relevant to The Economist, the Business Cycle and Fertility

Barclay, George W. *Techniques of Population Analysis*. New York: John Wiley & Sons, 1958.

Becker, G. S. "An Economic Analysis of Fertility" in *Demographic and Economic Change in Developed Countries*. Princeton, N.J.: Princeton Univ. Press, 1960, pp. 209–21.

Easterlin, Richard. *The American Baby Boom in Historical Perspective*. Occasional Paper 79. New York: National Bureau of Economic Research, 1962.

——————. "On the Relationship of Economic Factors to Recent and Projected Fertility Change" in *Demography*. Chicago: American population Association, 1966, pp. 131–63.

Freedman, Ronald and Goldberg, D. "Current Fertility Expectations of Married Couples in the United States." *Population Index*. Oct. 1963. 29 (4), pp. 366–91.

Galbraith, V. L. and Thomas, D. S. "Birth Rates and the Interwar Business Cycles." *Journal of American Statistical Associaton*. Dec. 1941, **26**, pp. 465–76.

Grabill, M. H. and Parks, Robert. *Marriage Fertility and Childspacing*. Washington D.C.: U.S. Bureau of Census Current Population Report Series No. 108, July 12, 1961.

Grabill, M. H.; Kisser, C. V. and Whelpton, P. K. *The Fertility of American Women*. New York: John Wiley & Sons, 1958.

Hanson, W. L. "The Cyclical Sensitivity of the Labor Supply." *American Economic Review*. June 1961, **51**, pp. 299–309.

Jacobson, Paul H. *American Marriage and Divorce*. New York: Richard & Co., Inc. 1959.

Kirk, D. "The Influence of Business Cycles on Marriage and Birth Rates" in *Demographic and Economic Change in Developed Countries*. Princeton, N.J.: Princeton Univ. Press, 1960, pp. 241–60.

Kuczynski, Robert. *The Measurement of Population Growth*. New York: Oxford Univ. Press, 1936.

Lotka, J. and Spiegelman, M. "The Trends of the Birth Rates by Age of Mother and Order of Birth." *Journal of American Statistical Association*. 25, 1940, pp 595–601.

Morris, Judy K. "Changing Patterns of Fertility. A Study in Depth." *Population Bulletin*. Sept. 1964, **20** (5), pp. 113–39.

Ryder, Norman B. "The Structure and Tempo of Current Fertility" in *Demographic and Economic Change in Developed Countries*. New York: National Bureau of Economic Research, 1960.

Thomas, Dorothy. "The Influence of the Business Cycle on Certain Social Conditions." *Quarterly Publication of the American Statistical Association.* 1922, **18**, pp. 324–40.
Thompson, Warren S. and Lewis, David T. *Population Problems.* New York: McGraw Hill.
Westoff, C. F.; Potter, R. G., Jr., and Sagi, P. C. *The Third Child.* Princeton, N.J.: Princeton Univ. Press, 1954.
Whelpton, P. K. *Cohort Fertility: Native White Women in the United States.* Princeton, N.J.: Princeton Univ. Press, 1954.
Whelpton, P. K. and Kisser, C. V. *Social and Psychological Factors Affecting Fertility.* New York: Milbank Memorial Fund, 1951.
Yasuba, Yasukichi. *Birth Rates of the White Population in the United States 1900–1960 and Economic Study.* Baltimore: The Johns Hopkins Press, 1962.
Zelnick, Melvin and Coale, Ansley. *New Estimates of Fertility and Population in the United States.* Princeton, N.J.: Princeton Univ. Press, 1963.

Relevant to Economic Fluctuation in Israel

Cohen, A. *Cyclical Fluctuations in the Economy of Israel.* Sifrial Poalim, Merchavia, 56.
Gaathon, A. L. *Capital, Stock, Employment and Output in Israel.* Research Department Special Studies No. 1, Jerusalem 61.
Halevi, Nadav and Klinov-Malus, Ruth. *The Economic Development of Israel.* New York: Praeger, 1968.
Horovitz, D. *Structure and Trend in the Economy of Israel.* Massada, Tel-Aviv 1965 (Hebrew).

Journals, Abstracts

Bank of Israel Annual Reports.
Consumer Price Index, Report of the Public Advisory Committee. Technical Publication No. 5, Jerusalem, 1959.
Israel Economic Development, Past Progress and Plan for the Future. Economic Planning Authority, Prime Minister's Office, State of Israel, Jerusalem, 1968.
Labour Force Survey. Central Bureau of Statistics, Special Series No. 162, Jerusalem.
Review of Economic Conditions in Israel, Bank Leumi-Le-Israel, July 64.
Statistical Abstracts of Israel, Central Bureau of Statistics, Jerusalem.
Statistical Bulletins of Israel, Central Bureau of Statistics, Jerusalem.

16

Place Prosperity and People Prosperity: The Delineation of Optimum Policy Areas

MARINA v. N. WHITMAN

University of Pittsburgh
Council of Economic Advisers, Washington, D.C.

THE PROBLEM: DEFINING AN OPTIMUM POLICY AREA

In his recent textbook, *An Introduction to Regional Economics* [9, Chapter 9], Professor Hoover discusses the controversy over whether the targets of economic policy should be defined in terms of "place prosperity" or of "people prosperity." Although this succinct phraseology is apparently quite recent,[1] the question itself seems to be one of long standing, running through much of the literature on the formulation of goals for regional economic policy. The real issue is not, of course, a challenge to the general consensus among Western economists that individual economic welfare is the basic unit to be maximized. Rather, it is concerned with how well and under what conditions "place prosperity" serves as a proxy for "people prosperity"; that is, how effectively one can maximize the economic welfare of the particular group of individuals with whom policy is concerned by maximizing selected economic variables within a geographically-delineated area.

---

*The author is grateful to Norman C. Miller for his helpful comments and constructive criticism on a preliminary version of the paper; in August 1970 the paper was rewritten.

[1]Hoover attributes the first use of this terminology to Winnick [40].

Y

It is the contention of this paper that the controversy over the identification of "place prosperity" with "people prospecity" can best be systematically analyzed in terms of the concept of an optimum policy area. After making this connection, the analysis will proceed in several steps. The first step indicates how the existing concept of an optimum currency area can be broadened into that of an optimum policy area. The second surveys the existing criteria for the delineation of an optimum currency area in order to show why they lead to severe analytical difficulties. The third and fourth, finally, offer an alternative and more workable criterion for delineating an optimum currency and therefore an optimum policy area, and consider the role of regionally-directed policies in the light of the resulting analytical framework.

In attacking the question of "place" versus "people" prosperity, it is natural to look first to the literature of international economics, in which the coincidence of the two types of prosperity has long been taken for granted, when "place" is defined in terms of national boundaries. Three considerations have made this identification workable. First, the constituency of a national government, which determines the "welfare horizon" relevant to its economic goals, is quite clearly defined in terms of the nationals[2] of that country, and the relative weakness of sub-national or supra-national governments prevents the problem of competing constituencies from posing a serious challenge. Second, the constituency so defined remains relatively fixed over a considerable period of time, particularly if we expand the definition to include the offspring or descendants of present nationals. Or, to put it the other way around, the identification of the two types of prosperity requires the assumption that international migration is insignificant. The assumption of international immobility of people, which has long been recognised as one of the major distinctions between inter-regional and international economics,[3] turns out to be at least as crucial for the theory of international economic policy as it is for the classical theory of international trade.

Finally, the international economists' identification of "place" with "people" prosperity rests on the assumption, explicit or im-

---

[2]The legal distinction between residents and nationals of a country will be ignored here.

[3]This distinction can be traced back at least to Ricardo; for the most exhaustive discussion, see Ohlin [27].

plicit, that a nation has the power to implement its national economic goals. That is, while external influences on a national economy are not ignored, it is generally assumed that they do not dominate the scene, and that they can be neutralized or offset by the proper use of the instruments of national economic policy.[4]

A number of economic trends, widespread in the Western world since World War II, call into question the implicit identification of place prosperity at the national level. This is most obvious in the relatively few cases where the movement toward international economic integration has been given *de jure* recognition, as with the European Common Market. Such a union creates a competing constituency; the economic goals formulated by member nations must take into account the economic welfare of the union as a whole which, of course, includes the welfare of the other member countries. More important, however, is the *de facto* integration which has been taking place on a much broader scale, as a result of the progressive liberalization of international commodity and factor movements. The potential impact of this liberalization is vastly enhanced by the rapid improvement of world-wide transportation and communications and by the apparent convergence of cost-structures in a great number of advanced countries, which together greatly increase the scope for economic transactions among them.

Such economic integration, whether accompanied by legal and institutional recognition or not, has at least two important implications. First, insofar as it is accompanied by an increase in migration, it reduces the extent to which a fixed constituency can be defined in geographical terms. Even more important, it is likely for a variety of reasons to weaken the effectiveness of traditional macroeconomic policy instruments in achieving economic goals delineated in terms of geographical boundaries; economic openness and economic sovereignty must inevitably conflict.

We will not tackle here the question of what the constituency or "welfare horizon" should ideally be; insofar as this question is amenable to economic analysis, the relevant concerns are with economies and diseconomies of scale in the implementation of

---

[4]This assumption does not exclude, of course, the recognition of such constraints as possible retaliation, nor the existence of "trade-offs" between various goals such as, for example, the relationship between the rate of inflation and the rate of unemployment represented by a Phillips curve.

economic policy and with the impact of distance, as distinct from size, on the effectiveness with which this function can be carried out. Nor will we be concerned, except occasionally in passing, with the question of the constancy of a constituency. Rather, attention will be focused in this paper on analyzing the conditions under which the identification of place prosperity with people prosperity is a workable one, meaning that the policy-making authorities can effectively utilize the economic instruments at their command to achieve economic goals aggregated over the geographically-delineated area under their jurisdiction. One might term the area over which such effectiveness is at a maximum the "optimum policy area."[5] From this vantage point, the controversy over place versus people prosperity resolves itself into the problem of defining the economic characteristics of an optimum policy area.[6]

TOWARDS A COMPLETE DEFINITION: SOME BUILDING-BLOCKS

At least three analytical concepts current in the literature can be brought to bear on the problem of defining the optimum policy area. One is the literature on the customs union, defined as a group of nations characterized by trade among partner countries, unhampered by any explicit barriers to the movement of commodities across national borders, and by the maintenance of common barriers to external trade with the outside world. Analysis of the static welfare implications of such a union is generally carried out in terms of the difference between total trade creation, defined briefly as the reallocation of production from higher-cost to lower-cost partner countries, and total trade diversion, defined in terms

---

[5]The term "effectiveness" is here defined primarily in macroeconomic terms, i.e., in terms of the achievement of specified aggregate target or goal variables. We will occasionally be concerned also, however, with its microeconomic aspects, that is, with the impact of a particular policy-making regime on the efficiency with which resources are allocated: a question closely related to this one, Lanyi [15] distinguishes between the microeconomic and the macroeconomic costs and benefits of flexible exchange rates.

[6]This whole discussion refers, of course, to a market-oriented economy in which the government's direct involvement in allocational decisions is minimal. For a discussion of some similar questions in terms of a planned economy, see Balassa [2].

of the reallocation of production from a lower-cost outside country to a higher-cost partner within the union.[7] When dynamic considerations are introduced, the analysis becomes more complicated; then considerations of economies of scale, the stimulus of greater competition, of changes in the growth rates of income and of investment, all enter into the evaluation of the welfare impact of a customs union, both on its member countries and on the rest of the world.[8]

The second strand in our delineation of the optimum policy area is the concept of the optimum currency area—the phrase from which the broader concept of this paper is obviously derived. The question of the optimum currency area, as posed originally by Robert Mundell [25], addressed itself to the following question: Under what conditions or over what area (defined abstractly in terms of certain economic characteristics) are economic targets most effectively pursued in the framework of rigidly and immutably fixed exchange rates, operationally equivalent to a common currency?[9]

Finally, there is the question of the optimal domain or scope of monetary and fiscal policy in their roles as policy instruments directed toward income-stabilization and economic growth. That is, we are concerned here only with the macroeconomic aspects of these two major policy instruments and neither with their impact on the distribution of income, neither nor on the allocation of output between investment and consumption goods or between the public and the private sector.

The first step in applying the various concepts just described to the analysis of the optimum policy area must be to show that such a composite makes economic sense. This amounts to showing why a customs union, a single-currency area (defined in terms of immutably fixed exchange rates), and the jurisdiction of monetary and fiscal policies directed toward stabilization and growth should all have the same domain if logical contradictions in the functioning of the economic system are to be avoided.

---

[7]A good survey of this literature is provided by Lipsey [17].

[8]Balassa [3] still contains the most complete discussion of the dynamic aspects of the customs-union question.

[9]This statement ignores, for the sake of simplicity, the small transactions costs which would be entailed in converting between different currencies under fixed exchange rates. This simplifying assumption makes no substantive difference to the analysis which follows.

The first link in this chain, the geographical coincidence of a customs union and a common-currency area, is implied by the requirement that there be no *special* barriers to the movement of commodities across national boundaries within a customs union. This definition would seem to exclude the particular risk of exchange-rate variation as well as the barriers erected by commercial policies.[10] The logical prototype of the customs union must be characterized by rigid and permanent links between the exchange-values of its members' currencies, however much the real-world approximations of such a union at present deviate from this ideal.[11]

Concerning the next link in the chain—that between a common-currency area, in the exchange-rate sense, and the domain of monetary policy—there is a good deal of controversy. Some economists have argued that a common currency area requires a common monetary policy; others insist that fixed exchange rates can be maintained without difficulty, even in the face of independent monetary policies, if there is a sufficiently high degree of capital-market integration within the area.[12] Such integration, the latter group argues, implies the existence of a stock of privately-held generally-acceptable financial claims, large enough to ensure stabilizing capital flows that would offset potential balance-of-payments difficulties and thus obviate the need for exchange-rate variation to restore payments balance. It seems likely, however, that such stabilizing flows can provide for short-run financing but not for medium- or long-run adjustment of imbalances. And it is hard to see how a pledge to eschew both commercial and exchange-rate policies, that is, to avoid trade restrictions and at the same time maintain fixed exchange rates, could remain credible in the face of independent monetary policies.[13] It is worth noting, in this connection, that the interregional adjustment process within the United States, to which the supporters of capital-market integra-

---

[10]Lanyi [15] argues, on the contrary, that the maintenance of fixed exchange rates represents a *subsidy* to international transactions. This difference stems from different views about what constitutes *neutrality* of treatment of domestic *vis à vis* international transactions.

[11]The events of 1969 made clear how far the European Common Market, for example, is at present from being a single-currency area. However, plans for the creation of a common Europan currency by 1980 have recently been announced. See e.g., *The Wall Street Journal*, June 1, 1970, **165** (106), p. 7.

[12]For the former view, see Meade [22]; for the latter, see Ingram [11]. The controversy is summarized in Willet and Tower [38].

[13]This is the view taken by Willett and Tower [38, p. 8].

tion as a sufficient condition for a common-currency area generally point as their model, is characterized not only by the existence of a large stock of privately-held generalized claims but also by a more or less common national monetary policy.

Finally, there is the question of the relationship between monetary and fiscal policies directed toward income stabilization and economic growth. The general argument for a common domain for such policies can be expressed in terms of the well-known proposition that multiple economic goals require multiple policy instruments for their achievement.[14] Unless the various macroeconomic targets of an economic system have significantly and systematically different welfare-horizons, the concept of an optimum policy mix requires that both monetary and fiscal policy (as well as other available tools of macroeconomic policy) be directed at the achievement of such targets. Also, the practical problems which would interfere with the effective application of monetary and fiscal policies to this end if their domains differed are myriad.[15] This does not imply, however, that *all* fiscal policy must be conducted at the same level as monetary policy. Most countries have several levels of fiscal jurisdiction; and it is perfectly logical, for example, for differences in tastes between groups within an optimum policy area to be reflected in differentiated fiscal policies at the sub-area level, leading to different allocations of output between the public and the private sector.[16]

In the above discussion, we have attempted to establish the proposition that several conceptual strands, each one concerned with the proper domain of a different facet of economic policy, can profitably be combined into the single, composite concept of an optimum policy area. But what criteria can be used to define such an area? And what guides to the establishment of such criteria can we find in the literature of either regional or international economics?

---

[14]The seminal statement of this proposition is by Tinbergen [34]. For a survey of the entire targets-instruments literature, see the paper by Whitman [35].

[15]For a discussion of some of these problems, see Kenen [14, pp. 46–47].

[16]That is, the proper domain of fiscal policy in its stabilization role may differ from the domains appropriate to its allocation and distribution roles. For a thorough analysis of these three roles in a Federal system, see Oates [26].

PROBLEMS OF DEFINITION: THE
MUNDELL-McKINNON PARADOX

Among the criteria suggested for the delineation of an economic region, four appear to be given the widest consideration. They are: distance, homogeneity, economic interdependence, and scope of policymaking jurisdiction.[17] Of these four, we shall dismiss the first and last from consideration—the first because it is based on questions of location and information theory outside the scope of this paper and the last because it is predicted on having an answer to the very question with which this paper is concerned, which is not yet even fully defined.

Of the remaining two criteria, we shall argue that the concept of homogeneity is something of a dead end in the search for criteria to define an optimum policy area, while the question of economic interdependence turns out to be central to the analysis. However, full discussion of the role played by these criteria will be postponed until it can be incorporated at the appropriate points into an analysis which takes as its starting point the concept of the optimum currency area. It is convenient to use this strand as a starting point rather than either of the other two—the concept of the customs union or that of the domain of monetary and fiscal policy—simply because it is in these terms that the question of defining an optimum area has been most fully and explicitly articulated in the existing literature.

In introducing the concept of an optimum currency area, Mundell [24] defined it both in terms of immutably fixed internal exchange rates and of a centralized monetary policy. Offering this concept as a blade with which to cut to the heart of the bewildering controversy over the relative merits of fixed versus flexible exchange-rate regimes, he argued cogently that monetary policy alone could never achieve income-stabilization in an area simultaneously experiencing unemployment in some regions and inflation in others. The income-stabilization target could be approached in all regions, he argued, only if the terms of trade between those regions suffering from unemployment and those experiencing inflation were changed by means of exchange-rate adjustment so as to shift aggregate demand away from the products of the latter group and toward those of the former. The optimum

---

[17]See, for example, the book by Seibert [31, pp. 16–22].

currency area, Mundell concluded, must therefore coincide with the area over which labor can move freely, out of regions of the unemployment and into those experiencing inflationary pressure.[18]

One of the implications of this labor-mobility criterion, as Mundell himself pointed out, is that the optimum currency area is likely to be small. Indeed, by pushing the idea to its logical limits, one might argue that every rural or ghetto pocket of persistent unemployment should constitute an optimum currency area, empowered to alter the value of its currency *vis à vis* the outside world. In addition, close scrutiny suggests that, although Mundell used the geographer's language for convenience, his regions are actually defined, not in terms of geography, but of product-mix;[19] his world consists of two regions: "the East, which produces goods like cars, and the West, which produces goods like lumber products" [25, Mundell, p. 659]. When viewed in this light, Mundell's requirement of perfect interregional labor mobility implies perfect occupational mobility. His optimum currency area must be perfectly homogeneous; "It must, indeed, be coextensive with the single-product region" [14, Kenen, p. 44].

But, as Mundell anticipated and others were quick to elaborate, the identification of a small, homogeneous region with the optimum currency area is fraught with contradictions. For such a region will inevitably be extremely open, in the sense that the foreign-trade sector represents a large part of its economy which, in consequence, will be heavily dependent on and sensitive to influences from the outside world. And, as McKinnon [19, 20] pointed out, the use of exchange-rate fluctuations as a means of maintaining external balance is incompatible with the maintenance of price-level stability in a small, highly open economy, since such fluctuations cause direct changes in the domestic prices of exportable and importable goods, and the prices in this foreign trade sector are the major determinant of the general price level.

---

[13]Mundell speaks of "factor mobility" but, in context, it is clear that he is really talking about labor mobility. Since, in the Ricardian theory which he takes as his framework, the two are the same, this imprecision is understandable. For the same reason, perhaps, Mundell can ignore the problem that arises in a multifactor world: If factor proportions differ in different industries and regions differ in their industry-mix, no amount of migration may be able to eliminate entirely the unemployment in some regions and the inflationary pressure in others.

[19]This point is made by Kenen [14, p. 44].

The high welfare costs of such an adjustment technique in a very open economy are reflected in a variety of ways: the waste, including frictional unemployment, involved in induced shifts in the allocation of production when the foreign-trade sector is large; the loss of liquidity-value and the resulting unacceptability of the currency which must accompany loss of control over the domestic price level; and the inflationary bias imparted to such an economy by exchange-rate changes if prices are flexible upward but sticky downward—subject to the so-called ratchet effect.[20]

When exchange-rate changes lead to roughly proportional changes in the domestic price level, as they will in a very open economy, they are not likely to be as effective in inducing changes in the terms of trade and thus in the trade balance as they are in cases where the foreign trade sector is a less dominant part of the total economy.[21] This means that exchange-rate policy cannot be counted on either as an effective means of stabilizing domestic income by causing expenditure shifts between foreign and domestic goods, nor as a means of maintaining trade balance and thereby

---

[20]The first and third of these effects, taken together, imply that, in an open economy, the best attainable combinations of inflation and unemployment—the Phillips curve—may be worse under flexible than under fixed exchange rates. For a fuller discussion of this point, see Lany [15, pp. 11–12].

[21]There are at least two reasons for the inverse relationship between the size of the foreign-trade sector and the effectiveness of exchange-rate variation in altering the trade balance: (1) The fact that, for given underlying elasticities of demand and supply for a commodity, the elasticity of import demand, or export supply, for that commodity will be lower the larger is the ratio of imports and exports to domestic consumption and production of that commodity. To put the same point somewhat differently, the impact of exchange-rate variation depends on its ability to switch domestic expenditure from traded to non-traded goods. The smaller is the non-traded sector relative to the tradeable-goods sector, the smaller is the scope for such switching, and the more inelastic, therefore are the domestic demand schedules for imports and supply schedules for exports. (2) The efficacy of flexible exchange rates in altering the trade balance is predicated on the existence of money illusion: The assumption that domestic residents will accept reductions in their real incomes via changes in the terms of trade that they would not have accepted directly. The more important are import prices in the determination of the domestic price level, the greater, and therefore the more implausible is the degree of money illusion required to make this process affective. On these points see Mundell [25, p 663], McKinnon 19, 20, Willett and Tower [38, pp. 18–19], and the references cited in this last paper.

freeing monetary and fiscal policy to be directed at the achievement of domestic stabilization. For these reasons, as well as those described in the previous paragraph, a small, highly open economy is not likely to function very effectively as a currency area, with a currency whose value fluctuates *vis à vis* the outside world.

ACHIEVING INTERNAL AND EXTERNAL BALANCE: THE PARADOX AGAIN

This paradox inherent in the various criteria offered for the delineation of an optimum currency area can also be seen from the illustration in Figure 1.[22] In this simplified Keynesian framework, the twin goals of internal or domestic balance (full employment with price stability) and external or payments balance are maintained by means of two policy-instruments: the rate of exchange and the level of domestic expenditure or absorption—the latter regulated via appropriate combinations of monetary and fiscal policy. The DD line is the locus of policy combinations consistent with internal balance; it is negatively sloped because a depreciation of the exchange rate, which is assumed to induce a shift in demand from foreign to domestic goods, must be accompanied by a reduction of domestic absorption if internal balance is to be maintained.[23] The EE line, analogously, represents policy combinations consistent with external balance; its positive slope reflects the fact that exchange-rate depreciation, which leads to an improvement in the trade balance, must be accompanied by an increase in domestic absorption, and thus in imports, if external balance is to be maintained.[24]

By the same reasoning that permits us to draw the internal and external-balance lines, we can determine the particular type of imbalance that characterizes the areas on either side of them. All points above and to the right of DD represent policy-combinations

---

[22]This type of graphical analysis was popularized by Mundell in his numerous articles on the optimum policy mix, most of which are reprinted in his 1968 book [24]. This particular variant is introduced by Snider [32].

[23]This assumes, of course, that the Marshall-Lerner stability condition is fulfilled, so that an exchange-rate depreciation does, indeed, lead to an improvement in the trade balance.

[24]This is under the usual Keynesian assumptions, that exports are exogenously determined, and imports are a constant proportion of income.

whose net impact is inflationary: those below and to the left, combinations leading to inadequate demand and therefore to unemployment (recession).[25] Similarly, at all points above and to the left of EE there would be a trade surplus; at all points below and to the right of that line, a trade deficit. Combining the requirements for internal and for external balance, we have the four zones of disequilibrium labelled in Figure 1.

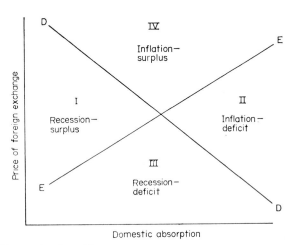

Figure 1   Conditions for Internal and External Balance

Given the assumptions of this model, it follows that the disequilibrium positions characterized by Zones I and II could best be eliminated by expenditure-altering policies operating in the framework of fixed exchange rates. This is because policies directed toward restoring internal balance in these zones will tend to restore external balance as well. The expansionary policies required to eliminate the unemployment of Zone I will also tend to reduce the payments surplus; contradictory policies will likewise tend to alleviate both the inflationary pressure and the payments deficit of Zone III. If flexible exchange rates are used as the adjusting variable, on the other hand, any movement toward one goal represents a movement away from the other. The exchange-rate depreciation called for by the unemployment in Zone I will tend to increase the payments surplus; the appreciation needed to relieve the inflationary pressure of Zone II will aggregate the payments deficit.

In Quadrants III and IV, by contrast, we have what Stein [32] has called "conflict economies," referring to the fact that, with exchange rates constant, the use of expenditure policy to restore internal balance will aggravate the external imbalance, and vice-versa. This conflict can be avoided, however, if exchange-rate variation is used as an instrument of adjustment. The implications of this line of reasoning are clear: an economic system in which inflationary pressure tends to coincide with payments surplus, and unemployment with a deficit, should form a currency area, using changes in the exchange-value of its currency *vis à vis* the outside world as a major instrument of economic adjustment. The next step is to investigate the conditions under which an economy is likely to display this set of relationships between domestic income and the trade balance.

Keynesian multiplier analysis offers a clear-cut answer to this question. In the multiplier framework, autonomous changes in any component of domestic spending ("internal disturbances") will have the same effect on the domestic economy as autonomous changes in exports (external disturbances) of the same size and in the same direction. But the two types of disturbance will lead to exactly opposite changes in the trade balance. Thus, if the initial disturbance is in the foreign-trade sector, the Keynesian analysis implies a coincidence between inflationary pressure and current-account surplus, and between unemployment and current-account deficit. If, by contrast, the initial disturbance occurs in some component of domestic expenditure, a situation of prosperity-cum-deficit or of recession-cum-surplus is implied.[26]

This line of reasoning suggests that open economies, where disturbances originating in the foreign-trade sector dominate those arising from fluctuations in domestic expenditures, should experience coincidences of recession and deficit or of prosperity and surplus more often than relatively closed economies less sensitive to changes in the outside world. There are several reasons why one might logically expect a relatively self-sufficient region's exports to decrease during booms and increase during slumps, leading to

---

[25]Strictly speaking, the regions labelled "inflation" in the diagram must be interpreted as situations of "inflationary pressure," with excess demand at full employment prevented from raising prices by some form of rationing device. A situation of dynamic inflation, with continuously changing price levels and expectations, cannot be handled with such a model.

[26]For a more complete discussion, of which this paragraph and the one following are a summary, see Whitman [37, pp. 6–7]. See also Yeager [41, pp. 91–94].

the imbalance combinations of Zones I and II. Changes in relative prices, affecting the competitive position of exports adversely during booms and favorably during recessions, and the possibility that during periods of inflationary pressure potential exports will be bid away by internal demand are two of the more obvious factors tending in this direction. But this kind of reasoning assumes a chain of causation running primarily from changes in the domestic economy to changes in the export sector. In highly open economies, however, where autonomous fluctuations in exports are large in comparison with fluctuations in investment or other autonomous components of domestic expenditure, the chain of causation will more probably run the other way, from the external sector to the domestic economy. And, in such instances, a deterioration in the trade balance will contribute heavily to a general slump and unemployment; conversely, an export increase leading to a current-account surplus will contribute heavily to internal prosperity.

If open economies are indeed characterized by concomitant expansion or contraction in net exports and in the domestic economy, as represented in Zones III and IV of Figure 1, whereas the opposite pattern of Zones I and II is more likely to prevail among more closed, self-sufficient units, we are back to the Mundell-McKinnon dilemma. Our analysis of the optimum adjustment process in terms of Figure 1 suggested strongly that flexible exchange rates should be utilized as the primary tool for achieving internal and external balance by economies in which unemployment tends to coincide with external deficit and inflationary pressure with external surplus. But it turns out, on further examination, that such imbalance patterns are most likely to occur in open economies which, for a variety of reasons discussed earlier, are poorly suited to the maintenance of flexible exchange rates against the outside world. We are still faced with a mutually contradictory set of criteria for the delineation of an optimum policy area.

Twice, now, we have worked through alternative chains of reasoning, only to encounter the same impasse. An optimum currency area should be characterized by a high degree of internal labor mobility or of homogeneity of productive resources [25, Mundell] or, alternatively, by a general coincidence of internal prosperity with external surplus and internal unemployment with external deficit [32, Snider; 33, Stein; 41, Yeager]. All these criteria suggest a small, highly open economy, extremely vulnerable to influences from the outside world because of the dominance of its foreign trade sector. At the same time, as McKinnon [19, 20] and others have pointed out, flexible exchange rates are consistent with control over the domestic price level, and can be counted on as an effective means of influencing the trade balance, only in a relatively closed, self-contained economy. The literature of the optimum currency area offers no solution to the Mundell-McKinnon paradox.[27]

FROM PARADOX TO UNCERTAINTY: SOME EXTENSIONS OF THE ANALYSIS

Besides leading to the dilemma just mentioned, the theories of the optimum currency area discussed so far suffer from some analytical weaknesses worth noting—weaknesses that stem, in the main, from the assumptions underlying the widely-used model on which these discussions are based. First, however, there is a much simpler problem with the Mundell analysis: It is based on the implicit assumption that, apart from exchange-rate variation, monetary policy is the only stabilization tool available. Actually, of course, the automatic stabilizers inherent in the fiscal policies of the United States and many other advanced countries have an important regional dimension[28] and, in addition, there exist a number of discretionary instruments that can be exercised so as to alleviate both the unemployment in some regions and the inflationary pressure in others. There are serious difficulties associated with the use of stabilization measures in highly open economies, some of

---

[27]We have omitted discussion here of the criterion suggested by Kenen [14]: that the more diversified is an economy, the less will be the cost to it of maintaining fixed exchange rates. Close examination suggests that Kenen is really talking about self-sufficiency (the opposite of openness) rather than diversification, and his point is essentially that the less open is an economy, the less vulnerable will it be to external shocks transmitted through the trade sector under fixed exchange rates, against which flexible rates offer more protection. This is a valid point, but one which would appear to deepen rather than alleviate the paradox, since it implies that open economies should maintain flexible exchange rates and self-sufficient economies, fixed rates.

[28]Kenen [14, p. 47] amplifies this point, noting that "when a region or community suffers a decline in its external sales, a trade-balance deficit, and internal unemployment. . . . its federal tax payments diminish at once. . . . There is also an inflow of federal money—of unemployment benefits."

which will be discussed later. But the incorporation of these problems into the analysis will not necessarily give the same results as Mundell obtains when he omits from consideration all policy instruments other than exchange-rate variation and changes in the money supply.

More fundamental is the fact that the analysis so far has been conducted entirely in terms of simple Keynesian multiplier analysis. In its exclusive focus on demand phenomena, this type of analysis leaves out of account changes in capacity and all related factors affecting conditions of supply; Keynesian economics is essentially the economics of the stationary state.[29] As a corollary, such analysis generally defines external or payments balance as it has been defined here so far, in terms of the trade-balance alone. A framework that generally ignores growth, changes in capacity, and the determinants of investment (which, like exports, is generally taken to be exogenous in multiplier analysis) is poorly equipped to incorporate a theory of autonomous capital movements.[30]

If we now look at the relationship between the foreign-trade sector and the domestic economy in terms of changes on the supply as well as on the demand side, by incorporating the output and capacity effects of changes in the trade balance, the analysis becomes more complex and the conclusions far less certain. One convenient way of incorporating these effects into the Keynesian framework is in terms of a simple model of export-led growth (or decline), which takes as the major source of "disturbance" in a highly open economy changes in the marginal efficiency of capital (MEC) in the export sector, stemming from shifts in demand schedules for its exports.[31] In such an economy, there is likely to be an important "accelerator-type" link between changes in the level of exports and in the level of domestic investment, a link created by shifts in the MEC originating in the export sector. Both because

---

[29]For the difficulties associated with using the Keynesian formulation for short-run analysis when growth (positive net investment) is taking place, see Mundell [23]. Mundell there shows that the resulting increments to the real stock of wealth cannot be ignored in determining the rate of interest or the equilibrium level of income, even in the short run.

[30]This approach can, of course, incorporate short-run accommodating movements of financial capital. But, for the difficulties involved in regarding such capital movements as a flow rather than a stock phenomenon, see Whitman [35, pp. 23–25] and the literature there cited.

of this link and because of the high mobility of capital across regional boundaries, a significant proportion of any increase or decrease in exports and the rate of domestic investment is likely to be matched by corresponding inflows or outflows of capital. Finally, to the extent that labor is also interregionally mobile, capital flows that alter the capital-labor ratio and thus affect labor productivity and the wage rate can be expected to induce reinforcing labor flows in the same direction.

This approach implies that there are interactions between real income and the balance of payments, not merely via the export multiplier in an underemployed economy, but also, through the migration of factors of production, on the capacity side even at full employment. For an economy which can pull in labor and capital from the "outside," it is not inconsistent to assume that the real-income adjustment mechanism operates and, at the same time, to postulate a close link between shifts in investment and in exports via capacity changes, which come into play only when production has reached full-capacity levels.

The various "steps" in the process of export-led growth or export-led decline characteristic of an open economy have been outlined in detail elsewhere [37, Whitman, pp. 15–18] and will not be repeated here. Rather, we will focus on one important implication of this model, namely, that there is nothing implausible about the coincidence of prosperity and deficit, or of recession and surplus, in an open economy. This is in sharp contrast to the conclusions reached via the simple Keynesian multiplier formulation, which regards changes in investment and in exports as independent exogenous disturbances and takes into account the effect of investment on income and thus on imports but not its longer-run effect on the capacity to supply exports. The formulation discussed here, on the other hand, explicitly recognizes an accelerator-type link between exports and investment and also takes account of the effects of investment on output as well as on income, and on exports as well as on imports. These additional relationships make all four of the disequilibrium zones of Figure 1 plausible for an open economy.

Specifically an "overbalancing" of the initial disturbance, causing export-led prosperity to coincide with a current-account deficit

---

[31]The discussion of this and the following three paragraphs is taken from Whitman [37].

z

(and export-led recession with a current-account surplus), will occur when the accelerator effect originating in the export sector is strong enough to cause an open economy to be unstable in isolation. That is, it will occur when the multiplicative effects of investment augment aggregate demand and imports more than— or more rapidly than—that same investment generates additional capacity, output, and exports.[32] This overbalancing may, indeed, be a requirement for the maintenance of overall payments balance; an initial deficit on current account serves to "finance" the capital inflow often associated with export-led prosperity, and a current-account surplus balances, analogously, the capital outflow resulting from export-led decline.[33]

With respect to open economies, the extension of the Keynesian multiplier model to incorporate accelerator and output effects has made the relationship between domestic income and the trade balance conditional upon the relative magnitude of certain key parameters. This particular model does not itself imply a symmetrical modification of the multiplier-based analysis of a closed economy. In such an economy, which is by definition unable to pull in factors of production from the outside, "overbalancing," implying a marginal propensity to spend greater than one, must be excluded by assumption; a closed economy which is macroeconomically unstable cannot be handled with the analytics of this model. However, the modifications implied by the very modest extension of the Keynesian analysis attempted here suggest strongly that, were we to embed the analysis in a genuine growth model, the relationship between domestic income and the trade balance would become as uncertain for a closed economy as it has already become for an open one.

We have completed our rapid aerial survey of the existing criteria for defining an optimum policy area, culled from the literature on the optimum currency area: Mundell's labor-mobility-cum-homogeneity criterion, McKinnon's self-sufficiency criterion, and the internal-external balance criterion, the com-

---

[32]In terms of a simple algebraic model, this overbalancing can be shown to depend upon the relationship among three parameters: the domestic savings rate, the output-to-capital ratio, and the relationship between net investment and the increase in exports. See Ingram [9] and Whitman [37, Appendix].

[33]Such a disinvestment process is likely, of course, to proceed more slowly than the investment process associated with export-led prosperity.

posite work of several authors, illustrated in Figure 1. The result is a jigsaw puzzle of partial relationships whose pieces cannot be fitted together. If we take the criteria that have been offered for delineating an optimum currency area at their face value, we are faced with the apparently unresolvable dilemma which has here been called the Mundell-McKinnon paradox. When we broaden the analysis to take into account some of the gaps in both the Mundell and the internal-external balance analysis, the hard out-lines of this paradox are softened, but only at the cost of creating so much uncertainty that the criteria themselves vanish. The argu-ments of McKinnon and others that the optimum currency area should be as self-sufficient as possible stand unchallenged; but this criterion by itself is inadequate to determine the optimum cur-rency and thus the optimum policy area, unless we are willing to agree that it is the world. Something more is needed for a unified theory of the optimum policy area, incorporating a mutually con-sistent set of criteria for determining the maximum as well as the minimum size of such an area.

AN ALTERNATIVE CRITERION FOR DEFINING
THE OPTIMUM POLICY AREA

The starting point for an alternative to the Mundell or internal-external balance criteria can be found in the observation, occasion-ally noted but little developed in the literature,[34] that the macroeconomic costs of maintaining fixed exchange rates, that is, of being part of a larger currency area, are proportional to the degree to which the desired rates of inflation and growth in the economy under consideration diverge from those in the rest of the currency area.

The central role assigned to the rate of inflation in this approach requires a few words of explanation. Actually, we must distinguish two situations, in terms of the somewhat different roles played by the rate of inflation in each. In the case of separate nations, where there are likely to be barriers preventing the equalization of com-modity prices by market forces even if the countries are members

---

[34]This point has been noted by Scitovsky [30, p. 167]. The most extended previous discussion of the question, as far as I know, is to be found in Lanyi [15, pp. 17–21].

z*

of a common policy area, the simplifying assumptions of the Keynesian model make equal rates of inflation a necessary condition for the maintenance of payments balance under fixed exchange rates. In the case of regions which are part of the same nation, on the other hand, balance-of-payments problems as such do not arise. But this is, in part, precisely because when commodities are interregionally very mobile and regional demand elasticities consequently extremely high, market forces operate in such a way as to ensure that rates of inflation in the component regions can never diverge very much.[35] For somewhat different reasons, then, nations and sub-national regions are alike constrained to rates of inflation commensurate with those prevailing in the rest of the currency area of which they form a part.[36]

If we again abstract temporarily from growth considerations, this discussion can be formalized in terms of Phillips-curve analysis.[37] The optimum rate of inflation is then determined, for any economic system, by the point of tangency between the Phillips curve, representing the attainable combinations of unemployment and inflation determined by the structural characteristics of the economy, and the community indifference curve representing, in this case, the politically-determined trade-off function between unemployment and inflation. Deviations in the optimum rates of inflation among different economies can be caused either by differ-

---

[35]Equalizing forces operate on the supply side also: "With or without migration, the market mechanism ensures a parallel development of wage costs, and . . . capital movements ensure the equality of . . . capital costs among regions . . ." [6, Giersch, p. 146). See Scitovsky [30, pp. 18–19] or Whitman [37, pp. 8–9] for fuller discussions of these points.

[36]This distinction between nations and regions is, of course, a simplification, a shorthand for the distinction between situations in which substantial barriers exist to price-equalization via market forces and situations in which such forces are effective. Extreme distance or other factors leading to inaccessability may create such barriers even between regions of a single nation; prices and price levels in Alaska and Hawaii, for example, can and often do diverge substantially from these prevailing in the rest of the United States.

[37]We will not review here the current theoretical controversy over the stability of the Phillips-curve relationship, but will merely note Willett and Tower's observation that ". . . even if the Phillips Curve is not stationary, desired rates of inflation may still differ between economies" [38, note 32]. For two of the major arguments against the existence of such a stable relationship, see Phelps [38] and Lucas and Rapping [18]; for a recent justification of its use, see the article by Holt [8].

ences in their Phillips curves, or in their trade-off functions, or both.

The point we are making is demonstrated graphically, for the two-region case, in Figure 2. We assume that deviations in optimum inflation rates are due to differences in the underlying Phillips curves, that the trade-off preferences of *both* regions can be represented by the same family of II curves. (The case where the deviation is due to differences in the shape of the trade-off function is much more complex since the outcome then depends, among other

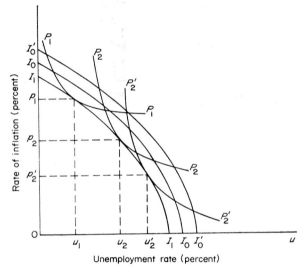

Figure 2 Harmonizing Rates of Inflation: The Welfare Effects

things, on the distribution of adjustment costs among the partner economies.) Note, incidentally, that, since both unemployment and inflation are presumed to bestow disutility rather than utility, the curves of our trade-off map represent higher levels of welfare as they approach the origin, the point where unemployment and inflation are both zero.

Just what common rate of inflation will prevail if the two regions join a common currency area depends upon how the burden of adjustment to the new situation is distributed. In the special case where the adjustment burden is equalized, in the sense that both regions have the same rate of unemployment after joining the common currency area and thus both undergo the same welfare loss, the common inflation rate can be found in Figure 2 by locating the point where the two regions' Phillips curves intersect, and then extending a perpendicular to the vertical axis on which the rate of inflation is measured. It is then clear that the cost of maintaining a common currency area is greater, the greater is the discrepancy between the optimum rates of inflation in the two regions. When the optimum rates of inflation are p_1 and p_2, based on the underlying Phillips curves P_1 and P_2, the maintenance of a common inflation rate will reduce total welfare in each of the two regions from the level represented by I_1 to that represented by I_0. If, however, the Phillips curve of one of the regions were P'_2, the comparable costs would be represented by the movement from I_1 to I'_0, clearly a greater reduction in welfare than in the previous case.

This conclusion is not confined to the special case of an equalized burden of adjustment. Assume, on the contrary, that the prevailing rate of inflation in the common currency area is p_1, implying that region 1 bears none of the adjustment cost, remaining on the same indifference curve as before. (This means that, once they are part of a common curreny area, region 2 will have a higher unemployment rate than region 1.) Then, the total burden of adjustment borne by region 2 will be greater, in the sense of movement to an indifference curve representing a lower level of welfare, when the relevant Phillips curve is represented by P'_2. Analagously, when it is region 1, which bears the full burden of adjustment, that burden will be greater when the common rate of inflation is p'_2 than when it is p_2. However the burden of adjustment is distributed, the total welfare loss involved in moving to a common rate of inflation will be greater, *ceteris paribus*, the greater is the initial discrepancy between the optimum inflation rates in the two regions.[38]

From this simple analysis, we derive yet another criterion for the delineation of an optimum policy area in a world without growth: the regions comprising such an area should vary as little as possible in their optimal rates of inflation. For regions with substantial differences in economc structure leading to substantial differences in the loci of attainable points represented graphically by Phillips curves, or in the preferences which determine their subjective-trade-offs between unemployment and inflation, the costs associated with the maintenance of internal fixed exchange rates and of a common monetary-fiscal policy are likely to be high. Such regions should belong to separate policy areas.

Some empirical support for the assertion that the costs of regional adjustment within a common policy area will vary directly with the degree of variation in the optimal rates of inflation in the regions comprising the area is offered by Archibald's statistical analysis [1] of "The Phillips Curve and the Distribution of Un-employment" in the United Kingdom (1950–66) and the United States (1959–67). As we have already noted, observed rates of in-flation can differ very little among regions of a single country. Since the mobility of goods among such regions is apparently much higher than the mobility of factors of production, particularly labor, the burden of adjustment to differences in the underlying

---

[33]To understand the significance of the *ceteris paribus* assumption, con-sider the following counter-example·

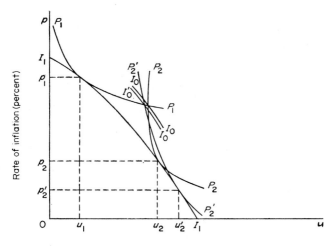

Unemployment rate (percent)

Clearly, the adjustment-cost of maintaining fixed exchange rates in less when the relevant curves are P_1 and P_2 and the movement it from I_1 to I_0, although the relevant curves are P_1 and P_2 and the movement is from I_1 to I_0, although the optimum rates of inflation in the two countries are further apart in the first case than in the second. The reason is that the two cases are not really comparable, because the elasticity of substitution of the curve P'_2 is much greater than that of P_2. (Again, the point is a general one, even though we have used in our example the special case of an equalized adjustment bur-den.)

structural and preference relationships will automatically be shifted onto the unemployment rate, even without the emergence of any visible signs of payments imbalance. For this reason, any such regional differences which lead to different tangency points in Figure 2 will be observed primarily as differences in regional unemployment rates rather than as divergences between regional rates of inflation.[39]

Two of Archibald's major conclusions bear directly on our hypothesis. The first is that he finds a significant positive relationship between the national average unemployment rate and the regional variance in unemployment rates. The second is that, despite the multicollinearity implied by the relationship just described, his analysis also reveals a significant positive relationship between the rate of wage-price increase and the regional variance in unemployment rates. Together, these findings lead Archibald to conclude [1, p. 129] that ". . . reduction in the regional dispersion of unemployment in the United Kingdom would move the fiscal policy frontier in a favorable direction." He reports similar findings for the United States if the regional dispersion variable is lagged one quarter, to take account of the fact that the British data are annual and those for the United States, quarterly. Insofar as findings based on time-series analysis can be extrapolated to cross-sectional relationships, Archibald's findings provide strong evidence of a relationship between the costs of adjustment and the degree of similarity in the underlying Phillips curves and trade-off preferences of the constituent parts of a policy area.

A GENERALIZATION OF THE PHILLIPS-CURVE CRITERION

Our survey of the criteria yielded by the literature on the optimum currency area, and of the analytical difficulties associated with their use, has made it clear that any attempt to move away from stationary-state analysis to incorporate dynamic elements requires a broader focus than any single partial relationship, however carefully selected, can give. We are therefore forced to move away from the analytical simplicity which might enable us to define a

---

[39]"If there are interregional differences in Phillips curves, they must result in different employment levels and not in different labor costs" [6, Giersch, p. 146].

criterion for the optimum policy area in terms of a single index or relationship.

Specifically, when we incorporate economic growth into our Phillips-curve approach to the delineation of an optimum policy area, it is no longer sufficient to define our criterion simply in terms of the difference between the optimal rate of unemployment in a particular economy and the rate determined by the constraint that all regions within a policy area must have the same rate of inflation.

For regions of the same country, the incorporation of economic growth into the analysis in no way vitiates the assumption that there are strong market pressures tending to enforce a common rate of inflation. But two additional relationships must now be incorporated into the analysis. The first is the relationship between the rate of inflation and the real growth rate. It is generally assumed that the rate of inflation will be less, for any given level of unemployment, the higher is the real (productivity) growth rate in the economy. The second is the relationship, generally assumed to be negative, between the unemployment rate and the real growth rate. The pressures for productivity increases are expected to be greater when the economy is operating close to capacity than when there is substantial slack.

Where significant barriers to equalization of inflation rates through market forces exist, as is likely between nations even when they are members of a common policy area, the operative constraint is defined in terms of the requirements for payments balance under fixed exchange rates. Now a third new relationship must be incorporated, namely that between real growth and the balance of payments at constant prices. Even with prices constant or increasing at the same rate as in the rest of the world, the output-elasticities of supply and income-elasticities of demand will not always take on values such that their net effect is to make the growth process *trade-neutral,* that is, consistent with continued maintenance of balanced trade. Their net effect, may rather be to create a) growth process which is *export-biased,* leading to a trade surplus, or b) one which is *import-biased,* leading to a trade deficit.[40] In these last two cases, the maintenance of uniform rates of inflation is neither a necessary nor a sufficient condition for the

---

[40]The Major articles on this point are those of Hicks [6] and Johnson [12, 13].

maintenance of external balance among the constituent parts of a policy area.

Once again, the incorporation of growth considerations has forced us to move away from a simple, single-index criterion for the delineation of an optimum currency area to a more complex composite involving several relationships. What is required here is a multidimensional "possibilities surface" representing all possible combinations of the rate of inflation, the unemployment rate, and the real growth rate and, in some cases, the trade-balance as well. The difference between the optimum values of these target variables, determined by the point of tangency between the possibility surface for each economy and the corresponding indifference surface representing the community's subjective trade-off among these same variables, and the required values determined by the relevant market or balance-of-payments constraint, could then measure the welfare costs associated with membership in a common currency area.[41] This is on the assumption that the indifference surfaces are the same for each economy in the area; if they are not, the *distribution* of the adjustment burden will also play a role in determining the total welfare costs entailed.

Even this rather elaborate set of conditions is, of course, a simplified example, in that we have selected for discussion only a few of the most commonly accepted macroeconomic targets in a market economy. In using such an approach to analyze the costs of entering into a common policy area in any specific case, all the major goals or targets which enter into the community's welfare function would have to be incorporated, along with the associated structural characteristics. The analytical jigsaw puzzle still has many pieces; the difference is that it is no longer impossible to fit them together.

To put the point another way, this alternative approach does appear to offer an escape route from the impasse of the Mundell-McKinnon dilemma, in the sense that the range of possibilities it encompasses is far less restrictive. Certainly, requiring a high degree of economic homogeneity or of factor-mobility throughout a currency area (the "Mundell criterion") is one obvious way to increase the likelihood of similarity in the underlyng Phillips-curve relationships, if not necessarily in the preference functions.

---

[41]Note, however, that the welfare *benefits* of belonging to such an area cannot be measured in terms of these surfaces.

But it is not the only way. There can be a variety of conditions under which the structural characteristics of different regions would lead automatically to similarity in the attainable combinations of inflation, unemployment, and real growth rates, even if the resource and product mixes of these regions differed considerably and in the absence of a high degree of factor mobility among them.

More to the point, since our problem is one of developing a criterion useful for policy-formulation, is the fact that it is conceptually possible to design area-wide policies which would effectively narrow the degree of divergence among the possibility surfaces of the area's component regions, without requiring either the extremely high degree of labor mobility implied by the Mundell criterion nor the regional application of those macroeconomic adjustment tools which would force each region to become (or remain) a separate policy area. To outline specific policies of this sort is beyond the scope of this paper, but some examples are given in the following section. They suggest that it is indeed possible to delineate optimum currency areas which conform to this new criterion of "structural similarity," yet which are neither so small nor so open as to vitiate the use of flexible exchange rates as a major mechanism of adjustment. It is this possibility that removes the stumbling-block on which the criteria previously offered in discussions of the optimum currency area appear to founder.

THE ROLE OF REGIONAL POLICIES IN AN OPTIMUM POLICY AREA

The development of a workable criterion for delineating an optimum currency area does not, however, eliminate the scope or the need for regional economic policies, that is, policies directed toward economic goals defined in regional terms, whether under the jurisdiction of regional or of national governments. (Having established the concept of an optimum policy area, we now revert, for convenience and out of force of habit, to the use of the word "nation" in referring to such an area, without thus implying anything about the extent to which *existing* national boundaries conform to the boundaries of our theoretical construct.) This assertion may seem to be merely a reiteration of the obvious. But the fact is that the demand-oriented multiplier analysis which has so far formed the basis for much of the theory of economic policy itself provides no justification for regional economic policies directed at macroeconomic targets. It is worth explaining that this is so, before we go on to discuss the basis on which such policies *are* justified and to give examples of the types of regional policies that can serve to make our "structural similarity" criterion for the delineation of optimum policy areas operational.

We have already indicated a number of reasons that, in terms of the Keynesian framework, the conventional tools of macroeconomic policy will not be effective in an open economy under flexible exchange rates. But the situation is no better under the régime of fixed exchange rates which would apply to regions within an optimum policy area. Recollection of the simple open-economy multiplier, $1/(s+m)$ (where s is the marginal propensity to save and m the marginal propensity to import), indicates why openness will tend to vitiate the effectiveness of fiscal policy as an instrument for stabilizing domestic income. The larger the foreign-trade sector and, therefore, the marginal propensity to import,[42] the more will changes in the level of government deficit-spending (or in tax rates) exert their impact on the demand for foreign rather than for domestic goods, thus spilling over into the balance of payments rather than affecting employment or prices in the domestic economy.

The impact of economic openness in weakening the effectiveness of fiscal policy as a stabilization tool is enhanced when we take into account the role played by financial-asset balances in the determination of expenditure and income. So far, such balances have been ignored in the analysis but, as Oates [26, p. 39] has pointed out, ". . . for small, highly open communities, it is dangerous to ignore movements of financial assets in response to trade flows." For any region which is highly open in the commodity-market sense is likely to be open in the capital-market sense as well.[43] And the drain on financial assets which accompanies a trade-balance deficit, or the inflow of such assets accompanying a surplus, will affect the level of domestic expenditure and, therefore, of domestic income.

---

[42]This assumes that the average and marginal propensities to import are not widely divergent.

[43]For a statistical investigation of the correspondence between commodity-market and capital-market openness, see article by Whitman [36].

Oates [26] has shown that the incorporation of these portfolio-balance considerations leads to conclusions quite different from those yielded by the usual Keynesian analysis.[44] Specifically, in the limiting case of perfect capital mobility, when domestic and foreign assets are assumed to be perfect substitutes for each other so that the interest-elasticity of capital flows is infinite, his model yields a deficit-spending multiplier of $(l-m)/m$,[45] obviously far smaller than the conventional open-economy multiplier. In this limiting case, the multiplier ". . . depends solely on the relative openness of the system; it bears no relation to the marginal propensity to save" [26, p. 43]. Furthermore, Oates points out, deficit spending will in this model be accompanied by the creation of external debt for the region as a whole, since the government debt created by deficit spending will be held largely outside the region. Not only is the effectiveness of fiscal policy severely reduced in an open economy but, if undertaken by the regional government itself, it will be constrained by the willingness of that government and its constituency to incur external debt.

In an economy, open in terms of capital as well as commodity flows, monetary policy can fare no better than fiscal policy as a stabilization tool. In essence, this is because monetary policy is assumed to exert its influence on domestic income through its effect on interest rates and thus on the level of investment.[46] The investment multiplier will, of course, be reduced by commodity-market openness, just as was the deficit-spending multiplier in the discussion of the previous paragraph. Even more devastating, however, is the impact of capital mobility. The greater the responsive-

---

[44]The Oates model includes, in addition to the usual equilibrium equation for the commodities market, a second insuring equilibrium in the financial-asset market (i.e., that the demand for financial assets equals the supply), and a third constraining the trade balance to zero. This last equation reflects the fact that, if the trade balance were not equal to zero, the stock of financial assets would be changing and income could not be in stationary-state equilibrium.

[45]This simple form of the multiplier also requires certain symmetry assumptions: that the marginal propensity to import be the same whether expenditure changes originate in the public or the private sector, and whether they are stimulated by an increase in income or in wealth (asset balances).

[46]The argument remains essentially unchanged by incorporation of alternative or additional relationships between the money supply and the level of investment other than through the rate of interest, e.g., through the impact of monetary policy on the availability of credit.

ness of such capital flows to regional differentials in interest rates, the less effective can monetary policy be in altering the level of the domestic interest rate. In the limit, when the interest-elasticity of capital movements is infinite, this interest rate cannot move at all; and the only impact of monetary policy will be on the size and direction of capital flows into and out of the economy in question.[47]

In the face of the impotence of conventional fiscal and monetary measures as instruments of income stabilization, the only instruments available to highly open economies would seem to be those which attract new spending away from the outside world. But such policies, when viewed from the vantage point of Keynesian stationary-state economics, are beggar-thy-neighbor in character; one region's gain must be another region's loss.[48] If one takes into account the likelihood of retaliation, or takes the broader perspective of a number of open-economy regions all trying simultaneously to exercise such policies to their own advantage, the apparent futility of pursuing internal balance in the context of a high degree of economic openness becomes clear. And, were such policies to be undertaken on behalf of certain regions by the national government, justification would have to be made in terms of interpersonal equity or perhaps of political expediency; Keynesian macroeconomic analysis offers no support for such policies in the name of maximizing total economic welfare, defined in terms of such national aggregates as unemployment, price stability, and the real growth rate.[49]

It is logical, in the light of the foregoing discussion, that regional economists should have cast their arguments about the definition of appropriate goals for regional economic policy in terms of their impact on factor *supplies*. The question is frequently argued in terms of "additivity," that is, of the extent to which regional increases in income, employment, and growth rate can be expected to contribute to national increases in these same aggregates by

---

[47]The model on which this discussion is based is given in McKinnon and Oates [21, pp. 3 and 6–9]. It assumes [21, p. 3] that the region in question is small enough to be considered a price-taker in the world market for financial assets.

[26]See Oates [26, p. 44].

[49]Even when the context of economic growth is substituted for that of the stationary state, Leven [16] points out that there may be inconsistencies and therefore conflict between maximizing the real growth of a nation as a whole and the pursuit of the same goal defined in regional terms.

increasing either the volume of productive resources or the efficiency with which they are utilized.[50] To what extent can one attribute additivity to the policies generally directed toward regional development, particularly of backward or distressed regions? Such policies include increasing publicly-financed social overhead investment, subsidizing the availability of low-cost capital or of technological assistance, and upgrading the quality of labor and the efficiency of regional labor markets?

The answer is the subject of much controversy, but there appears to be general agreement that such policies will be additive to the extent that they lead to total output increases via one of three effects: 1) a decline in regional unemployment below that which would be produced by outmigration to regions of labor shortage; 2) an increase in labor force participation rates, on the assumption that there would be no significant outmigration and subsequent employment elsewhere on the part of those not in the labor force; and 3) any transfer of those already employed, and therefore unlikely to migrate, to more productive employment.[51] On the assumption that interregional migration will never completely eliminate excess unemployment in depressed or backward areas, supply considerations do offer a justification for a regional dimension in the formulation of economic policies in an optimum policy area. This argument is strengthened when we take into account the possible costs of the social disruption associated with large-scale selective outmigration in response to economic incentives.[52]

One can easily translate the foregoing discussion about the merits of regional policies into the framework established here for the delineation of optimum policy areas. For, by and large, the types of regional policies listed above, on which the discussion has tended to center, are examples of the policies alluded to in the preceding section, ones which could be effectively utilized to bring about convergence between the possibility surfaces (the generalized Phillips curves) of regions within an optimum currency area. To the extent that they promoted this convergence, such

[50]Chinitz [4] discusses the conditions under which regional growth policies are additive.

[51]See, for example, the paper by Wilson [39].

[52]Among the difficulties associated with such outmigration is likely to be a lowering of the quality of the remaining labor force, leading to a persistent and perhaps cumulative unemployment problem. See Hoover's 1971 book [9, pp. 9–36].

regionally-oriented policies would reduce the costs of the automatic interregional adjustment process, and would thus enhance the economic welfare of the area or nation as a whole.[53]

POLITICAL AND ECONOMIC SOVEREIGNTY: SOME CONCLUDING COMMENTS

The discussion has proceeded so far with only occasional reference to the purely political dimension, particularly to the distinction between a nation on the one hand and a region, be it sub-national or supra-national, on the other. Such considerations are, of course, crucial to the question of defining an optimum policy area,[54] partly because of their impact on the economic variables we have been discussing. A region, for example, is always more open than a nation of the same size, and a region lacks the legal means to impose barriers to commodity or capital movements. Nor is it likely that a nation could ever bestow monetary and fiscal independence upon regions within its borders and retain its nationhood. However much the United States may appear to diverge from being an optimum policy area [32, p. 16], the question of how it might best be carved up into such areas is a whimsical one. Political sovereignty is surely an essential determinant of economic sovereignty.

The point at issue is rather that, while political sovereignty is a necessary condition of effective economic sovereignty, it may not be a sufficient one. As Cooper's [5] major study has shown, one of the accompaniments of increasing economic integration, both formal and informal, in the postwar world has been a weakening of economic self-determination, an erosion of the ability of nations to implement independent economic goals. As the mobility of goods, of capital, and of technology has increased, and as the domain of international capital and international corporations has

---

[53]Wilson [39, p. 10] cites as one of the reasons why regional policies may benefit national development as a whole ". . . it would be easier to maintain a high level of national employment without incurring the risk of inflation if labour were more evenly distributed relative to the opportunities for employment."

[54]E. A. G. Robinson notes that: "The boundary of the nation represents a point of discontinuity; it represents a change in the degree of mobility of almost all the factors of production . . . it represents above all a discontinuity in the mobility of goods" [29, p. xiv].

come often to exceed that of nations, the sort of jurisdictional "slippage" which has long constrained the freedom of states to pursue independent economic goals has come to affect nations as well. As the economic openness of nations increases, the choice may increasingly be between a retreat back toward autarchy and the increasing transfer of macroeconomic policymaking instruments to a supra-national level.

Finally, whether the closest approximation to an optimum policy area is achieved at the national or the supra-national level, the coincidence between place-prosperity and people-prosperity can never be complete. Within an area self-sufficient enough for macroeconomic policies to operate effectively, regional problems are almost certain to remain, and regionally-oriented policies will therefore have their place. The aims of this paper, formulated with this constraint in mind, have been, first, to indicate how the concept of an optimum currency area can be broadened to incorporate other dimensions, and thus to provide the optimum policy area as a framework for analysis. Building on this framework, we have suggested a criterion for the delineation of optimum policy areas, which avoids the dead-end of the Mundell-McKinnon paradox and which can be extended to incorporate a variety of analytical complexities associated with economic growth. Such complexities have generally been avoided in the literature on optimum currency areas, and it turns out that the two main criteria which have emerged from this literature for establishing upper bounds on the size of policy areas (the Mundell factor-mobility criterion and the internal-external balance criterion) are seriously weakened by the uncertainties which accompany these extensions of the analysis. The rationale for defining a workable alternative criterion is twofold: to minimize the discrepancy between place-prosperity and people-prosperity and, in addition, to provide an analytical framework within which the role and nature of microeconomic policies required to deal with the remaining discrepancy can be defined.

REFERENCES

(1) Archibald, G. C. "The Phillips Curve and the Distribution of Unemployment." *AER*, 49, No. 2, May 1969, pp. 124–34.
(2) Balassa, Bela. "Planning in An Open Economy." *Kyklos*, **19**, 1966, pp. 385–410.
(3) ——. *The Theory of Economic Integration*. Homewood, Ill.: Irwin, 1961.

(4) Chinitz, Benjamin. "Appropriate Goals for Regional Economic Policy." *Urban Studies,* 3, No. 1, Feb. 1966, pp. 1–7.

(5) Cooper, Richard N. *The Economics of Interdependence.* New York: McGraw-Hill, 1968.

(6) Giersch, Herbert. "Entrepreneurial Risk under Flexible Exchange Rates" in C. Fred Bergsten, *et al. Approaches to Greater Flexibiilty of* *Exchange Rates: The Bürgenstock Papers.* Princeton, N.J.: Princeton Univ. Press, 1970, pp. 145–50.

(7) Hicks, J. R. "An Inaugural Lecture." *Oxford Economic Papers,* 5, No. 2, June 1053, pp. 117–35.

(8) Holt, Charles C. "Improving the Labor Market Trade-Off Between Inflation and Unemployment." *AER,* 49, No. 2, May 1969, pp. 135–46.

(9) Hoover, Edgar M. *An Introduction to Regional Economics.* New York: Random House, 1971.

(10) Ingram, James. "Growth in Capacity and Canada's Balance of Payments." *AER,* 47, No. 1, March 1957, pp. 93–104.

(11) ———. "State and Regional Payments Mechanisms." *QJE,* 83, No. 4, Nov. 1959, pp. 619–32.

(12) Johnson, Harry G. 'Economic Development and International Trade." *Nationalükonomisk Tidsskrift.* 97, Nos. 5–6, Hefte, 1959, pp. 253–72, reprinted in H. G. Johnson. *Money, Trade and Economic Growth.* Cambridge Mass.: Harvard University Press, 1962, Chapter 4.

(13) ———. Economic Expansion and International Trade." *Manchester School,* Vol. 23, May 1955, pp. 95–112 reprinted in H. G. Johnson, *International Trade and Economic Growth.* Cambridge, Mass.: Harvard Univ. Press, 1958, Chapter 3.

(14) Kenen, Peter B. "The Theory of Optimum Currency Areas: An Eclectic View" in R. Mundell & A. Swoboda, eds. *Monetary Problems of the International Economy.* Chicago, Ill.: Univ. of Chicago Press, 1969.

(15) Lanyi, Anthony, "The Case for Floating Exchange Rates Reconsidered." *Princeton Essays in International Finance,* No. 72. Feb. 1969.

(16) Leven, Charles L. "Estabilshing Goals for Regional Economic Development." *Journal of the American Institute of Planners,* 30, 1964, pp. 99–105.

(17) Lipsey, Richard. "The Theory of Customs Unions: A General Survey." *Economic Journal,* 70, Sept. 1960, pp. 496–513.

(18) Lucas, R. E., Jr. and Rapping, L. A. "Price Expectations and the Phillips Curve." *AER,* 59, No. 3, June 1969, pp. 342–50.

(19) McKinnon, Ronald I. "Optimum Currency Areas." *AER.* **43**, No. 4, Sept. 1963, pp. 717–25.

(20) ———. "Optimum World Monetary Arrangements and the Dual Currency System." *Banca Nazionale del Lavoro Quarterly Review,* Dec. 1963, pp. 366–96.

(21) ——— and Oates, Wallace E. "The Implications of International Economic Integration for Monetary. Fiscal, and Exchange-Rate Policy." *Princeton Studies in International Finance,* No. 16, March 1966.

(22) Meade, James E. "The Balance-of-Payments Problems of a European Free Trade Area.' *EJ,* Sept. 1967, pp. 379–96.

(23) Mundell, Robert A. "A Fallacy in the Interpretation of Macroeconomic Equilibrium." *JPE*, 73, Feb. 1965, pp. 61–66.

(24) ——. *International Economics*. New York: The MacMillan Co., 1968.

(25) ——. "A Theory of Optimum Currency Areas." *AER*, 51, No. 4, Sept. 1961, pp. 657–65.

(26) Oates, Wallace E. "The Theory of Public Finance in a Federal System." *Canadian Journal of Economics*, 1, No. 1, Feb. 1968, pp. 37–54.

(27) Ohlin, Bertil. *Interregional and International Trade* (revised edition). Cambridge, Mass.: Harvard University Press, 967.

(28) Phelps, Edmund. "The New Microeconomics in Inflation and Employment Theory." *AER*, 59, No. 2, May 1969, pp. 147–60.

(29) Robinson, E. A. G. "Introduction" in E. A. G. Robinson, ed. *Economic Consequences of the Size of Nations*. New York: St. Martin's Press, 1960.

(30) Scitovsky, Tibor. *Money and the Balance of Payments*. Chicago: Rand McNally, 1969.

(31) Siebert, Horst. *Regional Economic Growth: Theory and Policy*. Scranton, Pa.: International Textbook Co., 1969.

(32) Snider, Delbert A. "Optimum Adjustment Processes and Currency Areas." *Princeton Essays in International Finance*, No. 62. Oct. 1967.

(33) Stein, Jerome. "The Optimum Foreign Exchange Market." *AER*, 53, No. 3, June 1963, pp. 384–402.

(34) Tinbergen, Jan. *On the Theory of Economic Policy*. Amsterdam: North-Holland, 1952.

(35) Whitman, Marina v. N. "Economic Goals and Policy Instruments: Policies for Internal and External Balance." *Princeton Special Papers in International Finance*, No. 9, Oct. 1970.

(36) ——. "Economic Openness and International Financial Flows." *Journal of Money, Credit, and Banking*, 1, No. 4, Nov. 1969, pp. 727–49.

(37) ——. "International and Interregional Payments Adjustment: A Synthetic View." *Princeton Studies in International Finance*, No. 19, Feb. 1967.

(38) Willett, Thomas and Tower, Edward. "The Theory of Optimum Currency Areas" *Harvard Institute of Economic Research Discussion Paper*, 1970.

(39) Wilson, Thomas. "Policies for Regional Development." *University of Glasgow Social and Economic Studies: Occasional Paper No. 3.* Edinburgh: Oliver & Boyd, 1964.

(40) Winnick, Louis. "Place Prosperity vs. People Prosperity: Welfare Considerations in the Geographical Redistribution of Economic Activity" in: University of California, Real Estate Research Program. *Essays in Urban Land Economics*. Los Angeles, Cal.: 1966.

(41) Yeager, Leland B., *International Monetary Relations*. New York: Harper & Row, 1966.

Publications of Edgar M. Hoover

BOOKS *(sole-authorship)*

Location Theory and the Shoe and Leather Industries (Harvard Economic Studies, No. 55). Harvard University Press, Cambridge, 1937. Japanese translation, Taimedo Publishing Co., Tokyo, 1968.

The Economic Effects of the St. Lawrence Power Project (Part VI of Reports of St. Lawrence Survey, U.S. Department of Commerce). Government Printing Office, Washington, D.C., 1941.

Economia Geográfica. Fondo de Cultura Económica, Mexico City, 1943.

The Location of Economic Activity (Economic Handbooks Series, No. 1). McGraw-Hill, New York, 1948; paperback reprint, 1963. Spanish translation, *Localización de la Actividad Económica.* Fondo de Cultura Económica, Mexico City, 1951. French translation, *La Localisation des Activités Economiques.* Les Editions Ouvrières, Paris, 1955. Polish translation, *Lokalizacja Dzialalnosci Gospodarczej.* Państwowe Wydawnictwo Naukowe, Warsaw, 1963. Japanese translation in press.

An Introduction to Regional Economics. Alfred A. Knopf, Inc., New York, 1971.

BOOKS *(part-authorship)*, CONTRIBUTED CHAPTERS

Industrial Location and National Resources (with others). National Resources Planning Board, Washington, 1942.

"Internal Mobility and the Location of Industry" in Harold F. Williamson, ed. *The Growth of the American Economy,* Prentice-Hall, Inc., New York, 1944; revised edition, 1951.

"The Significance and Implications of Cutthroat or Ruinous Competition" in *Papers on Price Policy,* issued by Conference on Price Research, National Bureau of Economic Research, Inc., New York, 1939.

"Shoe Manufacturing" in *Dictionary of American History.* Charles Scribner's Sons, New York, 1940.

"Research in Regional Economic Growth" (with Joseph L. Fisher) in *Problems in the Study of Economic Growth.* National Bureau of Economic Research, Inc., New York, 1949, pp. 175–250.

"Factors Influencing the Demand for Funds by Business Enterprises and the Problem of Projecting Business Capital Requirements—Analysis of the Problem and Discussion of Procedures" (with Burton H. Klein). *Conference on Research in Business Finance,* National Bureau of Economic Research, 1952, pp. 89–120.

Population Growth and Economic Development in Low-Income Countries (with Ansley J. Coale). Princeton University Press, Princeton, N.J., 1958. Published also in Portuguese, Spanish, and Arabic translations.

Anatomy of a Metropolis (with Raymond Vernon). Harvard University Press, Cambridge, Mass., 1959 (part of New York Metropolitan Study). Paperback reprint (Doubleday-Anchor), 1962. Japanese translation, 1965.

"People and Jobs" (Supplement) in Robert M. Lichtenberg, *One Tenth of a Nation*. Harvard University Press, Cambridge, Mass., 1960 (part of New York Metropolitan Region Study).

"Population and Immigration" (with Elizabeth W. Gilboy), in Seymour E. Harris, ed., *Amtrican Economic History*. McGraw-Hill, New York, 1960.

"Recommendations for the Michigan Tax Structure" in Paul W. McCracken, ed., *Taxes and Economic Growth in Michigan*. W. E. Upjohn Institute for Employment Research, Kalamazoo, Mich., 1960.

Projection of a Metropolis (with Barbara R. Berman and Benjamin Chinitz). Harvard University Press, Cambridge, Mass., 1960 (part of New York Metropolitan Region Study).

"The Economic Functions and Structure of the Metropolitan Region" in Harvey Perloff, ed., *Planning and the Urban Community*. Carnegie Institute of Technology and University of Pittsburgh Press, Pittsburgh, 1961.

"The Role of Accounts in the Economic Study of the Pittsburgh Metropolitan Region" (with Benjamin Chintz) in Werner Hochwald, ed., *Design of Regional Accounts*. Johns Hopkins Press, Baltimore, 1961.

"The Economic Outlook for the Region," *Proceedings of First Annual Conference of Southwestern Pennsylvania Regional Planning Commission*, Pittsburgh, 1963, pp. 10–17.

Economic Study of the Pittsburgh Region, Vols. 1–3: *Region in Transition, Portrait of a Region,* and *Region with a Future* (Study Director and part author). University of Pittsburgh Press, for Pittsburgh Regional Planning Association, Pittsburgh, 1964. Vol. 4, *At the Forks,* issued in mimeo by Pittsburgh Regional Planning Assn., 1965.

"Economic Aspects of Urban Research" (with Raymond Vernon) in Philip M. Hauser and Leo F. Schnore, eds., *The Study of Urbanization*. John Wiley & Sons, New York, 1965.

"The Role of the University in Economic Growth" in *Conference on the Role of the University in Economic Growth*. Indiana University, Business Paper No. 15, 1966, pp. 8–13.

'Spatial Economics—I: The Partial Equilibrium Approach" in *International Encyclopaedia of the Social Sciences,* 1968.

"Challenge of the Future" in Bernard J. Frieden and Robert Morris, eds., *Urban Planning and Social Policy*, Basic Books, Inc., New York, 1968, Chapter 18.

396   *Spatial, Regional and Population Economics*

"The Evolving Form and Organization of the Metropolis" in H. S. Perloff and L. Wingo, eds., *Issues in Urban Economics*. Johns Hopkins Press, Baltimore, Md., 1968.

"Some Old and New Issues in Regional Development" in E. A. G. Robinson, ed., *Backward Areas in Advanced Countries*. London: Macmillan, London, 1969, pp. 343–57.

"Introduction: Suburban Growth and Regional Analysis" in Dieter K. Zschock, ed., *Economic Aspects of Suburban Growth*. Economic Research Bureau, State University of New York at Stony Brook, 1969, pp. 1–11.

JOURNAL ARTICLES, ETC.

"The Location of the Shoe Industry in the United States," *Quarterly Journal of Economics*, 1933, 47: 254–276.

"The Measurement of Industrial Localization," *Review of Economic Statistics*, 1936.

"Industrial Location and the Housing Market," *Annals of American Academy of Political and Social Science*, 1937, 190: 138–144.

"Spatial Price Discrimination," *Review of Economic Studies*, 1937, 14: 182–191.

"Versuch einer Theorie der raumwirtschaftlichen Umgliederung," *Weltwirtschaftliches Archiv*, 1938, 47: 1–22.

"Interstate Redistribution of Population, 1850–1940," *Journal of Economic History*, November 1941, 199–205.

"Strategic Factors in Plant Location" (with Glenn E. McLaughlin), *Harvard Business Review*, Winter 1942, 20 (2): 133–140.

"Research in the Area of Productive Capacity and Investment," *Papers and Proceedings, American Economic Association*, May 1949, 39: 442–452.

"Capital Accumulation and Progress," *Papers and Proceedings, American Economic Association*, May 1950, 40: 124–135.

"The Outlook for Capital Expenditures," *The Analysts' Journal*, 1951, 7 (4): 37–38.

"Some Institutional Factors in Business Investment Decisions," *Papers and Proceedings, American Economic Association*, May 1954, 44 (2): 201–213.

"Whence Regional Scientists?" (Presidential address). *Papers and Proceedings, Regional Science Association*, 1963.

"Struktura przemysowa i potencja wzrostu we regionie Pittsburgha," *Przeglad Geograficzny*: 4, 1963 35 (4), Warsaw.

"Metropolis samochodu," *Biuletyn Komitetu Przestrzennego Zagospodaro-wania Kraju,* December 1963 (Warsaw).

"Pittsburgh Takes Stock of Itself," *Pennsylvania Business Survey,* January 1964. 4–9.

"Motor Metropolis: Some Observations on Urban Transportation in America," *Journal of Industrial Economics,* 13 (3): June 1965, 177–192. Italian translation in *Segnalazione Stradale,* 1967.

Statement in Arthur M. Weiner, ed., *Conference on the Role of the University in Economic Growth.* Indiana University, Business Paper No. 15, Bloomington, 1966, pp. 8–13.

"Economic Consequences of Population Growth," *Indian Journal of Economics,* July 1966, 47 (184). Published also in *Indian Journal of Public Health,* January 1968, 12 (1): 17–22.

"Measuring the Effects of Population Control on Economic Development: a Case Study of Pakistan" (with Mark Perlman), *Pakistan Development Review,* Winter 1966, 6 (4): 545–566.

"Some Programmed Models of Industry Location," *Land Economics,* August 1967, 43 (3): 303–311.
"Some Aspects of Educational Park Planning" (with Gordon Marker), Occasional Paper No. 1, Regional Economic Development Institute, 1968.

"Trendovi lokacije i teorija lokacije," *Economska Misao* (Belgrade), December 1968, 1 (4): 721–729. Also distributed as "Some Trends in Location and Location Theory," CRES Occasional Paper No. 6, University of Pittsburgh, 1969.

"Transport Costs and the Spacing of Central Places," *Papers, Regional Science Association,* 1970, 25: 255–274.

BOOK REVIEWS

Hans Richter-Altschäffer, "Volkswirtschaftliche Theories der öffentlichen Investitionen." *Journal of the American Statistical Association,* June 1937.

Glenn E. McLaughlin, "The Growth of American Manufacturing Areas." *Journal of the American Statistical Association,* December 1938, 38: 749–571.

Lloyd G. Reynolds, "The Control of Competition on Canada." *Journal of the American Statistical Association,* December 1939, 34: 757–768.

Allan Lyle, "Die Industrialisierung Norwegens." *Journal of the American Statistical Association,* June 1940.

Borge Barfod, "Local Economic Effects of a Large-Scale Industrial Undertaking." *Journal of Political Economy,* August 1940, 48: 592–593.

Herman F. Otte, "Industrial Opportunity in the Tennessee Valley of Northwestern Alabama." *Journal of Political Economy,* June 1941.

Laurent Dechesne, "La Localisation des diverses productions." *American Economic Review,* September 1946: 704–709.

Leo C. Brown, S. J., "Union Policies in the Leather Industry." *Industrial and Labor Relations Review,* October 1947.

F. C. Dewhurst and Associates, "America's Needs and Resources." *American Economic Review,* December 1947: 965–970.

P. Sargant Florence, "Investment, Location, and Size of Plant." *Journal of the American Statistical Association,* December 1948: 601–603.

Dexter M. Keezer and Associates, "Making Capitalism Work." *American Economic Review,* June 1951: 452–456.

Hans U. Meyer-Lindemann, "Typologie der Theorient des Industriestandortes." *Journal of Political Economy,* October 1952: 442.

Melvin L. Greenhut, "Plant Location in Theory and Practice." *Journal of Political Economy,* April 1957: 170.

Allan R. Pred, "The Spatial Dynamics of U.S. Urban-Industrial Growth, 1800–1914." *Journal of Regional Science,* Winter 1967: 193–195.

Martin Beckmann, "Location Theory." *Journal of Economic Literature,* June 1969, 7 (2): 488–489.

Harry W. Richardson, "Location Theory, Urban Structure, and Regional Change." *Journal of Economic Literature,* September 1970, 8 (3): 847–849.

ABSTRACTS

"The Location of the Shoe Industry in the United States," Harvard University, *Summaries of Ph.D. Theses,* 1932: 189–193.

"The Urban Economy of the Future," *The Problem of the Cities and Towns.* Conference on Urbanism, Harvard University, March 5–6, 1942: 1–5.

"The Significance and Implications of Cutthroat or Ruinous Competition," *Papers and Proceedings, American Economic Association,* March 1939, 29: 102–103. See Books (part-authorship) above.